Post to Post:
INSPIRATIONS ALONG
THE WAY
Book 4

By

Rayola Kelley & Jeannette Haley

Hidden Manna Publications

POST TO POST 4: INSPIRATIONS ALONG THE WAY

ISBN: 979-8-9893588-4-7

Except where otherwise indicated, all Scripture quotations in this book are taken from the King James Version

Hidden Manna Publications
P.O. Box 3572
Oldtown, ID 83822
www.gentleshepherd.com

Facebook:

https://www.facebook.com/HiddenMannaPublications/

CONTENTS

Introduction

This is the fourth book of Facebook posts by Rayola Kelley and the third for Jeannette Haley. Both have written posts for their Facebook page that have touched many, and this is the second book where it is a collaboration of both authors to preserve the posts by putting them in a book for others to benefit from them.

Both authors are diverse in their approach, subject matter, and presentation. Once again, the posts of Jeannette Haley serve as these priceless nuggets that are intertwined in between the posts of Rayola Kelley to add a change of scenery, a bit of adventure, and some spice to the journey. Some of the posts in this book will be for future use on Facebook, but have been set forth in this work in order to make a complete devotional book.

Since God brings people into our lives to inspire, challenge, and encourage us, we also want to encourage believers on their journey. All journeys are wrought with challenges, trials and temptations to take detours away from the course, sit under the cloud of depression while nursing some self-pity, sitting in the middle of the road of frustration, or under a tree of indecision.

It is for this reason we must keep our eye on the path before us, line up between the posts of Spirit and truth and walk out the course by faith towards the vastness of God character and work and in obedience to His Word. It is our prayer that the posts in this book can encourage those who are weary, inspire those whose vision is becoming dim, and challenge others to endure to the end regardless of the terrain.

May these posts inspire those who accept the challenge to walk by faith, stand by truth, and continue forward based on the many wonderful promises of God.

JANUARY

January 1

"Go to now, ye that say, To day or to morrow we will go into such a city, and continue there a year, and buy and sell, and get gain" *(James 5:13).* Every new year brings a glimmer of hope to many. Perhaps with the old ending, something new will take place and there will be an exchange.

With the new, we can make resolutions, set in motion plans to experience different horizons, finish up the old, and fulfill dreams of yesteryear. After all, we now have time ahead of us and not behind us. However, like the year before, time not only marches on but it actually will race past us without us even realizing that it is slipping through our fingers like the sands in an hour glass.

At the beginning of the year, we are looking at eleven months in which to accomplish something, and by August we are looking back at what we failed to do, and by the time December comes around we sit in wonderment as to where the time went, often leaving us in the same place we were at in the beginning of the year.

James is considered the New Testament book of wisdom and it tells us to hold plans lightly because we are not in control of either life or time. Circumstances often intrude into life and worldly demands undermine any plans.

The only sure thing we believers can trust is our faith towards God. He never changes and His plans are set in eternity, established by the blood of Jesus, highlighted by a cross, and guaranteed by His unfailing promises.

This is why we must make sure our plans for tomorrow will line up to His will, His way, and His plan and faithfully walk according to them on a daily basis.

Prayer: Lord, I know Your plan, Your way, and Your intervention is the only sure thing in my life. To look beyond and around Your plan is foolishness. Have Your way oh Lord! Amen.

January 2

"Take therefore no thought for the morrow; for the morrow shall take thought for the things of itself. Sufficient unto the day is the evil thereof" (Matthew 5:34). When you are a creature of time, tomorrow can become your best friend. After all, if you are a procrastinator, tomorrow gives you a good reason to put off the matters of today, because in your mind tomorrow is sufficient enough to start a new project and finish up the old, while settling down in today with good intentions that soothes any guilt about dropping the ball. The problem with such an attitude is that tomorrow will always prove to be a better day as responsibilities and plans are being kicked down the road; and, enough tomorrows can allow you to forget what you agreed to do or set out to do, leaving behind a string of unfinished projects and disappointed people.

If you are an emotional person your tendency is to wait until you feel right or good about what you should do. Tomorrow gives the promise that another day will provide the right environment in which your emotions will feel on top of a matter allowing you to zoom right through it with zeal. The problem with tomorrow is it always carries plenty of demands that will nudge out any yesterday plans, leaving you buried under a mountain of yesterdays' failures.

The only good thing about the tomorrows is that they give you the time to finish what you started today, otherwise they become the biggest indictor of wasted time and energy because the todays have been drowned out by the endless array of excuses and justifications, leaving much undone. When you consider that which is left undone, you must examine to see if there is some disobedience, some spiritual laziness, the lack of vision, or an unfaithfulness towards God in the things He has entrusted to you.

The truth of the matter is tomorrows are a test that will offer a way out or around the matters of grave importance to the kingdom of heaven, revealing unbelief and/or disobedience. These two fruits prove that today offers us enough opportunity to fail God, do wrong, do nothing, and become ineffective in one's calling and responsibility in His kingdom.

Prayer: Lord, I always would like to think that I have carried out Your will on a daily basis, but through the years I have tripped over little matters of today, thinking that I will be prepared to take care of greater matters tomorrow. How foolish I have been because You have given me today to carry out Your will and plan in order to prepare me for greater responsibilities for the tomorrows. Amen.

January 3

"But seek ye first he kingdom of God, and his righteousness, and all of these things all be added unto you" (Matthew 6:33). Yesterday I talked about putting off to tomorrow what could be accomplished today. Tomorrow becomes a wonderful excuse to kick the can down the road due to various factors that could include procrastination which often hides selfishness, laziness,

and a lack of vision. There are those who are waiting for the right timing emotionally, but their hope is based on vanity and wishful thinking.

I have learned that today is the only day I have to get matters done. Jesus reminded us that today is sufficient unto itself as far as the evil that can lurk behind such things as our attitudes towards the matters of His kingdom. We, as believers, need to realize today is the day to finish that which is before us regardless of how we feel. This is why the call to discipleship is daily. Paul admitted that he died daily to himself in order to run the race.

The kingdom matters, and sometimes the urgency of today, requires me to prioritize. At the top of the list are such things as my relationship with God which requires me to first seek His perspective. I must then be prepared to do His bidding and carry out His will. What follows, or could be included in His kingdom matters, are my responsibility and promises to others, and then my duties as far as the home front.

In order to make sure I am lining up to what is important to God, I must continually first seek God to ensure the integrity of righteousness will be upheld in all matters. As believers, we are constantly reminded today is the day of salvation. Whether a soul is saved today, a believer is delivered today in some way, or a saint spared from grave troubles today, God's work has to be done today to secure the heir of salvation in light of eternity.

Prayer: Lord, we know You have eternity to do something, but for us eternity is wrapped up in one day at a time. As creatures of time, we can't be assured of our time here, but we can be assured of Your work being done today on our behalf in light of eternity. Praise Your glorious name! Amen.

January 4

"Vanity of vanities, saith the preacher: all is vanity" (Ecclesiastes 12:8). Have you ever noticed that most of the New Year's resolutions begin from the premise of vanity? The premise is to look better, do better, be better, and actually accomplish something that adds a period at the end of some project or work.

Regardless of what we resolve to do, we find three hindrances: time, ability, and discipline. Time runs out, ability proves limited, and discipline an exercise in futility when it comes to that which is considered vanity.

Discipline can be an outward and inward discipline. Without the inward discipline, there is no real outward discipline. Outward discipline challenges the flesh, while inward discipline becomes a mirror of the soul. Temperance in any form reveals the weakness of the flesh and the unmanageable ways of the soul. Both must be disciplined to ensure establishment and endurance of character.

The idea of personal discipline is a big turn-off. When it comes to physical discipline, it takes every bit of determination we have to succeed in bringing our bodies into subjection. We all want to rejoice over success when it comes to physical discipline, but for many there is little rejoicing and a lot of frustration, disillusionment, and hard work. Behind the battle is the keen awareness that all is temporary and requires constant vigilance.

When it comes to physical discipline our ways must be regimented, but when it comes to inward discipline, our attitude must also be disciplined if we are going to not only succeed, but maintain any progress.

Admittedly, I get weary of trying to maintain the emotional battle and the intellectual challenges that must go with disciplining the body because it can prove to be an endless battle. However, if the inner discipline of the Spirit is not taking place, I will lose the real battles that count for eternity.

Prayer: Lord, thank You that You are the great I AM—the ever-abiding presence in our midst. Amen.

January 5

Sometimes it takes less than just a few seconds to have an experience that makes a lasting impression. I had just such an encounter the other day when I walked into a local grocery store.

A young couple with two little girls were coming out of the store. At a glance I could sense they were a happy family, but what caught my attention the most brought a smile to my lips and awakened my heart to a bit of heaven. It was extraordinary because, as you no doubt know, the world that we live is excessively evil, and reeling under a spirit of heaviness.

But what I saw was not just delight, not just happiness, but unbridled, sheer joy! Carefree, beaming joy radiating from the precious face of a toddler as she gleefully "steered" the grocery cart "wheel" of the children's "car" attached to the front of the cart.

In a quick glance at the biggest grin that you ever saw and her twinkling eyes, the radiant joy of heaven itself flooded my heart, and quickened my weary mind—so much so that I had to ask myself when was the last time my face reflected the unadulterated, pure joy of the LORD to others? I'm not sure if I can answer that question.

But I do believe that the LORD "spoke" to me through a little child to cause me to remember that not only is the "joy of the LORD my strength," but that if we come to Him "as a little child," we shall enter into His joy and go forth as lights shining in the darkness. *"A merry heart doeth good like a medicine: but a broken spirit drieth the bones." (Proverbs 17:22.)* – J. Haley

Prayer: Lord, we live in a depressing world, but if we look around, we will see that which serves as medicine to our soul, brings joy to our spirit, and inspiration to our minds. Amen.

January 6

"Thou tellest my wanderings; put thou my tears into thy bottle: are they not in thy book? When I cry unto thee, then shall mine enemies turn back: this I know; for God is for me" (Psalm 56:8-9). In our humanity we have a tendency to wander in the valley of uncertainty and despair. There is so much we can despair over. At times it seems as if everything is against us. Sometimes we come out with what appear to be losses that are too great to bear.

It is at this time that we become unsure about the path before us. We can find ourselves despairing over the cruelty and injustice that often abounds around us. Besides dealing with the challenges in our midst, there are also personal adversities that will test our resolve.

The truth is this world brings much sorrow to us. It is, after all, under a curse. Such sorrow will cause us to cry in silence towards our Lord. The tears that spill from our eyes will go into an unseen bottle to be stored for a future testimony of God's faithfulness to deliver us, even from our enemies.

It brings great hope to me when I realize that God will take care of all my tears. If He is not "storing them in a bottle," I know that He will ultimately wipe them away when He makes everything right. This is my promise and my future blessing.

Prayer: Lord, we have so much to be thankful for. You are the One who knows all of our tears, and You are the One who will address, take care of, and eventually replace them with joy and confidence. Amen.

January 7

"But every man is tempted, when he is drawn away of his own lust, and enticed" (James 1:14). When reading about the spiritual environment in the American colonies during the life of Jonathan Edwards in the 1720s, it was said that it was very low and there was a desperate need for revival. The reason for this situation has been described in this way, "Preachers were generally well-educated, but they lacked a burden for souls and power in preaching. Some were not even converted."

Today the environment is the same as in Edwards' time. History does repeat itself. The reason for this is because the cycle of sin remains the same. Man in his unregenerate state cannot help but go the way of darkness. Even though darkness is enfolding, it causes man to react the same way. He perceives his darkness to be light, his ways to be right, and his understanding superior. He does not realize that the darkness simply seduces him as he is tempted by the way of flesh, while being drawn away by lust or the possibilities of how such attractions will satisfy the flesh.

We are told that such darkness keeps people from being converted. They see no need to be converted to the light because their darkness serves as their light of understanding. As the Bible declares, if the Gospel is hidden, it is hidden to them that are lost because their minds have been blinded by Satan.

Prayer: Lord, You have preserved Your truth, but through the centuries people prefer their own take on spiritual matters. Thank You for penetrating my heart and life with truth and leading me to the revelation of it. As You stated, You are the truth and it will stand when all else falls before Your righteous, holy feet. Amen.

January 8

"Praising God and having favour with all the people, and the Lord added to the church daily such as should be saved" (Acts 2:47). In thinking about the Great Awakening which covered a period from about 1725 to 1760, there were two decisive camps that emerged. There were those who tried to downplay the harsh reality of sin and what it does to a man's conscience. In a sense, it sears it from being tender towards the truth. It will make a person feel good in their doomed state as they remain marked for death.

The other camp is the one that holds to the urgency for sinners to flee the wrath of God to come. Its message is clear, its call urgent, and its warnings sharp. It stirs the conscience of the soul to consider the terrible consequences for those who do not heed the Gospel.

What fruits can be expected from these two camps? In the Great Awakening, history shows that the churches that rejected the work of God and refused to examine people as to their spiritual experience eventually became more liberal, while those who remained true to the message of the Gospel witnessed the conversion of lost souls.

God is the One who adds souls to His Living Church. But, the environment in which He builds His church must be conducive for the Spirit to convince the lost of sin, convert the vulnerable to righteousness, and cause the seeking soul to flee from the judgment that awaits them.

Prayer: Lord, You always want to awaken Your people to the truth about Your commitment to save and deliver those who are lost and enslaved. However, they need to see their need to be saved in light of the narrow way, as well as the judgment that awaits them. Amen.

January 9

"But when he saw many of the Pharisees and Sadducees come to his baptism, he said unto them, O generation of vipers, who hath warned you to flee from the wrath to come" (Matthew 3:7)? A very important statement came to my attention while studying the lives of some of those involved in the Great Awakening, "An unconverted ministry and an unconverted membership are the devil's chief weapons in opposing the work of God."

We live in a time that much of the visible church walks the broad path of liberalism. It appears, for the most part, that their religious attempts are all quite religious, but the reality is that it is man-centered. These people's presentation of salvation is that it is about man's best which is nothing more than humanism. It is void of any real awareness that redemption is the work of God, and that it must address the utter despotism of the unregenerate human disposition. It calls for complete repentance by fleeing the wrath of God to come. It challenges quasi-religious environments, indifferent pious poses towards God, a worldly attitude, and a lack of passion for souls.

Today these two camps still exist, but on the liberal side, some camps take on a militant pose that proves cruel and mean-spirited. Regardless of the pose liberals take on, they are enlarging their path to embrace the very ways of hell.

The only way to heaven is narrow, and it does not embrace any other way but the way of redemption that was wrought on the cross by the Lord Jesus Christ.

Prayer: Lord, I thank You for leading the way to redemption. You not only lead the way to it, You provided it. If I am asleep to You, awaken me to that narrow way, and cause me to rise up with an urgency and to walk in it. Amen.

January 10

"For to me to live is Christ, and to die is gain" (Philippians 1:21). Matthew Henry said to a friend when he was on his deathbed, "You have been asked to take notice of the sayings of dying men—this is mine: that a life spent in the service of God and communion with Him is the most pleasant life that anyone can live in the world."

I have spent much of my Christian life trying to establish a mental epitaph as to my goals on earth that will follow me as a witness into heaven. I really wanted my life to become a witness that will shine in the next world to come. I have since come to understand that when this life is over, my witness will merge with the great cloud of witnesses that will speak of God's wondrous majesty and greatness.

In my examination of my initial epitaph, I realized it spoke of my pride, and the second one of my grandiose hopes, but the latest one speaks of a simple truth that marks my state, my reality, and the essence of my future hope. The epitaph simply reads, "Forgiven."

My past life is dealt with because of God's forgiveness of my sins through justification, and due to His ongoing mercy and His abounding grace, I presently walk in His forgiveness through repentance. It will be because of His love that I will experience the promise of forgiveness in the next world as I experience the fullness of my redemption.

It is true that godly service and sweet communion with Him should be our ultimate goal, but I realize without forgiveness that comes from my sins being remitted by the work of redemption done on the cross, neither service nor communion are possible.

Prayer: Lord, we so appreciate Your ongoing kindness. You are the one who gives us a life that can leave a witness or epitaph behind of the impossible, the incredible, and the glorious. Praise Your holy Name. Amen.

January 11

"That ye be not slothful, but followers of them who though faith and patience inherit the promises (Hebrews 6:12). I have often pondered what I call the "Hall of Fame" in *Hebrews 11.* These are the people who left behind a great cloud of witness. Whether it was in word, deed, or example, their faith towards God would end up shining through the darkness of their time.

These saints who have gone before us, preparing the way by faith, showing us the way of faith, and leaving us with the example of faith have in many ways become more real and personal to me than many people I know. God allows us to see their human factor that often put them at odds with themselves and others, but they held onto what they knew was true about God and persevered until the end.

In my spiritual journey, I have also noted those who are part of my growing process, my learning times, and my challenging periods. Some of these people have formed what I call my personal "Hall of Fame." They have encouraged, inspired, and sometimes challenged me. In essence, they have been an important part of my journey, and at times my encounters with them have left a lasting memory or memorial in my life that I have visited at different times to bring some perspective to me.

These people would shrug off any important role they might have played in my life and prefer that I would not even give them any recognition. However, each one reminds me that I am to impact the lives of others with the great revelation of our Lord to become part of a great cloud of witness that left a lasting spiritual legacy behind for those to consider who will come after me.

Prayer: Lord, everyone You bring my way will leave some mark on my life. Lord, the marks may identify me to Your suffering, perhaps they will be plow marks that show where You plowed up some fallow ground in my life, cut marks where some scrab from a festering womb had been, or bring the healing balm of Your truth and love. Whatever, the mark is I can trust You are guiding it with Your own hand. Amen.

January 12

"Salute one another with an holy kiss. The churches of Christ salute you. Now I beseech you, brethren, mark them which cause divisions and offences contrary to the doctrine which ye have learned; and avoid them" (Romans 16:16-17). Who has influenced your life? There are those who touch our lives with kindness, others who touch our hearts with love, our souls with nourishment, and our spirits with inspiration. We also encounter those who God allows to humble our pride, hurt our soul, wound our spirit, and challenge our resolve. Such people use the tools of rejection, cruelty, accusation, and judgmentalism.

When God brings people my way, I am very aware that there is a reason and most likely some test attached to it. Most of the time I look for ways to minister to them because I do not want to waste an opportunity to bring a bit of heaven to their lives. However, God will usually use them in some way to enlarge me on a personal, emotional, and spiritual way. The encounters may not always be pleasant, but they are each necessary. Lives touching lives, lives effecting lives, lives leaving marks or footprints somewhere on the terrain of our souls.

The reality is people are people regardless of past influences, present circumstances, and future hopes. They may vary in temperament, character, attitudes, and ways but nevertheless they are God's creation who have gifts, callings, purpose and potential when it comes to His kingdom.

When I consider Jesus, Paul, Peter, and John they mentioned the people who they encountered whether for good or for bad. They used their lives as examples for us to consider. In this devotional book, I felt the need to share about those who inspired me and what I have learned from them.

Perhaps you need to take time and identify those who became a personal "cloud of witness" to you in your spiritual journey. Of course, we all know who must and will have the greatest and ultimate influence on us: the Lord Jesus Christ.

Prayer: Lord, people come and go but they will leave some type of calling card or footprint. Lord, I want to leave a calling card that will make me part of the greater "cloud of witness" in this world that will continue on into eternity that will bring glory to You. Amen.

January 13

"Make a joyful noise unto the LORD, all ye lands" (Psalm 100:1). I have always enjoyed beautiful Christian music with sound theology. It soothes the soul, calms the mind, causes frayed emotions to land, and the heart to look up with hope. Since music has so ministered to me, I always wanted to be able to sing praises to God with everyone else without causing others to cringe, some to step away from me so they could stay in tune, and a few to slip away to save their ears.

Those who have tried to encourage me to sing unto the Lord always reminds me that to God my singing is a joyful noise. After all, He looks at my heart and sees my desire to lift Him up and worship Him. I am so thankful that God is not looking for professional singers but seeks those who worship Him in Spirit and truth.

I must admit God has solved the problem when it comes to me enjoying singing on earth. He sent in a songbird, Carrie Seaney, to be part of the ministry team. Her voice is a gift, her ability an incredible talent, and she offers her songs from the altar of a pure heart. Sometimes her songs even cause me to feel as if I am sitting in heaven listening to her sing unto the Lord with the angelic choir.

Carrie continually reminds me that the key to a joyful noise is not based on whether you can sing, but on your heart. I realize that the condition of my heart truly determines if a beautiful melody comes forth that is backed up by the symphony and choir of heaven itself.

Prayer: Lord, I am so thankful that You listen to my heart for it is there You have prepared an altar, planted seeds of life, and garnished hope everlasting. Praise Your holy name. Amen.

January 14

"Blessed are the pure in heart: for they shall see God" (Matthew 7:8). I love that which inspires me before God. When I was first a Christian, what I heard and learned inspired me to learn more about God. I was avid in my pursuit. However, I found that I did not spiritually mature. Yes, I had much conceit as to my knowledge of spiritual issues, but I sensed my person, my being, and my soul were going backwards. I was not advancing in my walk of faith.

It was not until I had been broken over my spiritual poverty that I realized it was not enough to learn about the Lord. I needed to know Him in a personal way. In reality I needed to be as Job who said, *"I have heard of thee by the hearing of the ear: but now mine eye seeth thee"* (Job 42:5).

The whole purpose of advancing in my spiritual life is to see the Lord. However, only those who are pure in heart will see Him. It is up to me to ask the Lord to search my heart to ensure that the eyes of my heart are capable of seeing Him with and through, purity.

Prayer: Lord, there is so much I need to know when it comes to You, but I need my heart pure so that the spiritual eyes of my soul are capable of seeing You in a greater way. Make my heart pure and take away the blinders from my eyes so I can see You. Amen.

January 15

Follow peace with all men, and holiness, without which no man shall see the Lord" (Hebrew 12:14). As I consider my need to see the Lord, I cannot forget the two ingredients that need to be present in each of our lives to see Him. *Hebrews 12:14* tells us that peace and holiness must be present before we can see our Lord.

We are to follow peace with all men. However, there cannot be peace where there is no peace with God. Unless a soul is at peace with God, they will not have peace with those around them.

Today, there are many clamoring for peace, but it is based on a fantasy. In other words, it is based on the idea of absence of conflict. However, the world is embroiled in conflict because it is at odds with God. It embraces the practices of war as it uses the indifference of hatred, the oppressive rule of tyranny, the cruelty of prejudice, and the ways of destruction to stir up people into a fanatic zealousness.

Presently the world is catapulting towards complete destruction. It is bent on ridding itself of that which brings any type

24

of opposition to its fleshly, humanistic philosophies and godless ways. In its attempt to rid itself of God, it is pulling everything down around it, while sinking into the quagmire of foolishness, insanity, and hatred.

Prayer: Lord, we live in unusual times. Even though it can be frightening sometimes, it presents windows of opportunity for each of us to become more established in and on You as our foundation, cornerstone, and head. Lord, please become all in all so that I will see no need to chase the false promises of a world that has not only gone mad, but is on a course of self-destruction. Amen.

January 16

"But as he which hath called you is holy, so be ye holy in all manner of conversation; Because it is written, Be ye holy; for I am holy" (1 Peter 1:15-16). As I meditated on yesterday, there must be two ingredients present in my life if I am going to see God. One is peace. Such peace can only come through a relationship with God. It is as we have peace with God that we will have peace with others.

The second ingredient is holiness. This is one subject that Christians seem to avoid. They either swing in extremes about it or they hide in utter fear towards the possible implications of it. After all, holiness implies the one virtue about God that will make Him distinct from pagan idols, false religion, sinful man, and a perverted world.

Holiness speaks of separation that will take place between the wicked and the righteous. It often comes out of a state of brokenness over sin and the deep awareness that even the righteous are scarcely saved. It knows some type of judgment

25

awaits all, and in the end, what has not been cleansed and purged by the blood of Jesus will be burned up in the fiery ovens of wrath.

God is holy and He will never cease to be who He is. He will never lower Himself to the level of the profane, the fleshly, and the corrupt. It is for this reason that man must come to the state of holiness. It all comes down to what he prefers and exposes himself to.

He must expose himself to the fires of holiness before he can come to the state of holiness. He must be separated from that which is profane of this present world before he can embrace what has truly been sanctified by God.

Prayer: Lord, holiness is a difficult subject because it can be rendered into a mishmash of nonsense that can become overwhelming to the hearer. Lord, make the essence of Your holiness simple to the hearer as You unveil its distinctive qualities to our spirit. Amen.

January 17

Whenever a new art student would say to me, "I can't draw a straight line, but I really want to learn how to paint a picture," I knew that their potential to succeed was not so much in any latent talent they might have, but in their heart's desire to learn.

Through the years I taught oil, and then acrylic painting, I met some folks with an incredible amount of natural talent for drawing, (which is the basis of a good painting), and who were quick to learn and develop their own painting techniques. It was quite obvious that the learning processes the beginners patiently struggled with was no challenge for those with natural God-given talent.

However, much to my surprise, most of the time the ones with the greatest amount of talent and promise lost interest, and drifted away to pursue some other activity; while those who put into practice what they were taught and who were determined to "get it" and reach their goals actually became quite good at what they set out to accomplish. It all came down to where their heart's desire was.

The same can be said of God's "students" (disciples). Many who come to Jesus out of a self-confident zeal will gladly follow Him for a while. They enjoy the excitement of being in the crowd that follows Jesus when emotions are high, and everything is going well. They love the attention and popularity their gifts and talents (or money) brings their way. Being a "Christian" seems so natural to them that they're often exalted to some "ministry" in the church where they can "strut their stuff."

By now you might recognize that all of this is wrong on so many levels, for whom does God choose? *1 Samuel 16:7b, "for the LORD seeth not as man seeth; for man looketh on the outward appearance, but the LORD looketh on the heart."*

Again, whom does God choose? Consider the qualifications of whom God chooses as given to us in *1 Corinthians 1:26-29*, and see if you qualify. *"For ye see your calling, brethren, how that not many wise men after the flesh, not many mighty, not many noble, are called: But God hath chosen the foolish things of the world to confound the wise; and God hath chosen the weak things of the world to confound the things which are mighty; And base things of the world, and things which are despised, hath God chosen, yea, and things which are not, to bring to nought things that are: That no flesh should glory in his presence."*

That paints a pretty clear picture for us, doesn't it? – J. Haley

Prayer: Lord we always have our excuses for not stepping out into deeper waters out of fear, or enlarging our abilities because we can prove to be weak and a bit lazy when it comes to trusting You to always be there to catch us, pick us up, and do the impossible

27

to bring about Your promises in our life. All we need to do is choose to look, trust, and rely on You to do what is perfect and right. Amen.

January 18

"For unto us was the gospel preached, as well as unto them: but the word preached did not profit them, not being mixed with faith in them that heard it" (Hebrews 4:2). I have been thinking about the indifference of people towards God. Through the years I have occasionally struggled with my own indifference towards the matters of God.

As believers, we have much available to us but we often live like paupers. We become sulky because we don't get our way, mad because we are not immune from the sorrows and challenges of life, and defiant towards all spiritual matters because God will not bow down and serve us. After all, we have thrown our best crumbs at Him, put on our best religious, pious front to impress Him, do our duty by going to church, and ask Him to bless our attempts and prayers.

In my attempt to understand such a state, the Lord brought insight to it through the writings of A. W. Tozer. This godly man unveiled that the core of such indifference as being unbelief. Tozer stated, "Faith enables our spiritual sense to function. Where faith is defective the result will be inward insensibility and numbness towards spiritual things."

We are told in the Word that unless we mix faith to the truth and ways of God, it will not profit us. Without the pure intent of knowing and pleasing God that is found in the inspiration of blessed assurance of our Lord, we will never profit from the wisdom of heaven. We may intellectually know a matter is true, but if we do not walk in it, we will never experience the reality of truth where we actually come to a place of abiding in our Lord.

The place of abiding entails that blessed anchor of quiet confidence and joy in the Holy Ghost.

Prayer: Lord, unbelief is such a show of contempt towards Your character, Word, and plan. Forgive me for giving in to its shortsightedness and its ridiculous reality. Amen.

January 19

"For I am jealous over you with godly jealousy: for I have espoused you to one husband, that I may present you as a chaste virgin to Christ" (2 Corinthians 11:2). I cannot imagine the burden that the Apostle Paul felt over the condition and challenges some of the local churches were experiencing. For me I sometimes find myself in great distress over the condition of the church in America. I shake my head at the possibilities of how far away we have strayed from the course set for the new infant Church 20 centuries ago.

Admittedly, I have even been more so stressed when I have been accused of being radical in my faith. If only that was true, but I must honestly confess that I feel I fall quite short of the real mark set for the living Body of Christ. In some ways I would consider myself a bit warm compared to the bold preachers of old. There was such a fiery distinction in their manner of living. They had such a zeal because of the passion and power of the Holy Spirit. They were compelled by love, marked by righteousness, and led by a fire in them that burned brightly for the Gospel.

Christmas Evans made this statement, "The gospel, as a glass (mirror), should be kept clean and clear in the pulpit that the hearers may see the glory of Christ and be changed to the same image."

The true Gospel has been a casualty in the present religious environment. The light of it (Christ) has been alleviated by unbelief

29

and compromise. The warning of it (repent and flee the wrath of God upon all sin), has been done away with the hope of it (resurrection), that has been exchanged for wishful thinking. In essence, the glass has been fragmented by compromise, broken by heresy, and clouded by unbelief.

It is time for the mirror to be reestablished in its completeness so men can hear the message of life and hope and flee the wrath to come on all unbelief and disobedience to the Gospel.

Prayer: Lord, I am greatly concerned by my spiritual condition. I dare not test my present with how far I have come; rather, I must test my condition by how far away from the mark I am. Lord, I want to be ever so close to the mark that when I enter glory there will be no drastic change in my inner environment. I will know that I am finally home. Amen.

January 20

"He is the Rock, his work is perfect: for all his ways are judgment: a God of truth and without iniquity, just and right is he" *(Deuteronomy 32:4).* I was reading an article about the eastern way of looking at something versus the western way. For example, when it comes to justice, in the western world, we weigh judgments according to our sense of justice. However, the eastern way of looking at something is if God is just, then one must conclude that all God does is just whether or not it corresponds with our sense of justice.

The eastern way is the correct way when considering the attributes of God. God is just, and there is no room for questioning it because it will just turn into one judging God instead of trusting that in the end His justice will reign. Such judgments do not speak of wisdom but of unbelief. The eastern view is based on the character of God and not on His particular judgments. Clearly, the

Lord can never step outside of what is right or is considered a point of justice; therefore, all that He does is just.

I realize that my sense of justice is quite limited. God sees all and knows what is just. I see from a limited standpoint and must decide what is just. Clearly, God will do what is just, while I will maintain a limited understanding of what is right. It is for this reason that we often improperly judge God's ways as being unfair.

Prayer: Lord, Your Word is clear; we must not think so highly of ourselves that we end up judging You. In such arrogance we may believe we are right, but in due time Your Word will prove how wrong we are. Bring us up to the snubbing post of humility and break us in our stiff-necked ways. Amen.

January 21

"Whereas ye know not what shall be on the morrow. For what is your life? It is even a vapour, that appeareth for a little time, and then vanished away" (James 4:14). Today is my birthday. It is really just another day to me but it also marks a milepost for me to consider what kind of effect I have on those around me.

The truth is my life is a vapor. It is here one day and could be gone the next. I will only have this short time on earth, and possibly only one chance to impact a life. It all comes down to how I interact with people and whether I end up developing some relationship with them.

However, even what we consider to be good relationships are unpredictable and fleeing. The best relationship can hit a climax due to one situation that is acted out in a wrong spirit to topple it. When it comes to relationships with others it is risky business.

You may have a strong commitment towards certain individuals, but people have other ideas as to what they value. Once a relationship becomes upside down, it becomes that sting

31

of betrayal that leaves you raw, that judgmental arrogance that leaves your shaky, that fickle temperament that leaves you walking on eggshells, and that inward sense that the ball could drop at any time leaving you with a vapor of nothing when the smoke lifts.

My relationship with the Lord has taught me that every relationship has significance. Granted, it might not end on a good note, but as believers we must make sure that we do not create that sour note because of something foul in our character.

Prayer: Lord, I want this life to count for You. I know that my humanness has gotten in the way and left a foul taste, but Lord You know my weak frame, my heart, and my desire towards You. Have mercy on me at such times as I seek Your forgiveness and perspective. Amen.

January 22

Curiosity is basically the "desire to know." The good thing about curiosity from childhood to old age is that it can effectively lead us to learn something new every day; broaden one's interests; lead to growth in knowledge and understanding of what is good, practical, helpful, beneficial, truthful, inspirational, and spiritual (among other things) which can result in a person being far from dull and boring. BUT curiosity can also lead us down a dark pathway into dangerous and soul-damning knowledge, or even into another dimension.

In a broad sense, perhaps we could say that curiosity can be both a blessing or a curse, depending on where we allow it to take us—either to truth (good) or lies (evil). That is where I found myself one day back in the 80's when I visited a retired minister and his wife in their Christian book store in Everett, WA. As if reading my mind as I approached the pastor to pay for my purchases, he blurted out, "There's life on other planets, you know." I was stunned, and asked, "How did you know I wondered about that?" Then came the clincher, "God told me."

Since I was young and ignorant of the fact that not all people who claim to be a Christian are really what they claim to be, especially when they "hear from God just like that," I fell hook, line and sinker for his next sales pitch. "This book will tell you all about it," he said as he reached under his desk and pulled out a big, heavy book.

Curiosity plunged me into a whirlpool of excitement, so I squeezed out enough money to pay for it and hauled it home. When I asked him who had written it, he said nobody knows, but I figured if I searched through it enough, I would come up with the author.

The 2,097-page book seemed to "exude" something that I sensed was ethereal and different from regular publications. True, I could find no author, and it was also obvious to me that no human mind could configure and structure such unusual and unique verbiage. It had to have come from somewhere beyond this world. Proof of that manifested itself within three days of bringing that book into my home when I sensed I wasn't alone as I read it.

Their faint presence from another dimension grew stronger as fear submerged my sense of curiosity, replacing it with the knowledge that these beings were extremely tall, at least ten feet, that there were three of them, and that while they were celestial, they were definitely not "friendly" angels! Then I knew that these robed beings were silently waiting, and watching for me to make a decision—a decision as to whether or not I would deny the TRUTH of the Holy Bible and allow myself to be consumed by the lying spirit of that book!

Hastily, I flipped through it to find what it said about Jesus Christ, His incarnation, His death on the cross, and His resurrection. Somehow amidst all the copious "spiritualized"

33

language I got my answers, slammed the book shut, and marched it outside to the trash can. Once my decision was made and action taken, the ominous entities vanished.

And, that is the story of my encounter with the channeled "Mother book" of the popular, (also channeled) New Age book, "A Course in Miracles." The name of the mysterious and dangerous book that Satan wrote? It is simply called Urantia. *"But though we, or an angel from heaven, preach any other gospel unto you than that which we have preached unto you, let him be accursed. As we said before, so say I now again, If any man preach any other gospel unto you than that ye have received, let him be accursed"* Galatians 1:8, 9. *"BELOVED, believe not every spirit, but try the spirits whether they are of God: because many false prophets are gone out into the world"* 1 John 4:1. AMEN! – J. Haley

Prayer: Lord, how many times must we be warned about the end day deception before we tremble before Your Word, test the Spirit behind "so-called" revelations, and beware that there are seducing spirits in operation and doctrines of demons that will tickle the ears but cause a cold chill to run down the spine of any discerning saint. Forgive us for our arrogance and save us from our ignorance of You. Amen.

January 23

"For ye are dead, and your life is hid with Christ in God" *(Colossians 3:3).* The greatest challenge to any spiritual growth is one's ability to face reality for what it is. Once reality is faced, then there must be the necessary character to face it with clarity, grace, courage, and endurance. As we can see, real growth does not take place in the highlands of ecstasy, but in the valleys of drudgery, adversity, and humility.

I have to admit in my small world, it is hard to believe that there is a battle taking place in the valleys. I am sitting here in the peace and quietness of beautiful forests and mountains. I am aware that wickedness is raging, but God still sits on the throne. Evil has gained inroads, but God has a timing before He will show His unbridled wrath against all that is evil and opposes Him.

Meanwhile, I wait in a spiritual valley, but always seeking to occupy according to the highland of God's way that honors Him. Regardless of all that is happening, as a Christian I know where the eye of the storm is located. It is located in Christ. What a powerful word "in" is. It is all inclusive and it reminds me that Jesus is my blessed ark. In spite of how the storm rages around me, I am safe in Him. I will be lifted above the waves of judgment to endure to the end.

Prayer: Lord, we can walk with such great expectancy in You. Our lives are totally submerged in You and You are seated in high places. Lord, I am so thankful that You are my everlasting ark. Amen.

January 24

"For I bear them record that they have a zeal of God, but not according to knowledge" (Romans 10:2). As I consider the climate of religion, there seems to be much religious activity, but very little godliness. There appears to be much head knowledge, but no real heart revelation. There seems to be many characters who are zealously swinging from one popular religious movement to the next, but there is not much inward character that exhibits integrity.

It is easy to get caught up with the religious environment of the day, but in doing so we can easily miss what is real. Today our pursuit has become an intellectual one as a means to understand the things of God. However, understanding something does not mean it is a reality. In fact, to hold to something on an intellectual plane often means we do not hold to it in practice. We assume we know it, but until we apply it in practical ways, we do not know whether it is true or not.

A. W. Tozer relates how the scribe who appears knowledgeable tells us what he has read, while a prophet tells us what he has seen or experienced on the spiritual level. Clearly, there are grave differences between these two types of individuals. Tozer points out that we are overrun with orthodox scribes, but where are the prophets?

I agree with him. There are many scribes running through the religious world with their particular take on a matter, but there are few prophets who possess the necessary sling shots to aim the stones of truth at the heretics and their heresy in order to protect the souls of God's people.

It is obvious we have much lifeless and dangerous knowledge floating around, but there is only life in revelation that parts our limited understanding with a heavenly reality that will forever change our perspective about God.

Prayer: Lord, I know the traps of knowledge and I must often be snatched out of them. Thank You for directing my steps away from the temporary to bring me to the revelations that embrace the eternal. Amen.

January 25

"He is despised and rejected of men; a man of sorrows, and acquainted with grief: and we hid as it were our faces from him; he was despised, and we esteemed him not" (Isaiah 53:3). What are you majoring in? It is important to answer this question because whatsoever you are majoring in will also show you what you are probably minoring in.

It is important to keep in mind that you can only put your concentration and focus on one thing at a time or you will end up confused. What you emphasize, pursue, or count as significant, will indeed determine what you are majoring in. Everything outside of that perimeter will become a point of contention, resentment, and contempt because it is intruding into your reality and plan.

It is natural to put the emphasis on "good" things while missing the best. For example, we can put our emphasis on ministry, doing good, being Scripturally savvy, etc., and still miss what is important—that being Jesus Christ and His great work of redemption.

We can become quite romantic about Jesus, but when we taste the rejection of the world because of our association with Him, become identified with Him in His sorrow over lost humanity, know the grief of rejection, experience the sting of being despised because we won't fit in, and being cast aside by those who we thought were friends, that is another story altogether. That is when Christianity becomes serious and we have to count the cost of loving, walking with and becoming identified with our Lord and Savior. That is when many settle for the title, while running, hiding, and ducking from living out the life of Christ.

Prayer: Lord, we can talk big, act wonderful, pretend we have Your life and way of doing down pat, but when tested, it all becomes ash before You because Your life is nowhere to be found in any of it. Lord, I want to major in knowing You and stay away from anything that would cause me to minor in what is important to You. Amen.

January 26

"But exhort one another daily, while it is called To day; lest any of you be hardened through the deceitfulness of sin" (Hebrews 3:13).

As I have thought about the condition of the visible Church, I have come to realize that it reveals that sin is present. Sin has been greatly minimized and modified in much of the preaching that has been going forth from the pulpit. The subject of "sin" does not fit into the politically correct philosophy of this wicked world, nor does it set well with the feel-good taste buds of the worldly church in America.

Warren Wiersbe said it best when he penned this statement, "Remember this, that you cannot commit some preferred sin in private, and perform the work of the ministry in public, with facility and acceptance."

When sin was hidden in the camp of Israel, the army lost its battle. Today lives, homes, churches, and nations have been rendered inept in their duty, and powerless in the face of the enemy due to sin. The end result is a tragedy too great to imagine. Much of the Church lies powerless before an enemy that will eventually trample under any resolve that is left, as well as swallow up any fragile hope that remains.

All sin must first be exposed by the light and rooted out before our holy God can step on the scene to make matters right in our personal worlds.

Prayer: Lord, You are holy and cannot ignore sin whether it is hidden or blatant. It must first be dealt with before You can honor us with Your presence. Highlight my sin and root it out with the purging conviction of Your Spirit. Amen.

January 27

"And he spake a parable unto them to this end, that men ought always to pray, and not to faint" (Luke 18:1). Andrew Bonar believed that one of the greatest sins of omission was a prayerless life. I have to agree with his evaluation.

The Bible is clear that what is not of faith is sin. What most people fail to realize is that rebellion and lawlessness are the sins of commission. However, failure to apply faith in regard to obedience and doing what is right and honorable is a matter of unbelief. We do not believe God and obey Him when the opportunity presents itself to do what is right, and we choose to ignore it. Since we do not believe God, we will go the way of unbelief. We will fail to do right. Such failure is known as the sin of omission.

It takes faith to pray. It takes assurance to possess expectation that a matter will come to fruition. It takes confidence to move forward in steadfastness, knowing that the Lord will accomplish the feat according to His will.

God is faithful to keep His promise to each of us. However, nothing is accomplished without us first showing our confidence towards God in prayer that He will keep His promise and He will bring about a matter for His glory and purpose.

Prayer: Lord, it takes faith to persevere in prayer, the confidence of faith to wait, the assurance of faith to stand, and the steadfastness of faith to move forward in our spiritual walk. Lord, thank You for giving us the measure of faith to finish the course. Amen.

January 28

"Falling in love" may be a term used by most people older than a grade school kid, but nevertheless, that's what happened to me. Except, I didn't "fall in love" with a person and not even a wonderful pet in the same way that I "fell in love" with oil paints!

It all began when my parents bought me a paint-by-number oil paint set. The picture was of a bay mare and colt. Believe me, nothing could've made me happier, except maybe actually getting

39

a horse, but when you live in a city like Seattle, that's not going to happen.

I can still remember the "aroma" of those oils, the linseed oil, and the turpentine along with how the paint felt as it smoothly flowed off the tip of the paint brush onto the thin canvas. So that was the beginning of a love affair that lasted until 1995 because of the toxic heavy metals in the paints.

Through the years I had used other art mediums such as pencils, charcoal, watercolor, acrylics, and soft pastels but nothing held my heart like oils. Thus, it was like parting with a very huge part of my life when I had to give those precious tubes of oil paints away, but it was either that, or continue to physically suffer and deteriorate.

As Christians, we know that every talent and gifting we have is from the Lord whether it's in art, music or literature, or any other enjoyable occupation we may pursue. I think of the fishermen that Jesus called to follow Him. They had to leave their boats and nets behind to follow Jesus, and it wasn't easy for them either.

There's just something about the call of the wind and the water, the expectancy of a good catch, the robust challenge and joy of it all that can capture a fisherman's heart, but no matter what it is in this world that becomes a very part of our heart and innermost being, (and that can include ministry) the day will come when Jesus calls your name as He did to Peter and asks you, *"lovest thou me more than these?" (John 21:15-17).*

The question is, are you ready for His call? – J. Haley

Prayer: Lord, we think we can give everything up for You, until You touch the thing that brings us the most pleasure and purpose in life. It is then we realize that there are other things in competition for our devotion, affections, and pursuits that need to be directed towards You. Forgive us of our idolatry and deliver us from it. Amen.

January 29

"My voice shalt thou hear in the morning, O LORD; in the morning will I direct my prayer unto thee, and will look up" (Psalm 5:3). In meditating on prayer, I realized long ago that prayer is an entry way into fellowshipping with God. In regard to addressing this form of communication with God, Andrew Murray stated, "Christians do not realize that the aim of conversion is to bring them into daily fellowship with the Father in heaven."

I recognized that I need to begin my day entering through the door of prayer into the place of agreement with God about the matters that are important to His heart. I must walk according to what I have perceived in the place of sweet communion with Him; and, finally in the end come to a place of rest that the Lord had His way with me through the day.

The truth is I cannot freely enter into a place of prayer and communion with the Lord unless I am being constantly converted to the ways of God's righteousness. I cannot enter the place of fellowship with God if my conscience is disturbed by my attitude towards Him and my actions towards others. I must come to the Lord clean in conscience, pure in heart, and with clean hands.

Prayer: Lord, prayer is a privilege and a glorious opportunity wrapped up in one. As a result, in our foolishness we take it for granted and in our apathy we neglect it. Forgive us for being foolish in our attitude and silly in our actions about this gift. Grow us up in the sobriety of Your righteous ways in the hope of us gaining the type of attitude we need to develop in order to take advantage of entering into the entrance of prayer on a daily basis. Amen.

January 30

"I loathe it; I would not live always: let me alone; for my days are vanity" (Job 7:16). When one deeply considers the essence of their life, they will come to the same conclusion as Job, "for my days are vanity."

Life has made me a philosopher in many ways. When I consider the time man has on earth in light of eternity, I recognize he has so little time to become wise. As I consider man's limitations, he has very few means to get it right. In regarding the ways of man, they always prove foolish, and when I consider the end of man, nothing makes sense when it comes to this world and this present life.

The one question that caused me to consider that there must be more to this life was, "What is the purpose behind life if man is simply born to toil in this existence in order to die in the end?" This question makes man's existence seems useless, and in a sense, a terrible joke on him.

The questions simple, but thought provoking. If there is nothing past this life, we are the most miserable wretches because there is no real reason for life. If there is not some expectation past the end of man here, why not end the misery right off instead of struggling to live in the midst of death and destruction.

In my search to understand my existence, I discovered that there is purpose for this life, a reason for this odyssey I am on, and significance in the toil and despair I have experienced along the way. All of it was to bring me to the end of myself in order to discover my Creator.

The world is the testing ground to show us our lack, life the teacher to show us our need, toil the tool to reveal our ineptness, despair the reality of our existence, and hopelessness is what highlights the vanity around us. All of it is to cause us to look beyond the present world to know that our hope is in the unseen, our purpose has been established in the annuals of heaven, and our destiny established in the redemptive work that took place on an old rugged cross.

Prayer: Lord, the more I look for the purpose of life, the more insane the world becomes and the more precious Your truths become. Thank You for answering the important questions of life. Amen.

January 31

"(For we are but of yesterday, and know nothing, because our days upon earth are a shadow:)" (Job 8:9). To me one of the great philosophical books of all times is Job.

People do not need to go to some expensive secular college to learn about philosophy all they have to do is take the journey with Job as he struggled with all the issues of life. Even though Job was a man of faith, he expressed the great inward fight man has when he comes face to face with things that do not make sense, issues that seem unfair, and an existence that mocks man's inner core.

Instead of sitting in the mud of despair, pulling the blanket of depression over him and wallowing in the cesspool of self-pity, the man Job took an incredible journey that was frightening, overwhelming, and miserable. He treaded where few would dare go. He refused to accept the conclusion of man to silence accusations, and sought and waited for only one judgment call and that was God's take on the matter.

Every time I read Job, I am encouraged by his questions because he asked them in good faith. I am inspired by his courage to be honest about his great struggle in light of appearing weak, and I am blessed when Job comes out, not just knowing about God, but seeing Him in a personal way.

Job's great journey into the darkness of what we know to be God's sovereignty over all matters shows us that in the end God will reveal Himself to us. Once the light comes on everything will be clear, and there will be healing to the soul and restoration of the spirit.

Prayer: Lord, I love the book of Job because in the end you answered all of his questions by revealing Yourself to him. In light of You, even what we consider the most important matters of life become insignificant. Amen.

FEBRUARY

February 1

"Man that is born of a woman is of few days, and full of trouble. He cometh forth like a flower, and is cut down: he fleeth also as a shadow, and continueth not" (Job 14:1-2). The many questions I had about the struggles of life were answered in the book of Job. It does not mean I comprehended the answer, it is that I know the answer.

The answers are found within the sovereignty of God. Although God's sovereignty is the answer, it is what creates the darkness that prevents man from comprehending the intricacies to the many "whys" of a matter. What can be known when it comes to God's sovereignty is how man often reacts to it. The book of Job is all about man's reaction to the darkness of the unknown and mysterious workings of God.

Job had an incredible handle on man. In the delusion of man's self-sufficiency, he rarely understands the fragileness of his existence. To him the bad things of life happen to others because such individuals have no real face, name or identity, but never to him or his small world. Somehow, he thinks he is immune from it or is an exception to it.

Man lives in a type of reality that is, for the most part, divorced from the stark truth that man's strength is for a few days, his glory is like a vapor, his light shines for only a moment, and his life is like a shadow that is illuminated by the light above, but once the

45

light passes it becomes part of the shadows that fade into the darkness of the grave of death.

The life on this earth is part of a cycle that begins with great hope but ends in a lonely grave. In between the beginning of life and the end of it, man must discover the real source and purpose behind it (God), as well as the promise and potential of life (reflecting the Son) to experience its fullness.

However, to get from point A to point Z man must pass through the great darkness of what is unknown and accept that it will most likely remain so as long as he looks through the dark glass of his flesh. It is at this point he must trust that what counts is what he knows about the true God of heaven and His great work of redemption through His Son Jesus Christ.

Prayer: Lord, our time on earth is short, our opportunity to shine fleeting, and our moment to ensure our destiny is fulfilled is like a "flash in the pan," but you have recorded each aspect of our lives in the annuals of heaven to ensure they serve as an eternal witness of Your grace flowing downward, Your love reaching out, Your faithfulness to keep us, and Your powerful sovereignty to bring us home. Amen.

February 2

"And said, Verily I say unto you, Except ye be converted, and become as little children, ye shall not enter into the kingdom of heaven" (Matthew 18:3). As I have made reference to in one of my posts is that which has often inspired me in my spiritual walk has been certain friends. Friends come in all kinds of sizes, and shapes, as well as from different backgrounds. As a result, they have added different dimensions to my spiritual life.

This day marks a birthday of one of them. Her name is Gloria Craft, and as a ministry team we first met her in 1997. Gloria

46

inspired me about faith. She has a child-like faith that moves what seems like mountains and at times trusted God to straighten out some crooked paths that lay before her. Gloria and her husband once owned a Christian book store and she was the president of the Aglow in her community. I remember a situation where she was involved in scheduling a famous violinist to come and play for the community.

As the time approached, they realized a place for him had not yet been secured. I found myself witnessing faith in action as this woman with her child-like faith looked up to God and trusted Him to provide a place. He did not disappoint her.

I think the real power of Gloria's child-like faith has always been exercised in her prayer closet. Faith moves mountains before us but it often straightens out certain attitudes and ways in us as well. It is in prayer and by faith one learns how to fight the good fight and endure to the end until a matter has been completed.

Gloria will tell you that there are always matters that remain incomplete when it comes to the world, but child-like faith keeps trusting God to work out all matters for His glory. After all, what is so in heaven, will also be so on earth. We may not see it completed here but when we get to heaven, we will know that all matters will be as they should be.

Prayer: Lord, faith simplifies things and when we exercise it, it becomes simple as to what Your part is and that our part is to simply stand on what is so. Thank You for giving us sustaining faith to see us through to the end. Amen.

February 3

"Be still, and know that I am God: I will be exalted among the heathen, I will be exalted in the earth" (Psalm 46:10). As stated

yesterday, friends have served as points of inspiration along the way for me. It is amazing that two of our dear friends celebrate their birthdays in February, a day apart from each other. My next friend has inspired me with her courage.

Her name is Wanda Hiebert. I have known her since 2012. We met in a church and it was there that the Holy Spirit put a spotlight on her and drew us to her. She seemed shocked that we would even consider her, but we knew there was something special about her and that there was an immediate agreement in the spirit.

We have been on different paths with Wanda and she with us that included illnesses, inner struggles, broken hearts, and despairing circumstances. We know such adversities are part of the tools that the Lord uses to grow us up spiritually, but it is comforting to know that you have friends that back you up in prayer and are watching your backside.

The characteristic that stands out about Wanda is her inner courage. Courage is a matter of faith that finds the inner strength to stand on what is true. Even though courage would like to take a bow in order to cower in some corner, it refuses to because there is no victory in hiding from challenges, running away from what seems defeat, or giving up when the victory is ever before you.

Her inner courage is based on her faith towards God and in His Word. Through her difficulties she reminds me that strength is from God and that the greatest victories occur when one truly becomes still in their spirit and confident in their soul and knows without a doubt that God is God, and that no matter what, He has got it all under control.

Prayer: Lord, in a world where we are being constantly bombarded by every challenge possible, we still must learn to be still before You so we can discern Your intervention, recognize Your way in a matter, and be content with Your timing, knowing You are perfect in all Your doings. Amen.

February 4

"By this shall all men know that ye are my disciples, if ye have love one to another" (John 13:35). The shortest month of the year is known for "love." We have Valentine's Day coming up and I wonder how many couples are working their way up to something special as they plan how they are going to celebrate their love, time, and life together.

Let's face it, the world greatly benefits from the gestures of love from flowers to cards to romantic dinners. The question is how much does it personally affect, change, or strengthen the relationship of those who get caught up with this commercial wave and promotion of something that has been greatly corrupted?

How much of the hoopla about "love" is wishful thinking that will end in a big letdown or a branch of expectation that one swings from, but is unable to find another branch to catch in order to continue the ecstasy. Such a person will crash land on the rocks of disillusionment and disappointment. The question I have is when will we as Christians finally let go of the silly notions and sentiments we have about love and truly come to terms with love according to God?

The concept of love has been corrupted by romanticizing it. It has been exploited by Hollywood, commercialized by advertisement, and made sentimental gobbledygook that is heightened by tension played out in movies and in books that hits a climax, but has nowhere to go but down into oblivion.

However, God's love is not of this world. It has no agreement with it and passes it by when compared to it. Unlike God's love the world's love is based on fanciful notions and not commitment. It dances in heights of expectation instead of walking out love in sacrificial ways. The world's love flits about while God's love stands on, stands by, and stands for what is sure.

Sadly, there are those even in Christianity who want to hold on to the silliness surrounding worldly love, chase after the unfounded expectation of the ecstasy based on the pure lust of the flesh, and refuse to land on the reality of God's love. This should not be because it is God's love for one another that identifies us to the kingdom of God.

Prayer: Lord, I choose Your love that is lasting, sacrificial, and enduring. Thank You for displaying Your love on the cross, manifesting it in bodily form, and making it available to all who will come to You by faith seeking Your life. Amen.

February 5

Ever so sweetly one of our Bible study students took my hand, smiled into my eyes and said, "Your earrings don't match—they're different." Sure enough! I had done it again. Somehow, I always get my socks to match, but the part that's visible to the rest of the world can sometimes relay a different story. Another lovable sister said she had all her makeup on, but didn't realize she forgot to comb her hair until she looked in the mirror.

These little "flub-up's" give us cause to laugh at ourselves, and spread the joy of our common humanity to others. Try as we might, our outward appearance will most likely never look totally perfect in this fallen world, but what truly matters is how our "innermost man," that is, our hearts, appear to God.

When He looks at us, He doesn't turn away because of our physical flaws; rather, He resists pride (*1 Peter 5:5*) and sin (*Habakkuk 1:14*.) Our time on this earth is way too short to make our outward appearance our number one priority while forgetting that what is important to God is the condition of our heart.

Remember what the LORD said to Samuel, *"Look not on his countenance, or on the height of his stature; because I have refused him: for the LORD seeth not as man seeth; for man looketh on the outward appearance, but the LORD looketh on the heart"* *(1 Samuel 16:7).* – J. Haley

Prayer: Lord, we want to be perfect in this life and strive for perfection in preparation for the next, but the truth is we will only come to perfection when we see You face to face in Your glory. Meanwhile, thank You for Your Spirit's work of sanctification in my life. It reminds me that I must submit to it and that "perfection" is Your work. Amen.

February 6

"And we departed from Horeb, we went through all that great and terrible wilderness" (Deuteronomy 1:19a). The other day I started pondering how far the Lord has brought me in my spiritual life. As I considered the terrain of the past, I could not help but notice how rugged and challenging it has been.

There were the pinnacle points of my adolescent years, the deep canyons of uncertainties and struggles in my young adult days, the highlight of my salvation in my 20s, and the ascension up the spiritual mountain of discovery and growth in my 30s, to only encounter the shadows of the valleys in the initial years of ministry.

I would not trade any part of my journey, but I am so glad that I do not have to pass that way again. My hope is that I have learned the lessons of my past so that I can properly stand today and effectively move forward to my final destination.

Even though I have occasionally gone around the same mountain, my desire is to learn what life has been designed to teach me. The lesson is simple. I must ascend upward into greater revelation and not downward into a rut of utter dismay. Such a rut is present because I failed to heed the signpost marks provided along the way that warned me of detours of the world and the dead ends of the flesh.

Prayer: Lord, You have provided so many signposts along the way by Your Spirit and with Your Word, but in the past I have allowed the foolishness of my pride and the silliness of selfishness to sway me away from the warnings. Lord, I may have gathered wisdom from such detours, but I prefer to avoid them and learn the ways of Your wisdom by treading down the path You have carved out for me. Amen.

February 7

"But his wife looked back from behind him, and she became a pillar of salt" (Genesis 19:26). Yesterday I paused to consider the past. Admittedly I had to stop as I passed the signpost of my past. You possibly know the post as "Memory Lane." I was thinking about the wondrous reality that God is the one who gives us the glorious opportunity to leave the past behind us. In a way, it is like being given a second chance to discover the life that has been designed for you.

As I thought about the past, images and people paraded through my mind. As I considered each image, I realized that even though the images represented different aspects of my life I had no desire to pass that way again.

Regardless of what was, it can never be again. The past has receded into the vast wilderness of what was in order to prepare me for what can be. But, to discover what can be, I must not look backward, but forward.

The one lesson my life in Christ has taught me is that my life in Him will always be before me. After all, the failures of my past have been forgiven, my present is in the hand of my ever-present God, and my future is already secured in the corridors of heaven.

Therefore, I stand in assurance of today and in the abiding confidence of what tomorrow holds for me.

Prayer: Lord, You are precious. You have gone before me in order to meet me at the end of my journey. I am looking forward to being in Your presence and glory forever. Amen.

February 8

"And of his fullness have all we received, and grace for grace" (John 1:16). Andrew Murray wrote that Jesus Christ gives grace each new day, and our faith must reach out according to the needs of the day.

There is some confusion about how grace and faith work. Grace is God's part where He shows favor to undeserving man, while faith is our part where we believe that He has shown us grace and act upon it by allowing it to transform our lives before Him. We must keep in mind that each time faith acts upon a matter, it is not only reckoned for righteousness by the Lord, but it also speaks of conversion.

We are always being converted to the righteous ways of God. Each step of conversion leads us up the path of righteousness to that place of quiet confidence and rest in the Lord.

As you realize that Christ gives us the necessary grace to be converted to the ways of righteousness, it becomes obvious that God has given us everything that pertains to life and godliness. We have need of nothing, and yet many of us live as cringing beggars because we do not apply His instructions by faith, thereby, experiencing the spiritual blessing and promises that come with it.

Prayer: Lord, I thank You for all You have done for me. You have shown me grace beyond any measure. My prayer is that when I encounter Your grace, it activates the faith that is present to not only embrace it in the right way, but to assimilate it in my life as truth in order to walk it out to experience Your life in me. Amen.

February 9

"(Praise the LORD) Mountains, and all hills; fruitful trees, and all cedars…Let them praise the name of the LORD; for his name alone is excellent; his glory is above the earth and heaven" (Psalm 148:9, 13) (Parenthesis added to ensure intent.) Fall is absolutely beautiful here in northern Idaho. The colors reveal the artistic ability of our great Creator.

What a magnificent Spirit He has to express the beauty of His very being. I can only relate it to two maple trees that mark the entrance to our garage at our former residence. These two trees stood distinct among various bushes and other leafy trees displaying yellow, yellow green, orange, peach, and brown leaves along with green pine and fir trees. What causes these maple trees to stand distinct is that their leaves emit a blazing color of red. Even though there is beauty all around them, these two trees would immediately catch your eye. You couldn't help but notice them.

Like the maple trees, God in the midst of His beautiful creation stands distinct. Such beauty does not compete with Him; rather, it speaks of His majesty. As I used to gaze upon these most glorious trees, I'd ask myself if my life in Christ stood distinct. Was His glory obvious or did my life fade into the background because it had been made drab by compromise and worldliness? Therefore, I must remember that I'm called to be erect like strong trees that are rooted deep in the foundation of God while they reach high into the sky towards the life-giving rays of the sun.

Prayer: Lord, Your heavenly beauty is beyond description. It is for this reason I believe that the beauty of Your creation simply reveals the greatness of Your majesty, but it will never be able to describe the immensity of it. If it could, You would not be God. Amen.

February 10

"Therefore if any man be in Christ, he is a new creature; old things are passed away; behold, all things are become new" (2 *Corinthians 5:17).* When we lived by Priest River, I would rise up every day with the expectation of seeing the beauty of the river that we had the privilege to live alongside. I was fascinated by the incredible inspiration it displayed by its splendor and ever-changing appearance. In a way, I watched the constant flow of the seasons of life that occur during the year.

From the slow-moving river of summer, it suddenly immerged as a fast-moving river in the fall. Once hindered by a submerged sand bar, it would forge its way around that obstacle as it gained momentum. Unlike in the summer, you could hear its pulse as it rushed to its destination.

In springtime and summer there would be more water making its way down the corridor between the banks of the river. It began to cover up the sand bar. Whether the volume of water was due to a rainstorm or a change of volume from the small dam upstream remained unknown to me. Nevertheless, the river seemed to reinvent itself.

As Christians, the flow of God's living water has the capacity of causing newness or revival to our lives. In a way, the pulse and movement of the water from heaven will reinvent the person we are becoming. Therefore, let the storms come and the dams be opened to let the water from heaven have its way in my soul.

Prayer: Lord, prevent me from allowing the flow of Your water in and through my life to be hindered by any obstacles left behind by self or the world. I need to ensure the current of Your life is freely flowing through me. Amen.

February 11

"For we are his workmanship, created in Christ Jesus unto good works, which God hath before ordained that we should walk in them" (Ephesians 2:10). Rivers always make an impression on me. They express the type of terrain they move through, whether through reflection or through their speed and rapids. One element that causes a river to become mysterious is fog. It's hard to see the clear movements of the river when fog hangs over it. I had to note in the past that fog creates its own beauty when it comes to a river.

The type of beauty it creates is a mystical environment. However, the beauty of the fog is not really evident until the rays of the sun part the gray curtain, exposing the magnificent colors and shapes of the landscape.

It seems that there is often a blanket "of fog" upon my soul. I must trust that God is doing a deeper work and that in time His light will push back the blanket that covers my innermost being, revealing His magnificent handiwork. I also know that I can live in expectation of seeing His artistry upon my life, recognizing that His light will emit the warmth of His love, mercy, and grace.

I must remember that once the curtain of fog is parted, the warmth of God's light will penetrate my soul. However, the depth and color it will bring to my life will be beyond description. But, once the light floods my soul, it will once again revive my spirit and restore my confidence in Him.

Prayer: Lord, I thank You for the light that will always penetrate the darkness of my soul to reveal Your glorious work upon the terrain of my soul. Amen.

February 12

"For God is not the author of confusion, but of peace, as in all churches of the saints" (I Corinthians 14:33). Fog not only makes the rivers mysterious, but it covers mountains as well. Beginning in the fall until early spring, the fog can lay low on the mountains, making them appear insignificant.

Fog is an interesting element of nature. When it rests or floats around the mountains, it adds a mysterious quality to the environment. Fog either hides or obscures something; therefore, it seems to add secrecy to the scenery. As you watch it, you must wait in anticipation as to what will be revealed when it finally lifts.

The other feature about fog is that it can blind a person as to where they are, as well as the right way to go. If the fog is thick around a person, they can actually become lost. It can endanger an individual if they are driving a vehicle within the confines of its thick blanket. It has caused horrible accidents which have killed and injured many people.

In the spiritual realm fog represents confusion. In the present darkness there is much fog hanging onto the souls of men. They are confused, often unable to clearly see through the fuddled reality that such confusion brings upon their minds. They struggle as they cannot see past the confusion to see where they are going, or what is in front of them, or what is to their side, and they don't dare stop because they don't know what is behind them.

God is a God of order. There is no confusion in His ways. His path is clear, and His course is set in light of His destiny for His people who are waiting for His leading. Therefore, confusion finds its source either in the flesh or in the spirit of the world. For this reason, before I can move, I need to discern the source of my confusion as I wait for God to bring clarity to the environment around me.

Prayer: Lord, help me discern my confusion. I know You are a God void of perplexity; therefore, all must fall into line with Your perfect order to cut through any fog or blanket of confusion. Amen.

February 13

"Wherefore, my beloved, as ye have always obeyed, not as in my presence only, but now much more in my absence, work out your own salvation with fear and trembling" (Philippians 2:12). Andrew Bonar stated that many want salvation, but they do not want the Savior. How true this has been proven to me time and time again. People want the benefit that is attached to salvation but they don't want the responsibility that comes with Jesus being their Savior and Lord. The responsibility comes out of what it means to have a relationship with the Lord.

The harsh reality of salvation is that people want to use Christ for their own purpose, abuse Him to ensure their own reality, and tack Him on to their life in order to give their ineffective religion some credibility. However, Christianity is about possessing the life, the person of Jesus. I am to be like Christ, my body should be His platform and I must become an instrument in which He can freely use me for His glory.

The real tragedy of this matter is that people may want to be associated with Christ for the benefits, but if they are not identified with His death, burial, and resurrection, then there will be no witness or assurance of salvation. We must remember that Jesus came to benefit us by saving us. This is the greatest gift of all and the very promise from heaven we cannot afford to miss, misuse, or neglect.

Prayer: Lord, we cannot afford to neglect Your salvation. Help me to value it above all else by valuing who You are. Amen.

February 14

"I have fought a good fight, I have finished my course, I have kept the faith" (2 Timothy 4:7). As I meditate on the Christian walk, I am always reminded of Paul's famous words in *2 Timothy 4:7*, and I ask myself, "How close do you want to be to the Lord?"

Some people are willing to walk parallel to the ways of God, but fail to line up to them so that they can be in His way. There are those who stand outside of the gate, hoping they are close enough but fail to enter through it to establish whether they are within the place of refuge and safety from the predators of this present world. There are some who enter through the gate but maintain their closeness with the world while avoiding consecrating their life to serving the Lord. There are also those who enter the door of service but remain in the shadows of religion so they can maintain their right to life and service on their terms.

The truth is we need to line ourselves up to the ways of the Lord Jesus Christ, put aside all worldly notions about serving Him and consecrating our whole heart and lives out of love in service to Him. And, it is in such consecration that we will have the confidence to enter through the veil of communion and worship where we can approach the throne in humility by seeking Him and His mercy, while knowing we will experience the abundant flow of His grace from His throne.

How close do you want to be to the Lord? It's not unusual to settle for just a glance at Him, a "brush" with Him, a quick encounter, or experience with Him. We must press forward like Paul and in due time we will be able to declare what Job stated in *Job 42:5, "I have heard of thee by the hearing of the ear: but now mine eye seeth thee."*

Prayer: Lord, Paul had it right. We must be willing to fight the good fight in order to advance forward on the course You have ordained, but it requires faith that stands, endures, and ultimately possesses the promises of heaven. Amen.

February 15

"Hearken, my beloved brethren, Hath not God chosen the poor of this world rich in faith, and heirs of the kingdom which he hath promised to them that love him" (James 2:5)? I love to watch creation in action. Today after a stormy day, the sun has broken through to reveal the shades, shapes, and colors of the countryside. I remember when we lived by the river that when it was cold, the mist would dance on top of the thin melting sheet of ice that would expose the river rushing towards its destination. The clouds were usually lying low on the mountains.

In my spiritual journey, I have seen many glorious sights and discovered many treasures when it comes to the examples of creation. As I traveled along the way, I realized that if the light of God had not broken through the darkness, I would never have seen such beauty or gained the insight to discover God's incredible treasures.

His treasures abound around us in so many ways. They cast shade upon our souls to bring relief from the weariness created by the journey. They shape us as we seek to find them, and they add depth and color to what appears to be our dreary existence. They bring hope and expectation back into our walk.

The only way we can gain such treasures is by faith. I must activate my faith to seek out and possess those treasures that God has planted in my path. However, in order to find them I must not veer away from the course He has set for me.

Prayer: Lord, you are forever gracing my life with treasures. You have planted them on the path You have ordained for me. Keep my feet on the course You have prepared for me and illuminate Your treasures. Amen.

February 16

"Not by works of righteousness which we have done, but according to his mercy he saved us, by the washing of regeneration, and renewing of the Holy Ghost" (Titus 3:5). February is a hard month. January proves to be a big let down from all the hoopla that has taken place for at least three months, but February is in between the darkness of cold and the breaking forth of spring time. Perhaps that is why February is set aside to celebrate "love."

It is in the month of February that three of our sweet furry companions met their fate of death. The memory of them often creates its own dark clouds, and the love that is felt for them turns into sorrow, an anguish of the soul that occurs after one loses the gem that gleamed with life and love, bringing incredible joy to the soul.

As I wrestle with February, I realize that there is much I can be thankful for. True, when I think of love, I am thankful for the love of God, the loving relationships in my life, and the fact that the sun is beginning to shine longer causing the darkness to flee. I realize that even though certain losses bring anguish, I for one could not imagine my life without such gems because they added so much to it.

February reminds me that the light is beginning to break forth and it will reveal the terrain of one's soul. It will show the marks of winter that are still clinging, and the barrenness of the terrain without the beauty and life that God provides, but for the Christian it does so in light of the regenerating work of the Holy Spirit.

February must come so that the terrain of the soul will give way to the new life being brought forth, revealing the deep work of God upon tender, immature, weary-ladened souls.

Prayer: Lord, we love the beauty of Your creation, but avoid, shun, and hate the process it takes to bring forth such beauty along with its glorious fruits. Lord, thank You for Your abiding care on and in my life in all of its different seasons. Amen.

February 17

"Guaranteed for Life." That's what the salesclerk in the men's department proudly told me, back in those long-ago days when stores actually hired people to help customers. I was out shopping for some gifts for my husband, and found a great buy on a pair of men's work socks. "Guaranteed for life," he had said, so I asked, "Who's 'life'—his or the socks?"

He was shocked into silence, and my question never got answered. Anytime I hear an ad on TV, (and that's what TV is most of the time, just ads) and the words "Guaranteed for life" are emphasized, I still wonder just whose or what's "life" and for how long.

When it comes to guarantees where our earthly lives are concerned, we soon learn that the world can't guarantee us anything, because no matter how you look at it, everything has a point of expiration. Only God Almighty knows how much time you and I have on this earth, but what He does tell us in *Ephesians 5:16 is "Redeeming the time, because the days are evil."* And, again in *Colossians 4:5* believers are urged to *"Walk in wisdom toward them that are without, redeeming the time."*

Therefore, before our "guarantee" runs out in this world, may we adhere to *Psalm 90:12, "So teach us to number our days, that we may apply our hearts unto wisdom"* and, concerning *wisdom 1*

Corinthians 1:30 tells us, *"But of him are ye in Christ Jesus, who of God is made unto us wisdom, and righteousness, and sanctification, and redemption."*

Thanks be to God, for His "guarantees" are eternal if we continue to abide in Him. – J. Haley

Prayer: Lord You are the only One that can guarantee anything not only for this life time but for eternity. Man's best is temporary and fading, but Your best is perfect and forever. Thank You for guaranteeing me eternal life. Amen.

February 18

"Let us come before his presence with thanksgiving, and make a joyful noise unto him with psalms" (Psalm 95:2). The other day I mentioned being thankful. We have to learn to be thankful before we can learn how to appreciate what is around us. So much of our life is stifled because we are not thankful and we can't appreciate the small gifts around us, enjoy the beauty that exists, and the life that we have been given.

The problem is that if thankfulness is missing, it creates a vacuum where discontentment, murmurings, and disillusionment takes up residence, making the person miserable. Misery is like a smelly swamp that one becomes more bogged down in as they struggle with the mire of it.

The other day I was wrestling over a matter concerning my physical well-being. As I was questioning the Lord why He seemed to remain silent about it, He asked me when I last thanked Him for my tabernacle, (my body) that He gave me. I have to admit I was a bit shocked because I am finding as I get older I have more and more limitation cropping up, and as a result I failed to see the many avenues I still can function in, in spite of my limitations.

I have always thought of myself as a "half-full" type of person, but I began to realize that by focusing on the limitations I was encountering, I was creating a vacuum in my soul that was being filled by the wrong attitudes. It was robbing me of the joy that I could have, preventing me from coming to a place of appreciation where I could see the many blessings I have been given, and thank Him for them.

Prayer: Lord, thank You for my tabernacle. It has endured the rigors of this world, the abuses of foolishness, and the tidal waves of time. I am still going, maybe slower, but even that is a blessing because I can enjoy longer the many different gifts You have graced my life with. Amen.

February 19

"And they lifted up their voice, and wept again: and Orpah kiss her mother-in-law; but Ruth clave unto her" (Ruth 1:14). One of my favorite Biblical people is Ruth. When we think of this Moabite woman, we think in terms of her giving up her gods, family, and home to follow Naomi. This sounds noble, but the reality is that Ruth was not pursuing just any god, she wanted to know the one true God of Israel, Jehovah God.

What we can easily overlook is that a clear, notable testimony had to first be established before Ruth would ever consider such a radical pursuit. She had to have a knowing that what she was witnessing in the life of Noami about her faith towards Jehovah was true.

When we consider the story of Ruth, we realize that we have two diverse examples presented to us. We have an Orpah who possessed a type of affectionate sentiment towards Naomi, but there was no real heart conviction; but, as for Ruth, she was not about to let Naomi leave without her as she literally clung to her.

Religion and sentiment without real conviction and conversion will produce various responses. There can be a zeal, but it will fade with the digression of emotional momentum. There is that emotional attachment due to some history or experience with a person, but that will flee when things become rough, causing one to run back to that which is familiar. There can be declarations of commitment, but they will become silent and are quickly dropped and left behind as one runs back to that which is understandable.

The question is, are we clinging to what is eternal or are we settling back into what is normal about our past life and familiar with when it comes to our religious influences.

Prayer: Lord, we all want to believe we are like Ruth when it comes to our life in You, but how many of us are like Orpah, with a tear of regret in our eye and a kiss on the cheek, we still go back to what was in order to avoid being exposed by the light of heaven? Amen.

February 20

"When she saw that she was stedfastly minded to go with her, then she left speaking unto her" (Ruth 1:18). Ruth and Orpah remind me of the two camps of Christians that I have observed. There is always a choice on each of our parts as to how far we will go in our Christian walk.

There are those who feel bad that they don't go all the way when it comes to following Jesus into a new, consecrated life and will even bemoan it a bit, but since it is sentiment, they will go back to what is familiar after a kiss, and never be heard of again. Then there are those like Ruth who cleave to Jesus with everything in them and will not let Him leave without them.

Ruth was introduced to the God of Israel and drawn to Him through Naomi. The simple truth is that there must be a Naomi before a Ruth can find her way to God and His redemption. This Moabite woman was willing to follow this Israelite woman through various trials and uncertainty to know this one true God of heaven. Ruth's faithfulness and desire brought her to the feet of Boaz, Naomi's kinsman redeemer. There, she was redeemed and placed at his table as his wife.

If we know Jesus, are we like Naomi, seasoned enough in our testimony of Him to attract the Ruths of the world to Him? Do we understand Jesus' redemption enough that we can instruct the Ruths of this age to seek it at the Savior's feet? If so, this will ensure redemption for all who choose the route of seeking the true God, because both Ruth and Naomi were redeemed, and it all happened because after being instructed by the "Naomi's", the "Ruth's" will find their place at the feet of "Boaz" (Jesus), who ensures such seeking souls that they will become part of His bride.

Prayer: Lord, help me to remember why I am here. Never let me settle for the waning sentiment towards You of an Orpah, but cause me to have the type of devotion of a Ruth who is willing to follow You while even trying see clearly through the maze of this world in order to come to terms with You as my true Creator. Amen.

February 21

"And it came to pass, when Moses came down from Mount Sinai with the two tables of testimony in Moses' hand, when he came down from the mount, that Moses wist not that the skin of his face shone while he talked with him" (Exodus 34:29). Living around rivers and lakes remind me that the color of the water comes from above. The color of the sky is what determines the color of the water.

Water is clear, therefore, it is transparent. It can only reflect that which dots the shoreline, rests on its bottom, flows through its currents, or resides above it. Clearly, water takes on a life of its own according to its surroundings.

I learned long ago that the extent of transparency in our lives will determine our surroundings. Like the water, we will in essence reflect what we expose ourselves to the most. This simple concept is hard for people to believe. They do not realize that we have been created to reflect the image of the type of life being formed in us. Our countenance, attitude, prevailing mood, and mannerisms reveal what type of life we are exposed to, and what type of life we are taking on.

I must consider what type of life I am being conformed to. It will not only reveal my inward environment, but my preferences as well. May my environment be humble and my preference holy and right.

Prayer: Lord, You are my preference. I want to expose myself to You in Your most Holy Place. I want to come out reflecting You and not my base self that has been influenced by the present age. Amen.

February 22

"A good tree cannot bring forth evil fruit, neither can a corrupt tree bring forth good fruit" (Matthew 7:19). Yesterday I talked about the type of life I am taking on at the present. The life I am living will say much about who I am allowing myself to become.

The problem with people is that they will not own the life they are living. They want to blame bad decisions, actions, and consequences on circumstances. They want to accuse others for their wrong attitudes, and they want to shift the evidence of foul moods onto their environment. In essence, they want to divorce

67

themselves from the reality of the fruits they are producing. These self-centered fruits prove to be unpleasant to others, foul to those who have a constant diet of them, and deadly to their own souls.

It has taken me years to own my life. The tendency of selfishness is to make such unacceptable ways noble, and the trend of the world is to blame such personal wrongs on others, while the ways of Satan are to seal such people in the darkness of deception. It is for this reason that I have had to learn to be brutally honest about what my life is telling about the inner environment that I now abide in.

It's up to me to take ownership of who I'm becoming. In the end, I will be standing before the righteous judge of the universe giving an account of who I actually allowed myself to become.

Prayer: Lord, it is hard to keep the integrity of the inner man when so much assails it from the flesh, the world, and Satan. However, You know how to keep us and do the miraculous by finishing the work You have begun in us. Praise Your holy Name. Amen.

February 23

Sometimes you just can't see what you're looking at. It's been months since our big beautiful Flamingo Dappled Willow bush was given a good "haircut." When we first planted it several years ago, it was maybe only a couple of feet high, but now it towers over our heads. When spring comes, it's fresh new leaves are a lovely blend of pale pink, white and apple green.

Now that most of the surrounding foliage is undressed for winter, trunks, twigs, and branches are easy to see. Here's the thing—because I assumed that all the branches had been pruned on that big bush, I failed to see one straight branch sticking straight out of the top of it that resembles an antenna. Now when I look out the window, that out-of-place "stick" is a very obvious and annoying flaw in the landscape.

The lesson here is what do we really see when we stop long enough to "examine" our hearts? Do we allow the light of the Holy Spirit to shine upon those things that we simply "assume" have been taken care of "way back when" or are there still residues of sin or shame, unforgiveness, fear or anger that need to be repented of and given to the Lord Jesus Christ to heal and cleanse us from so that there is nothing between our heart and His? *"Search me, O God, and know my heart: try me, and know my thoughts: And see if there be any wicked way in me, and lead me in the way everlasting." (Psalm 139:23, 24.)* – J. Haley

Prayer: Lord, we are told to examine ourselves, but so many times we assume we are alright because nothing has come against our bow to show us that we have become spiritually sluggish. Cause Your Spirit to stir us up to truly examine our spiritual condition. Amen.

February 24

"That we henceforth be no more children, tossed to and fro, and carried about with every wind of doctrine, by the sleight of men, and cunning craftiness, whereby they lie in wait to deceive" *(Ephesians 4:14).* The life I reflect has a lot to do with what I come into agreement with. The truth is, until I come into agreement with something, I will be like a tossed wave on the ocean, being driven by anything that comes along that takes my fancy captive. In such a state I will not have any idea where I will land until I hit the rocks or the shoreline.

The truth is many people are looking for a place of agreement in which they can confidently land. They are hoping something will attract or alert them to some type of purpose or place of significance. Once they come across such an attraction, they will fling themselves towards it in abandonment.

As a Christian, I must properly discern my restlessness. Only Christ can give my life meaning and purpose. He alone satisfies, but I must come into a place of agreement with my Lord. It is only by exposing myself to Him and His Word that I will be able to take on His likeness.

Prayer: Lord, You alone are the One who will give us substance and abiding confidence, for You serve as the glorious Rock that will never be moved from truth and righteousness. Amen.

February 25

"A friend loveth at all times, and a brother is born for adversity" *(Proverbs 17:17).* As I have stated through the years the Lord has graced my life with various people. They bring with them a fresh wind that sometimes serves as a breath of inspiration.

In ministry the investment in the harvest field can prove to be long and tedious. Sometimes you see fruits at different stages in the lives of God's people. Once in a while the Lord brings people into your life at different places and in situations that are seeking more of Him, and it is like being put in another field with different scenery and a whole new crop to deal with that will change up things and add a different type of flavor to the mix.

He has always brought such people our way. They have different names and callings in their lives, but they bring something into your life that will cause you to get out of the rut you may have been laboring in and take time to breathe in the sweet fragrance from His garden.

For example, there is Jessica Reed who, with her quiet sweet ways, remind us that the real work that takes place in God's people is often unseen and can't always be measured and appreciated. There is Carol Chicote who brings a greater awe back into worship with her inspired songs from Scripture; and Marjie Castle whose desire and search to know Jesus and His truth reminds us of what needs to be the essence of all of our searches in this world—to seek out and know Jesus.

There is Dianne Strand who reminds us that the joy of the Lord can manifest itself in laughter that uplifts, tears that steady one through the adversities of life, and an anchor that holds tight to the Lord when in the storms of life. There are also the talented Cathy Wendt and Dana Gamble. Both are artists that can create a masterpiece with paint. Cathy is a musician whose music reaches the heart and Dana has various experiences in life that ministers to the seeking and downtrodden.

Who has the Lord brought into Your life? In what way have they become His extension to You? Sometimes ministers can become so caught up with being an extension of Him to others, they forget He sends others to become an avenue of His blessings to them.

Prayer: Lord, there is so much that goes on in the harvest field. We forget that sometimes You call us to another field, insert another soul into the equation, and even bless us with tasting the fruit of Your work. Thank You for being such a faithful husbandman. Amen.

February 26

"Which hope we have as an anchor of the soul, both sure and stedfast, and which entereth into that within the veil" (Hebrews 6:19). As I considered my own personal devotion, I could not help but remember that Warren Wiersbe stated that devotion without disciplines can become shallow.

There are many people who are quite devoted to the Lord. They speak with such passion with tears running down their faces in such a convincing fashion. However, such displays could all be sentimental.

Sentiment is fickle at best and treacherous at worst. Therefore, sentimental devotion will cause people to swing from one sentimental limb to the next. But, let the winds of adversity come and then see what happens to such sentiment.

Genuine devotion is grounded by disciplines that keep it sharp when challenged by compromise, steadfast when shaken by uncertainties, and enduring when faith is being tested by the dark cloud of unbelief.

Such devotion will not be easily moved from the Rock it is standing on because it is disciplined by the Spirit and the Word of God. It is focused on the Lord, and as a result, a person can be sure about its foundation. Ultimately, it will not allow itself to be moved away from the path of righteousness as the person presses forward to reach the heights of the Lord's revelation, wisdom, and glory.

Prayer: Lord, save me from sentimental hogwash. Stand my devotion firmly on You and establish it in You. Thank You for Your faithfulness to bring me into these glorious places of revelation with You. Amen.

February 27

"That I may know him, and the power of his resurrection, and the fellowship of his sufferings, being made conformable unto his death" (Philippians 3:10). In my devotion reading of A. W. Tozer, he stated that in our modern Christianity, it is easy to completely miss having a consciousness of God, which causes many Christians to only know God by hearsay.

The Bible is clear that we must know God for ourselves. It's not enough to hear what others have to say about Him or read books about Him, we must take the personal ownership of our relationship with Him as a daily exercise of faith. This requires us to become serious students of His Word that walk in accordance to the spirit and truth of it. We must ask the Holy Spirit to unveil greater revelations of the Lord in His Word.

As a believer, I have learned that there are godly disciplines that must be instituted in the Christian walk to ensure the integrity of my Christian life. After all, how I walk will determine if I learn to come into step with Him in order to walk in communion with Him. And, if I remain one step removed from my Christian responsibility to know God for myself, I can easily lose sight of what it means to have a relationship with Him.

I must draw near to the Lord on a daily basis if I expect to meet Him in my walk and maintain a healthy relationship with Him. I must not let hearsay define my idea or understanding of God. I must develop a personal relationship with Him that will cause me to know Him in a personal, intimate way.

Prayer: Lord, You provided the way in which I can know You in a personal way. Help me to remember this when the way of religion offers me a path that knows about You, but fails to bring me to a place where I actually commune with You. Amen.

February 28

What an unforgettably hilarious sight. It was cleaning day, a day in which we pick up items in order to vacuum. So, when we looked down at our Yorkie-Poo and saw him lying in a perfect "Sphinx" pose squarely in the middle of impressions left in the carpet where his kennel usually sits, we burst out laughing.

Instead of jumping up to join us, he looked at us with a mixture of emotions that just made us laugh even harder. Every dog lover knows the incredible depth of emotions a dog can portray in their eyes and body language. In this instance, we got a good dose of communicated mixed messages that, being interpreted, said, "How could you? How could you put MY kennel with my bed, my place of security comfort, rest and privacy up where I can't get into it? Are you nuts? My doggie heart is sad, and it's all your fault, but I know this is MY spot, and I'm going to make the most of it anyway. Poor me."

The little lesson here reminded me of how, when things aren't going well for us as they normally are, our faith can be severely tested. Will we trust the LORD that He knows all about it, remembers our needs, and that He will never leave us nor forsake us? None of us have a guarantee that we will always experience smooth sailing, lavish living, or pantries of plenty, but we can sing and rejoice in the LORD GOD with the prophet Habakkuk who wrote, "*Although the fig tree shall not blossom, neither shall fruit be in the vines; the labour of the olive shall fail, and the fields shall yield no meat; the flock shall be cut off from the fold, and there shall be no herd in the stalls: Yet I will rejoice in the LORD, I will joy in the God of my salvation. The LORD God is my strength, and he will make my feet like hinds' feet, and he will make me to walk upon mine high places. To the chief singer on my stringed instruments.*" (Habakkuk 3:17-19.) – J. Haley

Prayer: Lord, we can become a bit edgy when something disrupts our routine and world, but we are reminded that You are in control and nothing gets by You unless it is for our well-being. Lord, when such disruptions come, may I be reminded to not wallow in what is not and rise up and praise and thank You for the change that is coming. It is bound to be an improvement in the end. Amen.

February 29

"Search the scriptures; for in them ye think ye have eternal life: and they are they which testify of me" (John 5:39). Herbert Lockyer said this about the Word of God, "The Bible is like a vast Hall of Mirrors reflecting Christ in a thousand ways for us to admire and appreciate."

I have sat in wonder before God's Word. I have discovered it to be like a fresh pool of water that I can drink from, knowing the water will never cease to be as it refreshes and gives me life.

God's Word has been like a gold mine that harbors riches beyond any imagination. At this time, I feel like I have already been greatly enriched by my many discoveries, only to realize that there are more nuggets to be dug up and more rich veins to be unearthed.

Exploring the Word has been like taking a great journey to beautiful places that cannot be described in mere words. At times I have caught glimpses of heaven's glory, and at other times I have witnessed the darkness enfolding Mount Sinai. Sometimes I have seen the burning bush in the wilderness and the parting of the Red Sea. However, through each terrain I have traveled, I have discovered more and more about Jesus Christ and the heavenly riches and promises attached with it. Obviously, you cannot go wrong when the Bible becomes your most sacred, prized possession that has been earmarked with fingerprints, weathered with use, and highlighted by years of study and discovery.

Prayer: Lord, thank You for Your Word. It is indeed a Hall of Mirrors that records Your infinite beauty. I am so thankful that You have graced my life in numerous ways with it. Amen.

MARCH

March 1

"The elders which are among you I exhort, who am also an elder, and a witness of the sufferings of Christ, and also a partaker of the glory that shall be revealed" (1 Peter 5:1). There are a few times I have contended with people who called themselves "pastor." In each case I had to greatly debate such a claim because there was one glaring aspect missing from all of these individuals' insidious ramblings, and that was the presentation of our glorious Lord and Savior, Jesus Christ.

According to the 19th century preacher, Robert Murray McCheyne, "A man cannot be a faithful minister until he preaches Christ for Christ's sake." There are a lot of different presentations of Christ being put forth. Some presentations are watered down, others present a stoic, lifeless Jesus, while others simply ignore Him altogether.

The truth of the matter is that all religious activities should be to present the Christ of the Bible in all of His glory. It is Christ alone who saves. He is the only antidote for all the ills of society and the world.

This brings us to the final aspect. Christ should be preached for the sake of who He is and what He did on the cross for each of us. He should not be preached for financial gain, or because of self-serving notions, or as a means to receive recognition.

Christians' lives are to be the platform in which Jesus is lifted up to draw others to Himself. With their lips of praise, in the environment of worship and service, they are ever putting the spotlight on the Redeemer. When people see believers, they should see Jesus being lifted up in glory and unadulterated worship.

Prayer: Lord, there are so many imposters out there, but You have left us with an indelible example that will never be erased from the annals of Your eternal Word. You have left us with the example of YOU. Amen.

March 2

"Feed the flock of God which is among you, taking the oversight thereof, not by constraint, but willingly: not for filthy lucre, but of a ready mind" (1 Peter 5:2). As I was thinking about false pastors, I could not help but remember Alexander Maclaren. He was a great Scottish preacher who lived during the 19th century. He stated, "To efface one's self is one of a preacher's first duties. The herald should be lost in his message."

Maclaren had it right. Too many pastors want to be remembered, idolized, and adored by their congregations. They want their followers to see them as being spiritually savvy, above average in their understanding about the matters of heaven, and all wise when it comes to the various challenges that may be rolling through their flock.

However, such notions often require these individuals to be "God", rather than serve as a messenger of God. Every real servant of God must first humble self in order to give way to the very flow of heaven.

It is from the throne of God that all matters close to His heart will be revealed as it flows down in wisdom and revelation. In such wisdom and revelation, the person of Jesus Christ will be lifted up in a majestic fashion, uncovering His glory. It is from the throne that all real servants of God are imparted with the spiritual food that has been designed to feed the flock and sustain it until each one of them enters into everlasting glory.

Prayer: Lord, we have such fanciful notions about serving You. However, they are not realistic and ultimately, they do not regard Your heart and will in matters. Bring me down to earth even if there has to be a crash to wake me up to what my real responsibility is towards You. Amen.

March 3

"But now we are delivered from the law, that being dead wherein we were held; that we should serve in newness of spirit, and not in the oldness of the letter" (Romans 7:6). There is a thin line that some preachers find themselves walking on. They can be considered too conservative for the liberals and too liberal for the conservatives. As a result, they find themselves in a crossfire, where they receive fire from both camps.

I can relate to this precarious place. That which drives the religious liberals insane is the holiness of God. He will never cease to be holy in His ways or approach to a matter. Regardless of how narrow and unbending His holiness may be, its righteous standard will never be brought down to man's best which is considered filthy rags. In the end, His holiness will bring an indictment against those who refuse to believe the complete Gospel that declares we are dead in sin and must be raised up in newness of life according to the righteous, perfect ways of God.

On the other hand, what drives the conservatives crazy is the Holy Spirit. He cannot be boxed in by rules, controlled by religious rituals, or corralled by doctrine. It is the Spirit who brings life to God's people to truly pursue their life in Christ, as well as putting life into their religious ways and activities. For the liberal, they end

78

up missing Christ altogether, but for the conservative, they fail to breathe in and out the life of Christ. Ultimately, their life becomes cluttered with dead-letter beliefs and useless activities bringing leanness to their souls.

Prayer: Lord, You are precious. You have given us the gift of Your Spirit to put life back in our religious ways. However, there are those who want to hold on to their dead-letter drivel, rather than embrace the fullness of the life You have for them. Save me from such religious nonsense. Amen.

March 4

"Neither as being lords over God's heritage, but being ensamples to the flock" (1 Peter 5:3). All real leaders in the kingdom of God should show themselves to be servants of their Creator. The only way they can display a servant's disposition is by serving others. In essence, they become examples in their service.

One of my tests in regard to spiritual leaders is how much of a servant they are towards others. There are a couple of different tests that I use to test the pastor's level of commitment to the flock of God.

Attitude: The first thing I consider is the pastor's attitude. Is he a caring shepherd or tyrannical, which makes him appear as if he is lording his position over others. Is his position a job or a vocation that is backed by a heavenly calling? Does he love the Lord by showing that he loves His Word? Does he tremble before His word and dread displeasing the Lord? Does he fear leading the sheep astray from God's truth and purpose?

Favorites: Another good test is if a pastor shows favoritism. To the Lord, His people are equally important. Each member is necessary for the function of the whole body.

Today there are many hirelings and wolves standing behind pulpits. But, the one thing I know is that there is one who is a true Shepherd. I can trust Him at all times. His name is Jesus Christ.

Prayer: Lord, I am so blessed to know You are my real Shepherd. I thank You for the men who possessed a Shepherd's heart and has led me to You, but I also am thankful for the discernment You gave me to recognize the counterfeits. Lord, You will never fail Your sheep and in the end, You will reclaim all of them for Your glory. Amen.

March 5

It was an unforgettable day in 1985, and the situation was dire. There was no one to turn to for help except God. My womanizing husband had left, leaving behind a stack of unpaid bills, so I went into the bedroom, spread them all out on top of the bed, and knelt down to pray in earnest.

"Lord," I began, "You see all these bills that I can't pay" --but before I could finish praying the doorbell rang. I couldn't imagine who it could possibly be, but to my shock and surprise it was a very close friend and her husband who lived about 50 miles from my house.

This was the only time she ever came to visit without calling first, but the Lord had sent them to buy enough dehydrated food we had stored to cover the cost of those unpaid bills! Praise the Lord, for how true it is (even for me) *"And it shall come to pass, that before they call, I will answer; and while they are yet speaking, I will hear" (Isaiah 65:24).* (See *Daniel 9:20-23; 10:12.*)

What a great God we serve! – J. Haley

Prayer: Lord sometimes the world crowds You out as our one and only great Provider; that is, until we fall into a great place of need and see that if You are not in a matter, we are doomed. Thank You for being faithful to show Yourself as our Solution and Provider before we even cry out. Amen.

March 6

"And when the chief Shepherd shall appear, ye shall receive a crown of glory that fadeth not away" (1 Peter 5:4). As part of God's flock, there is one thing I know, the Great Shepherd is coming back to claim His sheep and set all matters right. When he appears, everyone will recognize Him for who He is.

For those who have rejected His leadership, they will shake and tremble, while asking for the rocks to fall on them *(Revelation 6:15-17)*. However, they will not be able to hide from the righteous Lamb of God. He will judge them, and they will taste the bitterness of the death sentence that hangs over them.

For those who know Jesus as their Shepherd, His appearance will signal the beginning of a glorious existence. They will receive a crown of glory. What the crown entails is hard to say except that all glory is attached to the Lord.

As Christians, we are to reflect His glory on earth, but when He comes, we will not only reflect His glory but we will be enfolded and surrounded by it. As a result, I cannot help but wonder if the crowning glory we will receive is the fullness of Christ in all of His unhindered majesty?

Prayer: Lord, as an heir of salvation, I have so much to look forward to. I don't understand it all, but I know it will be glorious, too wonderful to describe, and too incredible to imagine. Thank You for the future promise of experiencing the fullness of the hope of Your glory. Amen.

March 7

"Woe unto you, when all men shall speak well of you! For so did their fathers to the false prophets (Luke 6:26). A great English preacher by the name of Joseph Parker wrote this statement, "Any pulpit that founds itself on personal invention, cleverness, ingenuity, audacity, or affected originality will most surely cover itself with humiliation and pass into merited oblivion."

I often wonder what kind of epitaph will be written on some of the more popular preachers' headstones. Clearly, TV has shot some of these individuals to the forefront of stardom. It has made them celebrities in their own right. Granted, I cannot know their motive, but occasionally I see their fruit and it proves to be anything but sweet and sustaining.

The tragedy is some of the most popular preachers may find all that they have obtained will be cast into the winds of judgment never to be seen again. For some, the merit system of weighing their deeds with their inner life may find itself falling off the edge and into the abyss, and ending up in a state of oblivion.

Faith will always actively express itself in some form of benevolence, but such deeds are not weighed in light of eternity. What must and will always be weighed in light of eternity is a person's hidden life before God. In the end, their life will speak of His work, not their deeds.

Prayer: Lord, I know that my life will be weighed in the balance of heaven. My hope is that Your life will be what is unveiled before heaven. I know that the balance will declare that I am redeemed and ready to enter into the place of eternal rest in You. Amen.

March 8

"My flesh and my heart faileth: but God is the strength of my heart, and my portion forever" (Psalm 73:26). I constantly struggle with the demands of my flesh and the emotional fickleness of my heart. So many times in my struggles I come face-to-face with my inability to keep my flesh on the cross and my heart steadfast towards the Lord. It is at such times that I realize how weak the flesh is and how unpredictable the heart can become when it is being overwhelmed by the depth of fleshly emotions.

However, in *Psalm 73:26* I am reminded that God is the strength of my heart. The truth of the matter is that God should determine the essence of my heart attitude, become the source behind my thoughts, and the inspiration behind my emotions. My heart should desire to please Him at all times. It should be completely devoted to serve Him. It must direct all affections towards Him and seek Him out in all matters pertaining to life.

If God becomes the essence as to my heart attitude, I will be assured that He will also become my portion forever.

Prayer: Lord, You are my portion. Such a concept reminds me that what I possess is eternal, complete, and satisfying to the heart, soul, and spirit. Amen.

March 9

"From the end of the earth will I cry unto thee, when my heart is overwhelmed: lead me to the rock that is higher than I" (Psalm 61:2). In yesterday's meditation I had to admit that due to the influence of the flesh and the world my heart can prove to be fickle and unpredictable at times. However, if God becomes the

complete sum of my heart condition, He is the one who will serve as the strength of it.

My heart should always be directed towards God. If it is inclined to believe and trust Him, it will be natural for me to cry to the Lord when I am overwhelmed by the circumstances around me.

If my heart rests in the Lord, I can trust that it will be sensitive enough to His leading. When the matters of life are swallowing me up, all I have to do is look up and allow Him to lead me to the Rock.

This Rock is not only higher than I am, but it will lift me above the matters that are proving to be such an affront to my soul. On the Rock I will find stability and in the Rock I will find safety and rest.

Prayer: Lord, thank You for being my Rock. You are my place of safety and rest. Help me to remember this when my world is caving in around me. Amen.

March 10

"But one of the soldiers with a spear pierced his side, and forthwith came there out blood and water" (John 19:34). Everything in this life is a gamble except the Lord. You realize that even relationships are a test to your character and that regardless as to whether the other person does right, it matters little because you are the one who needs to get it right since you will be standing before the Lord to give an account of your life before Him.

I have considered the possible impact I leave on others based on those who have had an impact on me. Granted, relationships are a two-way street but the type of investment each person puts into the relationship will determine the quality of it.

For me there are those who God gave me a great burden for. My desire was to see them win in their Christian life, but they did not value their soul as I did and walked away. There are those who come so far, and then turn on you because the cost to go all the way with Jesus is becoming too much. There are those who give the impression they want it all, but eventually decide Jesus is not worth it.

Your heart breaks for such souls. How precious those souls were to you, but then the light dawns on you that when the soldier pierced Jesus' side, the blood and water that came out pointed to the fact that Jesus' heart was literally broken because of similar rejection even as He was hanging on the cross.

This revelation does not take the hurt away, but it allows you to realize that you have become identified with Jesus in a special way and that the scars left behind, whether on the heart or elsewhere, are special badges that will be highlighted as the light of heaven shines upon them, exposing the incredible impact of Jesus' life on you. After all, it is all about the impact of His life on others through us and not about our life that must be cast constantly aside to ensure He is glorified.

Prayer: Lord, Your scars are precious to me and I pray that the scars that originated because of Your life in me will prove to be as precious to You. Amen.

March 11

Opinions. We all love our own opinions, but shy away from the opinions of others that don't line up with ours. I have to admit, being opinionated is part and parcel of my all-too-human make up, and throughout my life many opinions that have shot out of my mouth have not ended well in "making friends and influencing people."

Be that as it may, however, there's one opinion that surfaced today as I stood in the kitchen refilling a number of spice jars, and that opinion goes like this: great cooking means plenty of herbs and spices (and good salt.) Not just a wee pinch, or a timid little sprinkle mind you, but a rather lavish amount added on to your meat and vegetables, pastas, sauces and salad dressings takes the flavor up to the next level. Or, maybe even higher.

The thing is, when you're busy preparing a meal and you're in a time crunch, it becomes more than exasperating to reach for some of your favorite herbs or spices only to discover their container has an inadequate amount, or is empty altogether because you neglected to refill them. Perhaps we can compare this to our spiritual life—you know, those times when a perfect opportunity presents itself to share the "spice" of the life of Christ with someone, but you're unprepared and empty because you got caught off-guard. Your "spice jar" is full of nothing but air (self), and your mind and emotions feel "off-key" (flavorless) so the opportunity passes you by.

The disappointment in yourself that you feel inside leaves a bad taste in your mouth, but the Lord knows. Just as good cooks learn by their mistakes, so too, the Lord's children learn by theirs. *"But sanctify the Lord God in your hearts: and be ready always to give an answer to every man that asketh you a reason of the hope that is in you with meekness and fear"* (1 Peter 3:15).

"Awake, O north wind; and come, thou south; blow upon my garden, that the spices thereof may flow out. Let my beloved come into his garden, and eat his pleasant fruits." (Song of Solomon 4:16.) – J. Haley

Prayer: Lord, You are the One who spices up my life and it is because I impart Your life to others, I am the one who is to be the salt to them. Lord, make me the salt so I can add the touch of heaven to people's lives. Amen.

March 12

When Jesus knew in himself that his disciples murmured at it, he said unto them, Doth this offend you? (John 6:61). The one thing I keep in mind when ministering to people is that often truth will offend them. Truth is meant to awaken, shake, and cause some type of discomfort.

Whether a person is in delusion, denial, or rebellion about their spiritual life, they must be challenged in some way. However, to avoid conflict, we try to take the sharp edges off of truth so we are not embarrassed or left feeling uncomfortable because some conflict has arisen or the person becomes silent. But, without the sharp edges, a person will be left in the same lost, miserable state as before because they have not really been awakened or challenged to see the urgency to address their state.

It is easy to be a side-line quarterback in every move that is being made, but until we are in the game, we have no idea what is really happening when it comes to another person's conviction. The truth is God enables each of us to be sharp in some way. For some their passion for truth can become abrasive and they will plow up fallow ground. For others, their authority in what is true can become abrasive as they become immovable in what is true, and there are those who have a type of indignation towards what is wrong that can be sharp to the hearer. Finally, there are those who are decisive and can do nothing more than lay out the truth as it is.

The Bible tells us that when delivering unpopular truth to do so in meekness, but I have also learned to never apologize for the truth. However, there are times when I am caught off guard by the truth, and at such times, I must avoid becoming embarrassed by its sharpness. I must stop a critical attitude from taking the judgment seat towards the vessel God uses to penetrate the grave darkness of someone's soul with the type of necessary sharpness that allows life and hope to take root in their barren soul.

Prayer: Lord, we are comfortable with what we know about You, but we can easily become uncomfortable when it comes to others being exposed to it. Regardless of the vessel You use to awaken or challenge a soul, unfeigned truth never changes, nor does it lose its sharpness. Instead of judging such times, I will choose to trust You to have Your way in the situation. Amen.

March 13

"Think not that I am come to send peace on earth: I came not to send peace, but a sword" (Matthew 10:34). Yesterday, I talked about the sharpness of truth and how it can and will offend those who are not prepared to hear it or do not want to hear it. The reality is truth will not only offend others but will test us as well.

We often become embarrassed by how others present the truth because the reactions of those being challenged may be unsettling even to us. We often fear that the person who is hearing it may be driven further away from God, but what would we do or say differently that would cause that person to even respond in a positive way?

Then it begs the question, why were we not in the place to be the one to ministered to that individual in the way we think best? After all, were we willing to be truthful with a person in the first place about their soul or their sin? Perhaps it was not the right timing for us to speak the truth, but when would the timing be convenient, especially in light of the day possibly being the day of salvation for that person. It's true it may not be our timing because there is no leading or conviction to do so, but who is to say it was not the right timing for the person who is speaking the truth?

When I feel uncomfortable during the times of someone speaking the truth, I realize it's not the vessel God is using that makes me uncomfortable, it is truth itself because I can't control how it is delivered and how it will be received. I then ask myself, are you embarrassed because of TRUTH itself? The honest answer in many cases is "yes!"

This reveals how pious, judgmental and hypocritical I can be. I want people saved, but I don't want the birth pangs that must occur first. I want people to hear the truth, but I don't want the turf tore up too bad, causing them to react negatively to it because I may have to stand on it and give a defense for it. I want people to be brought into the kingdom of God, but according to my ways, my thinking, and my doing.

Prayer: Lord forgive me for being judgmental towards Your instrument who speaks the truth and being embarrassed by the reaction it may cause. I must trust that it's You who will bring in the harvest and You will use whatever instrument is available. Amen.

March 14

"Know now that God hath overthrown me, and hath compassed me with his net. Behold, I cry out of wrong, but I am not heard: I cry aloud, but there is no judgment. He hath fenced up my way that I cannot pass, and he hath set darkness in my paths" (Job 19:6-8). As a believer are you ready to be misunderstood by those who "supposedly" know better? When you walk in the path of righteousness, stand for truth, and do not compromise your faith, be prepared to be cruelly judged even by those closest to you when your faith is being tested with great darkness.

Job's companions knew him as a righteous man, and yet in his great test they accused him of having sin. They assumed God had overthrown him and compassed him with a net because of some hidden sin. Job gives us insight into his own struggle with his plight. He was willing to face any deviation in his character but there was no conviction. He was willing to be righteously judged, but there was no pronunciation of guilt. On both counts, God had remained silent. He recognized that the Lord had allowed him to be fenced into his plight and that darkness, and not light was in his path.

It was becoming clear that Job's faith was being tested. Exercising genuine faith begins where darkness covers the way. That faith is not based on what we know of God but on what has been established as being true about God's character. Darkness plagued Job's understanding and there was no light penetrating it to bring clarity, and at such times all you can do is cling to what you know is true about God's character. Job was trying to come to rest on who God was/is, but his companions would not let him rest in God as they flung one false, slanderous accusation after another at him.

It looks like Job was trying to defend his character, but in many ways I think Job was trying to cling to God as he waited to hear from Him to clarify what was so, but instead he was bombarded by the false accusations of those who should have known better.

Prayer: Lord, it's natural to go against what we know if what we see is not lining up to what we understand. Lord, we can only see when Your light finally parts the darkness to bring clarity to a matter, but during the time of darkness, I can choose to trust You because You are trustworthy. Amen.

March 15

"But without faith it is impossible to please him: for he that cometh to God must believe that he is, and that he is a rewarder of them that diligently seek him" (Hebrew 11:6). Do you really believe God to be who He is? Many would with absolute clarity say, "Yes!" However, when things are challenging and ready to bury you, do you believe God cares and hears your despairing cries?

When things are falling apart, do you still trust God's intentions towards you? When life deals you an unfair blow, do you believe He is fair and just? When what He tells you to do goes against your logic, the world's way of doing things, and the advisers around you, do you go forward in obedience while trusting Him with the details as to what doors He opens and closes or do you veer off to wait for another day and time when things make sense?

It is easy to say we believe in God, but do You believe Him? The only way you can please God is by directing your faith towards Him based on who He is, putting your faith in His Word because of who He is, and resting on His promises because He will always prove to be true to who He is. When a person can truly put all their assurance in Him, that is when they believe without any doubt that HE IS!

I say all of this because God introduced Himself as the "I AM," and the only response we can have towards Him as the "I AM," is that "HE IS!" When I was a new Christian, I debated about what His Word said about certain subjects. As I grew in the knowledge of Him, I debated with others about the theology of a matter. When I became more mature in my Christian walk, the debates ceased as I began to realize that at the end of all debates stood the great "I AM!" It was then that all I could do was declare that HE IS and humble myself in order to align all matters to who HE IS, while

91

obeying His truths and resting in His Promises because HE IS the one who will fulfill them.

What about you? It's easy to say you believe in God, but faith is active and it will naturally respond to Him because HE IS the only true God who can deliver, save, and bring us into the fullness of His promises.

Prayer: Lord, we can take so many detours in Your Word, but when it comes to You there are no detours. At the end of all spiritual searches, we must silently stand before You in complete awe and worship and declare the simple truth about You to all who would dare to veer off of what would establish them in their real faith, and that truth about You is, "HE IS who He says HE IS!" Amen.

March 16

"Wherefore by their fruits ye shall know them" (Matthew 7:20). Most people's concept in pleasing God has to do with works. It is natural to think, surely, God will note us by our works, but Jesus told us we will be known by our fruits, not our works. Fruit does not develop itself. It must first have some source, a seed, water, and investment. This is to ensure that the type of ground and environment is present in which the seed can germinate and grow.

As believers we know the source for life is what God did through His Son on the cross. We know the seed is the Word of God and His Gospel, water the Holy Spirit, and the investment comes down to what will cultivate our faith towards God. Cultivation involves the trying of our faith, the testing of our character, and the revealing of any deviation from God's truth and righteousness in our character and ways. The right investment will become obvious for it will produce godly disciplines established through obedience.

When you read *Hebrews 11:6* God rewards those who diligently seek Him. Again, it has nothing to do with works but truly seeking to know Him so that we can know what pleases Him. We are, by faith, to search for Him with all of our heart, trusting and knowing that He will be found by us. After all, our rewards are not crowns but the Lord Himself, and that is why we diligently seek Him.

Man's idea of God and what pleases Him are so earthbound and entangled in religious notions and lifeless ideas while the reality of God requires us to look up, seek what is heavenly and excellent, and land on what is established by the Holy Spirit as being truth and life.

Prayer: Lord, You have provided us with not only our needs, but also treasures that will equip and enrich our lives in our journey through this world. However, remind me Lord that my true treasure is You, my real gem is You, and my search for riches mean nothing if they do not lead me to knowing YOU! Amen.

March 17

Remember that old cliché, "Don't be such a pansy?" As children, we never wanted to be taunted by a little gang of daredevils calling us a "pansy". After all, the end result of trying to prove we were big, bold and brave could not only cause us some bodily injury and pain, but even worse, the shedding of real tears in front of everybody as we ran home to mommy.

However, the truth is pansies are a whole lot tougher than they look! The pansies we buy early in the springtime do well even if some nights still get frosty, and later, as long as they aren't directly exposed to the hot summer sun, they hang in there, and continue to linger and delight the eyes after their annual companions bowed when fall arrived. Yes, they're tougher than you think! If I neglect to water them, they wilt and droop, but a few minutes after watering them, they are all perked up and standing tall again. Even when an occasional deer munches them down for a midnight snack, they recover and come right back.

One thing about pansies that I've come to expect is, they will always turn their faces, as if in unison, to the position of the sun. I would love it if they "turned" to face the window so I could admire them from the dining room, but no! Even if I turn their planter around, they will somehow maneuver back to face the sun.

Pansies remind me of a happier time when, as a small child, Grandma taught me how to pick them and put them into a small vase. She assured me that it was okay to pick them, because that just made them bloom all the more.

Perhaps that little fact calls to mind how the hand of God "picks" or "prunes" us in life's journey, and how painful and unfair personal losses can seem to be. But it's all under His watchful care and always for our good and His glory. Therefore, it's okay to be like a pansy if you're always beholding the Son, seeking the light, patiently overcoming the indifference of "coldness," enduring the searing heat of trials and tribulations, and never giving up, *"For ye are dead, and your life is hid with Christ in God" (Colossians 3:3).*
– J. Haley

Prayer: Lord, You use Your creation in such wondrous ways to teach us impactful truths that inspire us. Thank You for the many examples that teach me that You are a God who knows how to bring forth beauty and perfection in Your creation and that it is those things that seem weak that prove to be strong because Your grace is always at work. Amen.

March 18

"Though he were a Son, yet learned he obedience by the things which he suffered" (Hebrews 5:8). In my last post I talked about obedience. Some Christians would have us believe that any such obedience to the Word of God points to earning one's salvation. Needless to say, the obedience I am talking about is a natural response of love for the Lord. This love's one great desire is to please Him because He is worthy.

It is important to point out that the work for our salvation was done on the cross. The redemption was complete and the work finished, and by child-like faith we receive eternal life. We can't add or take away from this work. We simply have to decide if we receive the gift of life by faith. It is active faith that begins to walk this life out in obedience to what has been established in God's Word.

Obedience is a discipline of the Christian life. As already pointed out, this obedience finds its source in faith that wants to please God. This faith is established on the Word of God because faith comes by hearing and hearing by the Word of God.

We must remember that active faith will end in obedience to God's Word out of love for Him. Jesus said it best in *John 14:15,* *"If you love me, obey my commandments."* He also asked the question in *Luke 6:46, "And why call ye me, Lord, Lord, and do not the things which I say."*

It was in His humanity that Jesus learned obedience through the things He suffered. When the self-life is fighting hard against denying itself and allowing the lusts and affections of the flesh to be put on a cross, it will experience the wounding of the self-life and the adverse effects of the cross each time the person decides to do right according to God's Word. When one does right, they do not see it as obedience but their reasonable service. They know the only reason any believer makes such a decision is not because they are wonderful and honorable in themselves, but because it is the right thing to do. As believers of His Word, our present lives must be about pleasing God and not ourselves.

Prayer: Lord before I knew You, I lived for myself and ended up empty, miserable, and hopeless. The flesh still can tempt and the world continues to subtly draw me back into its evil webs. When I feel the lure pulling me back to fleshly ways and the draw of the world, remind me of the type of miserable fruit that will result which will cause me to flee from the vanity of it all. Amen.

March 19

"And being made perfect, he became the author of eternal salvation unto all them that obey Him" (Hebrews 5:9). When you meditate on *Hebrews 5:8-9*, you begin to realize that in His deity, Jesus was the essence of perfection in holiness, but in His humanity, He had to come to perfection. We are all born in a fallen state and Jesus' example in His humanity is that we can and must likewise come to a place of perfection. And, how was this perfection accomplished? It was learning obedience by the things our Lord suffered in the flesh.

Obedience that comes out of faith requires one to deny themselves of their right to life on their terms. It can prove to be a bit painful when we hold tightly to things that are attached to the old life. It is almost like a severing, a tearing, or a ripping of the old that at times leaves us feeling wounded and vulnerable. However, it is through such separation that we begin to discover the freedom to walk out the incredible Christian life.

It is through the perfecting of His earthly life, that Jesus became the author of eternal salvation because He truly became the perfect Lamb of God, tried, found sinless and prepared to be

96

offered up in His human body as the ultimate sacrifice for all of us. It is important to not stop at this part because the last part of *Hebrews 5:9* shows us we must become identified to Him to receive the fullness of salvation. Note what it says, that this eternal salvation is available to all that obey Him.

This is not a condition to salvation; rather, it is the preparation that is needful to walk in this new life in order for it to be established in us. As believers, we receive all of His commands and instructions by faith and out of love we walk in obedience to them, knowing it is the right thing to do. Obedience is the discipline that gets rid of the rough edges, along with the old decaying garbs of the world and the stench of fleshly ways.

Obedience is not about earning our salvation; rather, it is about gaining the fullness of a new life through godly disciplines that are liberating, allowing us to take on more of Christ's likeness in a dying world that desperately needs to see Him.

Prayer: Lord, we are told if we abide in You, we will walk as You walked and You went the way of Calvary, the way of the cross. Help us not to think in terms of losing anything of worth when it comes to our old life; rather, help us to realize we are gaining what is truly valuable and wonderful. Amen.

March 20

"Examine yourselves whether ye be in the faith; prove your own selves. Know ye not your own selves, how that Jesus Christ is in You, except ye be reprobates" (2 Corinthians 13:5). Faith towards God is a topic that can never be exhausted no matter how many books are written on the subject. However, Andrew Murray summarized the walk of faith in this manner, "The life of faith is a life of obedience."

When I examine my spiritual life, I cannot help but examine my faith. Every mountain I climb requires me to exercise the sturdy cords of my belief. Every challenging wave that I encounter on the ocean of life tests the steadfastness of my confidence towards my Creator. Every storm I have had to endure exposes the source of my faith. Every time I encounter calm waters, the sharpness of my faith is tried.

It is at such times that I must question my faith. Will I maintain the balance in my life because my faith is directed and founded in the character of God, or will I find it running amuck in the midst of the encroaching darkness of the world. I must always test my loyalty, point of confidence, and place of assurance and rest to maintain my ways before the Lord.

Prayer: Lord, I know my faith is what I must keep to stay on course. Help me to remember to look up and not down or around me. I do not want circumstances, challenges, or situations to take my eyes off of You and put them on the shifting sands of the world. Amen.

March 21

"And this is life eternal, that they might know thee the only true God, and Jesus Christ, who thou has sent" (John 17:3). There are so many presentations of what it means to be saved. These presentations may be valid or weak, realistic or deceptive. However, A. W. Tozer stated it best when he said the experiential knowledge of God is eternal life.

To receive Jesus is to receive eternal life. After all, Jesus is eternal and the life which is given to us is His life. It is the gift of the Holy Spirit who works that incredible life in us and through us. The problem is that people separate Jesus from the life. They intellectually accept a theological presentation of Jesus, but they

98

don't receive the whole package in their heart as truth. After all, there is no life in the theological Jesus, there is only life in His person.

Therefore, we receive the person of Christ in our inner man. Granted, we must put on His life by submitting to the work of the Spirit, but nevertheless, we must assimilate our Lord's life in our inner person and ways through faith knowing that such an unseen work is so, it must be so, and it will be so.

Prayer: Lord, I so much appreciate the gifts of Your life and Spirit. It's easy to take so much for granted, but the truth is everything is being offered to us because of Your redemption. Praise Your Holy Name. Amen.

March 22

"God setteth the solitary in families: he bringeth out those which are bound with chains; but the rebellious dwell in a dry land" *(Psalm 67:6).* As a believer, I have enjoyed a sense of liberty that has come at different times throughout my life.

When I was born again, I was set free from the tyrannical grip sin had on my conscience and soul. The initial liberty was utterly glorious and beyond words. I also found myself part of a great family. This proved to be a consolation to me. Our earthly families often represent the old, idolatrous ways. As I determined to follow Jesus, the earthly ties that bound me began to be severed. Although it proved challenging and at times hurtful, it was necessary so that I could secure a new identity.

The other liberty I found was the freedom to discover who God designed me to be. The more I discovered about how the very life of Jesus would define my own personality, the more I became secure in my position in Him.

The final freedom is found in the promise of future glory. The rebellious will dwell in a dry land that has no semblance of life, liberty, or spiritual blessings. They will know the emptiness of their own vain life, while I will know the fullness of His life.

Prayer: Lord, I have so many promises to rest on that I don't need to worry about the fact that I live in a world that can only promise sorrow, toil, struggle, and death. I am so glad my life is hid in You. Amen.

March 23

"The righteous shall be glad in the LORD, and shall trust in him; and all the upright in heart shall glory" (Psalm 64:10). As Christians, we bear the glorious title of being saints of the Most High God. However, the real test is do we live like saints when the rest of the world is not looking our way?

Saints are called to holy living. To live a life set apart from the world means to live an upright life before the Lord. It seems that there are always certain subjects I must come back to in order to gain dimension about the Christian life. These subjects include redemption, salvation, resurrection, faith, and righteousness to name a few.

Once again, I must consider the subject of righteousness. Psalm 64:10 tells me that one of the fruits of the righteous is gladness. The reason for such a feeling is because the Lord will bring it to the heart of the one who not only trusts Him, but takes great pleasure in Him. Such upright individuals will be able to experience the unseen glory of heaven in their hearts.

Prayer: Lord, I know positionally I am Your saint, but I must live like one. It will take the power and influence of Your Spirit and Word to cause me to live a holy life before You. Amen.

March 24

"For every house is builded by some man; but he that built all things is God" (Hebrews 3:4). The one thing that changes the landscape around us is the light. It always amazes me how the light changes the scenery by how its highlights the surrounding. It also determines the color of the water in the rivers and how it reflects or mirrors the countryside.

After a storm, it seems that the light always broke through at one spot at our former residence along Priest River. Amazingly, what it often highlighted was a particular house. It was a white house that was surrounded by the beautiful décor of a well-groomed landscape, but it had no real distinction until the sun highlighted it. Once the light parted the clouds, you could not help but notice its surrounding beauty highlighted by the landscape.

The only right angle to consider anything from is God's Word. This allows us to stand assured that its light possesses integrity. The Word of God tells us that God builds all things, but from experience I know it depends on the extent as to how much the life of Christ is being worked into believers.

It is the work of sanctification that will determine whether a believer will stand distinct in this dark world. It is the Lord's life in us that serves as the light in us, breaking forth to reveal the beauty of God's handiwork in our temples. I must consider if such light is obvious in my life, and what kind of distinction it is bringing in light of the present darkness that is invading the hearts and minds of people.

Prayer: Lord, I want to stand distinct. I want Your life to illuminate me in this darkness. I want Your beauty to shine forth for Your glory. Amen.

March 25

"For as I passed by, and beheld your devotions, I found an altar with this inscription, TO THE UNKNOWN GOD. Whom therefore ye ignorantly worship, him declare I unto you" (Acts 17:23). I have been thinking lately about my personal devotion. It's easy to erect some type of altar and put an inscription on it in relationship to my devotion, but do I know who I am devoted to? Is my devotion mechanical, or is it inspired by what is real and eternal.

The world would have me believe that it is the type of deed I do that will ultimately count. However, deed means nothing unless true heart-felt devotion is present. Devotion is not inspired by deeds; rather, deeds become an expression of devotion.

As a seventeenth-century Anglican by the name of Jeremy Taylor stated, "If thou meanest to enlarge thy religion, do it rather by enlarging thine ordinary devotions, then they become extraordinary."

The truth of the matter is that the extraordinary Christian life comes out of extraordinary devotion. It is birthed with the power of the unseen, the incredible, and the unimaginable. Such devotion is also bathed in love, enfolded by the Spirit, highlighted by heavenly wisdom, touched by a bit of eternity, and marked by the very likeness of Christ.

This is the beauty of heavenly devotion. It exposes us to the eternal, making our lives extraordinary and our ways straight and narrow, leaving a powerful testimony behind for others to consider and meditate upon.

Prayer: Lord, we can become impressed with our devotion, but will you consider it noteworthy? Lord, I commit my life to You as a living sacrifice in the hope of discovering what true devotion is. Amen.

March 26

"And another also said, Lord, I will follow thee; but let me first go bid them farewell, which are at home at my house. And Jesus said unto him, No man, having put his hand to the plough, and looking back, is fit for the kingdom of God" (Luke 9:61-62). It is amazing what certain days mark for you. Take devotions for example. On the day of my birthday, I want to see what special insights God has put in that devotion for that day just for me. I know it seems a bit silly, but I also know God can highlight certain times with some special revelation or insight.

I have to admit when I write devotions, I consider the day according to birthdays of those I know. Today would be my mother's birthday. She passed away in 2014. I don't believe in wishing my mother a happy birthday in heaven because there is no time in heaven, and her time on earth was one of great struggle that I know she does not miss or wish back for herself.

She struggled with regrets of her past, disillusionment with the present due to emotional despair, physical struggles with such things as pain and losing much of her eyesight, and dealing with my father who had Alzheimer's. I know that I did not realize the depths of my mother's struggles; therefore, I could never really judge her emotional or spiritual state when she was wrestling with the "whys" at her lowest points.

My mother taught me many things, but the one lesson that stands out the most had to do with personal growth. My mother wanted the best for me, but to her that meant she had to try to direct my life. We struggled with our roles because as I grew as a person and adult, our relationship found itself in many different crises.

She thought of me as someone she always had to influence or have a say over to somehow protect or ensure my well-being, and

I had long ago left that position in order to follow the Lord. In the end it was hard for my mother to recognize and accept the changes and growth in my life because that would result in developing a different type of relationship with me that she was not familiar with. In essence, she could not simply let things be so that she could have a constructive relationship with me.

As Christians, we go through various growing pains and stages in our lives with the Lord. If any problem in our relationship crops up, it does not rest on God's end, but ours because we often want to direct our relationship with Him. We want to make sure He does it according to our ways and perception.

What many of us fail to understand is that the essence of faith is expressed in the most honorable way when we simply trust the Lord's character, abide in His Word, and rest in His promises while we simply let Him be GOD.

Prayer: Lord, You use others in our lives to teach us very important lessons. Give me the wisdom to recognize them and learn them so that I can let go of the old in order to embrace the new that often comes out of the ashes of what has already been consumed by the fires on Your altar, where all has been offered up for Your purpose and glory. Amen.

March 27

"Think not that I am come to send peace on earth: I came not to send peace, but a sword. For I am come to set a man at variance against his father, and the daughter against her mother, and the daughter in law again her mother-in-law" (Matthew 10:34-35). In yesterday's devotion I talked about my relationship with my mother. A mother will always be a mother, but as a child grows into adulthood, the relationship must also grow and change if it is going to prove to be beneficial for both parties.

My mother would always be my mother, but a mother must accept the fact that each adult child must seek out their own life. Each offspring must experience the different upheavals that life can bring in order to grow up and take responsibility for the type of person they are becoming. If the growth doesn't happen because there is one who wants to control or maintain the former influence, then the relationship will morph into an unhealthy existence that will become sour to both parties.

My mother wanted to have a say in my life, but at the same time she wanted to live her own life. To me it was quite unfair of her to try to direct my life while claiming autonomy to live her life as she saw fit.

When parents become too involved, almost obsessive with their adult children's lives, they will often provoke them to anger. After all, as an adult, their children are at that stage in life where they are trying to forge their own path.

All good relationships are forged through growing crises. The biggest challenge to any relationship is to let it grow and to have enough wisdom to adjust attitudes and if need be, change approaches to ensure that the relationship is reaching heights of excellence and not becoming stagnant in some lifeless pool of past memories.

This also applies to our relationship with the Lord. It must be forged through the crises that comes with the walk of faith. Jesus must become more than Savior to us, He must become our all in all.

Prayer: Lord thank You that You are always calling me higher and that regardless of how I might kick and scream, You hold the line that eventually will force me to get up and grow up. Amen.

March 28

"Iron sharpeneth iron; so a man sharpeneth the countenance of his friend" (Proverbs 27:17). I have been talking about relationships. There are those who test your character, some who spice up your life, and others who encourage you to grow, but the one thing that is obvious is that people will create some kind of stimuli in your life that will cause growth to take place if properly assimilated in your life.

For my mother and I, our relationship reminded me of Esau and Jacob struggling in the womb of Rebekah. Each person had their place but it would require a struggle to find it. Through much struggling my mother and I did come to a place of understanding and acceptance, and our relationship was better for it.

The struggle in relationships can be compared to Ishmael and Isaac. One of the things that creates the greatest problem in relationships is jealousy. Ishmael was jealous of what Isaac had and out of it came mocking. There must be respect for a person's place in the scheme of things, to ensure that jealousy never inches its way into the midst.

Another good example of the struggles that take place is between the Spirit and the flesh. All struggles in relationships begin in the flesh. The flesh wants to rule, subdue, and control, while the Spirit wants to set the person free from the tyranny of the flesh in order to reach their ordain potential. The flesh makes for a base man and a miserable existence, while the Spirit ensures the necessary liberty to become a spiritual man that no longer gives way to the flesh.

The key is it is our choice as to what level our worldly relationships operate in.

Prayer: Lord, I know there must be struggles for growth to take place. It is clear You never waste relationships, Lord. Some struggles end in separation but my desire is to do right in every relationship because each one is meant to sharpen me in some way. Thank You for Your many special tools. Amen.

March 29

If you grew up in the era I did, when the Saturday matinée at the local theater consisted of a double feature of riding the range with Gene and Roy, plus a cartoon in between, then you probably developed a deeply held belief that the good guys always win in the end. The inner satisfaction of consistently seeing right win over wrong in those old western movies, at least for some of us, had a profound influence on our worldview when we were young. After all, the weekly western heroes always caught the bad guys, rescued the pretty ladies, and rode off into the sunset on their fancy horses.

For some, such as myself who had a decent homelife, it took longer for the "Happy Trails" bubble to burst, but burst it did when eventually cold, crude and cruel reality hit squarely between the eyes. Not all good guys win, not all victims are rescued, not all problems are solved, and not all endings are happy.

This is the crises point we all hope to either be able to ignore or somehow avoid, but in this world, there is no escaping the inevitable. Sooner or later, we are brought to the place of decision where we are forced to decide, for once and for all, whether or not we believe and trust God, trust His Word, and trust Jesus Christ concerning the final outcome of all things. And, sometimes the Lord lets people hit bottom, and hit it hard, knowing that it is the only way they will ever look up, give up, and step up into the loving arms of Jesus Christ.

"Wherefore seeing we also are compassed about with so great a cloud of witnesses, let us lay aside every weight, and the sin which doth so easily beset us, and let us run with patience the race that is set before us, Looking unto Jesus the author and finisher of our faith; who for the joy that was set before him endured the cross, despising the shame, and is set down at the right hand of the throne of God. For consider him that endured such contradiction of sinners against himself, lest ye be wearied and faint in your minds" (Hebrews 12:1-3). – J. Haley

Prayer: Lord, we want to believe the good guy will always win, but when it comes to this world, there is nothing fair, pure, or really good unless it comes to You. Lord, I know You are the victor and meanwhile if I want to believe that good wins out I have to keep looking up to the only One who is good and that is You! Amen.

March 30

"But the God of all grace, who hath called us unto his eternal glory by Christ Jesus. After that ye have suffered a while make you perfect, stablish, strengthen, settle you" (1 Peter 5:10). As a believer, I am constantly being called by my Lord. I am being called to service to come higher, to press forward to heights of excellence, and to come to a place of fellowship and rest to name a few. In this Scripture, I am being called unto eternal glory. It is obvious that when the Lord calls an individual, it is to that which is worthy of all consideration.

Obviously, He will never call any of us to that which is base and unacceptable. He will not invite us to taste that which is bitter or touch that which is unclean. He calls us to a life that will speak of His glory. It will be marked by eternity and will be pure and sweet.

Adhering to His call will bring me to perfection or maturity in my spiritual life. It will bring me to a high place that will establish me on the Rock, strengthen me in my inner man, and cause me to settle in the pavilion of His protection, rest, and peace.

Prayer: Lord, as believers we have so much available to us. We have been provided with the means to survive this present world in order to enter into Your blessed promises. Thank You for providing us with all that we have need of. Amen.

March 31

"The righteous shall flourish like the palm tree: he shall grow like a cedar in Lebanon, Those that be planted in the house of the LORD shall flourish in the courts of our God" (Psalm 92:12-13). The Bible says much about the promise and inheritance that will be given to those who are righteous. I cannot help but meditate on what it means to be righteous.

Righteousness comes down to the bent a person will have towards the matters of life. The flesh is bent towards the world prompted by the temptation that weighs heavy upon the appetites, and is easily moved by the selfish disposition to experience the happiness of the present age.

Righteousness is bent towards God. It is right standing in Him. Regardless, of how much the winds of temptation cause those who are righteous to sway, they will automatically come back into right standing with God. They cannot be moved from what is right. They stand erect in character and draw their strength from the throne of heaven. They reach towards the Sun of righteousness as they strive for what is excellent, while they reach deep into the promises of God that firmly establishes them on the Rock. As a result, they do grow as strong trees that are productive and bring glory to the Lord as they ever point heavenward.

Prayer: Lord, we are blessed people. We stand on everlasting promises as we look towards our future inheritance. Thank You for being true to Your Word. Amen.

APRIL

April 1

"Blessed is he that considereth the poor; the LORD will deliver him in times of trouble" (Psalm 41:1). It can be hard for people in a prosperous country to understand the spirit of real giving.

It is easy to give in a time of abundance. Granted, there are those who become quite stingy in their times of prosperity. Such people truly represent the misers of the world. They prove to be the most miserable in their greed and lack of character.

The real spirit of giving can only be made obvious when people give out of their need to those who are less fortunate. In my experience, those who are wealthy can afford to be philanthropists who do good on a national or international scale. Such giving often serves as a platform to exalt social reform and godless causes. But real need is never met on such a scale, for it is the personal plight of those who often appear insignificant. Their cries are rarely heard and their needs overlooked.

I am thankful God hears the silent cries of the heart and meets us in our needs. That is the essence of the spirit of giving.

Prayer: Lord, You have shown us what real giving looks like. It comes from a selfless, pure heart, is benevolent in attitude, and sacrificial in conduct. Lord, I want to have a charitable disposition like Yours. Amen.

April 2

"He sent from above, he took me; he drew me out of many waters" *(2 Samuel 22:17).* It is interesting to watch the seasons change, and when we lived by Priest River we could watch it change day by day. In the summer it appeared docile as it quietly flowed to its destination. It almost seemed as if in certain places it was a bit lazy, stifled by the heat and not in any hurry to reach the next body of water.

In the fall it begins to recede, exposing the hindrances so that it can once again flow freely. However, in the winter it goes through various stages. Once again, I cannot help but relate seasonal changes to my spiritual life.

My life is always going through an array of changes. I can see the heat of summer dwindle my strength, and the fall season causes me to redefine my time and responsibilities. During the winter I try to finish projects and in the spring I can hardly wait to enjoy the sun on my face.

I can see so many similarities between my spiritual life and the changes of seasons along with the flow of the rivers around me. However, what catches my attention the most are the flow of the rivers. In the summer the river may appear consistent and in the fall it is establishing its own boundaries, but in the winter, it is going through different phases that are happening on a daily basis. Each phase represents the phases I find myself going through on a regular basis when it comes to the flow of the Holy Spirit in my life.

Prayer: Lord, You give us priceless examples that can give us glimpses into the inner work You are doing in our lives. Thank You for such examples. Amen.

April 3

"And if the righteous scarcely be saved, where shall the ungodly and the sinner appear?" (1 Peter 4:18). Every time I read this Scripture, I am reminded how precious grace is. It is clear we are saved by grace. It is nothing we can do to save ourselves except by faith to throw ourselves on the mercy of a loving, forgiving God. However, I have to admit, I become a bit concerned when I hear people who call themselves a Christian appear to be flippant about salvation when we are warned to work out our salvation with fear and trembling and that we must not neglect it (*Philippians 2:12; Hebrews 2:3*). I rarely see sober attitudes about the matters of God, hardly hear any exhortation about living a godly life, and somewhat am overwhelmed when Christians speak of the things of darkness as if it is not a big deal because "God loves us" and will "understand" our indiscretions (*Ephesians 5:6-13; Hebrew 10:25; 1 Peter 5:8-9*).

However, this Scripture reminds me that I am scarcely saved. It is not a matter of being saved by the "skin of my teeth" because there is none, and it is not a matter of barely squeezing into heaven, because the door into eternity will be opened to me or tightly shut against me depending on what I have done with Jesus in this present life. Rather, it comes down to the fact that I have been translated from the kingdom of darkness into the kingdom of life.

This translation points to not walking according to the dark ways of the old man, but walking in the ways of the new man. The new man will not be casual about sin, and as he matures in his faith, his attitude, even about the shades of questionable "grey's" when it comes to unbecoming speech and conduct, will line up to an unyielded stance of righteousness.

Wisdom should dictate that if we are scarcely saved that we must be aware of how we are walking and living out our Christian life. We should value salvation as being precious and remember that the fine line between grace and God's wrath towards the ungodly and sinner is narrow and sobering.

We must not live in constant fear of falling over the line into judgment because we possess unfeigned faith towards God, but we must have the fear of the Lord which will wisely discipline our attitude and cause us to walk in the ways of righteousness so that in the end we do not bring shame or reproach on the Lord and our testimony.

Prayer: Lord, the way is narrow and we are told to walk in it. As long as we are in the way, Your way of righteousness, we have nothing to fear. You are the One who not only saved us, but You preserve our soul and keep our feet from slipping into the abyss. Thank You. Amen.

April 4

"And we desire that every one of you do shew the same diligence to the full assurance of hope unto the end" (Hebrews 6:11). When I consider the fine line between that of grace and judgment, I must examine if I am operating in the faith that was first delivered to the saints (*2 Corinthians 13:5; Jude 3*). This causes me to think about the assurance of salvation. It's natural to resent anyone who would challenge any believer about salvation. Through the years I have become aware of people operating according to assumptions about salvation, instead of having the assurance of salvation. It is, after all, natural to make assumptions about many things.

We assume we know something when in reality we really don't know the whole story. We assume we understand, but when challenged we are not even close to the mark of what is really going on. We assume our conclusions are right, but when the truth of a matter finally comes out, we realize we knew enough to make us look foolish in the end, causing a bit of embarrassment.

The Bible is clear that we can be assured of salvation, but how many are living under assumptions about salvation rather than walking in assurance of it? As a result, they silently wrestle, question, and debate whether they are saved.

The Bible tells us we must be born again to enter the kingdom of God. Being born again is an actual experience and not some intellectual consensus. We are told we must receive the truth of redemption in our hearts to be saved, but how many assume, since they have a head knowledge about salvation, that they are saved but it is not a heart revelation. There are those who went forward and said some sinner's prayer but how many have truly confessed their sins and called upon the name of the Lord Jesus Christ to save them from not only the claims of death upon them by showing great mercy, but from themselves by showing them His incredible grace by giving them a new life? How many have also truly changed their master and owner by confessing that Jesus is Lord, knowing life will not make sense outside of living for Him, serving Him, and following Him.

Assumptions or assurance? When it comes to salvation, assumption will leave you deluded or doubtful, but assurance will leave you standing on what is sure, walking in what has been set forth as righteous, and pressing forward to what has been established in eternity as being immutable truth.

Prayer: Lord, I have operated in so many assumptions but because of receiving a new life from You, I walk in assurance of the salvation that You have secured for me on the cross. I may stumble, trip, and fall over my assumptions in my journey here but because of You, Lord, I stand assured in my salvation in light of my future home with You. Lord keep me from assuming what is not so and presuming what will never be and help me seek You daily to keep all matters right before You. Amen.

April 5

There's one place where I'm rarely alone, and that is the kitchen. Our Yorkie-Poo can be snoozing, playing with his toys, barking at the dog next door or busy chewing on his Chewie, but when he hears the refrigerator door open followed by the scent of beef, chicken, turkey or fish, he makes sure he's planted right next to me. He never says anything, but those shiny, hopeful and pleading eyes are hard to ignore, and he usually always gets his "bite" either before or after his hoped-for snack is cooked.

One day as he and I were in our usual spots in the kitchen, I glanced into those bright, expectant eyes and thought to myself, "If only Christians had as much enthusiasm, hunger and hope for God's Word as this little dog has for each and every tidbit of food, how much stronger, better and more powerful the Body of Christ would be!"

Where has the great hunger and thirst for the Word of God, and God Himself, that existed decades ago gone? Are we all so mentally saturated with our mind-bending technological social media options for entertainment, information, tantalizing tales, and the world's vanity that we have no appetite for the only source of Truth in the world?

If we ever needed men and women, boys and girls to love, desire, believe and live by the Spirit-breathed Word of God, it is NOW! *"Blessed are they which do hunger and thirst after righteousness: for they shall be filled." (Matthew 5:6).* – J. Haley

Prayer: Lord, give us a love for Your Word that turns into an appetite for Your righteousness and a relentless pursuer of Your truth. Amen.

April 6

"Keep back thy servant also from presumptuous sins; let them not have dominion over me: then shall I be upright, and I shall be innocent from the great transgression" (Psalm 19:13). In my last post, I spoke of assumptions. When I think about assumptions, I am automatically reminded of presumptions.

A presumption is an assumption with an attitude. The reason an attitude is present is because presumption is a matter of the will. It has basically adopted an assumption as being the truth of a matter, when in reality it is still an assumption but now it stands on shaky ground because there is nothing to really back it other than a person wills a matter to be so.

When it comes to salvation, I must consider if it is a matter of presumption on my part or if it is the essence of my testimony. What is the difference between a presumption and a testimony? A presumption assumes a matter is so, while a testimony stands as a record that a matter is so because a person has personally experienced it. *1 Peter 3:15* tells us we must give an account, or a defense, of the hope in us. To be able to give an account of something points to having a testimony. And what is the believer's hope? *"Christ in us is the hope of glory" (Colossians 1:27).*

My question is how many people who call themselves Christians presume they are a believer but when questioned they have no real testimony of Jesus? They, in essence, do not have a record of that point when they crossed over the Jordan River from an old life that was corrupt and a stench to God into His promises to walk in the new life of the Son of God. This is clearly an assumption with a stiff-necked attitude that something is so, because that is what I determine to believe is the truth of a matter.

Prayer: Lord, I am beginning to realize that assumption is silly and presumption is foolishness. Please give me a greater love for the truth so I can cast any assumption aside and declare presumption to be nothing more than foolishness opinion on my part. Amen.

April 7

"So I spake unto you; and ye would not hear, but rebelled against the commandment of the LORD, and went presumptuously up into the hill" (Deuteronomy 1:43). It is dangerous to operate in assumptions and presumptions when it comes to our spiritual well-being. However, assumptions are natural and presumptions become our preferred reality. We can't help believing what we hope is so and insist on such hope as being true even if it is not.

When a person presumes that they are saved because of some religious association of the past and/or present, they are in essence putting God to a foolish test because they presume He will save them when they have not even been born again.

They are like some of the children of Israel when faced with wandering in the wilderness for forty years after failing to enter into the Promised Land by faith: they presumed that if they simply apologized to God for their unbelief, they could then rise up and take the land. The children of Israel met with utter defeat.

Presumption allows one to stand on the wrong side of Jordan while believing they have crossed over into salvation, but the bridge of faith is missing and they remain on the other side of God's promises. I have a record of my salvation and if you ask me, I will testify of that time in my life when I experienced real salvation. Do you have such a testimony?

Prayer: Lord, it is easy to stand on the shaky ground of presumption in different matters, but when it comes to salvation You provided the bridge of faith to cross over into life everlasting; therefore, for those who remain on the other side trusting their presumption that they are alright, they will sadly meet with a closed door to Your promises. Lord, I have crossed over because of faith in You, and now I can stand on the promises attached to eternal life. Praise Your Name for Your great work of redemption. Amen.

April 8

"But the soul that doeth ought presumptuously, whether he be born in the land, or a stranger, the same reproacheth the LORD; and that soul shall be cut off from among his people" (Numbers 15:30). As already stated, it is dangerous to operate in assumptions and presumptions when it comes to our spiritual well-being. Assumptions reveal the maturity of our faith and presumptions test God. The truth is both are based on false or misdirected hope.

It is easy to put our hope in what we think we know about God instead of putting our hope in who we assume He is. Once we put our hope in what we perceive God to be, we naturally can put our faith in what He can do regardless of His will. We can declare that nothing is too great for God without considering whether it is part of the perfect plan or work of our great God. Clearly, presumption sets us up to fall into disillusionment and despair.

Hope in another god other than the one of the Bible is idolatry. Faith directed towards a god of our own creation who will fit into our formulas that serve our whims is nothing more than some "Sugar Daddy" or "Santa Claus," that solely exists in the imagination but is not the God of the Bible.

To have misdirected hope is to operate in assumptions about our salvation, but faith in a god of our own creation is a presumption that will end in bringing a reproach on the Lord and our testimony. In the end, such a person will hear those terrible words from the Lord, "I know you not."

Prayer: Lord it is easy to let you pass by us when we make assumptions, and in our presumptions, we try to get ahead of You and direct You in the way we think You should go. Either way Lord, we will miss You. Forgive us for our arrogance. Amen.

April 9

"Thou wilt shew me the path of life: in thy presence is fulness of joy; at thy right hand there are pleasures for evermore" (Psalm 16:11). In the last post I spoke of presumptions. The foundation of presumption is that of wishful thinking. The Bible speaks of knowing something to be true.

We can know if we are saved because we have the witness of the Holy Spirit in us. We must know we are saved so we can stand on immutable promises, and we will know we are saved because we personally know the One who saves. We not only know the Lord Jesus Christ, but we believe His Word is true and we line up our life to it to ensure the integrity of our walk before Him to avoid any reproach or shame when we do stand before Him.

Before I received Christ, I lived on wishful thinking. I would wish a matter to be so and occasionally life would throw me a small bone when something actually turned out the way I wished it. However, such bones were far and few in-between and always left me empty. It seemed I was always wishing for that small morsel to keep my wishful thinking from crash landing in the swamps of despair and hopelessness.

I eventually ended up in the swamp of despair because in all my wishful thinking true hope was absent. I would wish a matter so, but there was no anticipation that it would ever be so. The small morsels I encountered along the way eventually led me to the swamp of despair, but it was there I looked up in desperation to see that real hope is not around me, before me, or in front of me. Real hope is above me sitting on the right hand of majesty, Jesus Christ.

Prayer: Lord, keep me looking up. I know that as long as I look up, I can't look anywhere else. Oh Lord, keep my neck from sagging in despair. Remind me of Your promises as a means to inspire me to look up and know my hope is in You. Amen.

April 10

"And hope maketh not ashamed; because the love of God is shed abroad in our hearts by the Holy Ghost which is given unto us" *(Romans 5:5).* It is easy to fall into despair. All we have to do is look around us and become overwhelmed by the great darkness that is enfolding the world. Hope can flee in such darkness, faith can tremble as it looks for a way out, and truth can be knocked down. This is where we can go into unbelief or choose the way of faith. I choose to put my faith in Christ, and when I do hope comes into my spirit.

True hope lives in anticipation of what has been promised by God. It is not wishing for small morsels along the way where life turns out according to wishful thinking; rather, it is walking in the eternal life that is present in anticipation of seeing the author of life in which all the riches, promises, and heavenly pleasures will be realized and experienced.

Today, I fear some who call themselves Christians are standing on the small "mount" of wishful thinking. They wish to be saved because they do not want to experience the real bitterness of a lifeless, hopeless existence in hell until they stand before the Great White Throne Judgment to face the Judge of all. However, such wishful thinking will not save a person, because there is no legitimate anticipation on such a person's part that when Jesus comes, His saints will be ushered into His presence because He knows them and they know Him.

Prayer: Lord, I know You. I understood my need to be saved because of my despair, and I found hope because Your Word told me about redemption, but today I stand in great anticipation of my future with You because I know You according to Your Spirit and in light of Your truth. Lord thank You for causing the shifting sand of my wishful thinking to sink in the swamp of despair so that when I looked up and cried out for You to save me, You reached down and took my hand and placed me on the immutable Rock of Ages. Amen.

April 11

"In a moment in the twinkling of an eye, at the last trump: for the trumpet shall sound, and the dead shall be raised incorruptible, and we shall be changed. For this corruptible must put on incorruption, and this mortal must put on immortality" (1 Corinthians 15:52-53). At one of our Bible Studies, we heard the phrase "Resurrection or Rapture?"

These two words made me think about meeting Jesus. Since I am a believer, will I meet Him through the door of death or in the air? If I meet Him through the door of death the Apostle Paul assures me in *2 Corinthians 5:8* that my spirit and soul will be ushered into His presence.

To add to "Resurrection or Rapture," we must consider redemption. There can be no hope of a better resurrection or rapture without the work of redemption. The apostle talks about the far-reaching work of redemption in *Ephesians 1:11-14.*

Redemption is a complete work. I was redeemed through justification wrought on behalf of my wretched soul, I am being redeemed through sanctification of the Holy Spirit in my inner being, and I look forward to my redemption being complete when I receive my new glorified body. If I should be alive when Jesus comes then that means I will meet Him in the air where the corruption of my dying body will immediately be put off for it can't inherit the kingdom of God, and in the twinkling of an eye I will come forth in a new, glorified body.

Prayer: Lord, what great promises we have before us. Cause me to remember them when the world begins to drag me down in order to bury me under its temporary glitter and demands. Amen.

April 12

"And the city had not need of the sun, neither of the moon, to shine in it: for the glory of God did lighten it, and the Lamb is the light thereof" (Revelation 21:23). As Christians we are so earth bound, we have a hard time remembering that the promise of the next world is far greater than the fading glory of this world. We often get caught up with the glitter of this world while missing the glory of the next.

We know about the work of God on the cross, but we become hum ho towards it, often forgetting that the fullness of redemption is not just our spirit being revived by the Spirit of the Living God upon being born again and our soul redeemed by the blood of the Lamb of God, but that the fullness of redemption is when we gain a new body.

It is true that in God's presence, the spirit freely worships and the soul freely blesses the Lord in praise and adoration, but until I am brought forth in a new glorified body, my service before the Lord will not be complete. After all, we are told we will be serving with the Lord in the millennium age to come. To do that we will need a body that will be able to interact with both the spiritual and the physical worlds.

The body I am in now is dying, but the new body promised me will be perfect and will live forever. Meanwhile, as a believer, I need to press forward for a better resurrection by occupying in light of preparing to be in the incredible presence of the Lord when this body gives way to that which is miraculous, eternal, and glorious.

Prayer: Lord, no matter how bad it gets here, I have a glorious future awaiting me. I don't know if I will meet You through the blessed door of death or in the air, but I know with confidence that when I do meet You, I will see You as You are, beautiful, wonderful, and beyond description. Amen.

April 13

"So I spake unto you; and ye would not hear, but rebelled against the commandment of the LORD, and went presumptuously up into the hill" (Deuteronomy 1:43). There are various Scriptures that make me sad, and it comes down to man's lack or unbelieving response towards God.

I know God's heart towards mankind but it is often left broken by their rejection, as well as their end, if they don't repent. It is all quite sad and tragic. For example, in one incident in *John 6:60-66* because of hard sayings, many of Jesus' disciples departed and no longer walked with Him. However, there is one phrase that when I read it, I feel like I have either been shot out of the air of expectancy, fallen off the cliff of hope into great darkness, or heard the sour note of doom. This phrase is, "and ye would not."

Consider what God offers mankind. There is salvation, but how many would not even consider it because it seems foolish to them. There is joy, but how many shun it because it doesn't fit into their concept of "happiness and fun." How about peace? All a person has to do is come to the Prince of Peace, but how many will not because it seems too lame or too easy? We could go down the scale of the wondrous promises of God if only man would come to Him in brokenness, repentance, need, faith, and obedience, but, HE WILL NOT.

Man can justify why he will not come to God. He can excuse why he puts it off until possibly another time when it fits in with his life and circumstances. He can dance around the matter of his soul as he parlays with the world, plays footsie with Satan, and placates the flesh. However, the real reason he will not come to God is because it is not in his heart, according to his will, and in light of his selfish pursuits to do so. Therefore, his will, will not be moved by any prompting, his heart will not relent to any conviction, and his soul will not be humbled by truth that is contrary to its selfish preferences.

Since man has a free will to do as he chooses, he will not come to God; rather, he chooses to go his own way regardless of the warnings of Scripture, the consequences of bad decisions, and the judgments already pronounced on all disobedience.

Prayer: Lord, I have insisted on my own way and found out it was the wrong way. Lord, have Your way in my life regardless of how my pride resents it, my flesh resists it and Satan mocks me for giving way to You. Your way is right in every way, perfect in all ways, and liberating to the soul. Amen.

April 14

"Notwithstanding they would not hear, but hardened their necks like their fathers, that did not believe in the LORD their God (2 Kings 17:14). It would be wise of man to come to God, his Creator. It would benefit him greatly, bring satisfaction to his soul and revive his sagging spirit if he would choose to hear him, but he will not.

At this time, we could be critical of such a person, but stop and consider your own life. How many times have you heard one of the Lord's invitations, felt the nudging of His Spirit, had your conscience pricked by truth, or knew you should have done something but grabbed the first fleeting boat of justification so that you could merrily go down the river while you cover up with the fig-leaves of flimsy excuses for not doing it. In other words, "you would not" accept the invitation, repent in light of conviction, or do what was right when given the opportunity to do so.

There are reasons "we will not" properly respond when it comes to God. There is rebellion, pride, independence, compromise, worldliness, and fear, but the real culprit behind the lack of response is UNBELIEF.

Unbelief is the result of not loving God with all your heart, soul, mind, and might. We refuse to respond because it's not worth it to us. We would feel foolish responding to matters that don't benefit us, fit into our narrative, serve our purpose, or make us look or feel a certain way up front.

The next time you come to this phrase in the Bible, stop and consider if you would do what was asked of you without debate; or did you let the "buts" or the "ands" get in the way of your faith and obedience as you found some means of self-justification to cover up your unbelief and lack of love for the God of heaven and earth.

Prayer: Lord, I have had plenty of "buts" and "ands" give me a leg up in avoiding what was right before You, but Lord, I give you permission to cast my "buts" into the abyss, knock away my "ands" and cause me to make the choice to rest in You as my Savior, have peace in You as my Lord, and experience quietness of spirit and soul because You are my God. Amen.

April 15

"Repent ye therefore, and be converted, that your sins may be blotted out, when the times of refreshing shall come from the presence of the Lord" (Acts 3:19). When I read Scriptures such as this one, I am reminded that something must be blotted out when it comes to my life in God. The Bible is clear, my sins must be blotted out or my name will be blotted out in the Book of Life (*Revelation 3:5*).

I believe that everyone who is born into this world has their name written in the Book of Life. However, it is when one refuses to repent and seek Christ's redemption to be saved from the wages of sin, neglects to confess and make Jesus Lord of their life and be turned from their old ways with the intent of being converted to the ways of righteousness that their name will be blotted out of the Book of Life. We must remember Jesus' death on the cross dealt with sin.

The Lord did not die so we could live in sin without consequences; rather, He died so our sin could be taken away to avoid God's wrath on all disobedience. We must be ever ready to confess any sin in order to be cleansed from all unrighteousness so we can stand before Him without shame and reproach.

Today, I fear that some want the benefits of Christ's death on the cross, without dealing with the reason He had to go to the cross as the sinless Lamb of God. We might frown on certain sins while parlaying with what we consider minor sins that in our mind surely God will overlook. We can console ourselves that God loves us and will not hold us to such a high standard over such silly discrepancies, especially when He is a God of grace.

However, we can't really experience God's love unless we come by way of Christ's cross to lay all of our sins before it and tearfully embrace it as liberty and forgiveness enfolds us like a warm blanket. We must recognize that grace only abounds where sin used to and can only reign through righteousness that is accounted to us because of faith. If we want to experience the refreshing of His presence in our midst, then sin must be dealt with because His Spirit can't move when the profane is present.

Prayer: Lord, we want Your blessings, but they can only come through Your Spirit from the Father. However, if the profane, the unholy, and the perverted are present, He will not come. Let us not be neglectful, unthankful, and unwise when it comes to our salvation and walk before You. Amen.

April 16

"And at that time shall Michael stand up, the great prince which standeth for the children of thy people: and there shall be a time of trouble, such as never was since there was a nation even to that same time: and at that time thy people shall be delivered, every one that shall be found written in the book" (Daniel 12:1). I am human and I'm aware of the deviant ways of the old life that is only subdued when I firmly nail it to the cross, but I also know that it does not take much for it to raise its head to blindside me with some folly.

I don't know how many times I had to wrestle the old man down to the ground, drag him to the cross, and nail him there as he cried "foul," shed tears of worldly remorse, declared his rights, promised to reform, and accused me of being unfair and too rigid in my thinking. After all, a little fun won't hurt me.

There is always some logic to the arguments that often take place in the courtroom of our minds with the old man, but in the end, it always proves to be vanity. The issue always comes back to what is being blotted out in my life. Is the old man being blotted out by the cross? Are my old ways being blotted out by the grave? Is my old way of thinking being completed blotted out by a complete transformation of the mind? Are my sins being blotted out in true confession and by the glorious work of redemption?

As long as I breathe, I am choosing what is being blotted out. I choose to blot out the old with self-denial and the cross as a means to ensure that my life in Christ is not some waste, that my soul does not become lost in the folly of the world, and that my name is clearly present in the book of life. As one of the posts on my Facebook states, "When we draw our last breath only one thing will matter. That our name is written in the Lamb's Book of Life."

Prayer: Lord, I want to know the abundance of Your life here, experience the presence of Your Spirit now, and know when all is said and done, my name will be clearly written in Your precious Book of Life. Amen.

April 17

The determination, diligence, dedication and devotion of a pair of robins that return each spring to build their nest and raise their young in our backyard is amazing as well as uplifting because it is a living display of God's order. It's also amazing in the respect that their predictable commitment stands in stark contrast to the disinterest and disdain of most of the world's masses whose indifference toward living a life with such orderly and commendable qualities has pushed them to the outer limits of God's commandments and purpose for mankind. But in spite of the suffering inflicted upon all living creatures because of the disorder, destruction and death caused by the fall of man, day after day, year after year, God's creatures continue striving to fulfill their original purpose.

Sadly, it's not so with lost mankind whose natural bent is a state of rebellion. As humans, our grasp on the reins of freewill is the greatest temptation and test that any of us must face. *Romans 8:6, 7* tells us, *"For to be carnally minded is death; but to be spiritually minded is life and peace. Because the carnal mind is enmity against God: for it is not subject to the law of God, neither indeed can be."*

There is no "life and peace" when we refuse to submit to God's will and order for us, and we will always feel "out of joint" with life and at odds with God; that is, until we surrender at the foot of the cross and submit our entire being to the Lord Jesus Christ, the Son of God. He promises, *"A new heart also will I give you, and a new spirit will I put within you: and I will take away the stony heart out of your flesh, and I will give you an heart of flesh."* (Ezekiel 36:26.)

Call on the Lord while He is near! – J. Haley

Prayer: Lord, we want life but on our terms. We want peace but our great struggles are usually inner struggles with what is right. We want assurance that all will be right in the end, but unless we end with You, Your work of Redemption can't bring completion to our lives. Lord, You provided all and I must believe You, trust Your work and obey Your instructions. Amen.

April 18

"Behold I give unto you power to tread on serpents and scorpions, and over all the power of the enemy: and nothing shall by any means hurt you. Notwithstanding in this rejoice not, that the spirits are subject unto you; but rather rejoice, because your names are written in heaven" (Luke 10:19-20). In my last post I spoke of the Book of Life. When you study this subject, you will find this book mentioned through both the Old and New Testaments. A good example of this is found in *Daniel 12:1.*

It is important to recognize the priority that Jesus put on this book. As humans we can get caught up with sensationism that can be a result of being exposed to unseen power. Sadly, it appears as some in the religious realm seek after sensational experiences.

For them it is like swinging from one limb to the next through ether waves of religious ecstasy. The problem is sensationalism can become a drug to these people. They must have it to believe that their Christianity is valid and that they must constantly experience it to maintain a religious appearance and zeal to others.

As a result, they can find themselves living for that next experience, that next miracle, and that next supernatural intervention. If they don't get it, they almost let a yawn of boredom out when they don't have their senses heightened by some supernatural event.

I have witnessed the miraculous many times and in many different ways, but what changes my perspective, is that simple revelation of Jesus that causes me to fall more and more in love with Him. The truth is everything has a pause in it. For Christians it doesn't mean the Spirit is not present or moving, rather, it could mean there is a pause because the Lord wants us to come apart and sit with Him a while in sweet communion and worship.

Prayer: Lord, I am aware that religion can be a fleshly experience, a deadly exercise, and a tool of Satan to undermine the true faith of the saints, but I choose You, knowing You are the bread from heaven that can satisfy my soul. Amen.

April 19

"Yea, though I walk through the valley of the shadow of death, I will fear no evil: for thou are with me; they rod and they staff they comfort me" (Psalm 23:4). The reality of the Christian life is that it is not experienced in the tree-tops of sensationalism; rather, it is lived out in the demon-possessed valleys of this world.

The power we possess does not consist of limbs that cause us to swing above the present world; rather, it enables us to walk through this world, while giving us the means to be overcomers and victorious. We must be earthbound in our discernment, heavenward in our perspective, and standing in the gap in our prayer. We must avoid trying to ignore the valleys, while staying long enough on the mountains that we are prepared to minister in the valleys. We must be ever mindful that our journey here is not about power, authority and being a big shot; rather, it is about gaining Christ to ensure our heavenly destination.

Jesus is clear we must not rejoice because we have power over our enemies; rather, we must rejoice because our names are written in the Book of Life. The Lord is trying to bring His disciples down from the great heights of power allotted to them to the reality of what is important to heaven itself.

It is clear, when the roll is called up yonder, He wants to be assured that our name will be called out as we rejoice with the rest of heaven that we have finally finished the course and are now truly home in His presence, where we will experience His glory for evermore.

Prayer: Lord, we humans can take all kinds of detours, get caught up with all kinds of emotional experiences, and become quite zealous about religion, but in the end it will all come down to whether our name is written in the Book of Life. Lord, keep me grounded on Your Word, realistic about Your life, and holding onto to Your eternal truth. In essence, keep me in the narrow way of Your path that will lead me to You and life everlasting. Amen.

April 20

Flushed faces are probably what observers of Jesus' disciples witnessed when He set a small child in their midst, and told them *"Verily I say unto you, Except ye be converted, and become as little children ye shall not enter into the kingdom of heaven. Whosoever therefore shall humble himself as this little child, the same is greatest in the kingdom of heaven"* (Matthew 18:3, 4). After all, even though Jesus had chosen them to be His disciples, (which should have been humbling in and of itself), they were still human and human beings are naturally self-exalting and competitive.

Let's face it, wanting to be seen or heard, noticed or admired, exalted or even famous is a natural tendency. Perhaps that is one reason a sermon I heard about 40 years ago preached by the head chaplain of the Arizona women's prisons has stuck in my memory.

The bottom line of it was the importance of not being outwardly important and the illustration he used was "countersunk nails." I remember him stressing that a house couldn't stand without all the countersunk nails, and that there were untold numbers of them in a sound structure. He compared that to the unseen and unknown "countersunk" Christians working in God's kingdom—people who are unnoticed, ignored, unappreciated and usually forgotten by all except the Lord.

All the strife and struggle so many self-important, zealous people put themselves through to build a "big ministry" that just "has to get out there" by means of TV, Internet, Radio, conferences, rallies, or any other "over-the-moon" modern method available to make sure they're a "household name" is not worth it in the end because Jesus never calls us to be "great" in the kingdom of God, but rather to be a faithful servant who is working for the Lord of lords, and King of kings in order to bring all glory to God, not to him or herself. How many of these famous, super rich, "big names" who draw huge crowds of adoring fans because they know how to whip up people's emotions and flatter their egos truly belong to the real Jesus?

Here is a TEST: How many of the "rich and famous" with a so-called "ministry" would sell all that they had and put their money (which is usually in the millions) into a fund for the spread of the Gospel, and for the poor and needy? How many would literally give their life for the sheep? How many would resist the temptation to sell their soul in order to gain the whole world? How many truly walk in humility and love as our Savior walked? How many are investing their time, energy and money into discipling the saints and establishing them upon the Rock so when the storm comes (and believe me, it's coming) the people will be able to stand? How many of the false prophets mouthing lies in the name of the Lord for notoriety and "filthy lucre" would be willing to repent and become a "countersunk nail"? That's something to think about. *"Humble yourselves in the sight of the Lord, and he shall lift you up" (James 3:10)* – J. Haley

Prayer: Lord, we thank You that You measure greatness, not according to the arrogant superiority of the world, but according to how humble Your servant is before You and others. There can't be such humility unless there has been brokenness where Your restoration took place, repentance where change is obvious, and grace where Your life is present in the person. I praise You for bringing me to all the low places so that I can experience Your sweetness in high places. Amen.

April 21

"Then said David to the Philistine, Thou comest to me with a sword, and with a spear, and with a shield: but I come o thee in the name of the LORD of hosts, the God of the armies of Israel, whom thou hast defied" (1 Samuel 17: 45). Every time I come face to face with the inept spiritual condition of what we could call "Modern Christianity" by encountering its foul fruits of confusion, division, perversion, the absence of testimonies, and the evidence of worldliness, I am reminded of a couple of things. The first one is that Jesus was concerned that when He came would He find true faith?

The second truth I am reminded of is that there is always a remnant, whether it is the 7,000 during the days of Elijah who never bowed their knee to Baal, Daniel and his companions that would rather face the ovens and the lions than pay homage to a false god and their altars, the Noahs that are ever preparing the arks of safety, and the Davids that will face giants, take on kingdoms, and finish as overcomers.

I must be honest as to what is so, but I must do it in light of my own spiritual walk. The issue will always come down to whether I am part of the remnant that refuses to be part of the flow of this present world.

I must be the one pressing forward to ever do the will of the Father for His glory and the sake of His Son. This is the one way I can ensure that I will be part of the great cloud of witnesses.

These stout witnesses were willing to suffer the loss of this present world in order to obtain a better resurrection when it came to the future glories of the next world. As a result, they knew their God, and they could not be moved from their hope. In the end, they were overcomers and left a witness behind.

Prayer: Lord You are always trying to bring us higher, but we need to adhere to the call of separation from that which is base, idolatrous, profane, and worldly. Lord, I want to adhere to Your higher calling in order to experience the excellency of Your ways and inherit Your promises. Amen.

April 22

"And whosoever shall compel thee to go a mile, go with him twain" *(Matthew 5:41)*. How many times have you heard that we need to go the "extra mile" in something? The problem is that many consider that doing what is needful as constituting the extra mile. They think "reasonable service" is sacrifice, and doing right is excellence, but in reality, in each case it is the least a person can do to ensure the integrity of their testimony and service before God. There is nothing sacrificial, extraordinary, or excellent about doing what is needful and necessary.

When this example of going the extra mile was given, it was in relationship to the Roman law. If a soldier came upon a person while carrying their backpacks, the soldier could legally demand that the person carry it a mile for them. Can you imagine not being prepared, strong enough, or big enough to carry such a load even a mile, but because of the law you were required to do so?

As I thought about the extra mile, I realized that Jesus indeed went the extra mile for us. In fact, He came down from the glories of heaven, was lifted up on a cross for us and ended up going into the very depths of the earth. He did it to satisfy the Law which required us to come under its burden and carry it even though it was too great of a burden to bear.

This holy Law condemned us because we continually broke it, and it mocked us because we were weak and inept before it. The reality is that we could not even go a mile when it came to the Law and our sin. Jesus not only went the distance for us, but He went the extra mile. To me that extra mile is probably the greatest example of how grace works. It not only reaches the mark, but it abounds beyond it.

Prayer: Lord thank You for not only going the extra mile of redemption, but You went beyond because of grace. Amen.

April 23

He (John the Baptist) answered and saith unto them, He that hath two coats, let him impart to him that hath none; and he that hath meat, let him do likewise" (Luke 3:11). (Parenthesis added.) This was made in regard to repentance. The fruit of true repentance is benevolence that can't ignore being part of the solution if one has the means to do so. It can't be content with simply wishing someone the best when they possess the means to provide the solution.

Yesterday I talked about the concept of going the extra mile. With this example in mind, what would constitute going the extra mile for the believer?

If you are not prepared, the first mile would leave you breathless. If you were not strong enough, it would leave you weak, and if you were not big enough the load would become too great to bear, and yet when you struggled to finish the mile, your Christian duty was to carry it another mile and to do it cheerfully and not complaining or whining about it.

Let's face it, any act of sacrificial benevolence or carrying a load the first mile could easily enough produce the foulest temperament possible, the biggest whiney baby around and the most pathetic victim. We humans are basically lazy and don't want to be inconvenienced about anything outside of our routine and our comfort zones.

As I consider the extra mile, I realize that the mile is the least I can do, but to go beyond it is where the real sacrifices occur, exceptional service is rendered, and God is glorified. The extra mile is that sweet savor that reaches the throne of God and brings such pleasure to Him. It is a lot like the widow with her mites. She gave out of her lack and Jesus acknowledged it as being the greatest offering.

The mile represents our responsibilities, but the extra mile is a matter of grace for that is what comes out of one's lack, weakness, and ineptness. It is grace that emits the type of sweetness that only God can take pleasure in.

Prayer: Lord, I know past my doings, activities, and strength, I have nothing of value to offer except that which is a matter of Your grace. Help me to get past the drudgery of self, the mile-long lists of excuses, and endless whining of my rights, and compel me to go the extra mile with the right attitude. Lord, I realize even when I do go the extra mile for Your kingdom, it is still the least I could do in light of Your great sacrifice. Amen.

April 24

"And why take ye thought for raiment? Consider the lilies of the field, how they grow; they toil not, neither do they spin" (Matthew 6:28). My desire is to glean from the many examples of the creation around me. There are rivers that freely flow through the terrain. I must admit the rivers have brought such awe and

excitement to my spirit as I have observed how they reflect the landscape around them.

The Lord used sparrows and lilies of the field to bring home spiritual truths. For me the ospreys and eagles add such simple but majestic beauty to my life. The beauty around me at times has cut through the times of storms and darkness to bring inspiration to my soul.

God gives us all of creation to glean the inspirational nuggets of His truth. It speaks of unchangeable factors that usher in the environment to ensure the different cycles of life. It graces the cycles of life with loveliness that inspires and highlights the simple and practical. Some of its changes are subtle while others are blatant.

One of the lessons the terrain around me continues to reaffirm, is that the visible changes are only brought about by the unseen hand of Providence. So much that impacts change is hidden from sight, but it either reaches down into the deep canyons of testing or it reaches upwards to the heights of revelation, but it remains unseen until it breaks forth in the dawning of a new day of hope.

This dawning only occurs because the best of the day is first prepared in the obscurity of darkness. In the end, its fruit will speak of the depths it plummets to, as well as the heights it has reached in light of the glory of heaven. It is for this reason God's inspiration will never leave you in the states of stagnation, being in limbo, or remaining the same. It will change the terrain of your very soul.

Prayer: Lord, as Your children we always have the hope of the dawning of a new day. One day all darkness will flee when Your light breaks through the darkness of the present age to reveal the end to all deception, rebellion, and hopelessness. So be it.

April 25

"While he yet talked to the people, behold, his mother and his brethren stood without desiring to speak with him" (Matthew 12:46). Today is my brother, David's birthday. We mark the lives of those who are important to us so we can acknowledge their significance with a card or a present. We want to let them know we remember the history we had with them of yesteryears, and that much of the present is what it is because they have had some type of impact on our lives.

As we get older such relationships can become dearer to us because we know that in the busyness of our lives, we can take them for granted. We live in light of the assumption that these people will be around in the future, but the truth is we do not know how long they will walk among us.

Jesus had siblings who did not buy into His importance. They even sought an audience with Him thinking that they would be escorted through the crowd to Him, but instead, Jesus told the crowd whoever does the will of His Father comprises His family.

As I thought about how we go out of our way to let others know we care and love them, I wonder how many of us take such time with God. How much do we supposedly go out of our way to commune and worship God? How many of us obey Him?

It is easy to take our relationship for granted with the Lord but the main fruit that identifies us to Him is our love for Him and for others. You can't fake love, and it is that compelling draw it has that brings us ever closer to the Lord as we continually draw near to Him because we can't live without Him.

Prayer: Lord we can't live without You, but we don't always know what to do with You. We love all the possibilities surrounding You, but we often find only notions of sentiment where You are concerned, and not love. Forgive me for my shortsightedness when it comes to You. Amen.

April 26

"My words shall be of the uprightness of my heart: and my lips shall utter knowledge clearly (Job 33:3). It is my heart to write those things that reveal God's inspiration, His truth that challenges, His words that bring edification to others, and His ways that show forth His incredible wisdom.

This is so when it comes to my journals. I have written many journals in the past to record my spiritual journey. I have given them names. My first journal was "Bits And Pieces." Life is made up of bits of memories and pieces of lessons and experiences. In a way it is a mosaic that only God can bring together to form a beautiful picture of His work of redemption and grace in the lives of His people.

My latest journal is titled, "Audacity of Hope." Because of Jesus, we believers have the audacity to hope even in the midst of great darkness. We have such boldness to believe that no matter how hopeless this world is, we possess the essence of all hope. Regardless of the doomsday predictions, like the children of Israel at the Red Sea, we are in the light, waiting for the sea to part.

I say all of this because it often appears that our hope in the unseen hand of God is foolish to the world, a bit radical to that which is nominal, and a bit lame to those who see themselves rational, but I know it is the only place where real wisdom can be seen through the eyes of blessed faith. It is in the bosom of such faith that lasting hope serves as an anchor to hold me to what is sure and eternal in spite of the raging storms that are around me.

I am thankful that I have hope in what appears to be ludicrous to the world, but the hope that I possess is bold and steadfast every day. It inspires my soul and feeds my spirit in the barren, dry, spiritual wilderness of this present world.

This hope causes me to focus on future promises. The fulfillment of these promises will cause my wandering soul to finally land in Beulah Land where I will come to rest on the blessed assurance I have in my precious Lord and Savior, Jesus Christ.

Prayer: Lord, most words on paper or coming from lips, will prove to be idle if they do not bring people back to You. Lord, *Job 33:3* was Job's prayer and it is mine as well. Let all of my words be upright and may I utter the knowledge of Your truths in such a way that it will set captives free. Amen.

April 27

"And I will put enmity between thee and the woman, and between thy seed and her seed; it shall bruise thy head, and thou shalt bruise his heel" (Genesis 3:15). Amazingly, our first introduction to our Redeemer, Messiah is in the Garden of Eden.

Eden was also known as "Paradise." God had placed man in the midst of perfection, but our first parents disobeyed Him and ate of the fruit of the tree of knowledge of good and evil. Paradise ceased to be "good" as man fell into the state of darkness, death, and separation from God. In the midst of it, the Promised Seed of woman, the Messiah is lifted up as the only way for man to find his way back to light, hope, and life.

We would see this same scenario in the Garden of Gethsemane as Jesus was crushed by the great cost of sin that lay before Him. He willingly traveled by way of Calvary to be hung on a cross so He could die for our sin, and it was by way of the empty tomb that He proved victorious over sin and death.

Today man still looks for "Paradise" in spite of the depravity, sorrow, and consequences of sin. The tragedy is he looks outside of God and His redemption, and as a result is always running into the temptation of the serpent. He continues to taste the bitterness of the curse where toil produces vanity, tears bring a stain, and sorrow causes silent cries. Man fails to realize that he can only find redemption and hope in the midst of this cursed world at the foot of Jesus' cross.

Where are you looking to find paradise? Are you looking in this present world, in relationships, in things, or in pursuits to establish your own paradise? Keep in mind, outside of God, paradise will always elude you. Paradise can't be found in this material world, but only in relationships. And, if you do not have a relationship with God, your other relationships will leave you empty, frustrated, and disillusioned.

Prayer: Lord, we think we are so clever in our pursuits, right in our thinking, and self-sufficient in our worldly accomplishments, but if You are missing from the equation, we will find ourselves being fools in the end. Lord, I have been foolish in so many ways, but I know You are the only way to obtain wisdom and I humble myself before You as I seek to do it Your way in order to find real life. Amen.

April 28

He conned and lied to me again. You'd think I wouldn't so easily cave in to his demands, but how could I resist when his shining eyes were so full of joyful expectation? His voice was soft and low, as his body language expressed the strong emotions of his heart. How could I say "No", especially when all four paws were perfectly choreographed with his furiously wagging tail!?

I tried to explain to him that even though it was Friday, and he would get his "chickie chew" treat as usual when Rayola began recording her weekly sermon in our fellowship time, he still

143

insisted it had to be NOW. The clincher was when he sat down, and did his professional right paw beggar act. He always knows just how to get me to comply.

So, that evening I got into trouble because after all was settled and Rayola began her message, little liar RayRay sat up on Carrie's lap, looked me square in the face with those bright eyes, and began his low voice "talking." Not yipping, yapping, barking, whining or howling, mind you, but talking about not getting a "chickie chew" treat! His false accusations had to be quickly hushed, so I hurriedly found him another type of treat. Was he thankful? Not one bit, but after shooting a look of disgust at me, he ate it anyway and finally kept quiet through the sermon.

We can laugh at this scenario, especially if you've ever experienced being "owned" by a dog, but it can also serve as a lesson too. The question is, can you remember a time when you used a similar approach to God when you really wanted something? And, if you got it, then what happened? I know for me it wasn't always God's perfect will. It's far better to deny the urgency of the flesh, and consider a wiser approach. Jesus said, *"If ye abide in me, and my words abide in you, ye shall ask what ye will, and it shall be done unto you" (John 15:7).* – J. Haley

Prayer: Lord, I know You can't be moved by such antics as we are when it comes our children or pets, but Lord You do hear us and at times give us what we desire. However, we easily enough forget to thank You and remember all good things come from above because of grace and goodness. Thank You. Amen.

April 29

I Jesus have sent mine angel to testify unto you these things in the churches. I am the root and the offspring of David and the bright and morning star" (Revelation 22:16). We are living in trying times. The spiritual darkness is so stifling that it lays heavy on many hearts. The evil is so thick that it can be cut with a knife and the wickedness so great that it can take your very breath away. It is clear that with the physical eyes we can see nothing that would inspire hope in this present age, but when it comes to the eyes of faith, there is hope, but it is not of this world.

What lies on the horizon for every believer? When we go to bed, we know by faith that a new day is ready to make an appearance within hours. When the darkness of a storm is upon us, we have confidence that the sun will break through. When the fog lays heavy on the landscape, we know that eventually it must give way to the rays of the sun. When the great night of the soul is upon the saint, we are assured that the glorious light of the Morning Star (Jesus) will break through the darkness to bring hope into the dry, lean places left by the lack of light and nourishment.

Today we do live in the midst of grave darkness. Evil, dark hearts abound, but one day Jesus, His light, His glory will part the sky and He will not only break the power of the darkness of evil, but He will set matters right. He will judge the darkness and it will flee before Him, for the wicked with their deeds will not be able to hide from His wrath, while the saint will bathe in His glorious light.

Prayer: Lord, You do not rejoice in the death of the wicked, or in executing the just judgment upon that which is evil. Nor do You want to see the sinner die in their sins knowing judgment awaits them. You have made provision for all to escape Your judgment and wrath, but they will not respond. Lord, it is my heart to see all saved, but the darkness is great; therefore, in my heart my cry is, "Even so come Lord Jesus. Amen!"

April 30

"And it was so, that when he had turned his back to go from Samuel, God gave him another heart: and all those signs came to pass that day" (1 Samuel 10:9). This chapter was all about the heart. People may have a calling, but lack the heart to fulfill it. God was giving the Jewish people a king, but it would prove to be a form of judgment for the nation, an ongoing bitter cup for them to drink from.

God clearly gave them the man who would look the part of a king, but lacked the heart to be one. As a result, God gave this man, Saul, another heart, not a new heart, but a heart to be king for he was hiding from his calling and the people.

How many people are like Saul, hiding from their true calling because they lack heart to do it? They are divided in their heart towards God as they grasp at the world, proving to be half-hearted in their fickle loyalties. They may feel convicted but ignore it, justify or excuse it away, rather than give in to the sweet conviction of the Spirit.

The other part is that God also touched the hearts of others to follow Saul as king because, for the most part, the people were not ready for a king (*1 Samuel 10:26*). After Saul was crowned king, and the rejoicing was done, the people went back to their tents not realizing everything was about to change for them.

If you are truly born again, God gives you a heart to follow Him, but after conversion, it is a natural tendency to go back to our old life as if nothing of significance really happened to us. It is for this reason Christianity can be bittersweet. It is always sweet up front, but then comes the calling to come apart which results in the battle between the Spirit and the flesh.

There are the promptings of the Spirit to follow Jesus, but we must first deny ourselves which is contrary to the world's philosophy. We must apply a cross which seems radical in a world that mocks such sacrifice, and then by faith we follow Jesus into a new way of life that is foreign to us and will test every aspect of our character and faith.

Prayer: Lord, You did not call us to a life that would be easy, fun, glamourous, or wonderful; rather, You called us into a life that will undo our best, test our limits, and call for our demise to the old. Give me the heart that will endure, the Spirit that will empower, and the love that will compel me until I finish the course You set before me. Amen.

MAY

May 1

"And Joseph dreamed a dream, and he told it his brethren: and they hated him yet the more" (Genesis 37:5). God is always setting up circumstances to bring about a matter. He may give us insight into the future, but it may take years of wandering in some barren wilderness before God sets up certain events to bring about the promise that was revealed in a vision of the past and make it a reality of the present.

The problem with most of us is that if we receive some vision or promise from God in light of the future, we think it is going to happened the next day, perhaps a week later, and maybe a month later, but to wait for years for it to come to fruition is unthinkable, unacceptable, and just plain ridiculous in our way of thinking. After all, where will be the strength, the zeal, and the clarity of it to carry it out if we have to wait for years to see it come forth?

We fail to realize at such a tender time that we must be prepared for that vision or promise before it can be brought forth in our lives. What takes time is always the preparation for the event. It is hard to accept that we must be brought to a place of humility before we can handle the vision in the right way.

Until we cease to be a novice who stands high on the pinnacle of pride, we remain unusable. This was true for Joseph. What he saw about his brothers in the dreams was true, but his lack of wisdom due to his youth made him seem like a braggart rather than one sharing what the Lord had shown him.

It took an extreme process, but through it all Joseph became a mature leader that, even as a relatively young man, displayed great wisdom to the point that he was unrecognizable to his brothers. We must keep in mind that God equips those He calls before He sends them forth.

Prayer: Lord our youth assumes things will happen yesterday because of impatience and our immaturity presumes it is going to happen today because of foolishness but wisdom teaches us it will happen when we have been prepared and according to Your perfect timing. Praise Your holy name for being perfect in all of Your ways. Amen.

May 2

"And he said, Peace be to you, fear not: your God, and the God of your father, hath given you treasure in your sacks..." (Genesis 43:23). One of the people who influenced my life was my stepfather, Lester Kelley. His life reminds me a bit of Joseph when it came to his challenges. He was the man who raised me from the age of 10. He left home when he was fourteen to discover his lot in life. As a man who was in the Merchant Marines, he was an adventurer on the high seas; as a mountain man in the backcountry, he was explorer; and as a man with limited education, he spoke before congress about life-changing issues.

Lester Kelley inspired me to dream again and caused my imagination to take flight after it had been doused by the darkness of infidelity, divorce, dishonorable conduct, uncertainty, fear, disillusionment, and loneliness. It was clear that at age nine, innocence was no longer, and the hard cold reality of selfish human nature had taken center stage in various ways.

My new father was very human, but he taught me that defeat is a stepping stone and one must never give up on what they believe is true and right. To surrender in such a way would be giving up on yourself before you discover your own strength of character and potential. He also helped me understand my relationship with my Heavenly Father.

You may be a biological child, but if the emotional attachment and commitment are missing this vital relationship will be missing as well. And when it comes between the parent and child relationship, and the type of interaction that takes place is what forms many of our attitudes about life.

It is my relationship with my Heavenly Father that gives me the greatest type of inspiration as I move through a world that is full of darkness. He gives me the means to see beyond this present life to regard all matters from His heavenly perspective. Regardless of the darkness of this world, the light of hope outshines it and inspires me to reach beyond the stars to grasp the unseen and the eternal.

Prayer: Lord it is obvious You have directed my life in order to save me and bring me to this place in You. Thank You for being faithful to set the stage in my life so that I could discover You. Amen.

May 3

"And there was there with us a young man, an Hebrew servant to the captain of the guard; and we told him, and he interpreted to us our dreams; to each man according to his dream he did interpret" (Genesis 41:12). We often receive such promises in our youth or at the peak of our zeal, but we are too immature to properly handle them. As novices, our pride can set us up for a fall, our flesh can set us up to take endless detours away from it being fulfilled, and our emotional zeal for it can quickly wane with the affronts of life itself. It is only the sheer commitment to trust God in it all, that one can endure until the vision and promise are fulfilled.

For Joseph he was 30 years old before he began to see the fulfillment of what God had shown him in his tender youth. He had been sold as a slave and put in prison before all the circumstances came together for God to establish him in his calling. During that time his pride was brought low in betrayal and slavery, his resolve shaken in temptation, and his commitment towards God challenged in prison. When Joseph was brought forth, he was no longer a brash upstart, he was a man seasoned in the ovens of affliction and would be exalted as a great leader.

When Joseph was ready, God brought him forth in an incredible way. The Creator of the universe actually inserted himself into the dreams of the leader, Pharaoh to bring about the vision of a young Jewish boy, who had been forsaken by many, but not forgotten by the Lord.

Prayer: Lord, I don't want to be tossed on the ocean of life by fickle emotions and I do not want circumstances to define who I become. Lord, my life is hid in You. You are my Rock and I know You control the waves and tides that come my way. Place me where I am prepared for Your calling on my life to be brought forth for Your glory. Amen.

May 4

"Rejoicing in hope; patient in tribulation; continuing instant in prayer" (Romans 12:12). As considering prayer, one of Andrew Murray's statements caused me to meditate on how much prayer gives access to God to plumb the depths of my person. He said,

"Prayer in secret will be followed by the secret working of God in my heart."

The Christian life is based on the deep working of God in our very souls. It is easy to get caught up with religious activities, but the truth is the perfecting of the Christian life is born out of travail that begins with humiliation that finds one wrestling before the Lord, while choosing to walk through the prevailing darkness that is upon the soul and clinging to the unseen hand of promises.

It is only in such travailing of prayer that the wind of hope is allowed to lift up the weary sojourner to experience the glorious light of expectation. At such times the spirit is quickened and the soul stirred up to realize such travailing is worth it. After all, it will lead into the secret place of blessed communion where one will be able to look into the wondrous face of our Precious Lord and Savior, Jesus Christ.

Prayer: Lord, I have travailed in prayer, rejoiced in it, soared because of it, and used it as a torch of hope to help me through the dark times of the soul. In it all I knew that You were the platform that held me up, the wind that caused me to rise up, and the light that guided my steps. Thank You for being the One who hears, as well as catches my prayers and meets me in my plight. Amen.

May 5

Earthquake! After experiencing a severe one on April 29, 1965 in the Seattle area, I decided it might be a good idea to be prepared, just in case so I packed a little bag with my idea of "survival" items and stashed it away with the hope that if "the big one" ever hit that I'd be able to grab my "survival bag."

Years later, and long before I moved to Idaho, I found my so-called "survival" stuff when cleaning things out. Thoughts and emotions collided as I removed my assortment of "important" items from the bag causing me to question myself on several fronts. First, was it pride or sheer ignorance that I didn't know squat about disasters or how to properly prepare for one; and secondly, why didn't I take the time to go to a library (no Internet back then you know) and find out just what to do beyond saving a few band-aids? But, here's the clincher—I call it vanity for, believe it or not, I had packed cosmetics!

Not a lot, of course, but just enough to "fix" myself up so when the young, handsome search and rescue man peeked down through all the rubble I would surely be under, my hair would be combed and I would at least be wearing lipstick. Humbled by my lack of genius, I never put together an earthquake survival kit again, although somewhere around here I do have a "bug-out bag" even though now I'm so old I can hardly huff and puff my way down the street and back in a ten-minute outdoor excursion while only carrying a tissue.

Seriously, however, preparedness is one of the things we hear a lot about in these uncertain days, but the most important preparedness is spiritual preparedness. Is your church preparing you for overcoming life today, and how to stand in the days to come?

Jesus warned, *"And take heed to yourselves, lest at any time your hearts be overcharged with surfeiting, [overindulgence] and drunkenness, and cares of this life, and so that day come upon you unawares. For as a snare shall it come on all them that dwell on the face of the whole earth. Watch ye therefore, and pray always, that ye may be accounted worthy to escape all these things that shall come to pass, and to stand before the Son of man" (Luke 21:34-36).* – J. Haley

Prayer: Lord, You told us everything that can be shaken will be and I have certainly been in places where I felt it. However, You were with me in each shaking and are ever preparing me for future ones. I am so glad You are my Rock and Your Spirit is ever preparing me to stand, withstand, and continue to stand on You each time my life is shaken by challenging events. Amen.

May 6

"Now therefore ye are no more strangers and foreigners, but fellowcitizens with the saints, and of the household of God" *(Ephesians 2:19).* I have, for the most part, avoided the world of technology for years. It was Jeannette who treaded into the confusing world of the internet while I happily remained in my small, limited operation of computers. It was later that we both jumped feet first into Facebook.

It was on Facebook where I began to gain a greater reality that the household of God is international, and that the family of God is not only around and about, but abounds. The connection is the Holy Spirit, the hope is Christ and Him crucified, and the beauty is connecting with people who have the same spirit and heart.

There are five people who come to mind, and they reside in such states as Florida, Tennessee, Ohio, and Texas. They have experienced great losses, know the depths of suffering, encountered overwhelming challenges, and faced some incredible unseen forces.

There is Anna Schwery. She has gone home to be with the Lord but she challenged and encouraged us in our walk, and even helped me with editing one of my books. Another is Charlotte Haas who has encouraged us in various ways, from using our books as resources to going out of her way to share valuable information with us. There is Sonja Penniman who, as a faithful, committed friend, has been supportive in so many ways, but her greatest ministry to us has been on our behalf as she has faithfully prayed for us. There is also another prayer warrior, Cindy Dooley. She has a beautiful heart towards God, a sweet spirit, and a gracious way. To me she often speaks the loudest in quiet ways by the examples she sets, the stands she takes, and the burdens she is willing to come under in prayer. And, there is Lynette Hughes, who has a passion for truth, is a warrior against heresy, and a teacher who knows how to effectively wield the sword of truth.

I have never personally met these ladies, but I know we are part of that great household of the Lord, and it will be in glory, where we will not only meet, but we will have no problem recognizing one another.

Prayer: Lord, thank You for getting me out of my small world so that I can be challenged and encouraged by others who are part of the universal Body, serving in Your national household, and ministering to Your family. Amen.

May 7

"But as for you, ye thought evil against me; but God meant it unto good to bring to pass, as it is this day, to save much people alive" *(Genesis 50:20)*. Famine had come to ravage the landscape and Joseph knew the score about the events that were now plaguing the land. He had the hindsight to know God used the wicked, jealous ways of his brothers to send him to the land of Egypt. Granted, Joseph was taken as a slave, wrongly accused, and imprisoned, but God's hand was in all of it. God would prepare Joseph to lead a foreign nation and then He would place him in the place of authority to save his family from future famine and death.

When we go through challenges that seem so unfair, it is not unusual to ask why, to question the fairness of it, and to speculate the reasons for it, but as believers, we must trust that what is upon us and before us has been designed by God for a reason. We need to stand still when we are in the darkness of despair, knowing nothing will make sense and that we are not meant to see where it is leading us because our faith is being tested in the fiery ovens. At such times we may feel the heat but we will not see the light.

We must encourage ourselves in the Lord as we trust Him to work out the details. At such times what will encourage us greatly is to remember the Father sent the Son into the wilderness of this world to go before us in preparation of securing His ownership of us through redemption. He now preserves us because He has not only been placed over us as our owner, but our Intercessor and High Priest.

Jesus was clear that just as His Father sent Him, He sends us out into the barren wilderness of this world. His Spirit will lead the way, but we must follow to become a Joseph to others, to prepare the way of life for those seeking it, to nurture His lambs with His Word, and to watch over souls until the great Shepherd calls us to follow Him elsewhere as His Spirit is ever preparing us to take our place among the great cloud of witnesses.

Prayer: Lord, You are always calling us. We need to learn to hear Your voice and follow You, while trusting Your leading, ever being pulled with strings of love, nudged along by the gentleness of grace, and looking forward with the eyes of faith, as we spread out the wings of hope to take flight in trust and obedience. Amen.

May 8

"And because iniquity shall abound, the love of many shall wax cold" (Matthew 24:12.) The Bible talks about men's hearts growing faint and cold. It is hard to believe that a heart that once was warm towards God could become cold, but fear will always

chill any hope, and darkness will make that which was warm turn cold and become iced over with indifference.

It is obvious we live in great darkness. It's hard to look into the darkness of the world without being tempted to live in the memories of the past when days seem more innocent, or skip the present altogether and cling to the dreams, hopes, and promises of the future.

Regardless of what tense we try to live in to cope with the present, we know the darkness of this age exists and that ignorance may be bliss upfront when it comes to trying to ignore it, while holding on in the midst of evilness. Obviously, we don't have a time machine where we can miss what we don't like and insert ourselves back into history when it finally agrees with our way of thinking. Even if we look ahead towards matters, we will still fall into despair about the present. We can look behind, knowing that there is no reason to linger in the past because there is no means to capture or change what has been.

As we face the present, it is clear that the light of justice has almost been put out by the insane reality of the lawless environment that is present. Everywhere we look, the coldness of the present darkness is like vice grips that are squeezing many as they find themselves drowning in utter despair.

I am so glad my hope is in God alone. It is obvious death abounds in this dark culture of death and destruction, despair is heavy, and the coldness of hearts are manifesting themselves in wickedness, but we as believers have hope in Christ, and we have a sure future in Him.

Praise the Lord for the warmth of His love, the light of His truth, and the bright way of His glory. In such darkness, it is vital to consider only one day at a time. We are not meant to live in any other tense but the present. The present may seem overwhelming, but it is the only time we have to work with truth, work within faith, and come to terms with the life God has given to us in order to be an overcomer and set free from the present darkness.

Prayer: Lord, You alone help us to accomplish what we can in the present, as well as give us the means to learn from the past in order to become wise enough to make sound decisions as we face an uncertain future here in light of Your promises. Amen.

May 9

"He that is faithful in that which is least is faithful also in much: and he that is unjust in the least is unjust also in much" (Luke 16:10). There are always small details that keep us busy through the day. We want to conquer big things to feel as if we accomplished something, but the truth is there are always those details that must be dealt with to accomplish bigger things. Details are the steps necessary to climb mountains of accomplishments, to forge deep rivers of growth, descend into canyons of enlargements, and walk through valleys of despair and refinement.

I have always waded through the details and tried to jump the chasm of big accomplishments in order to walk in light of vision and purpose. I know without the details, accomplishments will prove to be illusive and failure imminent.

The problem with many people is that they live in a type of "Hollywood mentality" that comprises nothing but a fantasy that denies reality, while ignoring the details of the matters around them. Unabated fantasy turns into torment and madness, while fantasy that is given a platform often turns into a nightmare.

Life can only be discovered in the now. The past may influence it by its lessons, but it must never define our attitude towards the present. The present does not operate according to the future and the future will always fail to address the present in realistic terms. We often miss the nuggets of the present when we strive to adjust the future to any fantasy we may have about life. Those who miss the nuggets often end up living in regrets that they missed the small blessings of life, as well as disillusioned because they could not direct their life in the way they wanted to.

In heaven the future has already been secured for saints and the only way we can be assured of this future is to be hid in Christ. In these days it is even more important to keep your focus on Jesus, be faithful with the small details attached to your faith walk, and walk the straight narrow paths of righteousness, knowing that the Lord will go before you. He is the One who will straighten out the crooked paths and flatten out the elevated places.

Prayer: Lord, I need to be faithful with what is in front of me, while trusting that Your redemption took care of my past and Your promises assure me that You will work out all the future details of my life. Amen.

May 10

"If the world hate you, ye know that it hated me before it hated you" (John 15:18). How much do you look to the world for your needs, ways, and purpose? Let's face it, we want to get along with the world so we can get on with our life without any challenges and interferences. We do not want to think about being an offense to the world that ends in a hate relationship, especially since we are dependent on it in many ways.

When I first started my faith walk, I had no idea how much I was depending on the world for the essence of my life. I didn't realize that the world has no life to give. It had managed to entangled me in many of its lies and false promises. All it could offer me was some type of lifestyle that left me empty, dissatisfied, and ever seeking for some type of substance that would bring real meaning to my life.

We must face the harsh reality that we live in a world that is an enemy of God and designed for destruction by His wrath. It is dying and all creation moans underneath the great weight of sin. The god of this world, Satan, uses every device to spoil what is true, pure, and righteous. His great goal among his minions, slaves, and useless peons is to establish his kingdom where he serves as god, while in a sense taunting the God of the Universe as to the miserable failures His people prove to be in their weak, insipid humanity.

Prayer: Lord, we do in a sense choose our enemies by the lines we draw in light of righteousness and what we come into agreement with. Lord, I do not want to face You as an enemy but as my Savior, Lord and God. Amen.

May 11

It was with a calm feeling of satisfaction that I put the small mesh bag of six avocados into the grocery cart. They all felt and looked good, and the price was fairly decent as well. But, a couple of days later as I cut one of them in half to serve with lunch, disappointment and disgust momentarily arose for the inside of it was completely rotten.

I tossed the brown, mushy mess into the garbage can, and took out another. Any hope I had that it was a good one instantly dissipated as the horrible rotten interior displayed itself. One by one the remaining four avocados likewise made a quick exit into the trash. They were all rotten to the core—every-single-one-of-them.

Needless to say, these phony avocados reminded me of some folks I've met through the years—people who appeared to be "very good" on the outside—you know the type—they look "normal," they can even act decent and upright, "talk the talk," and seem to "fit in" with the Christian crowd. Sooner or later, however, their real character (fruit) is exposed, and easily seen just as the rotten figs were in *Jeremiah 24:2-10*.

Oh! Let the Lord's people pray in these evil days, *"Search me, O God, and know my heart: try me, and know my thoughts: And see if there be any wicked way in me, and lead me in the way everlasting" (Psalm 139:23), 24.* AMEN! – J. Haley

Prayer: Lord, David's heart-felt prayer in Psalm should be the cry of every heart of those who love and want to obey You in Spirit and Truth. Thank You for being faithful to bring forth the light. Amen.

May 12

"For ye are yet carnal: for whereas there is among you envying, and strife, and divisions, are ye not carnal, and walk as men? (1 Corinthians 3:3). Do you know people who love to stir the pot? They may be few in number, but they know how to bring forth the right ingredients to end up pulling everyone into their wretched pot of witchcraft. In fact, they will defile and pull everything good, right, and honorable down around them because the reason they stir it is because of jealousy and they possess a contrary spirit.

There is a craft in stirring the pot. You have to have the right ingredients and know when to add them to the mix at the right time in order to bring it to a boil. The ingredients are found in abundance. They are lies, innuendoes, accusations, and undertones of slander.

The inspiration behind this pot stirring is demonic because it is divisive and will result in sowing seeds of discord, something that God hates. It entails ensnaring silly people who lack wisdom, but they prove quite useful because they have loose tongues to pass on the lie. There are those who can be easily stirred up by any inconvenience to add their sour flavor of opinions to the mix. Others who have that board in the eye will be stirred up to see those things that seem hypocritical to them, and since it does not line up to the interpretation of a matter, they will advance the environment in the pot with judgment.

The truth is, this is the way of the flesh that Satan uses to bring division. However, God hates such tactics. It is an affront to His ways that will ensure wisdom, love, and peace. However, to ensure this type of fruit, we must love God's way of peace, do God's way according to the meekness of His love, and uphold the integrity of God's way with the wisdom of His truth.

Prayer: Lord, I have been a troublemaker in the past and managed to step in the hornet nest by opening my mouth. I have caused problems and upset at times because of my foolishness. Thank you for saving me from myself and bringing me into a place of peace so I no longer seek it elsewhere. Amen.

May 13

"That we henceforth be no more children, tossed to and fro, and carried about with every wind of doctrine, by the sleight of men, and cunning craftiness, whereby they lie in wait to deceive" *(Ephesians 4:14)*. What many people rely on for their reality are emotions.

I have watched some people emotionally fling themselves in the waters of the world to partake of something that they perceived would make them feel a certain way, but feelings are like the waves of the ocean. Sometimes they hit great heights of "ecstasy" only to crash on the shoreline of reality with a roar; while at other times they are erratic, rolling from one side to the other; or, sometimes all they amount to are small ripples moving with the currents. The reality of all waves is that eventually they are going to wash up on some shoreline, impeding their momentum and perhaps causing them to cease altogether.

Many people don't realize that much of the propaganda and ways of the world and, in some cases religion, are like a big subtle hook that is ready to grab the emotions in order to take people on some sentimental ride. Whether it is heartwarming, scary, sensational, soulish, religious, or gross, it stirs people up, reminding them that life is still present.

However, emotions cannot be trusted. Emotions may cause the momentum but they aren't the force behind the waves. They may cause heights of ecstasy but they can only come down to the depths of despair, and to operate in the nominal proves unbearable. There must always be some life, purpose or stirring to keep the emotions going.

The key is to find God is not in the heights where He is experienced or in the depths where He is sought, but in the nominal where His life can be experienced and walked out by faith. It is on the level ground of God's truth that stability reigns.

Prayer: Lord, we would all like that rush, but we are not built to live in the high or low places but on the plateaus where rest can be sought, in the valleys where victory can be obtained, and in the quiet places of the wilderness where fellowship with You can be experienced. Amen.

May 14

"A double minded man is unstable in all his ways" (James 1:8).
Yesterday, I mentioned how some people are driven by their emotions. Notice the word "driven." The Holy Spirit leads, but the emotions often drive a person to pursue something, only to wane and cause them to be driven another way or come to some confusing stop where they have no idea where they are or where they are going.

There is no stability in the fickleness of feelings and it makes people become doubleminded as their emotions go with whatever is affecting them at the time. However, there are many that define their reality according to their fickle emotions and they often find themselves being taken away with the changing of the winds and the waves.

When it comes to the religious world, emotions are often attached to experiences and fleshly worship. Fleshly worship lacks the right spirit, but it can become like a preferred drug that must be sought out and obtained every week to give that sensational edge of religious zeal to one's emotions that will hold them over until the next wave of emotional hype comes along.

There is nothing more dangerous than religious experiences. These experiences may be genuine, but if they are not anchored in the Rock and soberly weighed according to the full counsel of the Word of God, they become the measuring stick and authority as to how people see their religious life and even interpret God's Word. The subtilty of experiences is that people will often seek and believe them, instead of seeking the Lord Jesus Christ and believing His Word.

Prayer: Lord, I know all about the waning zeal of the flesh and the overwhelming power of experiences, but in the end, if they fail to lead back to You in greater love and devotion, they will prove idolatrous and vain. I desire to seek, know, and see You at the end of every journey, experience, and search. Keep me close, ever so close and anchored to the Rock. Amen.

May 15

"And he called unto him the twelve, and began to send them forth by two and two; and gave them power over unclean spirits" (Mark 6:7). This particular day marks some very important events that have clearly proven significant for my spiritual life. This same day in 1948 something of great importance took place in light of heaven and earth, Israel became a nation fulfilling prophecies and setting it on course to fulfill its destiny.

Five years before the event of Israel, another event took place that would greatly impact my life and set in motion an incredible spiritual odyssey. It certainly was not noted by the world, but it was within the annuals of heaven. That event was the birth of my friend and co-laborer, Jeannette Haley.

It is important to point out this happened almost twelve years before my entrance into the world. Who would have thought that two distinct lives such as a Seattle girl who was being trained to be a debutant, whose heart was in Montana, and a girl from a small sawmill town in Idaho would be brought together by circumstances in 1987. They would be forged by an unseen hand to form a ministry in 1989, and traveled many roads together, contended with many souls through the years, fought many battles back-to-back, and in 2024 both are still running the marathon together as their faces become more set towards heaven.

The Bible is clear that what God has put together, no one should separate. God put both of us together and there have been various attempts on the part of Satan and people to separate us, but by grace, God has held this team together in spite of the assaults and winds that have blown across the bow of our ship.

As I consider the events, trials, and challenges that we have encountered along the way, there are a few things I am certain of. 1) There is a God for only He could have situated the events that brought us together. 2) That God put us together before the foundation the world, He knew we would have the same heart, calling, and determination to serve Him. And, 3) being in God's will with the right co-laborer is a perfect place to be when tested, challenged, and overwhelmed. God will carry you through uncertain terrain while your co-laborer will take your hand and ride out the stormy waves with you until you come to that place of rest.

Prayer: Lord thank You that Your ways are righteous, Your work perfect, Your choices right, Your judgments correct, and Your will glorious. Amen.

May 16

"In God have I put my trust: I will not be afraid what man can do unto me" (Psalm 56:11). This psalm reminds me there is always one decision we as believers must choose to make and stand on, "is the only one who can be trusted is God." It is so simple to put my trust and confidence elsewhere.

I can put my trust in the false or illusive promises of this world, government, or man. I can put it in technology, education, or the wit of man. I can put it in military might and political savvy. However, history mocks such attempts as the sands of time mark the burial site of former civilizations which were great and had prided themselves in their glory and might, but are no more.

Personally, I have lived enough years to know that any point of reliance and confidence outside of God is going to end in utter disappointment and disillusionment. I have been immature or foolish enough to put my confidence in other things but God. I have also hit dead ends and immovable walls, as well as fallen into ditches of despair and pits of depression. To trust God is a choice, and to walk in such confidence serves as an antidote against fearing that which is temporary and powerless to destroy that which is heavenly.

Prayer: Lord, You are our point of trust and confidence. We praise You for all You have done for us. You are the One who keeps and preserves our very lives and souls. Amen.

May 17

Here's what happened, in one long sentence: How would you feel if your dear mother, who lived far away in her own home, (and for physical and financial reasons you were an only child and unable to personally care for her) passed away; and the "self-appointed" care-giver, who had taken advantage of her for two years until her death at 100, was given the responsibility to notify you in the case of death, deliberately defied those instructions, and even illegally and fraudulently signed the Death Certificate as the deceased's "only daughter," never notified you that your mother was gone, or told you what had happened to her?

When I turned 80 on May 15 of this year and there was no birthday card or call from my mother, nor had there been an acknowledgment of the Mother's Day packet I sent to her, I knew something was terribly wrong. Thank God, the LORD intervened for me by giving me the thought to go on Mom's FB page and ask if anyone knew where my mother was, and a day or so later, her wonderful neighbor left me a notice that she had passed away on April 23, almost a full month ago!

The LORD is good to give me great peace, and comfort at this time. But to one and all, may I say, please be very discerning and aware of the wiles of the devil who comes to "kill, steal and destroy" from vulnerable people, such as the elderly, because wicked predators will do anything to gain wealth from the unwary. *"For the love of money is the root of all evil: which while some coveted after, they have erred from the faith, and pierced themselves through with many sorrows" (1 Timothy 6:10.)* – J. Haley

Prayer: Lord, You warned us we would not be received by our own family. In fact, Your sword of truth will bring division between those of the world and those of our heavenly family. No matter what I still choose You because losing family is sorrowful to the heart, but losing You would be unbearable to the spirit and soul. Amen.

May 18

"Hell is naked before him, and destruction hath no covering" (Job 26:6). It is natural for wicked men to try to hide their wicked deeds, whether it be behind some covering of religious activities, necessary evils due to the circumstances, or what they consider a logical solution to a bad situation, their wicked deeds have been made justifiable in their minds; therefore, acceptable in their way of thinking. They will not be taken up with the casualties or destruction they leave behind them. After all, everything is expendable when it comes to them carrying out their evil plans.

The darkness is the lies that blind them to the insanity of their deeds and the wrath that abides on them. They prefer darkness because their deeds must be hidden in darkness so that their real plans are not discovered. No doubt they are saying to themselves, there is no God and if there is, He will surely not care what we are doing. It is true that man may not see their deeds, but these deluded individuals don't realize that God is light and there is no darkness to Him. He sees all from their attitudes and thoughts to their deeds and it has been recorded.

It's also clear that it doesn't matter how deep they go to hide from God, how far into the cave they tread to plan their deeds, or how thick the darkness is that they create with their delusion, God still sees it all. This is confirmed in Job where he states that hell is naked before the Lord and destruction has no covering.

Job was accused of hiding sin, but He knew nothing could be hidden from God. When you read the different replies to accusers as in the case of King David, it was obvious he had asked God's light to come on and reveal any wicked way in him. He also knew that God would be faithful to do so, but He hadn't revealed any real deviance in his character or ways.

Since the Garden of Eden, man has been hiding from God for different reasons. Perhaps he is hiding because of shame, or he doesn't want his sin to be exposed. He may be hiding so he can do that which is unbecoming and abominable to God without consequences, but God still sees it all.

Prayer: Lord, our selfishness wants to do what it wants to do, our human nature wants to get by without any repercussions, and our mind wants to be right about our conclusions no matter how wrong, but each path leads to death and destruction because Your thoughts and ways are higher than ours. Lord, turn on the light and reveal any wicked way in me so that I will stand justified before You and my accusers will stand silent in the end. Amen.

May 19

"And I will betroth thee unto me for ever" (Hosea 3:19a). Have you ever read Hosea? It is about a godly prophet who, on the Lord's instruction, married an unfaithful woman.

This union was to reveal to the people of Israel that when it came to their devotion to God, they were like an unfaithful wife. No one can describe the terrible sting of betrayal that a faithful spouse feels when they learn of the unfaithfulness of their mate. The betrayal is like an earthquake that shakes every fiber of trust, bringing great sorrow to the spirit, anguish to the soul, and despair to the mind.

The greatest sin that we commit against our body, which is to serve as the temple of God, is fornication. It represents the flesh being driven by the profane, the affections being corrupted by that which is perverted, and an unholy agreement with darkness. It speaks of the complete ruin of the soul as it robs it of any purity, kills any testimony, and destroys all hope.

The desire for God to be our loving husband is His heart's cry, but so many of us are married to this world, to lifeless idols, and to selfish ideas of happiness, which constitute a miserable existence that we settle for because it is all we know.

Granted, we may feel some guilt here and there, struggle with condemnation at times, but what we fail to do is REPENT by turning away from unholy unions, CONFESS it is foremost a terrible offence against God and a great wickedness leveled at those that will be greatly hurt by it. We must SEEK mercy and HOPE grace meets us in our brokenness.

Prayer: Lord, I know what is important to Your heart and sometimes I choose to forget it in light of pursuing after that which is foolish because of the desires of my flesh. It is sin. Forgive me for being a fool in such times. Amen.

May 20

"For their mother hath played the harlot: she that conceived them hath done shamefully: for she said, I will go after my lovers, that

give me my bread and my water, my wool and my flax, mine oil and my drink" (Hosea 2:5). It is important to note what Hosea was to say to his children about their mother's adultery. She pursued after the lovers who would give her all of her worldly desires.

Most people are blinded because they are selfish and stiff-necked and feel either deserving or justified in committing fornication with the unholy. They pursue these "lovers" according to their fleshly appetites and are not willing to let go of the world's false promises of satisfaction and happiness.

They are also fearful of how the light of truth might cost them. They fail to realize they aren't in control and eventually what is done in darkness will be brought to the light and truth will serve as a sharp sword that will expose, undo, and silence the offender. In essence, such individuals are blinded by unbelief and are standing on the lie that no matter the cost, the fleeing moments of fleshly ecstasy with the unholy will be worth whatever the cost is in the long run.

God has been my husband for years, but I can't count the times I have taken my eyes and focus off of Him. However, I am always comforted *by 2 Timothy 2:13*—when I am faithless or unfaithful—the Lord is faithful and remains faithful because He can't deny that which is attached to Him by way of covenant and spirit.

I am so thankful God is faithful and will keep the integrity of the covenant regardless of how, in my rebellion, I might have trashed it. However, I must not assume He will strive with me always. My opportunity to be reconciled back to God is now and I must be wise enough to seize upon it in true repentance.

Prayer: Lord, help me and show pity towards me. My eyes wander, my thoughts flit, and my focus changes with the terrain. Forgive me for my pathetic, faithless ways. Amen.

171

May 21

"Therefore they enquired of the LORD further, if the man should yet come thither. And the LORD answered, Behold, he hath hid himself among the stuff (1 Samuel 10:22)." I always smile when I read the word "stuff" in Scripture. In fact, at one of our meetings I asked the people what they had learned after I shared this particular scripture with them, and one individual responded, "I learned they also had 'stuff' in the Old Testament days."

The reality is all the world can offer us is "stuff." Like Saul, who was called to be king, we can hide in and among our stuff to avoid responsibility, calling, and even reality. In some cases, people actually become hoarders and become LOST in their stuff.

As we consider the word, "stuff" it appears to have very little meaning or significance. It almost a generic term and it seems that it implies to some type of nirvana that ends in an endless reality of nothingness, or as in the case of "hoarders," filth which points to obsessions and an unclean spirit.

"Stuff" is just things of the world, but your attitude towards it might reveal a spiritual problem. Granted, we need the things of the world to function in this world. Some things are necessary for the essence of life, while other things are for use, and some for pleasure, but like the world, these things are only temporary at best and can add great burdens to you at worse.

The world's "stuff" has a tendency of holding onto us when we try to rid ourselves of the weary responsibilities that come with it. After all, stuff in the end clutters our life with non-essential junk that adds no real substance or value to our lives. At such times such articles prove to be nothing more than "stuff."

This brings us back to the question, are you caught up with stuff, a form of idolatry, hiding behind it due to some type of fear, or being buried by it because of covetousness?

Prayer: Lord, we need to be delivered from our self-serving Western perspective and from the "stuff" we accumulate in our lives that bury us instead of satisfy or add to our life. Forgive us for valuing that which has no value. Amen.

May 22

"How sweet are thy words unto my taste! Yea, sweeter than honey to my mouth! (Psalm 119:103). You never know which Scripture or set of Scriptures with it stories and examples are going to minister to your spirit and uplift your soul. God's Word contains wisdom, revelation, and insight that end in surprises. These surprises serve as those "wow" moments, those times of "awe," and those humbling experiences that quiet your soul and causes your spirit to silently sit before God in adoration.

There are certain days that reading the Word of God brings special pleasure and delight. It is because it is God's personal diary to each of us and His Word that "hits the spot" at just the right time. Most of my time involves serious study of the Word of God; but in times of leisurely reading it I experience a satisfying sweetness. The "meat" of studying is lasting, but the "milk and honey" of it brings immediate satisfaction to the soul.

When I am in a personal struggle, the Word reminds me that God is for me and the victory is already at hand. When I am emotionally distraught, the Word reminds me He is still there. When I am overwhelmed, I am promised that deliverance is already so, and when I need wisdom, God opens the storehouse to it so I can stand in wonderment. The other thing is that God is really our portion and inheritance. I know this is true but it is satisfying to always be reminded.

Prayer: Lord, Your Word is sweet to my soul and You are bread to my existence, and the source all life. You alone satisfy my inner being. Amen.

May 23

"Behold, here I am: witness against me before the LORD, and before his anointed: whose ox have I taken? Or whose ass have I taken? Or whom I have I defrauded? Whom have I oppressed? Or of whose hand have I received any bribe to blind mine eyes therewith? And I will restore it" (1 Samuel 12:3). One might wonder why Samuel brought this matter up. It was simple. The people's excuse for wanting a physical king was because Samuel's sons were not honest men. Was their excuse necessary? No, it was not because God was the one who would raise up righteous judges such as Samuel.

I love this part where Samuel challenges the people to present a witness against his character and conduct as to whether he has done anything wrong as a judge and prophet against the Jewish people to reveal their true motive. If they can present any indictment, he declared he would do all he can do to make it right to take away any false accusation. Since the people could not bring any indictment against Samuel, he established their testimony as a witness before the Lord to avoid being falsely accused; thereby, bringing a reproach to the Lord.

Samuel wanted to establish that he judged righteously and was fair towards the people and their desire for an earthly king was unwarranted, unjustified and unfounded. He then stated that the Lord was a witness to them, along with him.

It takes two witnesses to establish a fact and bring forth an indictment. On that day, an indictment was being leveled at the children of Israel. The truth is our life will testify of our character and it will be established by and in heaven and used as an indictment against those who are truly guilty of rejecting the true king of Israel.

Prayer: Lord, we are forever justifying our sin at the expense of others so we don't have to deal with You. However, Your light will eventually expose the wickedness behind our attitudes and ways. Lord thank you for the light that will reveal any wicked way in me. Amen.

May 24

"And said unto him, Behold, thou art old, and thy sons walk not in thy ways: now make us a king to judge us like all the nations" (1 Samuel 8:5). By revealing that the real motive of the people of Israel had nothing to do with inept leadership, immoral judgments, or shady dealings but with them preferring the ways of the pagan nations highlighted their own sin. They were rejecting the leadership of their true king, Jehovah.

They were indirectly giving God's leadership a black eye to hide their dark designs to be like the pagan nations. They were using Samuel's sons as an excuse for their own rebellion and worldly preferences.

As Christians the greatest affront usually comes against our testimony. Those who oppose us are waiting to jump on some imaginary bandwagon to bring an indictment against our life so they can put a black eye on our testimony as a means to discredit and silence us. Those affronts come by way of small minds that are often petty, jealous and have nothing better to do than stir the pot when it comes to other people's business.

The Bible refers to such people as gossipers who are not only foolish with their tongue, but murderous in their hearts as they try to murder the reputation of others without a cause to make themselves look bigger or better than those they are accusing. In the end, those who are righteous and manage to maintain their integrity and authority will bring judgment on such people.

We clearly reap what we sow.

Prayer: Lord, our lives will stir the wicked up against us, bringing an indictment against themselves. It is never easy to be a target, but I would rather be a target standing on the right side of eternity than be a fool standing against Your kingdom and servants. Amen.

May 25

And Samuel said unto the people, Fear not: ye have done all this wickedness: yet turn not aside from following the LORD, but serve the LORD with all of your heart? (1 Samuel 12:20). In these Scriptures Samuel has just revealed that the desire of the Jewish people for a king in order to be like the rest of the pagan nations was a type of rebellion against and rejection of the Lord being their king.

The truth is that the people did not want to rely on an unseen king of heaven; rather, they wanted to have a king they could see. Even though God had shown Himself mighty, they still wanted to rely on the arm of the flesh.

The people of Israel realized their sin, but it was too late to reverse the consequences. They would have their king, but at what expense? They would come out from the perfect, just reign of their King and God to come under the imperfect reign of a man who could prove to be fickle, tyrannical, and foolish, leading them as sheep to the slaughter for no good or honorable reason.

In spite of having a king, Samuel instructed them to not turn aside from serving the Lord because if they did, they would chase after other gods. We are all serving something, but we must make sure we are serving God. If we aren't, we will naturally turn aside and chase after others gods with the intent of putting our faith in them and serving them.

Prayer: Lord, I give you permission to keep me sharp and to keep my feet in the right path so I will not turn aside from You to only find myself chasing after the illusive Baals of this world. Amen.

May 26

Thus saith the LORD; Cursed be the man that trusteth in man, and maketh flesh his arm, and whose heart departeth from the LORD" *(Jeremiah 17:5).* When I meditate on the incident in Samuel where people chose man over God to serve, lead, and keep them, I realize how man clearly does not want to trust what he can't see.

It is natural for us to trust what we can see and scoff at what we can't see. It is normal for us to look for man's way to save us and his strength to deliver us, but when we look to man in any way, we stand cursed. Clearly man is limited when it comes to strength, incapable of doing the impossible when it comes to deliverance, and inept to be the ultimate solution. Yet, we would rather put our faith in man's fading strength, false promises of deliverance, and man's profane ways in deliverance than to God.

In fact, man silently resents the idea that he has to look outside of what he can see and trust in what he not only can't see, but cannot control. He believes as long as he can see a matter, he can at least understand or control his reality. However, man refuses to face the fact that what is not seen is what really affects and controls his world.

We are to walk by faith which means we must choose to trust the Lord. I thought about faith. Faith sustains us—that is if our faith is towards God. The mustard seed of faith involves a choice to trust God with a matter. Such a choice is accounted for righteousness. God then gives us a measure of faith to take that step of obedient confidence towards Him.

Faith that is established will always be tested and refined in the fiery ovens of temptation and trials. I so much want a child-like faith towards God because outside of it I will stand cursed. The Lord is the One that all of our reliance belongs too. Praise His holy Name. I must always thank Him for being my point of reliance.

Prayer: Lord, there are always struggles, but You are close at hand to deliver us when the challenges are too great. Meanwhile, man can witness Your work on behalf of Your saints if he is willing to see, while heaven keeps the score as to those who cry out to You in faith, flinging themselves on You in utter abandonment and reliance. Amen.

May 27

"If thou hast run with the footmen, and they have wearied thee, then how canst thou contend with horses? And if in the land of peace, wherein thou trustedst, they wearied thee, then how wilt thou do in the swelling of Jordan?" (Jeremiah 12:5). Yesterday I talked about the fact that any reliance on man stands cursed.

Man is weak in one major area that is often exposed by his attitude and his pursuits. He is often pushed by ambition that is void of scruples, and desires a life that is exciting to the flesh, but not too challenging to the pride. Although his spirit is strong, his flesh is weak against temptation. Even though he may be determined to hold some line, he can easily enough be blindsided by the unexpected. He can take all the precautions, have the greatest intentions, stand at the highest peak of self-sufficiency and confidence but fail miserably in accomplishing the task before him.

The scripture in Jeremiah reveals the struggle. It doesn't matter how much one desires to reach greater heights, if they are not capable of withstanding the present matters of life without becoming bored in attitude, then emotionally weary with the drudgery, depressed with the nominal, and resentful of the mundane, there is no real preparation to endure bigger challenges. With such ineptness to see something through to the end, how can they expect to endure the next test that comes their way that will require more inner stamina to bear greater challenges.

The reason man is unable to stand the next test has to do with moral weakness. Moral weakness points to weak character. Physical strength without character lacks endurance, and determination without upright conviction will not be able to hold the line. Truth without integrity will be rendered into a muddled reality and abilities without moral temperance will end in apathy and burn out.

I could go on and on with examples that reveal that the greatest weakness of man is due to the lack of moral character. Man may want to do good, but often lacks the right spirit. He may want to do what is right, but lacks the right focus and clarity. He may want to put his best foot forward, but begins on the wrong footing. He may want to present his best, but discover it is filthy rags to God.

The only strength that endures is the strength of the Lord. It is only when we realize that in our weaknesses, we will see the need to seek the Lord. It is in seeking the Lord that we will discover and know His goodness and strength through His work of grace, the joy of our salvation, and the peace that passes all understanding.

Prayer: Lord, we so thank You for offering us Your best when we think the rags of our best is sufficient. Thank You for never waning in bringing me to the realization that I am nothing without You. Amen.

May 28

It happens every time I manage to do some organizing. Inevitably, organized items seem to take on a whole new identity just because they're placed in a different manner in a different location. It's like deliberately hiding your stuff from yourself so when you have to use something that you assume will be easy to find, you can't find it, resulting in mounting frustration.

This happened to me the other day and if the dog could talk (which he tries to do, by the way) I'm sure he would've agreed when I loudly called myself an "idiot." Finally, the missing items were found in plain sight, right in front of my nose and all was well. Besides, I realize that being an idiot occasionally is normal if we're honest with ourselves, and it hopefully helps to make us more tolerant and understanding of others.

However, when it comes to our spiritual lives, none of us wants to end up feeling like an "idiot" or fool or failure because we've ignored the warnings, instructions, precepts, and wisdom contained in God's Word. Regret is a terrible thing to live with. Concerning serious regrets, many Christians live with nagging regrets because of wrong decisions they've made simply because they failed to guard their minds and hearts against assumptions.

It's easy to float through life assuming we know what "God thinks" about different situations; therefore, we make decisions without praying for wisdom, discernment or direction, which could very well end up in disobedience. The regretful consequences can be a whole lot more disastrous than momentarily forgetting where we put something.

God tells us, *"Where no counsel is, the people fall: but in the multitude of counsellors there is safety"* (Proverbs 11:14); *"If any of you lack wisdom, let him ask of God, that giveth to all men liberally, and upbraideth not; and it shall be given him"* (James

1:5); "I will instruct thee and teach thee in the way which thou shalt go: I will guide thee with mine eye" (Psalm 32:8).

The truth is, no matter how much we think we know, and no matter how many experiences we have had, we still need to seek the mind of the Lord in making critical decisions, because "who has known the mind of the Lord?" – J. Haley

Prayer: Lord, thank You for keeping my feet in the way of Your path of righteousness and from slipping from the heights of Your truth. After all, You are honoring my heart desire to know only and nothing but the truth. Amen.

May 29

"And I say also unto thee, That thou art Peter, and upon this rock I will build my church; and the gates of hell shall not prevail against it" (Matthew 16:18). The visible Church appears as if it is becoming powerless and lost in the midst of man's various inspired doctrines, movements, and entertainment. Sadly, much of the Church stands naked, stripped of its armor, and unable to withstand the attacks of the devil and the onslaught of the powers and rulers of darkness.

Without power and authority, many will not be able to stand in the midst of wickedness. Although there are those in the organized Church that claim they have the armor in place, it is clearly missing.

The belt of truth has become tarnished with compromise and the breastplate of righteousness weak with worldliness. The feet are becoming lame and tormented because the power of the Gospel is absent, while the shield of faith has been rendered into a pretty paper shield of pseudo-faiths that blow away with every wind of doctrine.

181

The helmet of salvation is no longer in place. It has been put aside to accept the false security of man's coverings or the latest attempts to make himself righteous, holy, or immortal.

The sword has been rendered useless, dissected in many pieces in the name of intellectual and religious pursuits for so-called "truth" and sadly replaced with man's watered-down Bible versions, false teachings, traditions, and theology.

Prayer: Lord, we allow so many substitutes to replace the means and tools You have given us to stand in these times in order to function and get along with this world. However, it is time to cast aside the substitutes and put Your life and armor on. Lord, give me the boldness to stand no matter what, trusting that You are fighting the battle that already has been won. Amen.

May 30

"But I fear, lest by any means, as the serpent beguiled Eve through his subtilty, so your minds should be corrupted from the simplicity that is in Christ" (2 Corinthians 11:3). The simplicity of the Christian life is often buried under endless doctrinal debates, good deeds, and religious pride where one's particular understanding and way is the only "right way." I often wonder how new believers wade through the constant yo-yo affect caused by petty differences and the idolatrous exaltation of certain theology, denominations, and religious camps over God's Word.

However, the Christian life is not about getting everything right, but lining up to what is right. It is not about being in the right group but being on the right side of eternity. It is not a matter of what you know, but whether you know the true God of the Bible.

When you consider what the Bible emphasizes, it is the simplicity of heaven that keeps us grounded. Paul's concern was that people would be drawn away from the simplicity of Christ. For example, unless you have faith like, and are converted as a child, you will not see the kingdom of heaven. When it came to parables only the pure in heart would see their real meaning. A cup of water to the thirsty is as important as offering the Living Water to those who are dying in their spiritual thirst.

Finally, there is that simple truth about what God will accept and not accept. Jesus stated clearly, only those who do the will of the Father will be known by Him. The Bible is clear about God's will. He wants us to believe Him about His Son's great work of redemption so we can be saved. He wants us to trust Him and obey what we know is Scripturally right so He can show Himself mighty on our behalf. He wants us to have the right attitude to approach Him in authority, the right spirit to be empowered, and to be ready to repent in order to avoid perishing.

The simplicity has been for our benefit and complicating it has greatly served Satan. Let us come back to the simplicity to discover the sweetness of our Christian life that only can be enjoyed by those who are pure in heart.

Prayer: Lord, I have complicated so much most of my life, but I have discovered if I come back to the simplicity of a child, I can once again land on Your many promises and believe they are for me to rest in regardless of what is going on. Amen.

May 31

"Nay, in all of these things we are more than conquerors through him that loved us (Romans 8:37). Are you a victim or a victor in light of the present world? Are you conquering or being conquered by the darkness that is becoming greater? Are you overcoming or being buried by the demands of this world?

There are so many demands on my life at times, that I feel that I am being "piecemealed" out. I often feel I have to accept that which is inferior and give in to the inevitable reality that I must just go with the current of hopelessness, as well as resolve to accept that death works in me and will ultimately end up winning.

However, I must remember with God I can swim against the current of the inevitable and fling hopelessness to the wind in light of the promises of God. I can push the members of my body back and beat them into submission. I can refuse the inferior and insist on what is right and superior to the flesh and the world. This is how I can take my life back. I do not have to live as a victim, but I can claim the victory the Lord has secured for me on the cross.

Praise the Lord for all avenues, tools, and promises of victory.

Prayer: Lord, You have given me this life and it is up to me to daily dedicate it back to You for Your use and glory. Give me the vision and strength to joyously, and with great liberty abandon all to You exhibiting great confidence and showing forth wondrous celebration, that in the end I will not only gain life, but I will discover the abundance of it. Amen.

JUNE

June 1

His lord said unto him, Well done, thou good and faithful servant: thou hast been faithful over a few things, I will make thee ruler over many things: enter thou into the joy of thy Lord" (Matthew 25:21). So much of our service to the Lord can become a type of duty or even a way of "keeping God" off our back when it comes to doing things our way. After all, we can delude ourselves that if we throw enough good things at God, He will give us leeway to do what we want to do and not hold such selfishness against us on that day when we have to face Him.

We need to keep in mind God sees our heart attitude behind everything we do. He is looking for the motivation of love, the inspiration of faith, the expectation of hope, and the anticipation of Him fulfilling His promises. However, the glue that holds the right disposition together is faithfulness.

Love inspires faithfulness, doing good things in faith is the springboard to it, hope is the strength of it, and promises disciplines the focus to enable it to be steadfast until the goal is reached.

We must throw in another ingredient: that of thankfulness. Faithfulness finds itself in the current of thankfulness because it sees the hand of God in every situation, allowing one to truly benefit from God's goodness and faithfulness to His people that is constantly being shown through His grace.

Prayer: Lord, we can't begin to understand faithfulness until we see how Your faithfulness works in our life. You prove faithful in all matters and reveal that faithfulness towards You will always benefit others and bring glory to You. Amen.

June 2

"O love the LORD, all ye his saints; for the LORD preserveth the faithful, and plentifully rewarded the proud doer (Psalm 31:23). One of the qualities that sticks out on believers is their faithfulness to support God's work and kingdom in any way they can. They are often the unsung heroes of faith that are often overlooked. They steadily advance the work of the kingdom while quietly passing those who seek accolades.

These individuals have taught me a lot about faithfulness. For example, our friend Nancy Brown's faithfulness is expressed in sacrifice and I sense the Lord readily accepts her offerings with a smile as it comes to His throne as a pleasing savor.

Our dear supporters Pearl and Chuck DeMaris have shown me that faithfulness in itself is a sacrifice that speaks of God's grace in action. There is our sister in the Lord, Nisa Clarke who has revealed to me faithfulness is a point of identification in the Lord's work and household.

The key about faithfulness is that there is a call and a burden that comes with it. As God's saints are faithful with what God calls them to, they realize He is faithful to supply the means in which they become part of the blessing and work of His kingdom. Although they are overlooked and unknown by even those around them, they are known in heaven because their faithfulness is the expression of their love for the One they are serving.

Prayer: Lord, Your faithfulness proves Your abiding care on us, while our faithfulness towards You shows we do love You and that

You are worthy of all of our consideration. Thank You for Your example of lasting commitment. Amen.

June 3

"It is the LORD'S mercies that we are not consumed, because his compassions fail not" (Lamentations 3:22). To be touched by Jesus serves as a point of great comfort emotionally, mentally, and spiritually. It is almost like putting balm on an open wound, causing the pain to flee, the swelling to recede, and the healing to begin. That touch is known as compassion.

Compassion is made up of grace that tastes sweet, kindness that can show empathy, and genuine care that notices when one is struggling in their plight. Compassion speaks through the touch, whether it is a touch letting you know one truly cares, a hug that embraces you with comfort, or taking your hand to let you know you are not alone.

This touch is what I experienced from my nephew Benjamin at the funeral of my father. I walked in the door of the funeral home and was greeted by my brother with a hug, but it was his son, Ben who came over to me and without a word hugged me in such a tender way. It was as if Jesus was using him to enter in with me with the special balm of compassion in my time of loss.

For many people when they are struggling, hurting, or feeling vulnerable they put on a mask so they do not have to experience the sting of indifference, the cruelty of being judged, the smugness of "oh well," or "pity" that is a mere veneer because it is void of real compassion.

At such times there are no words to calm the soul, take away the sorrow, or make it better. That is why only that simple, caring touch can prove to be the balm of sweetness to the soul which makes such times of bitterness to the spirit, bittersweet to the heart.

Prayer: Lord, I want to be the extension of Your compassion to others. Take away the selfishness that keeps me from seeing the struggles of others who need to feel your touch. Amen.

June 4

And our hope of you is stedfast, knowing, that as ye are partakers of the sufferings, so shall ye be also of the consolation (2 Corinthians 1:7). In my last post I talked about the ministry of consolation. If you are like me, I shy away from the idea of experiencing any kind of adversity. However, if I am going to be effective in ministry, I must partake of suffering for the sake of Christ to become identified with Him. I must experience its darkness, its despair, its hopelessness, and its anguish to become identified with others in their plight.

Jesus never said we would be without tribulation in this world. We are told trials are necessary for testing, temptations are reality of life, adversity a tool of necessity for growth, suffering a means of preparation and persecution the badge the righteous will end up wearing. We can get angry at such means, cry foul, stomp our feet, scream at the inconvenience of it, and become angry and accusing towards God, but we have been told such things are necessary for our spiritual growth and to be effective in ministry.

Whether such tools of God have their way in our lives comes down to whether we resist them in belligerence or give way to them in good faith that God knows what He is doing. I have learned the biggest obstacle in ministry is selfishness and the greatest freedom in one's personal life and ministry comes when self is cast to the side, the will is lined up to God's will, the focus is turned from the inward to the upward, the affections set above and the mind has become settled on the Word of God.

In essence, once I get past myself to make it about the other person, I am set free to receive the sweet healing balm from above.

Prayer: Lord as long as I am focused on me, I will never be available to become an extension of Your love, grace, and ministry to others. Lord, help me to remember that when I need some type of healing that I can experience it once I become the avenue and extension of Your healing to others. Amen.

June 5

It happened again! In fact, it happens so often whenever I go shopping—especially grocery shopping—that it has become a "slogan" of sorts at our house. It goes like this, "I got the last one."

The community in which we live may be small, but the Super 1 grocery store is quite substantial. Even so, there are usually more than at least one to half a dozen items on my grocery list that are "the last one" and today was no exception.

The 21-pound turkey, however, is one that we refer to as a "miracle." It was the day after Thanksgiving and we had no turkey leftovers because kind friends had invited us to their lovely home for dinner. Besides, it takes a bit of energy for me to wrestle a huge turkey in and out of the roaster oven, but our younger co-laborer in the ministry (whom we live with) was home from work and went to the store and "just happened" to see a huge fresh Butterball turkey for 98 cents a pound. And, you guessed it—it was the last one! Even the checkout clerk called the butcher to make sure the price was right!

No doubt many would write all this off as just a bunch of "coincidences," but not so with us, for we know the joy and laughter that warms our hearts every time this happens is from above. And, it reminds us of the intimate guidance, love, and care of our ever-present Lord (who really does have a sense of humor.) And, just so you know, that roasted turkey was one of the best, ever! *"But my God shall supply all your need according to his riches in glory by Christ Jesus" Philippians 4:19.* – J. Haley

Prayer: Lord, You always saved the last in order to reveal Your care and faithfulness. The other part of the saving the last for Your people is that it turns out to be the best in the end. Praise Your wonderful name. Amen.

June 6

"We are troubled on every side, yet not distressed; we are perplexed, but not in despair" (2 Corinthians 4:8). In my last post I talked about compassion. There are different types of ministries in the kingdom of God. There is the ministry of reconciliation between God and lost man that comes through the preaching of the Gospel. Man must see he is separated from his Creator by sin and the only way to be restored is through repentance, forgiveness, and salvation experienced at the cross of Jesus.

There is a ministry of helps where one comes under the burdens of those who need a caring soul to lend a helping hand in something that is beyond their means to address. So many times, these helps come down to practical ministry that causes weariness to lift from the burdened soul.

There is a ministry of encouragement. Those with this ability know how to encourage others with a smile, the right word, a caring way, or a simple touch that lets the person know that they are not alone. This type of ministry reaches the downtrodden soul.

Jesus is our example of meeting people in their plight and reveals how each ministry is able to meet a person whether they are in perplexity, overwhelmed, in despair or in complete hopelessness. True ministry reaches past the obvious and reaches into the soul, touches the heart, and awakens the sagging spirit with a sense of hope and expectation that there is a great Physician who knows our inner struggle, and is able to heal the heart and cause the soul to be restored and raised up, and the spirit to catch the wind of God's Spirit and soar in the currents of liberty to reach heavenly heights.

Prayer: Lord, I praise You for being the one and only true Physician of the soul and spirit. Thank You for Your constant abiding care and healing in my life. Amen.

June 7

"Who comforteth us in all our tribulation, that we may be able to comfort them which are in any trouble, by the comfort wherewith we ourselves are comforted of God" (2 Corinthians 1:4). There is a ministry of consolation where one enters in with the individual who is being challenged with great loss. That loss can be so deep it is consuming, so great that it is indescribable, and so far-reaching that it leaves a person feeling totally isolated. However, those with the ministry of consolation have the compassion to reach down and touch that place of sorrow with comfort.

God often allows us to experience the depth of our sin, the great need for intervention, utter desperation in times of despair, and the bitterness of great loss so that we can be used in a ministry of consolation. Such experiences either cause us to possess a type of sweetness that soothes the soul or we become bitter and hard.

The depth of which ministry can reach is determined by the depth of our compassion. Those with great compassion will be able to go deep and those with little compassion will barely touch the surface as they skip across the way with a certain conceit and aloofness.

191

Prayer: Lord, I never wanted to waste the times of trials by simply surviving them. I want to come out of each one with greater compassion so I can be effective in the ministry of reconciliation. Thank you for the trials and the training. Amen.

June 8

"If ye will still abide in this land, then will I build you, and not pull you down, and I will plant you, and not pluck you up: for I repent me of the evil that I have done unto you" (Jeremiah 42:10). What will be the choice of God's people, an inheritance that must be reclaimed or the world that seems intact? After all, our flesh does not like the hard way and our pride resents the challenging way, but a right spirit is ready to embrace God's way. The question is, will the driving fears of the flesh have a greater voice, or perhaps will the logic of pride win out in the courtroom of our fearful minds and cause us to leave our inheritance behind?

When you consider the main reason why people would leave their spiritual inheritance to go back to the world, it is because of fear. There is the fear of the unknown, the fear of losing one's life as they know it regardless of how inept and pathetic it has become, and fear that the obstacles are too great to overcome. The question in this case is, did the remnant of Israel have such fears prompting and driving them?

It is important to point out it is never God's heart to bring severe judgment down on His people for their sin. It is His heart to quickly repent or change course from showing His great displeasure as soon as His people repent and change their attitude and ways. As in the case of Sodom, He is always looking for a few to stand in the gap and give Him reason to show mercy, but sadly, there are very few with the vision and conviction to stand in such a gap.

The world may promise us an easy time, but what God promises us is that He will establish us in our inheritance, bless us in our works, and bring forth His promises in our midst—that is if we stay in our inheritance. God's way may be a bit hard and challenging but, in the end, we will be where we need to be to inherit the promises attached to our eternal inheritance.

Prayer: Lord, we fear everything but You. You are the one who brought the judgment on the land in the first place, you would think Your people would have a healthy fear of You and desire to please You, but sadly, once Your judgment passes and people survive it because of Your grace, they can cast aside the eternal as they consider the present without regard that You are the One who holds all events in Your hands. Forgive us for worshipping fear instead of You. Amen.

June 9

"*Seek him that maketh the seven stars and Orion, and turneth the shadow of death into the morning, and maketh the day dark with night; that called for the waters of the sea and poureth them out upon the face of the earth: The LORD is his name*" *(Amos 5:8).* It is easy to get caught up with ministers and ministries. The ministries are simple tools and the ministers clay vessels.

Regardless of the face of ministry, we must keep in mind that both man and ministries will eventually let you down because they are so very limited. Christians must ensure their focus is right, their faith is not misdirected, and their commitment sure in order to continue to stand when all religious, pagan, or worldly idols are brought down in judgment.

God made it clear that He does not judge according to the outward man, but by his inward character. The effectiveness of a ministry comes down to the unseen. One must hold onto and maintain the qualities that would help them endure to the end. One such quality that must be present in character is something called

193

tenacity. Once tenacity gets a hold of something it greatly values or desires, it will not let it go until it has obtained it.

Granted, this quality can be dangerous if it is directed in the wrong way, but tenacity is necessary if you are going to see an impossible matter through when it comes to God's kingdom. In a sense it is aroused when a person catches a vision of something of great value. This focus allows the individual to see beyond the present reality to consider the beneficial aspects of it.

Whether the person sees the need to obtain the jewel or gain greater riches from it, tenacity takes hold and with great resolve pursues it until they have been reached. When tenacity is present, these individuals will not let the prize go, and tenacity will not let go of them. In the end they must have the prize, and they will do everything to seek it out until they possess it.

This should be our attitude when it comes to seeking out the Lord. We must not let our focus land elsewhere, our pursuits be diverted from finding Him, and efforts wane in our commitment to know Him until we have gained that revelation of Him that will revolutionized our inner man and transform our minds in greater ways.

Prayer: Lord, in all my pursuits of You, You have allowed me to find You. Each time, my life has been enriched beyond any description. Thank You for taking the veil off my eyes so that I could search for You, and see You veiled in some way, but while drawing near with my whole heart actually finding You. Amen.

June 10

"Again, the kingdom of heaven is like unto treasure hid in a field; the which when a man hath found, he hideth, and for joy thereof goeth and selleth all that he hath, and buyeth that field (Matthew 13:44). God places the right blessings in your life at the right time.

194

When I consider the ways in which God brings people together it is easy to see His hand. However, there must be a boldness due to faith and a tenacity because of strong conviction for His people to knock on doors until He opens the right one for kingdom matters to come together.

When I think of tenacity, there is one individual that comes to mind. Her name is Kitty Miller and we met her in 1999. She loves books and one day she came upon our book *Hidden Manna* in a book store that sold used books. She had to be discrete in how many books she could buy and she was left with a choice between *Hidden Manna* and another book. She chose our book.

The book revolutionized her understanding about God and her perception about herself. From that point she began to tenaciously seek out the authors, Jeannette and myself. She had a pretty hard task ahead of her for we had moved from the location printed in the back of our book from the area of Kirkland, Washington to Houston, Texas back to Moore, Idaho and then we ended up in New Plymouth, Idaho.

Kitty had one clue from our book that could help her locate us and that was a small town where I grew up. She and her husband had a summer home there. She went to church in my old community and inquired if anyone knew where I was, and there was a woman who had my mother's address. Kitty wrote my mother and the rest is history.

The example that Kitty established for me was to never give up on God's truth. Sometimes a matter may seem impossible, unobtainable, and ridiculous but if you keep praying, knocking, and seeking ways around obstacles, God will open the door for you, and in the end, you will be satisfied as you discover that His truths and ways will never leave you empty and disappointed.

Prayer: Lord, we want the things of heaven to fall into our lap but if they do, we never learn to really appreciate them. And, if there is no appreciation, there is no place for satisfaction to reside. Lord, thank You for causing me to seek You out so that in the end I will be grateful and satisfied with Your blessings, answers, and revelations. Amen.

June 11

"But he answered and said, It is written, Man shall not live by bread alone, but by every word that proceedeth out of the mouth of God" *(Matthew 4:4).* I was reading about the temptation of Christ. I do not casually pass over His temptation because there is so much to learn from Jesus using the premise of the Word that leads us to who the Lord is which establishes His ultimate authority over all creation.

It is amazing to me that Satan thought he could cause Jesus to play His hand as God. However, Jesus would not succumb to temptation. In the first temptation He stood on truth, submitted Himself to the will of the Father and quoted the Word of God to Satan to stop that particular temptation from going any further.

The second temptation had to do with putting the Lord God to a foolish test. Every time I read this part of Scripture, I think of the first person of the Godhead, the Father. However, as I looked at it closer, I realized that Jesus was speaking of Himself.

He used the term Adonai (Lord), owner, which is in reference to Him, especially in certain Scriptures in the Old Testament such as *Genesis 18:1-3.* Then He said to Satan, "thy God" in other words, pointing out that He is Satan's Creator. We know that Jesus was Creator of all the things we see (*Colossians 1:15-16*).

Clearly, Jesus was saying to Satan, "Why are you proving your Creator, by putting (Me) to a foolish test." It was not the Father who was being tested, it was the Son. It always has been there, but the Lord was gracious in revealing it to me. It was a precious revelation.

196

Prayer: Lord, You are faithful to reveal nuggets of truth that reveal who You are in a greater way. Thank You for Your faithfulness to show Yourself in greater ways to seeking hearts. Amen.

June 12

"Jesus said unto him, It is written again Thou shalt not tempt the Lord thy God" (Matthew 4:7). In my last post I wrote about how Satan was tempting Jesus to prove He was God. The key is that Satan already knew who He was and Jesus knew that He did not have to condescend down to such foolishness and prove His identity to any of His creation. It is important to note that Satan did not argue or debate with Jesus as to His identity.

As I consider this simple truth, I realize the only one who debates with Jesus as to His identity is man. I can't tell you how many times I have to contend with people over their misconstrued, unbiblical, and sometimes anti-Christ take on Jesus. In many cases they refuse to see Him as God in the flesh because they can't rationalize it out in their carnal minds. The Bible warns that these unregenerated, godless minds often see the unseen world as being foolish in the first place.

There are also those who always want the Lord to prove He is God with some type of sign or wonder. It is a form of conning that declares, "If only God will do this, I will believe." Seeing is not believing; believing is a choice of faith based on the Word of God that will eventually, through the eyes of faith, see a matter as being so.

The simple truth is we walk by faith, not by intellectual understanding. We receive in simplicity because we believe that what God says is so. We don't need to understand how a matter works, because we know without a doubt that it is already so in light of God's plan and workings.

197

Prayer: Lord, I want to know things but when it comes to You, it is about knowing You that makes all matters regarding Your kingdom so. Amen.

June 13

"Then said Jesus unto the twelve, Will ye also go away? Then Simon Peter answered him, Lord, to whom shall we go? Thou has the words of eternal life" (John 6:67-68). We must approach God and His Word to believe. Those who do not approach God to believe will never believe who He is and what He says as being the absolute truth regardless of what they see. Again, believing is a choice, and it is based on child-like faith that is directed towards God because of His unchangeable character.

This reminds me of an individual who we contended with for her spiritual wellbeing. Her mother was a weak Christian and her father an avowed atheist. Depending on what was happening in her life, she would declare there was a God one day and the next day when things were not right, she was not sure there was a God.

It all came down to whether God was serving her purpose. It became clear that she had no real intention to get off the fence and choose who she was going to believe and serve. After all, if God was a fable, she would prove to be a fool to her unbelieving father and others, and since she had no fear of God she was not concerned about consequences.

One day she was swinging on her fragile limb concerning spiritual matters and was supposedly wavering towards God when the Holy Spirit rose up in me and sorely rebuked her for her wicked games. Needless to say, the limb broke and the fence she had tried to straddle, collapsed in a heap, causing her to go with her preferred choice all along: the world.

What can we learn from this example? God's proof was the sacrifice of Christ and as our Creator He has nothing to prove to

198

anyone. After all, He does not need our approval, but we do need His.

Prayer: Lord, it is easy to try to the walk the fence to see which side, You or the world, will serve our purposes the most. However, Lord, You are not here to do our bidding, we are here to do You honorable service that will bring glory to You. Lord, I choose YOU for YOU are the only One who deserves worship. Amen.

June 14

"You are your father the devil, and the lusts of your father ye will do. He was a murderer from the beginning, and abode not in the truth because there is no truth in him. When he speaketh a lie, he speaketh of his own: for he is a liar, and the father of it" (John 8:44). Since Jesus refused to step into Satan's trap to prove His identity, what was Satan's next move? He offered Jesus all the glory of the systems of the world if He would bow down and worship him.

Could Satan offer Jesus these systems? Yes, he could because he is the god, ruler, or prince over the systems of the world. As a liar would he have given these profane, anti-God systems to Jesus? Not hardly, he would have reneged and admitted he was lying as he mocked his Creator for being a fool for believing him in the first place.

Jesus did not come to take back the kingdoms of this world, He came to take away the keys of hell and death through His death, burial and resurrection. He came to establish an unseen kingdom in the hearts of men, and He knew that one day earth would become His footstool as all of His enemies are put under His feet and He comes back as King of kings, and Lord of lords to judge and rule over all.

There are songs that declare that as Christians we have the power to pull Satan off of his throne as god over the world's systems, but that is a lie. In fact, the god of this age mocks such unbiblical nonsense, but he does not mock when he is rebuked and pushed back from territories that have already been identified as belonging to God by His Spirit.

Prayer: Lord, we either have very small notions about You or exalted ideas about ourselves due to pride, but in the end, we lose credibility and fail to understand the authority we have in You. We end up with our ideas being deflated, and our notions about you failing us as we wallow in complete defeat. Forgive us for wanting to believe a lie over believing You. Amen.

June 15

"Love not the world…For all that is in the world, the lust of the flesh and the lust of the eyes, and the pride of life, is not of the Father, but is of the world" (*1 John 2:15a,16*). As we consider the temptation of Jesus in the wilderness, we can overlook little nuggets. We see Jesus overcoming but we do not consider what His victory was revealing for our edification.

First of all, it reveals the three areas of temptation. They are the same as found in the Garden of Eden. They are the lust of the flesh—the fruit looked good to Eve; the pride of life, that she shall be as God, and the lust of the eyes as to what she could possess if only she would partake of the fruit. Keep in mind Satan's insinuations in his temptation of Eve is that God's intention, instructions, and commands could not be trusted.

The real temptation in every situation is to believe a lie about what is really true about God, sin, and eternity. Temptation magnifies a lie in order for the flesh to desire the forbidden fruit, dares the pride to agree with it and entices the eyes to see how it can and will benefit the flesh and feed the ego of pride.

Sadly, we in our fallen disposition have a tendency to prefer the lie over the truth, because truth will not justify fleshly lusts, bow down to pride's touchiness, and give way to the false light brought on by the promises of Satan.

Jesus is the truth and when we prefer the lie, we are saying "Jesus You are not worth giving up the lie for in order to know, follow, and obey You." We are also saying the lie is worth selling our souls for, which will prove to be the ultimate lie.

Prayer: Lord, before I knew You, I bought all three of these lies at different times. However, I have bought some even as a Christian because the lie helped logic, reason out, and justify why going with the lie was not so bad after all and that surely You will overlook it. Lord, I choose to love You, and Your truth in order to avoid falling into the trap of lies. Amen.

June 16

"And saith unto him, All these things will I give thee, if thou wilt fall down and worship me" (Matthew 4:9). It is important to realize that what Satan was after from Jesus all along was worship.

Satan must magnify the lies to make them attractive because the reality is that the bread is temporary, and the idea of him ever exalting anyone is a mockery. Satan's kingdoms in the end will prove to be a façade that covers great darkness.

The truth is, selling your soul at any cost comes down to idolatry which leads to worship or paying some kind of homage and obedience to it. Giving way to the lusts of the flesh and eyes or the pride of life would have been a form of idolatry or worship.

When man becomes dependent or driven by the flesh for his life, the lusts of the flesh have become an idol. If Jesus gave way to the great temptation of pride it would be the same as submitting to the whims of the biggest idol of all. When you give way to the eyes, you are exalting something as God. Satan is behind all idolatry. His goal is to dethrone the true God of heaven and exalt himself as God.

When it comes to God proving He is God to mankind, it means that creation is demanding that God submit to its whims and its conditions in order to consider if He is worthy of worship. This is blasphemous, and it is for this reason only faith towards God is what can please Him.

Prayer: Lord, we think nothing of putting You to a foolish test until we by faith embrace that You alone are God and the only One worthy of true worship. Lord thank You for revealing Yourself to me by Your Spirit. Amen.

June 17

Every day they remind me of how fleeting this mortal life is. I've never seen a flower that fades from a deep crimson color to a light tan shade like one of my Cosmos plants does! Usually flowers just simply "bow their heads" in submission to their fate when their short lives are finished, while retaining their designated color.

On the one hand, I love the profusion of flowers Cosmos produce, but on the other hand, the daily chore of removing faded and finished flowers so the plant will continue to produce new blooms can become rather tedious. And, the older I get and the hotter the weather gets, the more exhausting that daily chore becomes.

The whole process brings to mind life's journey. Like the crimson Cosmos, our youth blooms bright with vitality and promise, but as the years fly by, we find ourselves beginning to "fade." Soon, we too, will be removed from this earth by the hand of the One who numbers our days. *("Seeing his days are determined, the number of his months are with thee, thou hast appointed his bounds that he cannot pass" Job 14:5.)*

Knowing this then, may we pray *"...teach us to number our days, that we may apply our hearts unto wisdom" Psalm 90:12.* Jesus Christ is our wisdom, *"But of him are ye in Christ Jesus, who of God is made unto us wisdom, and righteousness, and sanctification, and redemption: That, according as it is written, He that glorieth, let him glory in the Lord" 1 Corinthians 1:30, 31.* – J. Haley

Prayer: Lord at different stages of our life we are allowed to live in the world of fantasy and delusion about our lives, but the Bible tells us that in light of eternity our lives are a "flash in the pan." Help me to be wise about not the length of my life, but about redeeming the present time. Amen.

June 18

"There hath no temptation taken you but such as is common to man: but God is faithful, who will not suffer you to be tempted above that ye are able, but will with the temptation also make a way to escape, that ye may be able to bear it" (1 Corinthians 10:13). Many people read this scripture as there is no trouble that will come upon you that you will not be able to bear, but this Scripture has to do with temptation.

In any type of tribulation, we have Jesus assuring us that we can be of good cheer for He has overcome the world, but when it comes to temptation, He will provide a means to escape so that we can bear it to silence all lame excuses for giving way to it.

Jesus was tempted in every way we are tempted. In the wilderness His flesh was tempted to become a dominate, driving influence in His life. When it came to proving His deity, it was a form of mockery and blasphemy.

When it came to the kingdoms of the world, Jesus' position as king and Messiah were on the line because it was not time for Him to take the reins as King of kings. As far as being the Anointed One, He still had a mission to carry out that involved an old rugged cross.

Satan not only tempts us with lies, but he wants us to become anxious, and if anxiety is allowed to climb the heights of bad possibilities it will cause us to slide into unbelief. He wants us to jump in and try to control matters which is rebellion or get ahead of the plan instead of waiting on the Lord for instructions to ensure He is glorified. The devil wants us to drop the ball and take detours before a matter is finished so we will miss opportunities and open doors, resulting in failure to overcome.

Prayer: Lord, You have shown us the way, given us our marching orders in regard to the Gospel, left us with Your Word that has all the instructions we need to finish the course, but we must keep our eye on You to avoid falling into the snares of temptation. Amen.

June 19

"My brethren, count it all joy when ye fall into divers temptations" (James 1:2) What can we learn from Jesus' temptations? Our spirit may be willing to obey, but our flesh is weak in temptation.

Keep in mind, Adam had dominance in creation until he ate of the deadly fruit, and now as a result man is often dominated by his fleshly lusts. We must choose what we are going to believe when such temptation comes our way. Are we going to believe the Word that, "greater is He that is in us than he that is in the world," or are we going to allow the flesh to so drive and torment us that we give way to it because we have no real moral conviction to stand on the truth of the Word, ever ready to draw near to God in humility to once again overcome and dominate the flesh?

When it comes to the pride of life that demands we prove a matter that is already so, we must remember our position in Christ. There is no need to prove anything, and that pride is the greatest trap of all. It is when we give way to it that we lose our authority to stand against the wiles of the devil. Finally, when it comes to the lust of the eyes, we must remember that giving in to this type of temptation requires us to give up our heavenly inheritance for a worldly inheritance that is temporary and will prove vain and deadly in the end.

Jesus silenced the enemy with the Word, stepped over him with His authority, and overcame Satan by holding to that which was true, right, and eternal. In His humanity, He has shown us the way through temptation, and with His authority He has shown us what it means to overcome temptation, and in light of our inheritance, He has shown us why we must overcome in order to possess that which is truly worthy in light of a worldly inheritance that has nothing of value that can begin to compare to it.

Prayer: Lord, we are told to count the cost, but many times we value the world too much and value our eternal inheritance too little because we have failed to walk it out by faith in obedience to Your Word. Forgive us for being foolish about what is really important and lasting. Amen.

June 20

For a dream cometh through the multitude of business; and a fool's voice is known by a multitude of words (Ecclesiastes 5:3). It is not unusual to wake up from some dream playing out in your mind. There have been a couple of incidents where I woke up from a dream that was not going well for me. I would gain enough semblance to think to myself that I am glad that I am out of the loop I found myself in, and then I would go back to sleep and find the dream taking off from where I left it. It was then that I would think, "Why can't I direct my dreams so I can determine how they will turn out?"

Life is a lot like dreams. We want to control the outcome of it, but we find ourself in some cycle or current that is taking us in a direction that seems ridiculous, frustrating, and at times frightening. We want so much to change the direction, get off the merry-go-round, and step out of the drama it is playing on our emotions. However, like our dreams, life is what it is. It will take us where it so wills.

We are told here that dreams come out of business and a lot of times we get caught up with the business of this world, which can cause the matters of life to be buried by vanity, but the quality of life is not based on fantasy or business but on one's relationship with God.

Every current has a destination. Riding in the current of the life Christ has given me reminds me that life is an adventure in uncharted territories.

There is so much to discover about what we have in Christ, for He is eternal, but we can't until we trust Him with the life He has given us. As the Light, it is His goal to bring out the purpose and clarity of the journey in order to show us what He wants us to learn to obtain His wisdom, as well as the heavenly glory that we need to see in order to come higher in Him.

Prayer: Lord, thank You for the current of life. It has different speeds at times, but I know You are also controlling how fast the current runs. Amen.

June 21

"In a dream, in a vision of the night, when deep sleep falleth upon men in slumberings upon the bed: then he openeth the ears of men, and sealeth their instruction" (Job 33:15-16). In the last devotion I talked about how we can't direct our dreams. In many dreams I either am trying to accomplish something that seems endless and far away or I am trying to escape something that is disconcerting to my spirit. I so much want to be able to yell, "cut" so I can stop and rid myself of the last scene.

Once an unpleasant scene emerges, you can't forget it right away. It may not be carved into your psyche but it has left an impression on your emotions, leaving you a bit uncertain about the meaning or purpose of the dream.

Like our disconcerting dreams, we would all like to be able to determine where the current of life will take us to ensure the outcome. We want to feel good about our life in the midst of darkness, corruption, and death. However, life is not meant to be a sight-seeing tour, an amusement park, or an ongoing vacation that serves our pleasures and satisfies our desires.

We must remember if we are in Christ, He is in control of the current of our life and instead of trying to figure out how to try to control the current or step out of the cycle onto some sideroad, we need to lean back in faith and trust the Lord as to where the current is taking us.

Life is meant to be experienced and its current is meant to bring us to places of spiritual maturity. However, in these uncharted territories I have discovered the level of my faith towards God and the integrity of my character; and, when it comes to experiencing this life, it brings many rewards with it, mainly that at every place of growth I see my sweet Jesus with greater clarity.

Prayer: Lord, I know any successful spiritual journey will lead to a greater revelation of You. Keep me from straying from the narrow path and taking rabbit trails of vanity that leave me empty and frustrated. Amen.

June 22

"Who hath delivered us from the power of darkness, and hath translated us into the kingdom of his dear Son" (Colossians 1:13). There are days that mark certain anniversaries. This day is one that stands out the most to me. On this day in 1965, my whole life changed.

I can remember the sights, the sounds, the people, and the happenings that forever changed the direction of my life. The happening surrounded my mother marrying my stepfather.

On that day my brother and I suddenly found ourselves being delivered from a shadowy existence into a new world. The divorce of our parents had taken away innocence and flung us into a world of darkness and despair. We tasted many things from loneliness, to rejection, and fear, as well as witnessed sick games and moral compromise. Without knowing it we developed emotional mechanisms to survive the dark maze we found ourselves in.

Our new stepfather gave us hope and our new life opened up a new world of adventure, discovery, and purpose. I often relate that change to the wonderful change that took place in my life when I was delivered from the kingdom of darkness and translated into the kingdom of light upon receiving Jesus Christ as my Lord and Savior.

Salvation is not just about being saved from darkness, but it is also about being translated into a new life. "Translated" means to be carried away or exchanged. In essence, salvation is about gaining a whole new life in Christ.

Prayer: Lord, it is easy to stop at the place of being delivered from darkness, but we have been given a chance to exchange the old for a new life in You. This means I now can walk in the light. Forgive Your people for stopping at the gate of salvation while failing to enter into a new life. Amen.

June 23

"For ye have not received the spirit of bondage again to fear; but ye have received the Spirit of adoption, whereby we cry, Abba Father" (Romans 8:15). Yesterday I spoke of a new life opening up to me through the marriage of my mother to my stepfather. That identification with my new life in Christ did not just stop with salvation but continued on in many other ways.

For instance, I always accredited my stepfather with making another relationship possible—that being with my Heavenly Father. Because of my relationship with my stepfather, I no longer had vague notions about the care and protection of a loving father, but I actually knew what it looked like and the type of attitude it produced in me towards him.

For many Christians the bondage that keeps them from growing in their relationship with the Lord has to do with their images, notions and ideas produced in them by an unhealthy, wrong, or perverted relationship with their biological father. The trust factor is often missing and it puts them in a bondage that is tormenting.

We can only come to the Father by Jesus and nothing will happen or occur unless it goes through Christ. For those who are uncertain of the parental relationship with God, you can trust the way that opens the door to it and the Holy Spirit that leads you into that wondrous and glorious relationship. Jesus would not let anything corrupt pass His way and the Holy Spirit would not lead you into anything perverted and wrong.

Prayer: Lord, thank You for providing the way to our wonderful adoption into a glorious family who is headed by the most loving and compassionate Father. Amen.

June 24

"The people which sat in darkness saw a great light; and to them which sat in the region and shadow of death light is sprung up" *(Matthew 4:16).* Much of life becomes a blur. It seems that we are on a fast-moving train that leaves our head spinning because we would like to slow everything down so we can enjoy the scenery. Sadly, much joy is missing even for some Christians because the surrounding darkness is becoming great.

The problem with darkness is our eyes can adjust to it and as long as we can see something, we think we are seeing. It is true we might be seeing something, but in what form? Jesus said that darkness is light to those who are blinded by the evilness of the age they are living in. These individuals will insist that what they are seeing is light and truth, when in reality it is darkness and perversion.

Jesus is the great light who came into the world and until that light penetrates the darkness of our soul, we will only be looking into darkness that possess outlines of what we think we see, forms of that which will prove to be vague, and lifeless concepts that will lack true dimension. The light of Jesus will bring clarity to what is real, liberty through truth that will set free, and joy to those who clearly possesses the great hope of heaven.

Prayer: Lord, like every Gentile before me, I walked in darkness, but praise God, Your great light penetrated the darkness upon my soul and now I see what is true when I look to You, what is so in Your Word, and what will be so in Your promises. Amen.

June 25

"And the voice spake unto him again the second time What God hath cleansed that call not thou common" (Acts 10:15). Names, names and more names. As I mentioned before as I consider that which proves inspirational to me through the years, I can't help but think of the people that have left some nugget, valuable lessons, or examples behind. The lessons may not always be pleasant and the examples honorable, but God can use both to bring some needed wisdom and sobriety to our lives.

Most of the names you will read in this book are common, but behind each one is a person that is unique in their own way. They have played different parts in my life and serve as part of the mosaic that comprises my life. They may only comprise a small piece in my life, but without that dab of color here, that defined mark there, or that impression back when, there would be no dimension to my life.

As you read these people's names, they will remain faceless to you, but my goal is to highlight the fact that they are individuals who may have common names but were not considered common when they came into my life. They left a bit of self behind, marked an event that clearly changed the landscape of my soul, or caused me to become wiser about life and people.

Faces may change, names fade, and memories lose their impression but there is one whose face through the years has become more defined to me, His name creates greater awe, His character remains unchangeable, and His ways certain and that is the Lord Jesus Christ. When Jesus does something through others to bring clarity to our lives, we must never refer to it as being common and lightly regard it.

Prayer: Lord, we so need to realize what You have touched and prepared for us to partake of so that we can come to maturity in our life in You. Thank You for preparing my path and placing the right people and challenges in it to bring me to perfection in You. Amen.

June 26

"But all things that are reproved are made manifest by the light: for whatsoever doth make manifest is light" (Ephesians 5:13). All too often we stop at what we think we know or what we think is common and insignificant. Unless something jumps out at us, most of the time we push people and events aside and give it no more thought that people do leave certain impressions on us, events dispense definite marks on the terrain of our souls, and memories can become a movie that can be replayed whenever there is something that sparks it.

We often fail to realize that some of the past becomes baggage we carry throughout our life. However, the baggage seems part of the natural makeup of the terrain of our soul.

When I was 35, the Lord began to highlight the baggage from my past that left me utterly overwhelmed as to what seemed like the magnitude of it. He started to reveal how the baggage of the past had affected my attitude, the decisions I made, and the traps I would fall into because I was blindsided by it. After all, not only was I blindsided to the temptation dangling before me, but when I tried to step back to consider the landscape, the traps did not look like traps. They seemed normal enough in the terrain, as they made logical sense to me; and, even though they may have not seemed right at the time, they did not seem completely wrong either. In other words, I could cloud the terrain with points of justification because of my past baggage that hid the danger that each trap held.

It is natural to think we are over things from the past. However, if those things that cling to the soul are not brought to the light so the Lord can bring His perspective to it, healing to our soul, and liberty to our spirit, we will find that such things will not only haunt us but set us up to fall into the subtle traps that have become part of the landscape of our inner being.

Prayer: Lord, I really do not know how much baggage from the past I am carrying, but I do know Satan can use it against me. Turn on the light, and identify such burdens, and set me free from them with Your truth as I cast each one to the side to possess all You have for me. Amen.

June 27

"For ye were sometimes darkness, but now are ye light in the Lord: walk as children of the light" (Ephesians 5:8). So much of our past can define us if we fail to recognize that Satan will use unresolved issues of the past to set us up. Whether they were wrong attitudes, sins, condemnation, or a traumatic event, in the right situation and at the right time, Satan can use them to entrap us in a world of guilt, regret, torment, condemnation, and hopelessness.

We must remember wherever there is darkness in our souls and lives, the enemy can work under cover to rob, kill, and destroy. Since he is not subject to time, he can lie and wait until the environment is right to ensnare us. It is for this reason we must ask the Lord to turn on the light.

King David asked the Lord to search him and expose any wicked way in him. He knew that he had no idea of the quality of his faith, the strength of his inner character, and the wrong attitudes that were lurking until they were revealed to him. After all, none of us think badly of ourselves because we do not start out to be wrong, do wrong, or become wrong, but because of our fallen disposition, we end on the wrong side of a matter.

The key to knowing the liberty of the Spirit is for the light to penetrate the darkness and expose anything that has been hidden. This is what allows us to truly walk in the light of our salvation and all the promises that are attached to it.

Prayer: Lord, thank You for delivering me from darkness and translating me into Your light. Lord, reveal both the way to walk in and the aspects of the inner character that needs to be delivered, set free, and healed. Amen.

June 28

Even elementary school-age children, at least way back when I was a kid, can come face to face with two of humanity's greatest problems which can be summed up in just two words—addiction and finances. This happened to be my problem when the sugar craving for penny candy was mounting because of no penny cash flow. What to do? Get a job. But I was too young to get a job, even babysitting, so I hatched a plan to become a door-to-door saleswoman (which turned out to be just one door in the end.) What to sell?

It had to be something that a neighbor would like to put into their home, like a bouquet of Mom's big, bright, beautiful Nasturtiums. About then, along came a neighbor girl. Not a close friend, mind you, but somebody to maybe talk to about my business venture. She eagerly nodded her approval, so after Mom gave her permission for both of us to pick a small handful of her lovely flowers, we both began picking. I wanted to present the very best product possible, so I took my time selecting certain blooms while the other girl carelessly snatched at the flowers, and without a word suddenly took off running up the street to our targeted customer who happened to be our best donator on Halloween.

By the time I got my bouquet put together and started up the street, the little opportunist was on her way home. Over seventy years later I can still recall the sinking feeling I had when the lady opened the door, saw me standing there with the brightly colored Nasturtiums, and told me that she already paid 5 cents to the "other girl" and shut the door.

Crushed and deflated, I went home to my mom who put the flowers in a small vase while trying to comfort me. Needless to say, I learned some valuable lessons that day, one of which was you can't trust everybody with your plans and ideas, and it's best to use wisdom and discretion around untrustworthy people.

It seems, however, that such hard lessons are often repeated through this life and are the ones God uses to instruct us in the world's fallen ways while helping us to learn that through prayer and His Word we can gain the victory through our Lord Jesus Christ. *"Fret not thyself because of evil-doers, neither be thou envious against the workers of iniquity" (Psalm 37:1).* – J. Haley

Prayer: Lord, You use the greatest disappointments in our lives to teach us the most valuable lessons. The question is will we learn the lesson and become enriched, or will we become bitter and spiritual beggars? I choose to gain the wisdom of heaven over wallowing in some miserable cesspool of the world. Amen.

June 29

"Pride goeth before destruction, and an haughty spirit before a fall" (Proverbs 16:18). I have been considering the prevailing mood that reveals our inner character. One of the prevailing moods that frequently makes its appearance is self-pity.

Self-pity finds its origins in the state of ingratitude. It comes from a skeptical attitude that life is a harsh intruder because it rips away the whimsical world of nonsense such people hold to. It cuts away the limbs that enable these individuals to swing from the unrealistic heights of fantasy, keeping them from facing reality.

Sadly, most of these individuals insist on maintaining their fantasy. They create emotional ropes that allow them to climb upon the branches of fanciful notions so as to reach a type of utopia. It is from these limbs that these individuals can do their flying trapeze act. However, it is a dangerous act and there is no net to catch them. Once the winds of reality knock them off of their branches of silliness, their fall proves to be great because it has happened from the heights of arrogance.

I have had my bouts with self-pity, but I realize how insidious it is. It is made insane by selfishness and made to look foolish by arrogance. I, for one, will do all I can to resist it and not fall into its deceptive traps. After all, for the Christian there is nothing to mourn for we possess a bit of heaven, the life of Christ. We are therefore more than conquerors in Him.

Prayer: Lord Jesus, it is so easy to become an Esau when it comes to tasting and reaping the bitter ways of life. However, this is Satan's world and we live under a curse that leaves bitterness in our mouths; that is, unless we know You. You are God's sweetness to each of us. Thank You for the taste of the sweetness of Your life. Amen.

June 30

"To the praise of the glory of his grace, wherein he hath made us accepted in the beloved" (Ephesians 1:6). Everyone who crosses your path has the potential to impact your life in some way. Of course, those who are part of the inner circle of your extended

family are the ones with the greatest capability to do so. Some of the people who influenced me most in my younger years were aunts and uncles.

My mother's sister, Frances, taught me about acceptance and boldness. She made up a big part of memory lane when I thought of past events. She was always there to share in the most defining moments of my life such as High School graduation. My mother and I had the great honor to lead her to Christ. She proved to be a bold witness and defender of the faith.

There is Aunt Marjorie that, even in spite of a divorce from my uncle, has continued to be a supportive member of the family. She has taught me the bond of family is deeper than biological, it is a matter of heart and commitment.

My biological father's sister Judithe had polio that left her one leg shorter than the other one. She taught me that you must not let loss or handicaps stop you from experiencing the fullness of life. My father's sister-in-law Joan quietly shared her grace and faith with me, leading to my salvation.

My step-father's sister-in-laws, Doris and Juanita, a Choctaw Indian, taught me that regardless of race and background, people are people after all. Granted they can add some flavor here and there and some interesting perspectives, but we are all part of the human race and we all need the Lord.

The dynamics of relationships reveal so much about our personal character. We are being constantly reminded that healthy relationships are forged and it takes the parties involved to make the necessary commitment to ensure the quality of each one of them.

We often get too caught up with what people do for us instead of what they have taught us along the way. The real benefit of relationships is that they become a mirror of who we presently are, a compass as to the direction we want to go as a person, and the type of person we want to become in the end.

Prayer: Lord, we minor in the temporary and fail to learn from that which is lasting, and in some cases eternal. Lord, help me to gain heavenly wisdom that learns the lesson while establishing a living memorial of that which is eternal. Amen.

JULY

July 1

"For I have given you an example, that ye should do as I have done to you" (John 13:15). Yesterday I spoke of my aunts, but I also had uncles who greatly touched and influenced my life. Since my mother's two brothers, Merlin and Byron Jensen were not much older than me, they initially influenced much of my taste for music. My Uncle Merlin and I were both Vietnam vets. However, he witnessed the nightmare of war and I witnessed the nightmares that often haunted those who returned from such a conflict. In spite of the nightmares of war, he maintained a boyish mischievousness, a sense of humor, and a simple curiosity towards life.

My Uncle Byron taught me that much of life comes down to decisions. He accomplished much because he dared to dream, work hard, and risk it all to bring about his goals. It all paid off as he brought forth the fruition of his dreams. Ultimately, he taught me one of the most important lessons, that the accomplishments of this world will often prove empty and that it comes back to the quality of relationships.

I had other uncles. There was my Uncle Red Binam who taught me courage not only entails being calm under pressure, but making sound judgments when everything is falling apart, and then becoming a sacrifice if necessary to ensure the well-being of others.

Uncle Bob Meuleman was a nice man and committed to my biological father's welfare, but the real impression I had of him was

219

based on some of his later decisions in life. He taught me it is not the good start that you are remembered for, but how you finish the race of life. My dad's other brother Perry Meuleman, was a quiet man who proved to be helpful at a very important time in life, showing me, it is not the amount of time that leaves us with life-changing examples, but those moments when someone really comes through for you.

My step-father's brother Conrad Kelley taught me a sense of humor adds the spice to life that keeps on giving, while his brother Max impressed upon me to consider my attitude towards life because it will determine my approach towards it.

Each uncle reminded me in one way or another, you can't let your past define you, your limitations keep you from dreams, or your excuses as a means to cop out when the way becomes rough and hard. You must forge ahead regardless of the giant obstacles and challenges ahead of you.

Each of these individuals gave me glimpses into Jesus' influence in my life. As a Christian no matter how we look at it, we are to make like impact in others' lives as Christ has made in ours.

The question is are we making such an impact?

Prayer: Lord, we start out with big ideas as to how to save the day with those we care about, but I have learned from You, You are the only One who can save the day and the souls of those we love. Amen.

July 2

If the Son therefore shall make you free, ye shall be free indeed (John 8:36). In a couple of days is the 4th of July. Starting on July 1st I begin to think about what it means to be free. When we celebrated our 200th birthday as a nation in 1976, I had just gotten out of the Navy. One lesson I learned is that the country is only as strong as the character of its leadership and as good as the moral compass of its people.

The 4th is the day where we traditionally celebrate our freedom as a nation, but the questions are, are we free and if we are, in what way are we free? There are different types of freedoms but what most people don't realize is that every type of freedom has come with some type of cost.

As Americans we recognize our freedom came with the great price that our ancestors paid. We know this basic freedom is based on two principles: the freedom of speech and the right to bear arms in order to protect ourselves from tyranny, whether from oppressive governments or from lawless thugs among us. We know the first one protects our religious freedoms, keeping us from suffering persecution for what we believe and proclaim, the second one gives us the right to protect our families, properties, and way of life without being subject to unfair prejudices, biases, and injustice. The first freedom requires honor and respect for others in spite of disagreement, while the second one calls for moral restraint to ensure order and respect of others' right to life, property, and way of life to ensure that same regard for ourselves.

Both of these freedoms are under siege through oppressive taxation that enslaves initiative, godless education and philosophies that enslave the mind, along with a minority that rage against any moral or ethical restraints that disciplines the soul. This brings us to the harsh reality that freedom is not free.

Prayer: Lord, our spiritual freedom to discover the abundance of life we have in You cost You Your best, Your all. The key is are we willing to give up that which enslaves us to know real freedom in our souls. Have mercy on me, oh Lord, for slavery has been a constant companion in the past and only You can set me free with Your truth. Amen.

July 3

"And ye shall know the truth, and the truth shall make you free"
(John 8:32). In July I do a countdown to the 4ᵗʰ by meditating on
freedom. Through the years the people of America were told how
privileged they were because we were born in a free nation. I can't
tell you how many times patriotism would swell up within me when
the idea of that freedom was in some way threatened.

Freedom is a beautiful sounding word, but few know what it
feels like. When they think of freedom, it is in terms of doing what
they always wanted to do but couldn't because they lived under
tyranny or in light of laws or moral codes. However, we must
consider whether the people who see freedom in this term really
understand the true nature of it. Real freedom is not about doing
what you want to do, but having the freedom to do what is right
according to conscience, religious convictions, and honorable
conduct.

True freedom is a right and not a privilege. There are different
types of bondage such as spiritual oppression, emotional
enslavement, mental entrapment, and persecution. The greatest
bondage does not come from the tyrannical governments and
leaders of the world but from the bondage within our souls, minds,
and emotions.

This is why freedom is attached to truth and not deliverance
from some physical oppression. What I had to understand is that
America was not all that free, and that it is the bondage from within
that causes man the greatest despair in his soul. It is God's truth
that unlocks the prison doors, and loosens the shackles and
chains from off hearts, minds, and souls.

It cost Jesus His life to secure real freedom. Do we have to pay
some price to obtain it? Yes! Our cost is those things that enslave
us and are not beneficial to us. However, those things that enslave
us can represent small patches of nothing that we hold on to

because that is all we know. That is the worst bondage of all. It is the bondage of fear and unbelief.

Prayer: Lord, we believe that our notions about freedom are correct, but the oppression we taste tells a different story. The man that has the greatest liberty is one who You have set free with Your truth and Your life. Thank You Lord for setting me free from myself. Amen.

July 4

"For when ye were the servants of sin, ye were free from righteousness" (Romans 6:20). The truth is man is born into slavery. To Satan he is a mere slave to the systems of his world to do his bidding as he requires loyalty and worship. To wicked governments, man is nothing but a serf that is here to serve its evil agendas which requires one's soul, and to wicked leaders he is nothing more than an indispensable pawn that can be sacrificed at any time to feed their lust for power. These tyrannical leaders control through ignorance, fear, and intimidation which requires man to give up his right to pursue the life he desires so he can live under their miserable control and oppression.

There may be different kinds of freedom promoted in this world, but if a man is a slave to Satan, a serf to the world and a pawn in the hands of the wicked, he is a slave to all. There is only one place of freedom and it involves freedom from being a slave, serf, and pawn that can be readily sacrificed, and that is the spiritual liberty that is found in Jesus Christ. This liberty came with a great cost: God, out of love, gave His best, and His Son out of grace gave His all.

Jesus' death on the cross gave us the freedom to choose who we serve and how we serve. Our level of service will determine how free we are to worship God in Spirit and Truth. If you do not possess this wondrous spiritual freedom this 4th of July, instead of celebrating a veneer of freedom, choose the real freedom that came by way of an old rugged cross.

Prayer: Lord, I know what it feels like to be a slave to sin, a serf in this corrupt world, and a pawn in the hands of a few wicked tyrants and bullies. I was miserable but when I realized my sin, I called out to you in desperation to be delivered and be saved from it, You reached down and saved me out of the darkness. It was then that I realized I was blind to my slavery and it was also then that I felt the first glorious breaths of freedom and tasted its sweetness. Thank You for my true liberation. Amen.

July 5

The small, soft, white stuff that was furiously flitting, fluttering and flying horizontally past the window brought to mind an incoming blizzard. But the problem was the temperature outside hovered around 80 degrees in spite of periodic gusts of wind.

Perhaps it was a bug invasion I thought to myself as I stepped out to see just what had been unleashed on our neighborhood. The tiny invaders seemed to possess a fierce determination to fulfill their destination, but I finally managed to grasp one. Aha! There it was, a tiny little weed seed dangling from its gauzy "parachute."

But weed or no weed, I had to admire in awestruck wonder the greatness of God whose wisdom and power has created an endless array of visible and invisible things to discover, study and bring glory and honor to Himself. This seemingly harmless "invasion" caused me to think, though, how little unbidden thoughts that "softly blow" through our minds sometimes can lead to little sins.

Just as little weed seeds resemble harmless bits of fluff, if we're not quick to recognize them for what they are, they can take root, grow and eventually take over. A little lie leads to greater lies, a little rebellion leads to all-out rebellion, a little doubt can lead to disbelief, and a little wrong decision can lead to a totally destructive lifestyle.

The Bible warns us, *"For to be carnally minded is death; but to be spiritually minded is life and peace" (Romans 8:6).* - J. Haley

Prayer: Lord, Your Word reminds us of the utter failure of man to get it right outside of You. All of his understanding leads to darkness, his ways to death, and his practices to destruction. Have mercy on us oh Lord, for our frame is weak, our minds perverted, and our ways foolish. Amen.

July 6

"Though he slay me, yet will I trust in him: but I will maintain mine own ways before him (Job 13:15). I was meditating on Job today. If there was a person who exhibited the steps of faith during his grave trial of temptation, it was Job. Job revealed that there are six steps in faith before one can come to rest in the Lord. These steps include: the assurance of faith, the hope of faith, the expectation of faith, the reality of faith, the declaration of faith, and the fruit of faith.

The assurance of faith can be found in Job's choice to trust the Lord no matter what circumstances challenged his abiding confidence in his Creator. He knew that by trusting the Lord he would not be ashamed for believing in Him. His faith in Him would be confirmed and in the end, he would be able to defend or maintain his ways before the Lord because they were based on genuine faith towards Him.

I know, according to Scripture, that God reckons such confidence as being righteous. Therefore, Job stood upright before the Lord in the midst of his fiery trial.

Prayer: Lord, I thank You for Your timeless examples. They teach us we can overcome this present world by trusting You with our circumstances. Amen.

July 7

"For I know that my redeemer liveth, and that he shall stand at the latter day upon the earth: And though after my skin worms destroy this body, yet in my flesh shall I see God" (Job 19:25-26). In yesterday's meditation I talked about the steps of faith that were spotlighted in Job's fiery test. The first step was the assurance of faith.

This particular step is a choice. I must choose to trust the character of God in a matter and not the circumstances. After all, God is not distinguished by the great things He does; rather, He stands distinct because He is God. Everything He does is a natural extension of who He is. He does not do things because He is powerful, He does things because it is consistent with who He is as Almighty God. It is in line with His character, ways, timing, and plan.

The next step is the hope of faith. Faith is designed to cause us to look upward and remember the promise of hope. This hope is that we are simply sojourners on our way to a better city and a more excellent existence.

Job made mention of this glorious hope when he referred to the resurrection power that would raise him up on that last day to bring him face to face with his Redeemer. The hope of faith operates within the "Amen Factor." The Lord promised it;

therefore, it will be a reality in due time for it is so. In the end, such faith will assure me that I will see the Lord.

Prayer: Lord, I want to possess the same perspective as Abraham. He was looking beyond this world to a city You made. I too want that vision. I know the world will become dimmer in light of Your light and presence. Amen.

July 8

"But he knoweth the way that I take: when he hath tried me, I shall come forth as gold" (Job 23:10). The steps of faith can be challenging. They reveal where our real source of reliance is. Is it with self, the world, or God? As a believer, I would like to think that my reliance is in God, but in the fiery test I often discover that my faith has been foolishly placed elsewhere. This is an important matter because where I place my faith will determine whether I will endure the trial.

This brings me to the importance of the expectation of faith. Faith expects a matter to come to completion. It does not hope it will turn out well or will bring glory to God, it knows with unwavering confidence that it will be brought forth in the most admirable way. It walks in expectation of experiencing the excellence in the matters of heaven.

Job knew that God understood the way he had to travel to bring out the best in his faith and life. He believed that in the end he would come out possessing the faith that would endure to the finish, and that his character would be refined in greater ways.

In times of trial the expectation of faith can become quite tarnished, but in the end, it will come forth as pure gold. Ultimately, it will reflect the beauty of heavenly glory that is established in the refining fires of God.

Prayer: Lord, faith will lead us in some hard places, but in the end, it will bring us to that which is excellent: It will bring us to a greater revelation of You. Amen.

July 9

"Behold, I am vile; what shall I answer thee? I will lay mine hand upon my mouth" (Job 40:4). I have been considering the steps of faith. Faith will always lead each of us as believers to the reality or truth of a matter. We must come to this place if we are going to advance forward. Otherwise, we find ourselves barely keeping our heads above water. It is faith that allows us to face a matter head on in order to grab a hold of the only lifesaver available to each of us.

In Job's fiery test, he wrestled with the "whys" of his situation. He had done it right in regard to maintaining a right status before the Lord. Each time he wrestled with the situation he encountered greater darkness. Nothing made sense to him. All he could do was trust what he knew about the character of God.

However, when the light of understanding finally came on, Job did not see himself in light of personal righteousness, but in light of who God is. It was at this time that Job realized how inept, and far removed he was when it came to understanding God.

The reality of faith will bring us to an awareness of our great need for God. It will not condemn us, but it will put us in our place of weakness and vulnerability. At such times we will come out with the awareness of God's greatness, and the reality of our smallness.

Prayer: Lord, I am so small before You, but even in Your greatness I know that You fill those areas of smallness in me to lift me up in You. Thank You for being faithful. Amen.

July 10

'I have heard of thee by the hearing of the ear: but now mine eye seeth thee" (Job 42:5). I have been dealing with the steps of faith. It is interesting how far down we must come in order to develop a total reliance on the Lord.

We start out in light of self-sufficiency only to realize how inept we are to control our worlds. We have hope in our abilities, only to discover there is no power in them to bring a matter about. We have an expectation that all will turn out well for us in the end, but in the end, we realize that our expectation is unrealistic and misplaced. We strive hard to bring reality into line with what we declare about the matters of life, only to discover such declarations are nothing more than wishful thinking.

Job had been brought low by the sorrowful losses of life. He realized that no one was immune from tasting the bitterness of the curse that came upon every one of us through Adam. However, he also knew that his God was real, living, and aware of his plight. Because of his faith towards God, the Lord could reveal Himself to Him.

This brings us to the declaration of faith. Genuine faith will cause you to see God in greater ways. Job had an understanding of God, but when faith allowed him to see the Lord, his perception of Him was revolutionized. He would never be the same for he would never look at the Lord in the same way.

As a believer, I do not want to be content with what I have heard about the Lord, I want to see Him so that my understanding of Him will be enlarged as He goes deeper with the intent of bringing me higher in Him.

Prayer: Lord, I have heard a lot about You, but it was not until I caught glimpses of You in Your majesty that You become more real and living to me. Lord, I beseech You, show me Your glory. Amen.

July 11

"...the LORD said to Eliphaz the Temanite, My wrath is kindled against thee, and against thy two friends: for ye have not spoken of me the thing that is right, as my servant Job hath" (Job 42:5b). I have been considering the steps of faith. Faith leads us to discover God in greater measure. Faith will declare in the end that it has seen God. It will be humbled by His holiness and in awe of His power.

This leads us to the fruit of faith: that of being reckoned as righteous. Job's companions perceived that they were correct in their conclusion about Job's plight. They based this on their theology about God.

Their theology may have given them some understanding about God, but it did not reveal His heart or His ways to them in this particular matter. Their theology made them self-righteous and judgmental in their attitudes. They became indifferent towards Job as they improperly judged him.

When Job's great testing was over, the Lord made it clear that Job was right about Him, and they were wrong in their conclusions about what was going on. It is at this point you realize that Job was reckoned or counted as being in right standing because of his faith towards the Lord. He did not let go of what he knew about the Lord's character.

It is natural to regard what is happening instead of the character of God. Unpleasant events do not confirm a person's plight; rather, they are meant to test people's faith in order to reveal their real heart attitude.

Prayer: Lord, the matters of life have always tested my attitude about You and others. Lord, I don't want to be exalted in my understanding; rather, I want to be humbled by the reality of You. Help me to pass the different tests for Your name's sake. Amen.

July 12

I have a confession to make. Not long ago, while struggling to pour the special health drink I make through a sieve from an 8-cup measuring pitcher, I complained out loud, to myself, about the way "they just don't make things the way they used to." To be honest with you, if rewards were given out for the most articulate "complainer" I just might win the prize. In other words, I'm good at it. Of course, as a Christian, that means guilt followed by some repentance.

Nevertheless, in this case, I did have a valid point! Pitchers (of any size) don't pour nicely like the old-fashioned ones with bigger spouts do. And, that, as most of us know, goes for a long list of other things from small kitchen items to all kinds of appliances, vehicles, tools, building supplies, houses, and the list is endless. It's just downright depressing. Besides, the world is a big place, so how can a regular person who is just trying to survive it all without going nuts manage to "survive?"

Here's what happened, and to me it was straight out of heaven—a very personal "touch" from God, that brought tears to my eyes at how awesome, great, and intimately personal He is with His children. A couple of days after my little complaining spiel, our Gospel soloist and co-worker, Carrie, drove the hour-distance to a town to shop and visit a sister in the Lord to help her with a tech issue.

Now, keep in mind that neither of them knew of my "pitcher pouring problem," so when this sister, out of the blue, asked Carrie if we could use an old big glass pitcher that she was going to put in a thrift store, Carrie felt prompted to say "Yes" and brought it home to me.

When she came in and handed that pitcher to me, I almost burst into tears, for I knew that it was another of God's little reminders of how very close He always is, and He knows exactly "what we have need of." Jesus said, *"But even the very hairs of your head are all numbered. Fear not therefore: ye are of more value than many sparrows" (Luke 12:7).* – J. Haley

Prayer: Lord, I know You are faithful and even hear my complaints because You meet me in the smallest ways which proves to me You are aware of little old me, complaining or not. Clearly, out of grace You meet me in the smallest but glorious ways that remind me You love me and care for me. Amen.

July 13

"Now there arose up a new king over Egypt, which knew not Joseph" (Exodus 1:8). Have you followed the generations in the Bible? To many they think it is all quite boring and it can be if you are not considering what it says about certain tribes and individuals.

As I read this Scripture, I remember how each generation grows up with less and less of a sense and knowledge of God. There have been great moves of God in this country in the past, but because the generation that lived during those moves can't pass on the vision, are unable to share the passion, or failed to keep the revelation distinct with faith and godliness, it can prove to be hard to pass on a lighted torch to the next generation.

Each generation must have its own encounter with God, but the question is how did the last generation know God, and what did they pass on? Consider the generation that is taking the reins in this country. It appears to have no real good or substantial knowledge of God. In many cases it is void of any real light, passion, or conviction when it comes to God.

The generation we have now is a product of the digression of past generations. The present generation has become lost in the philosophy of the "me" generation where there is no consensus of integrity, respect, and sacrifice. This generation has been swallowed in the whirlpool of nothingness where reality is fragile, the selfishness of "me" is everything, where the great idol "I" demands to be obeyed, and the declaration of "my" way is the only way that counts regardless of the devastation it leaves behind.

Can this self-serving generation be saved? I believe there are heirs of salvation in this generation, but is it desperate enough to hear the warnings of a Joseph about the future famine, open enough to heed the instructions of a Moses about the Passover Lamb, aware enough to respond to a John the Baptist warning to repent and flee the wrath of God that is coming, and become broken enough to receive the instruction of Christ to repent or perish?

The Bible speaks of the last generation. In years past God has passed over generations to bring forth His plan, but if this is the last generation, there will be no upcoming generations that will come to fruition before the great judgment falls on the earth. Let that truth sink into our souls and spirits. As Paul stated, *"Today is the day of salvation" (2 Corinthians 6:2).*

Prayer: Lord, we live in a day of itching ears that do not want to hear anything that will not suit a fragile frame of reference that insists on standing upon the ground of shifting sand. Lord, I choose to love truth, trust Your character, and believe Your Word regardless of how unpleasant it may be now, for in the end it will prove to be sustaining and glorious. Amen

July 14

"Be not deceived; God is not mocked: for whatsoever a man soweth, that shall he also reap" (Galatians 6:7). Yesterday I talked about generations that are fed on the bread of ignorance, delusion, and seduction. Such generations are often brought to the height of abundance through the sacrifice of others without understanding there is a cost to possess that which is valuable. As a result, such a generation fails to develop character, the attitude of gratitude, and a willingness to sacrifice all to gain what is truly honorable and important.

The fruits of such a generation leave some to examine this matter. The question is simple, "how is it that this generation does not know God?" It comes down to the conditioning of the world, the indoctrination of education, and the visible church dropping the ball of truth to get along with the world. In other words, the attitude of a generation is determined by that which is the predominate influence in their lives. If the world becomes the dominate influence, the authority of parents will be undermined, and moral and ethical influences often adjust to fit a more tolerant attitude.

How do we know that man's digression begins and ends the same way? Because God and man never changes. It has to do with history repeating itself, revealing the digression of man into a chaotic cesspool or moral degradation.

It is obvious that much of this generation taking the reins of society don't know history. They don't seem to care to know what is really happening around them because of the ignorance that is present and the many sins that are being whitewashed by vain philosophies. They are unaware that a train of destruction is coming at them with such velocity that they will be quickly taken away in wrath. They have no concern about the eternity that follows because everything has been fudged and made acceptable to every taste bud, whether religious or secular.

This indictment that is being leveled at this nation will always fall at the feet of the past generations either valuing vanity over substance, preferring darkness over light, substituting righteousness with worldly tolerance, and chasing after the temporary while losing sight of the eternal. However, with the indictment comes a bitter cup of reaping the consequences for not just the past generations, but the present one as well.

Prayer: Lord, Your first command of discipleship is not picking up the cross, rather it is denying self. Oh, how we like to ignore the call to put down self, while jumping over that particular step and nobly picking up the cross. However, the work of the cross will be nullified in our lives unless we first deny self and give the cross a platform to be erected as a means to cross out the old life. It is Your perfect order and one we need to adhere to. Amen.

July 15

"For the LORD God is a sun and shield: the LORD will give grace and glory: no good thing will be withhold from them that walk uprightly" (Psalm 84:11). Saints have many promises that they can walk in. However, they must obediently walk out the righteous ways of God to possess them.

One such promise for the saint entails walking in the light of Christ. The light will protect and keep believers from falling into traps. In a way the light serves as a shield that guides our steps, but it also becomes a barrier to the ungodly. In a sense it becomes intense darkness to them to the point that they cannot even see where God's people are located. Because of the great darkness they walk in, they become blinded by the light.

At such times the Lord is showing His grace to His people who are often hidden in plain sight. He does not have to protect us. He does not have to save us, but He does. In so doing, He will reveal His glory to us in such situations.

As a believer, I am indeed blessed with all that I need to get through this present world. As a result, there will be no excuse as to why I would not finish the course set before me.

Prayer: Lord, You have prepared the way for me. However, I must walk in such a way that I will not veer off course. It is easy to take my eyes off of You and lose sight of where You are leading me. Keep my feet on the right course. Amen.

July 16

"And the angel of the LORD appeared unto him in a flame of fire out of the mist of a bush: and he looked, and behold the bush burned with fire, and the bush was not consumed. And Moses said, I will now turn aside, and see this great sight, why the bush is not burnt" (Exodus 3:2-3). Every time I come to this part of the Scriptures, I have to pause to consider how Moses turned aside to consider the burning bush. I sometimes wonder if I missed the opportunity to turn aside in order to speak with my Lord.

Moses was in the midst of a barren wilderness, tending sheep, doing what we consider to be mundane activities. He was not expecting anything out of the extraordinary to happen. Yet, he sees a burning bush that is not being consumed by the fiery presence of the heavenly.

I sometimes wonder if God needs to throw a burning bush my way so I will turn aside to meet with Him. How much do I tarry before Him in prayer, wait for Him to speak, and prepare myself to get up to do His business instead of carrying on my regular activities?

However, the other part of this incident is that once Moses turned aside to see the bush, that is when the Lord called out to him. The reality is that until we turn aside from our normal activities, the Lord is unable to call us because we are not prepared to hear Him.

It is rude to not turn aside when someone calls you, but how many times has the Lord called us, but we failed to turn aside because we had more pressing matters to deal with, yet there is no greater matter than our relationship with the Lord. Clearly, to hear we must truly be facing the one who is speaking.

Prayer: Lord, we are overwhelmed by the many obstacles before us, but occasionally You will send a "burning bush" our way to cause us to turn aside to hear what You have to say. However, I have to wonder if I am missing something because I have not allowed You to consume what is vain while waiting before You in prayer. We know You will move each obstacle aside when asked, and allow us to cross over the Red Sea into Your promises based on Your preparation and timing. Amen.

July 17

It came as a bit of a shock early one morning when I looked out the window to find they were all gone! After all, I had just planted the beautiful coral impatiens the day before, and it seemed to be the perfect solution for the pansy-petunia problem in one particularly well-shaded planter.

In it the petunia had languished from absence of direct sunshine during the day, and the pansy wasn't happy with the hot summer temperatures. To be sure, just because some little visiting deer during the night enjoyed the colorful snack, it didn't mean it was the end of the world. End of the world or not, however, it still didn't make me happy.

The whole gardening thing at our house, and then this incident, brought to mind just how challenging life is in general, and also painted a picture of the Christian life in particular. Jesus never promised His followers that life in this world would be a "bed of roses" in some happy "peaceful paradise" from start to finish. On the contrary, He said that He was sending us forth as "sheep among wolves," and that we would be persecuted, slandered, shunned, and sometimes martyred—that there would be trouble and tribulation.

It would be nice if we could just wish the devil away by pretending that he wasn't real, but the truth remains that Satan is the "god of this world" who comes as a thief to "steal, and to kill, and to destroy." (See *2 Corinthians 4:4; John 10:10*.) But praise the Lord! In the midst of all the turbulence of this present world, we have such promises as this: *"For which cause we faint not; but though our outward man perish, yet the inward man is renewed day by day. For our light affliction, which is but for a moment, worketh for us a far more exceeding and eternal weight of glory; While we look not at the things which are seen, but at the things which are not seen: for the things which are seen are temporal; but the things which are not see are eternal" (2 Corinthians 4:16-18).*

So, when the flowers vanish and hope begins to fade, turn your eyes upon Jesus and the eternal glory that awaits us. – J. Haley

Prayer: Lord, when it comes to this world our heart will fail, our eyes will land on darkness, our ears will tingle from hopelessness, and our minds will become a muddled mess of fear and confusion. However, I know Lord if I look up, the light of Your life will part the darkness, warm the heart, and cause me to remember the good news You brought to this dying world. Amen.

July 18

"Speak; for thy servant heareth" (1 Samuel 3:10c). Sometimes I suffer from a bit of insomnia. My normal practice is to get up and go into the living room, sit in my personal chair, and for the most part try to have a productive prayer time.

In order to see where I am going in the dark, I turn on the light in the dining room to retrieve such things as water. However, I realize that the lights can hinder the environment of prayer. The truth is we do not need to see the physical world around us at such times, but we do need to hear the still small voice of the Spirit to see into the spiritual realm.

It became obvious to me that to see in the spiritual realm, I needed silence to calm the soul and direct my attention and open my spiritual ears of faith. It was then that I remembered the greater the darkness, the greater the silence.

It dawned on me that even lights emit a sound. Granted, you cannot hear any real sound coming from them, but they can serve as an alarm clock by stimulating your brain in such a way that your mind cannot come into a calm place. Instead of your ears being open, your mind comes alive with thoughts surrounding activities and challenges.

Today we live in great spiritual darkness. We may not see things, but the darkness is encompassed by various obscure noises that create unrest in our spirit. It is clear we need our soul to be enlightened and not the physical eyes. Through the darkness, I eventually came to understand why God's light sometimes creates the greatest darkness in our souls. He is waiting for us to say, "Speak Lord, for I am ready to hear." How we need to hear what the Spirit of God is saying in these dark, trying times!

Prayer: Lord, I must be ready to hear You speak. Help me to know how to prepare myself to hear what Your Spirit is saying. Amen.

July 19

"When a prophet speaketh in the name of the LORD, if the thing follow not, nor come to pass, that is the thing which the LORD hath not spoken, but the prophet hath spoken it presumptuously; Thou shall not be afraid of him" (Deuteronomy 18:22). Many religious people think they know how something will play out when it comes to the prophecies of the Bible. Granted, we know certain things are going to happen because God's Word states so, but how they will be brought forth really rests with the sovereignty, ways, and plans of God.

The truth is that many of the conclusions we have about how the prophetic will play out are nothing but the theories of others that may turn out to be presumptuous. These theories may find some semblance in the Word of God, but how many of those conclusions have been revealed and confirmed by the Spirit and how many of them are based on man's limited understanding of what he was told by others was going to occur? In essence, how much of our understanding comes down to pieces of a puzzle that others have tried to logically insert into prophecies according to what they think it should look like when it actually happens?

The question is, how seriously can we take our understanding about that which is prophetic? Every prophetic detail must come together to confirm something is of God. Prophecy must interpret the events to see if everything is lining up according to the whole picture as revealed in Scripture in order to discern where we are as to the days we live in. In fact, looking back at what is happening helps us to see whether all prophecies are falling into place or not.

Prophecy may be about the future, but for those who are living in the midst of prophecy, they sometimes must walk through it before they realize that something is being fulfilled. Today we are living in prophetic times and more than ever we need to examine if we have bought misguided presumptions or whether we are prepared to properly discern the times.

Discernment is priceless if we are going to stand in the midst of great darkness holding high the light of truth, or whether we come under a heavy cloud of disillusionment because of misguided presumption.

Prayer: Lord it is easy to get caught up with presumption about the prophetic. It seems logical because it is based on limited knowledge that is either adjusted to what makes sense to us or it leaves us clutching onto wishful thinking, but the prophetic is to prepare us to stand on what is true while holding up the light of Your promises. Thank you for Your unchangeable Word. Amen.

July 20

"Howbeit when he, the Spirit of truth, is come, he will guide you into all truth: for he shall not speak of himself; but whatsoever he shall hear, that shall he speak: and he will shew you things to come" (John 16:15). It is natural to dissect prophecy with our limited theology, read the commentaries from respected Bible teachers to confirm what we have already been conditioned to believe, and interpret it based on indoctrination that has a particular emphasis or slant to it.

We may not be wrong or far off base, but the problem is we are looking for matters to play out according to our limited understanding. While we are looking one way, we may MISS what God is doing around us according to His way.

Since we can't imagine how some prophecies will play out concerning the times we are living in, we must be enlightened by the Holy Spirit as to the validity of our understanding and interpretation of the events that are happening before our eyes. We must keep in mind, only the Holy Spirit will show us things to come and make sense out of it.

We must also keep in mind that we see in part, and the prophecy we have is also in part. The truth is, we know very little when it comes to what is really happening in the spiritual realm where all matters are taking place in the unseen realm. Therefore, we must realize much of our theology on prophetic happenings will prove to be theories based on the changing times and not a matter of truth. We must come back to the simplicity of what is being said in God's Word and embrace it as being so in order to grab hold of His promises. Keep in mind, you can't take hold of promises if you are clinging to the fragile limb of theology.

We are told that the Holy Spirit will shew us the things that are coming. He is the one who must reveal how matters will be played out or whether they are being played out according to prophecy. We must not try to fit prophecy into our theological understanding; rather, we must allow prophecy to interpret whether all the events are coming together, while waiting for the Holy Spirit to illuminate how each event is lining up to the complete picture presented in Scripture.

The key to the Holy Spirit revealing a matter to us is we must be willing to hear what the Spirit is saying to us. Sometimes we are so busy clinging to what we have been told that we are not interested in what the Spirit is trying to tell us in regard to the days we live in. It is time to let go of the fragile limbs of what we have been conditioned to believe in order to grab a hold of what the Holy Spirit wants to reveal to us about the days we live in so that we can stand in these trying times

Prayer: Lord, we often stand in confidence on what we have been told by others instead of standing sure on Your Word and trusting the Holy Spirit to show us what we need to understand in the days we live in. Lord, I don't want to be grabbing at empty air in the end; rather, I want to be soaring in Your Spirit which will take me above it all and give me Your perspective. Amen.

July 21

"For we know in part and we prophesy in part" *(1 Corinthians 13:9)*. How many times has the Lord shown you something and then you found out down the line what He showed you was correct, but your interpretation of it missed the mark? I have had this happen a couple of times, and I must say it was a humbling experience each time and it caused me to go back to the drawing board as to where I missed it.

What I discovered is that God would show me one aspect of a matter, leaving out some of the details. One's tendency is to logically fill in the blanks, however, God's thoughts and ways are not our thoughts and ways.

It was at such times, I quickly discovered that I indeed knew in part, and past that is a vast region of speculation where I must trust the Lord to work out the unknown details until the Holy Spirit reveals what is so; or, I could end up going in the opposite direction and simply wander in its darkness while grasping at what it all means. Although God does not lose credibility when misinterpretations cloud the issue, for He is always right, my misinterpretation based on logic, assumption, or presumption will receive a black eye, discrediting my take on it and casting a shadow of suspicion and doubt on my credibility.

This brings me back to how man's interpretation about the matters of God often proves to be a mistranslation. God will show us what we need to know, but past the knowing is the unknown, and since it is natural for us to fill in the blanks with what we perceive to be logical conclusions, such conclusions often end up becoming presumptions based on the idea that our conclusions or theories can't possibly be wrong.

Prayer: Lord, anytime we humans try to put our take on a matter, we can quickly become lost or end up looking foolish because we really do not know the matters of Your kingdom. I choose to trust You with Your kingdom affairs. Amen.

July 22

"In hope of eternal life, which God, that cannot lie, promised before the world began" (Titus 1:2). Through the years reality has collided with my assumed beliefs about certain things such as Satan, the end days, and salvation matters. What I was encountering was not lining up to the interpretation I had presumed was correct. After all, it made perfect sense to me when explained, but reality was not only giving some of my assumptions a black eye, but it proved to be a complete knock out for many of them.

God never lies and when there is a discrepancy, it comes down to man's interpretation of His prophecies and truth, but many times the Lord gets the blame when the interpretations do not pan out according to man's theories. Sadly, some of these interpretations have been made into what we call "doctrines" and taught as if they are truths.

It is important that we discern if what we believe to be God's revelation is not man's interpretation. Keep in mind if the Spirit has not revealed a matter to your spirit and confirmed it with the Word of God that has been rightly divided, then you can't assume that such a teaching is valid or presume that it is truth and proclaim or teach others that it is so.

Prayer: Lord there is a fine line between presumption on man's part and Your unchangeable truth. I know that the line is made up of arrogance and pride. On one side of the line is the arrogance of presumption that this assumption is so at the present and will prove to be so in the end. On the other side is humility that declares what is not of the Spirit and truth is a lie and is WRONG; therefore, I have no choice but to choose the right side of heaven. Amen.

July 23

"This know also, that in the last days, perilous times shall come" (2 Timothy 3:1). No one would disagree that we live in perilous times. It can all prove to be quite overwhelming. We do not want to think the worst of this life, but we must be honest about what is going on in the world to be prepared spiritually.

Realistically looking about will cause hope to wane as the darkness becomes greater. We would all like to believe all will work out, but in all honesty everything is either going wrong or falling apart. We want to believe there is still some future we can look forward to, but the clouds are ominous and growing darker each day.

As I look at the dark clouds, I am reminded that one day soon they will be parted by the great light of heaven. As a believer in the Lord Jesus, the present environment and events remind me that my hope has never been in this world. The hope I have can't be moved because it is not planted on anything of this age. I may be a bit overwhelmed and even depressed at times by what I see, but the light that will part the dark clouds of this age has already parted the dark curtain over my soul, enabling me to walk out of darkness and into His glorious light.

God has promised His people, Israel and the church certain things. The world can curse us from various platforms, persecute us in different ways, and hit us from different angles, but God's promises to His people will stand. We need to stand by faith, withstand with truth, and continue to stand according to His promises. In the end, we not only will be standing on the side of truth, we will be standing on the victorious side of God.

Prayer: Lord, I walk in the hope of my faith that is directed towards You. I have joy that is anchored in You, and I have assurance that all of Your promises will be fulfilled because You never lie and will always keep the faith. Amen.

July 24

The hireling fleeth, because he is an hireling, and careth not for the sheep" (John 10:13). I have been a Christian since 1976, and since that time I have been involved in various churches and ministries, encountered religious leaders in numerous arenas, and heard the frustration of the sheep when it comes to the hireling shepherds and the wolves that stand behind pulpits.

Jesus warned us of both. He told us that hireling shepherds would be void of any love for the sheep and as a result would not properly care for the sheep nor give their lives for them. They would also prove to be self-serving.

Each time I encounter such a counterfeit, I would learn something new. I knew the different lessons I have learned during such times have been constantly reinforced with each encounter since a religious or anti-Christ spirit will always be present.

Jesus speaks of Himself as the real Shepherd, serving as an example of what constitutes a real pastor. His heart towards His sheep is evident for He not only cares for the sheep's well-being in every way, but He gave His life for them. He makes the best investment by leading them into places of nourishment and rest.

I have asked the Lord to help me discern the imposters, and show me my responsibility, first to the sheep and then to the imposter. The sheep either need to be taught how to discern or warned, but as Scripture states, the sheep that belong to Jesus will hear only His voice and follow Him.

Prayer: Lord cause Your sheep to become so acquainted with Your voice that when they hear another voice, they will flee it and truly seek You out. Amen.

July 25

"Behold, I send you forth as sheep in the midst of wolves, be ye therefore wise as serpents, and harmless as doves" *(Matthew 10:16)* As pointed out in yesterday's post, when we come to imposters in the Church there are two types. There are the hirelings. They are in the church for what they can get out of it.

The second group are the wolves who are a different type of creature. They are predators, while the hirelings are freeloaders. The wolves however, are not looking to just get by in the church. They are ravenous predators and would have no problem preying on the sheep. Sadly, you would like to think such imposters would be far and few but I could write a journal on those religious leaders who are either hireling shepherds or ravenous wolves.

When it comes to a wolf, those of this ilk have the same attitude of indifference and the same games of manipulation to seduce the sheep so they can prey on them. There is a similar hard glint in their eyes and a touchiness that can cause them to react in great anger towards those who dare challenge them.

The one lesson I've learned in one of the latest incidents of facing off with a wolf is that it is all about the image for these counterfeits. Since there is no real substance behind them, fear reigns behind façades of cruel pride. In the end, these individuals (counterfeits) do not care who they trample under foot or devour. If a sheep does not serve their purpose, they will set out to control them in any fashion they can or destroy them. If they don't feed their egos, they will become offended and will set out to make the person pay.

God will always give those of us who ask Him for the discernment to know who we are following and the necessary grace to do what is right in all matters to maintain our Christian witness before Him and others. I always ask the Lord to deliver His true sheep from the indifference of a hireling and the jaws of the wolf.

Prayer: Lord, we had much to combat our resolve. We wanted our spirits to soar and our souls to be compelled to excellence. Instead, our spirits are often robbed and our souls brought low in vexation by the imposters and hypocrites. Today we choose to praise You, knowing in the end You have and will continue to secure the victory on our behalf. Amen.

July 26

"Thou therefore endure hardness, as good soldier of Jesus Christ" (1 Timothy 2:3). Every once in a while, during my studies or meditations, the Lord will drop a bit of revelation into my spirit. I always know that such inspiration comes from outside of me because of how it impacts me. In many cases it is a known reality, but it becomes a confirmation that reaches right down into my spirit as truth and brings such awe to me that the Lord would insert a bit of heaven into my daily activity. However, the revelation may be a little challenging or contrary to religious notions.

The revelation goes like this, "The church today has pastors that are cheerleaders and not drill sergeants." This was in relationship to Paul's instruction to endure as "good soldiers." I realized that many Christians are not posed and ready to do battle because the attitude towards much of Christianity is that it is some game on some field or court that leaves no casualties. However, we are in an intense battle and souls hang in the balance.

It doesn't take much examination to recognize that the cheerleaders of today cheer us on as we, the church, are being defeated in the stadium of the world. These people are motivational speakers that are trying to motivate Christians who are being sucked into the quicksand of lifeless religion, making them a vulnerable target for the enemy.

As the enemy strikes blows against believers, the pastors keep cheering them on so they can "feel good" in their defeat. However, they are failing to train each of us (disciple), challenge us (to reach our potential), prepare us (to stand), and instruct us to effectively fight as soldiers against our enemies.

Sin clearly reigns, pride sits on the throne, immorality is spreading like a plague, righteousness is being sacrificed, and Satan mocks as the powerless, lifeless, worldly church sinks lower into a cesspool of foolishness and despair as it tries to console itself that it is okay after all. However, the fruits of the visible church are showing decay from within, homes are collapsing, and its witness has become a reproach since there is no real separation from the world.

Meanwhile, many Christians are lean in spirit. They are missing the voice of the Shepherd, looking for the right path, seeking out the nourishing pastures, and in a state of confusion and despair while falling through the cracks of repetitious, nonsensical rhetoric.

Prayer: Lord, only you can raise up an army out of the skeleton of that which has become lifeless. Have mercy on those who are struggling under the dead carcass of what remains of man's religion, and raise them up in resurrection power and life to become Your army. Amen.

July 27

"And he said, Lay not thine hand upon the lad, neither do thou any thing unto him: for now I know that thou fearest God, seeing thou hast not withheld thy son, thine only son from me (Genesis 22:12). The Bible reminds me that faith is a choice and it determines our focus, or at times our focus determines if our faith begins on the right footing in order to finish the course.

I read about the priceless story of Abraham not keeping his only son, Isaac, back from being sacrificed in *Genesis 22*. Just a couple of chapters before this situation, Abraham lied about Sarah being his wife out of fear for his life.

I realize that Abraham went through various changes in his life and grew in his faith towards the Lord, but even Abraham shows us that people of faith can become weak in their faith, making them fickle and appear cowardly. When you examine the reason why, it comes down to what they are focusing on.

It is always interesting to note that these contrasts in the previous chapter revealed that the fear of unbelief reigned because Abraham feared he would lose his life, yet in chapter 22, faith rises up in him and he is ready to offer up the life of his only son, who represented a miracle and a future legacy. It is clear in the first situation, fear of losing his life became his focus, while faith in the second situation caused him to look beyond this present world to what God had promised him.

Abraham could see that God would easily raise up his son, but in the previous chapter he could not trust God to preserve his life. We humans are indeed fickle and prove to be foolish at times when our focus is not heavenward, but God still remains the same and faithful to us in spite of ourselves.

Prayer: Lord, thank You for remaining the same when I am like a restless wave on the ocean. You never fall off the throne or are caught off guard in Your sovereignty. You remain the same Rock, the same pulse of life, and the same God Almighty who spoke the earth into being. Amen.

July 28

I remember standing there, dumfounded as the old man clamed up, quickly closed and locked his mysterious cabinet, and walked away. After all, he and his wife had been so friendly when they met my friend and myself in the Bavarian restaurant. This took place back in the 1980's when I traveled to touristy communities that hosted art shows and "artists in action."

The popular restaurant had been overflowing, so we had agreed to share a table with the older couple. Our conversations were most pleasant, but took an odd turn when the old man (whom we shall call Carl), told my friend she had "powers" because a teaspoon next to her hand moved without her touching it. She insisted it was just static electricity, but they both insisted she was magically endowed with "something" so they insisted we come to their home for a visit so they could show us something.

Since we had some time to spare before the art show began, we followed them the short distance to their Victorian style home. That is when something took place that I've never forgotten. Carl led me to an antique cabinet with locked glass doors. As he opened it, he told me that he was a Rosicrucian, (which, at that time I knew next to nothing about) and there were some powerful things he would share with me, but first he needed to ask me a couple of questions.

Was I a Christian, and which Bible version did I grow up with. That's when the "air suddenly turned chilly" as I innocently replied, "The King James Version." His entire demeanor changed and he snapped, "Since you 'cut your teeth' on the King James Version, it won't work for you. I can't show you a thing."

May I just say that after many miles, many years and many experiences in confrontations with Satan, demons, witches, and familiar spirits, we have discovered that there is no other writing, book, "method" or Bible version that contains the power and the authority of the KJV. – "*In the beginning was the Word, and the Word was with God, and the Word was God*" John 1:1. – J. Haley (Please note: This is not to say that parallel Bible studies and other references can't be helpful for study and teaching purposes.)

Prayer: Lord, we often stop with titles and presentations instead of discerning the intent, compare spiritual things with spiritual things, and make sure the Word of God is being properly handled and presented. Give me the clarity to properly discern the matters of Your truth and principles. Amen.

July 29

"*And Saul tarried in the uttermost part of Gibeah under a pomegranate tree which is in Migron: and the people that were with him were about six hundred men*" (1 Samuel 14:2). Saul was in a battle, but instead of seeking the Lord, falling before Him in great need, seeking mercy for his ineptness, and grace to secure victory, he is tarrying under a tree. Saul is waiting on Samuel, but he was not waiting before the Lord. He was not seeking personal guidance from the Lord, or the wisdom to lead, and the blessing to overcome the enemy.

Sadly, Saul's attitude is not unique even in the religious world. We assume much about God's blessings and promises. The attitude can be, "I don't have to wrestle before Him about gaining His perspective, because it will all work out some way in the end. After all, God would never let me down, right?" If we are not assuming things, we are hiding behind some vague notion about hope that we don't have to draw near to God; rather, He will send in a Samuel that will somehow make sense out of it and make it right.

Clearly, Saul was complacent about the whole matter. Due to assumption and wishful thinking, how many times, (in what is really spiritual laziness on our part) have we waited for our Christian life to fall upon us instead of humbly seeking it? By seeking it, it would allow God the means to send the message through His Spirit or via the Samuels because we have prepared ourselves to hear the words of the Lord and obey whatever instructions are given to us.

Studying Saul reveals he was never ready for victory, because he was casual about the battle and assuming much about the end results.

Prayer: Lord, there is much going on in the spiritual realm. Only You will give us the strength to face such matters. Lord, I do not feel equipped or enthusiastic about it, but I must continue on the course You have set before me. Amen.

July 30

"And went after the man of God, and found him sitting under an oak: and he said unto him, Art thou the man of God that camest from Judah? And he said, I am" (1 Kings 13:16) In my last post I talked about Saul sitting under the tree instead of seeking God. There was another individual who sat under a tree where

temptation caught up with him, and he sinned, and paid with his life because of his disobedience.

For Saul, he was waiting around for Samuel instead of seeking the Lord. In one incident, he ended up getting impatient and stepped into the forbidden territory of the priest and ended up losing the kingdom. The prophet in this incident took time out from fulfilling His commission and failed to finish the course. I refer to him as the "unknown prophet" because we never learn his name.

Saul was spiritually lazy and when he felt the pressure, he proved to lack the integrity to do what he knew was right. If he had only waited upon the Lord while waiting for Samuel, he would have been able to endure the test.

The prophet in *1 Kings 13* did everything right except complete God's instructions. He was told by God to go straight to Bethel and pronounce judgment on the king, and then return to Judah another way to avoid any confrontation. However, instead of returning back to Judah, he stopped and sat awhile under the tree. It would seem like an innocent enough action, but God's instruction to him was clear. He was not to stop because the Lord knew temptation would catch up with him.

Temptation did catch up with him by way of a prophet who lied to him by telling him the Lord had changed his instructions to him. The Lord never does, but once a person disobeys at one point, regardless of how insignificant it may be, they are open to fall into the trap of temptation.

Prayer: Lord, we take seriously some instructions, but ignore small details. As they say the "devil is in the details." You have taught me those details offer a crack for the devil to make inroads into a situation and set up the right trap to catch us in rebellion. Amen.

July 31

"Then they said to Jeremiah, The LORD be a true and faithful witness between us, if we do not even according to all things for the which the LORD thy God shall send thee to us" (Jeremiah 42:5). My co-laborer in the Lord, Jeannette reminded me of this Scripture. If you are not acquainted with it, you should read it. This happened after Babylon's third and final siege on Jerusalem at which time the Babylonian army literally destroyed it.

A remnant was left in the land and a fair man by the name of Gedaliah was sent to oversee them, but a wicked man by the name of Ishmael killed him and carried away some of the remnant into captivity. Those taken captive were rescued, but the remnant felt insecure so they came to the prophet Jeremiah to ask him to pray for them as to what they should do.

They felt that they had some options or they would have never come to Jeremiah. Options always confuse the issues, but when it comes to options it often comes down to man's understanding being pitted against God's all-knowing wisdom. The options were, 1) they could stay in a land that lay in ruin and toil with it in the midst of great destruction and reclaim it as their inheritance or 2) go to Egypt.

Most of the time man knows what the right thing is to do, but when the way is hard and he has the attractive option of the world, he becomes confused. In man's logic he concludes that God would not have him walk down a more difficult path; therefore, all that is needed is that God give His approval to go to Egypt which represents the world. This is what is natural for man to do when his choice is the narrow, hard path or the broad path.

The question was whether the small group of people were seeking confirmation as far as God's way or seeking His approval to go their own way. In our religious thinking we can convince

255

ourselves that we want what God wants, but in reality, we are moving away from God as we con ourselves that God would certainly understand why it is right to leave our inheritance and go back into the world.

Prayer: Lord, You have set before us our inheritance, but to get there we must choose the narrow way that is hard, constrictive, and challenging. Lord my flesh is naturally drawn back to the world, and my pride wants to be worshipped not ignored so it will choose the convenient way. But, Lord the call to discipleship of denying self and crucifying the flesh takes all options away and leaves me with the only and right choice and that is to follow You into the life You have designed for me. Amen.

AUGUST

August 1

"For our light affliction which is but for a moment, worketh for us a far more exceeding and eternal weight of glory" *(2 Corinthians 4:17).* This day marks the life of a very special person, Carla Kropp. She has inspired me with her courage, boldness, honesty, and sense of humor.

Most of the world has not had the privilege of meeting this special person, but perhaps they have had the blessing of meeting someone like her. She is one of those people that I can fellowship with in the spirit at any time. Such individuals are rare gems that God so kindly graces our life with to bring inspiration and perspective.

The two of us rarely talk on the phone, but when we do it is like time and space has never separated us. The reason for it is because when you fellowship in the Spirit, there is no time or distance. In the Spirit, it is as it always has been in the present, as it was in the past and will be in future.

The two of us often talk about challenging happenings with miraculous interventions, inspirational books that cause us to come higher, and God's grace that ever sustains us.

Like all of us, Carla has a history of darkness, but is now a child of the light who has been forged by the hand of God with the tools of suffering that has refined her. There is a sharpness to her that is discerning, that will not tolerate nonsense when it comes to her love for her Savior, that stands for truth regardless of the fallout, and displays an abiding loyalty to her family and friends.

Carla is a living witness of God's abiding care on His people's lives. The one thing that Carla has reinforced in my life as a believer is that some of the many gifts of God that will shine even through the tears, suffering, and losses are an abiding joy, a glorious hope, and a looking forward to experiencing His everlasting promises.

Prayer: Lord, out of grace You give us such glorious blessings which include priceless friendships. Thank You for always giving us the best. It is the big "I" of me that will pass over the best to settle for the scraps, but You have even taught each of Your followers to trust You because You have always proven that Your best for us will prove to be excellent in the end. Amen.

August 2

"And the LORD opened the mouth of the ass, and she said unto Balaam, What have I done unto thee, that thou hast smitten me these three times" (Numbers 22:28)? Who has God used to speak to you about the matters of heaven?

You have been reading about some of those who have spoken into my life. These individuals have inspired me along the way, and even though they sometimes are used to challenge me, I know their intentions are pure. During such challenges their words can be almost like a slap across the face to get my attention or a cut into my pride, but each point of challenge ends up becoming sweet to my spirit, a quick jerk to my soul to awaken me, and a reality check to my conscience.

However, how do you react when God uses an instrument that could insult your intelligence, take your pride down a couple of notches, put you in your place because you were out of order, or leave you silent because there is no recourse? These people do not really care about you and do not have your best in mind. They often end up being rude, crude, and downright disrespectful.

The truth is, God will use who He can to get our attention. In the case of a stubborn Balaam, He used a creature that is known to be stubborn when dealing with his ilk. Do you think God used a donkey as a mirror to show Balaam his stubbornness? The truth is the donkey showed more concern for Balaam than Balaam showed her.

This brings me back to the instruments God has used to get your attention. What do they mirror about your own attitudes towards the matters of God?

Prayer: Lord, we like to think more highly of ourselves than we should. We can become angry at a stubborn creature and fail to see that we are stiff-necked towards You. We can label something due to its prevailing temperament in a mocking way, while failing to realize we are putting a light on our own attitude. Forgive us for being blind to ourselves, and judgmental of others who possess the same flaws. Amen.

August 3

"Hast not thou made an hedge about him, and about his house, and about all that he hath on every side? thou has blessed the work of his hands, and his substance is increased in the land" (Job 1:10). One of the aspects of my Christian life I had to come to terms with was whether the people that came into my life was a matter of circumstances, fate, or a well-orchestrated plan. I had to believe that God was sovereign and had complete say over everything, or He was indifferent in some ways, powerless in others, and that His involvement in my life was off and on and that I am constantly being tossed to and fro by the world.

I chose to believe what the Bible clearly outlines about God, and that is He is sovereign and nothing gets past Him without His say so and approval. I must admit, the book of Job cleared up and firmly established to me the matter of God's sovereignty.

This brings me to the people that come into my life. Is it by chance or by design? Are they a test, a tool, or a troublemaker? Are they truthful, trustworthy, or terrors? Am I to pray for them, witness to them, encourage or learn from them?

It has been clear that people bring different equations to one's life and as I look back through the years of my life and see how each individual that crossed my path challenged me in some way, put a light on some character flaw, or encouraged me to come higher, I can see how God orchestrated their presence in my life for my spiritual good.

Prayer: Lord by faith I received Your salvation, but at times I have had a hard time accepting that You are directing the other parts of my life. Either I believe You are sovereign over all of my life, or I don't believe You at all. I choose to believe You are who You say You are and will trust You with every detail of my life. Amen.

August 4

"And the ass saw me, and turned from me these three times: unless she had turned from me, surely now also I had slain thee, and saved her alive." It is not unusual for us to resist those instruments that seem least likely to be used, hypocritical in their ways or even mocking towards us when it comes to instruction from the Lord.

Some of the greatest lessons I learned came from people that had very little influence in my life. They may have crossed my path in an insignificant way, but God used them much liked He did the donkey in Balaam's case. They may have only spoke once to me,

260

but God took that one sentence or word and wrote a volume that flashed before my eyes, challenging me or changing me.

There was a situation in the Navy where I worked with a "Romeo" type. He had a reputation with the women that was well earned based on his escapades. However, he was always respectful around me. When questioned about his attitude and conduct towards me and another co-worker, he spoke volumes. He told us he considered us his friends and would never cross the line. He showed me that if one has the proper respect towards someone their conduct will also be honorable.

In another incident I was working in the seed potatoes. There were a lot of rough people around me who were quite free in expressing themselves with explicit words. One day I was standing there and someone used the name of Jesus Christ in vain. Another worker who showed no religious affiliation silenced the man when he said, "He has nothing to do with it." This man showed me if the unlikely can be bold about demanding the proper respect towards my Lord, I should even be bolder. I have used his statement more than once to silence those using my Lord's name in vain.

The Lord will use unlikely people to catch our attention in order to instruct or give us a contrast. We must never disregard the instruction because the instrument He is using does not fit our qualifications. After all, to receive anything from the Lord, we must first humble ourselves.

Prayer: Lord, You are so faithful to teach us valuable lessons, but we have a tendency to judge the instrument You use before we discern whether it is Your truth. Forgive us for our small way of thinking that has been limited by prejudices. Amen.

August 5

"Hath not the potter power over the clay, of the same lump to make one vessel unto honour and another unto dishonour." (Romans 9:21). When God uses an instrument to bring some necessary insight, if they do not fit our standards, we have a tendency to question God's wisdom, debate the matter and in many cases dismiss it. There was one incident that stands out to me. I was sharing at a Gospel Union place at the request of a minister. Some men took issue with it because I was a woman. One of the homeless men came up to me and asked me a simple question. I was quick to truthfully answer.

The man's reply came across as a slap across the face by implying that God would never really used a woman to speak to men. In his book it was an affront to his manhood. However, I realized without discerning it that pride had subtly taken center stage and God was using this man to reveal it to me.

It was then that I understood that God can use the biggest hypocrite to challenge us, but it matters little as to their status if what they are speaking is revealing some hidden aspect about character. I am not responsible to give an account to a hypocrite, but I am responsible to receive correction from my Lord regardless of who He uses to humble me.

Prayer: Lord, we can become uncomfortable with a slap on the hand, embarrassed about a slap on the face, and appalled at a complete take down but such moments are to prepare us to examine ourselves to see if You are trying to reveal something to us about our own character or testimony. Amen.

August 6

Dreams! "The American Dream," night-time dreams, day-dreams, and nightmares. In recent years the "American Dream" has crumpled into a complicated nightmare for many which has given rise to something almost akin to a developing "movement" called "off-grid living."

Let me state, I have nothing against off-grid living. In fact, we live in an area full of what I'd call "hard core off-gridders." However, what has caught my attention lately on TV concerning this "off-grid" fad are the big dreamers with little, if any, experience. For example, let's just say that Uncle Bubba has given a very young married couple some acreage in the middle of nowhere for a wedding present. (And, every state has plenty of "nowhere.")

It's just so wonderful, you know, being out there with the bugs, bears, bobcats, and the woods, weeds, and weather. Never mind that there are poisonous snakes, poisonous plants, more ticks than stars, and blood-thirsty leeches in that cute little creek where you think you can maybe catch fish for dinner the size of a goldfish in a bowl. Even though most wanna-be homesteaders figure out some sort of shelter, without a power source there is no refrigeration for food, lights or appliances of any kind. Never mind that the bears can smell your food and garbage twenty miles away, and with no way to wash yourself and your clothes often, they can smell you too.

Then there's the problem of sanitation, potable water, and fire for heat and cooking—which reminds me, how many big dreamers are up to killing, cleaning and cooking their pet chicken? In order for such big dreams to be carried out, there has to be a lot of preparation which involves a whole lot more than reading one pocket-size survival book, three novels, and spending two hours studying a map. Watching a homestead TV series for six months does not properly equip you to head for the hills with your terrified wife and your faithful dog, even though you're "well-armed" with just one very small ax! It's just plain dumb and dangerous.

On the other hand, how many professing Christians these days (especially young ones) are dreaming big dreams about an earthly utopia they hope to build for themselves without nary a thought about what the Bible tells us concerning real life on the narrow road? The Christian life, just like off-grid living, is an hour-by-hour, day-by-day, every-day-of-your-life process. Both require awareness, understanding, diligence, concentration, wisdom, commitment, and conviction. Christian character is essential, and is built through daily obedience, just as off-grid survival requires adherence to basic survival "rules" and skills, including how to protect yourself.

You cannot expect to end your journey on the narrow road as a truly saved, overcoming, heaven-bound Christian if, after you receive Christ, you decide to maintain your right to your self-life and live however you please with Jesus merely tacked on while your guidebook (Bible) gathers dust on a shelf. Like it or not, such a decision immediately places you back on the broad road of the world that leads to destruction. *"There is a way which seemeth right unto a man, but the end thereof are the ways of death"* *(Proverbs 14:12).* – J. Haley

Prayer: Lord, we have such high, unrealistic ideas about everything pertaining to life. When we are young, we can dream, when we get older, we have to consider what it will take to obtain dreams and when we become adults, we either grow up about life where dreams are put in a realistic light or go into a delusion that keeps us from ever going forward in a state of disillusionment. In You we don't have dreams but promises. Keep me focused. Amen.

August 7

"I do set my bow in the cloud, and it shall be for a token of a covenant between me and the earth. And it shall come to pass when I bring a cloud over the earth, that the bow shall be seen in the cloud" (Genesis 9:13-14). People talk about looking for a silver lining in the clouds no matter how dark and foreboding they appear. Through the years I have discovered different silver linings.

First of all, we must consider what a silver lining represents. We know that even though clouds can prove dark, wherever the cloud is not weighed down with participation or the light hits it at certain spots, it can make the cloud look silver.

A silver lining reminds us that there is no burden that is too great for the Lord to help us handle. Granted, under clouds heavy with participation we can feel the downpour as if we are going to be consumed by heavy burdens, but in Christ we can know His protection and safety.

The other part of the silver lining when it comes to heavy dark clouds in our lives is that regardless of the darkness of a matter, the light is not far behind it. It reminds us that even storms must give way to it.

The silver lining in matters is a truth that believers can be assured of. After all, the Lord is light and eventually His light will shine on a situation once the storm begins to move through. The beauty about such light is that it often produces rainbows.

Rainbows are a token of a covenant that God made with creation. Every time I see a rainbow, it reminds me that God keeps everyone of His promises. Therefore, the storms will come, but in the end the covenant of His promises will shine forth as a glorious token of His incredible care on each of our lives.

265

Prayer: Lord, thank You for Your rainbows. The blue reminds me that it is of a heavenly design, red of Your glorious sacrifice, the yellow of Your abiding light, the green of the fruitfulness of Your Spirit, and if I see hints of purple, I am reminded of Your royalty as King of kings and Lord of lords. Amen.

August 8

"These things have I spoken unto you, that my joy might remain in you, and that your joy might be full" (John 15:11). The next type of silver lining in the storms of life is joy. People who are void of joy will find themselves succumbing to trying circumstances instead of passing through them and being overcomers.

Through the years I have discovered joy serves in various ways in a Christian's life. It serves as an anchor. Jesus made this clear when He stated that the things He spoke, His Word, could cause our joy to be full regardless of what affronts us.

However, the key to such joy is that His Word must take root in each of us by faith, and remain as truth in order to ensure its inspiration in our lives. Keep in mind without hope there is no sustaining joy. Without purpose there will be no joy to see beyond the storm and without promise there would be no joy that would endure to the end.

The words Jesus spoke were not only living but they brought the assurance of hope, the confidence of calling, and the abiding grace that is present when we truly land on God's promises.

Prayer: Lord, joy will elude us if we are looking for worldly happiness, fleshly contentment and emotional satisfaction based on circumstances. What a soul needs is the joy that only comes from knowing You, while standing on Your promises, and abiding by Your Word. Amen.

August 9

"...for the joy of the LORD is your strength" *(Nehemiah 8:10).* We have been considering silver linings. When times are challenging and the darkness of some event is about to swallow you up, there is nothing to grab a hold of but an anchor that can lead you back to the Rock to which it is connected by the strong rope of His Word and the enduring chain links of His promises. That anchor is joy.

As believers, joy is a silver lining in every challenge that comes our way. Granted, we may not note it is even around when we are busy trying to come up for air as the matters around us are consuming us. However, the real joy is found in the Lord, and I must seek Him out with everything in me to take hold of Him.

Sometimes, I must swim against the prevailing current of despair, wade through the swamp of endless vanity, and struggle in the quagmire of foolishness that abounds. However, when I come to the end of such challenges, I am reminded that I must look up to the only One who is the solution to find real joy, while choosing to trust what He has said about the matter in His Word, and come to rest in His promises.

I have learned that I can find the Lord in every situation if I care to look up with the eyes of faith, a trusting heart, and an open ear to hear the words of wisdom and consolation His Spirit wants to say to me to lift me up and set me free with His truth.

Prayer: Lord, You have provided everything we need to experience joy in the midst of storms. Instead of looking for a way out of storms, I need to rest in the confidence and rejoice that Your strength is what is keeping me safe in them. Amen.

August 10

"Behold, when we come into the land, thou shalt bind this line of scarlet thread in the window which thou didst let us down by: and thou shalt bring thy father, and thy mother, and thy brethren, and all thy father's household, home unto thee" (Joshua 2:18). There are many silver linings when it comes to the Word of God. However, the main silver lining is a thread that actually runs through the Bible; it is call redemption.

In the case of Rahab, it was a red thread (cord) that was used to identify her and her family, reminding us that redemption was secured by the blood of Jesus. It may seem like it is a thin thread but it is strong and capable of securing us to the promises of deliverance and safety like the rope that was used to let Paul down over a wall in a basket in *Acts 9:22-25* to save his life.

However, the metal, silver, was used to point to the price of redemption. The blood of Jesus may have secured our redemption, but the promise of redemption is that silver lining that enfolds us with such assurance and hope because we have been bought with an ordained price that God could accept and that would satisfy His holy Law.

Prayer: Lord, we can get so caught up with the idea of salvation that we fail to understand that it is all about redemption. You paid the ransom for our souls, secured our salvation, and one day You will bring us into the fullness of all of Your promises because of it. Thank You for redeeming my soul with Your precious blood. Amen.

August 11

"For thou, O God, has proved us: thou hast tried us, as silver is tried" (Psalm 66:10). In the last post I mentioned how the other silver lining in the Word of God is the metal, silver.

Silver is what it took to redeem the firstborn. To avoid pestilence a shekel of silver had to be given by the men before a census could take place. At one time God was displeased with Israel and allowed Satan to provoke King David to take a census without first collecting a silver shekel, causing Israel to taste the bitterness of a pestilence for three days (*Exodus 30:11-16; Numbers 18:15-16; 2 Samuel 24;1; 1 Chronicles 21:1*).

Silver points to the process God's people must go through and how their works will be tried in fire to purify them. The fire is what will bring the boiling process that will separate the dross from the metal to make it pure.

The process is necessary to rid us of the dross of sin that clings to different aspect of our character and lives. Until the dross is removed, the silver lacks value because it has not been brought to its state of purity.

I read about how a silversmith was asked how he knew the silver was ready. He stated when he could see his reflection in the liquid of silver. How do we know we are in the process: others can see Jesus in us.

The last point about silver in relationship to redemption is that it reminds us Jesus' redemption on the cross was completed on earth as He declared from the cross, "It is finished." You might ask why silver points to this wonderful truth, because there is no silver in heaven for the complete work of redemption was done on earth.

Prayer: Lord thank You that silver points to Your work being completed on earth and that my future are that of gold streets, pearl gates, and Your unhindered glory. Amen.

August 12

The man was wearing the usual familiar fluorescent jacket that roadcrew men wear when working on highways, so my friend and I listened to his warning. We had just pulled my small RV off of I-5 into a Rest Area for a few minutes before continuing south towards the Siskiyous mountain pass that's between Ashland, Oregon and Yreka, California.

The sun had already set, and it was cold and wet. The man assured us that they were warning travelers in RV's who were heading for the pass that they had closed the pass due to a snow storm, and so we needed to pull off on a certain road that went down a hill, and then park under a bridge. My friend and I, both in our forties at that time (mid-1980's), felt uneasy about his insistence that we be sure to do as he said, and took note of the pitiful, dirty condition of his "official" jacket.

We concluded he was not what he pretended to be, and was not telling us the truth, but rather trying to lead us into a nefarious trap. As we continued traveling south, we saw the turnoff and the bridge he had referred to, but the Lord warned us to keep going, which we did until we saw a small café, and we stopped there.

Upon entering it, we saw two state patrolmen having coffee, so we approached them and reported what was taking place back at the rest stop. They told us they would check it out, got up and left. Of course, we never knew what took place, if anything, and, there was no problem for us getting over the Siskiyous Pass that night.

To this day I am so thankful for the Lord's faithfulness to warn and protect, not only for our physical safety, but our spiritual protection as well. Even so, it's up to us to pray for discernment of spirits and it's up to us to study God's Word.

What the Apostle Paul wrote to the Corinthians is also written to us when he said, *"But I fear, lest by any means, as the serpent beguiled Eve through his subtilty, so your minds should be corrupted from the simplicity that is in Christ. For if he that cometh preacheth another Jesus, whom we have not preached, or if ye receive another spirit, which ye have not received, or another gospel, which ye have not accepted, ye might well bear with him"* (2 Corinthians 11:3, 4).

And, *2 Thessalonians 2:3, "Let no man deceive you by any means: for that day shall not come, except there come a falling away first, and that man of sin be revealed, the son of perdition."* Just because someone looks the part, or "talks the talk" doesn't mean the Lord knows them! – J. Haley

Prayer: Lord, Satan has set up all kinds of traps for us to fall into, but You by Your grace keep us safe, but we need to discern, listen for warnings and obey. Thank You for Your faithfulness to keep us. Amen.

August 13

"Man is like to vanity: his days are as a shadow that passeth away" (Psalm 144:1). There are various shadows we must contend with in this world. Shadows are often associated with death in Scripture, but it is also a place of protection and shade when it comes to God.

When it comes to man, shadows vary. They can be places where a person can somewhat hide to avoid any light or a place of protection when strong leadership is present.

There are reasons people prefer the shadows. It can prove to be a safe place where they can be without too much scrutiny. They can avoid unwarranted pressures while allowing the light to shine on others without worrying about becoming a point of focus, or the one who might get shot at if the results are not great.

When it comes to ministry, I have encountered those who are in the shadows. To me, my co-laborer Jeannette is in the shadows when it comes to ministry, and yet her ministry is what keeps so much going. There are also others who stand in the shadows when it comes to ministry.

My friend, Teri Rex, is one such person. She and her husband were a ministry team that often ministered in worship. He played the guitar and led worship while she played base and backed him up. However, Teri found herself flung into the light when her husband passed from this world to the next.

Without shadows, the light becomes intense. Much to Teri's surprise, God was putting the light on the fact that she had her own ministry. She has a tremendous gifting in music, and discovered that she prefers the 12-string guitar to the base. God has also given her a voice of her own and wanted to bring out the songs He has placed on her heart.

God prepares us in the shadows, but once He puts that light on us to reveal our calling and giftings, the only thing we can do is walk in the light while trusting Him; otherwise, trying to remain in the shadows will cause us to be miserable in our spirit as everything else becomes vain and insignificant before us.

Prayer: Lord, You may prepare us in the shadows but once the light parts the shadows, we must be ready to walk in Your light. Amen.

August 14

"Keep thy heart with all diligence; for out of it are the issues of life" (*Proverbs 4:23*). I have been thinking about moodiness. So many

people live swinging among the limbs of ecstasy. They want to swing from one branch to another in a state of elation, believing that all is well in their world. In reality they have no anchor of sobriety in which to hold them to any reality. As a result, they prove to be flippant in their attitude and prevailing mood towards God.

I realize that many do not understand what prevailing mood is. It is in actuality the prevailing attitude of the heart. Mood swings and attitudes change, but the prevailing mood of the heart is the constant current that runs through our soul. It is often reflected in our moods and attitudes. It will always be that part of our moral fiber that peers out from behind all that is said and done to reveal the real depth, or lack thereof, of our character.

It is my desire to always be discerning of my mood. Granted, sometimes it is concealed by some covering, but eventually it will raise its head to show its predominate influence on my attitude and emotions. I must learn to control it instead of being controlled by it. I must prevent it from becoming my reality.

Prayer: Lord, my heart is a dangerous place unless You have given me a new heart. However, with a new heart I need to make sure it remains cleansed from hypocrisy, purged of wrong influences, and separated from wrong thinking. Turn the searchlight on it, and keep it on because I can be easily deceived by the wishful thinking that comes from high opinions of myself and the lies and false promises of this world. Amen.

August 15

"My soul is weary of my life; I will leave my complaint upon myself; I will speak in the bitterness of my soul" (Job 10:1). Have you ever felt like a slug at times? It is not that you are lazy, but you are wearied from what you consider swimming against the currents of this present life. It is as if you are being buried by circumstances

how many people do not believe Jesus, even though He has risen from the dead? Faith is not a matter of seeing miracles, but of choosing to believe God and His Word.

No amount of miracles are going to persuade one who will not choose to simply believe God. When the circumstances are such, these individuals will insist on seeing one more miracle before they will believe.

Physical death is the final door of healing for the saint. The Lord sees the death of His saints as a homecoming. It will be our loss here, but heaven's gain. We need to realize that according to *Hebrews 12:1,* the witness we leave behind is not our death, but our life that was lived out by faith towards our God.

There is also an **ultimate healing** and it can be described as resurrection or rapture. Those who die in the Lord are already present with Him, but there will be a day when they will rise up in new bodies with those who remain alive, and together they will be caught up to meet the Lord. At that time all the saved will receive a new body. This is the ultimate redemption that ends in total healing.

Prayer: Lord, I know that I live under a curse of physical death, but in You I live in light of a blessed life that is full of promises, the greatest one is that one day I will see You as You are. Amen.

August 21

"Then spake Jesus again unto them, saying, I am the light of the world; he that followeth me shall not walk in darkness, but shall have the light of life" (John 8:12). In the past I have talked about the changes occurring in each new generation. I admit in my almost seven decades of living, I have considered the contrasts brought on by changes occurring in each generation.

280

People might debate with me about the innocence that seemed to exist in the 1950's. Granted, the 50's and 60's produced the social, radical, godless Marxists that are now running our government into the ground of destruction. However, during that time children in general appeared to be more innocent. They had not yet been seduced by the filth of Hollywood, indoctrinated by a Communist education, and corrupted by the wicked Internet and the media. Don't get me wrong. The younger generation during that time had its own display of rebellion, but their imagination had not been corrupted by blatant sexual immorality, pornography, abominations galore, and violence that are now constantly invading the air waves.

I realize that regardless of the innocent pose of former generations, sin has always reigned. Without the proper influence of God upon the hearts and minds of each generation, that generation will slide into the quagmire of lawlessness and hopelessness. It will become lost in the culture of death, the suffocating hypocrisy of liberalism, the skepticism of humanism, and the ridiculousness caused by the immoral insanity of it all.

The truth is, once a generation begins to slide into the pit of depravity, there is no stopping it as to the great depth it will fall. What will go with it are all innocence and purity, but as believers we must remember the light that came in the middle of grave darkness over 2,000 years ago to bring hope. That hope is still present and available to those of each generation who would choose to believe the Gospel message in spite of the tolerant pose and the lawlessness and hopelessness of the present age.

Prayer: Lord, You brought the real light back into this world when You came fashioned as a man. Enable me to walk according to it, walk in it, and be led by it. Amen.

August 22

"But all things that are reproved are made manifest by the light: for whatsoever doth make manifest is light" (Ephesians 5:13). Light will only cast a shadow when there is something in its path. In the summertime shadows are a welcome element because they can represent shade from the intensity of the heat of the sun.

Imagine the sun providing the heat while identifying cool places. For Christians, the shadow represents character. However, if there is no real character, there is no shade from the intensity that life can bring our way.

The light will always reveal if there is any real shade in which our soul can find the means to stand, withstand and continue to stand when the intensity of life hits us. We would all like to think we have the necessary character to stand, but in reality, many hide in dark places because they can't afford to be tested by the intense light of God's forms of testing, which comes with trials and tribulations.

Job was a man of integrity. The amount of integrity will determine the type of shadow that will be cast when the intense heat of trials hit us. Integrity is a combination of honesty and righteousness. One is brutally honest about what is really going on and righteous enough to stand by faith, withstand with truth, and continue to stand on what is sure and eternal regardless of the devastation left around them.

We are living in very dark times. We may be uncomfortable, fearful, or vexed by such darkness, but how many of us would be able to stand if the intense heat of God's judgment of His light parted and dissipated the darkness. Would there be a shadow to find relief or would it serve as a purging heat that would leave us completely exposed and undone?

Prayer: Lord, in our arrogance we all think we can endure, but in the testing we find out we have nothing in and of ourselves that could endure. I choose to trust You to lead me by Your Spirit, while standing firmly on Your Word and hiding in Your Promises. Amen.

August 23

(For we walk by faith, not by sight:) (2 Corinthians 5:7). Light is an interesting subject. We have a natural light that allows us to see the environment around us, an artificial light that in time can grow dim and eventually leaves us in darkness, and a spiritual light that can penetrate any and all darkness.

Sadly, the light that allows us to see with our physical sight is what we rely on the most but we only see in part; in fact, we only see our limited world that is very small when compared to the rest of planet earth. The reality of our smallness reminds us our life is a mere vapor that quickly disappears in light of the vastness of the Universe. Even though we have a limited perspective, we believe we see enough that we know what is true about a matter.

We can control artificial light, but eventually it will leave us in darkness. This is true for our take on reality. We try to control our reality, but eventually we discover that we know in part and what we do not know will change our perspective altogether. Therefore, if we are wise, we hold what we know lightly realizing that if we take it too seriously, we will end up looking like a fool in the end.

Then there is the spiritual light that can only be seen by faith. Faith creates a type of darkness where nothing makes sense. This is necessary if we are going to come down from our pinnacle of intellectual arrogance in admission that we really don't know what is true and we need God's perspective. Faith enables us to walk in the darkness based on the unchangeable character of God according to His Word which guides us in each step of obedience we take.

This world lies in darkness and the only way we are going to advance through it as believers is by walking by faith according to the light God has provided through the life of His Son in us, the indwelling presence of His Holy Spirit and His Word.

Prayer: Lord, we think we are pretty clever for the most part. We are loaded with our facts, confident in our conclusions, and assured that our understanding will pass any challenge, only to discover that we really do only know in part. God forgive us for our intellectual pride that we constantly bow down to while failing to seek Your perspective in all matters. Amen.

August 24

"My beloved is like a roe or a young hart. behold, he standeth behind our wall, he looketh forth at the windows, shewing himself through the lattice" (Song of Solomon 2:9). How do we combat darkness? Our understanding is what we consider to be light, but the problem is that what we think is light could turn out to be nothing more than darkness. However, in our arrogance we can deceive ourselves that we understand a matter even though we may be like the girl in the Song of Solomon who sees her beloved showing himself through the lattice.

Note how her beloved starts out standing behind a wall. What wall? We people put walls up when we do not trust someone. No matter what, that wall keeps them at a distance. Her beloved is looking at the windows in the hope of catching a glimpse of her or her seeing him. The point is how many of us are really seeking to see Jesus for who He is? That takes faith that trusts enough to push aside any wall, or settling for seeing Him through some small opening that allows us to control our reality about Him.

The wall hid the Shulamite girl's beloved, the window could allow her to hide or control what is seen or what she sees. Finally, her beloved showed himself through a lattice. She could only see bits of him and what did she see? We settle for seeing Jesus through various lattices of theology and doctrine. We think we know what He looks like, but do we?

Jesus is the light but our walls will keep Him obscure from us, the windows will keep our understanding of Him limited, and the lattices will keep us from looking fully into His face to see His loving eyes, His kind face, and His glowing countenance.

The one way we combat the darkness is to never settle for a tainted, perverted, limited perspective of our Lord. If we do not see Him, we remain in darkness and will find ourselves groping around in the dark as we seek a way out of it. We must never settle for seeing Him in the distance or seeing Him through some "lattice", we must look into His blessed face!

Prayer: Lord, we say we want to see You, and in reality, we must see You if we are going to have a right perspective, but there is much that keeps our understanding of You either dimmed down or hidden from us. Forgive us for settling for less because of fear and pride, and open our eyes of faith so we can see You for who You are. Amen.

August 25

"Because the carnal mind is enmity against God; for it is not subject to the law of God, neither indeed can be" (Romans 8:7). The Bible is clear: the carnal mind is at odds with God. It thinks itself to be too intelligent to believe in the unseen, too superior to be bothered with simplicity, and too wise to trust in something that does not confirm its own sense of justice and worth. It cannot imagine the best coming out of that which seems childlike, the excellent coming out of self-denial and sacrifice, or the most prized possession coming out of loss.

The Christian walk is contrary to the world. It values what the world discards, it pursues after that which seems foolish to the world, and it desires to gain that which the world holds in complete disdain.

It is for this reason that the carnal mind refuses to be subject to the Law of God. It cannot relate to that which is contrary to its very core. It cannot agree with that which marches to an unseen Spirit. It cannot flow with that which is spiritual, pure, and possesses eternal life.

As a believer, I desire the pure mind of Christ. It is single in focus, purpose, and service. It is not driven by the waves of the world, hindered by the storms of the age, or defeated by the darkness that surrounds it. It stands in clarity and hope.

Prayer: Lord, as believers we have much to be excited about. We are not subject to this present world. We belong to another one, and one day we will be walking in the glory of it. Amen.

August 26

"So then they that are in the flesh cannot please God" (Romans 8:8). There is a great war in the souls of mankind between the flesh and the Spirit. This reality is ever before me. I have had to learn not to take myself so seriously. I must honestly examine whether I am walking according to the flesh or in the Spirit.

It is easy to talk about mortifying the ways of the flesh and following after the Spirit, but the actual process can prove to be overwhelming. It takes a daily death to the flesh to walk in the Spirit.

This reality reminds me that as Christians we are always walking towards our demise. We cannot find life until we lose our present life that is attached to the world. We cannot be Spirit-led unless we first disown the claims of the self-life on us. And, this is necessary if we are going to please God.

I am aware of how easy it is to get caught up with the best the flesh has to offer, but in doing so, we will cause a breaking in our relationship with God. The ways of the flesh always run contrary to the Spirit. Ultimately, it will lead one into the very throes of failure and despair.

Prayer: Lord, I know there must be travailing that leads to death in order for life to come forth. I hate the travailing, but gaining Your life will be worth the dying out process. Amen.

August 27

"Henceforth I call you not servants; for the servant knoweth not what his lord doeth: but I have called you friends; for all things that I have heard of my Father I have made known to you" (John 15:15). The marching of time not only brings events, challenges, and changes but it brings an assortment of people your way. As I get older, I can see how the people of the past were used as part of my refinement, while the people of my present prove to be avenues in which God continually blesses my life.

Admittedly, the people of my past also serve as a bridge to my present. I would not be where I am if God had not used them to create the necessary ingredients to establish me in my life in Him. However, there are few individuals of my past left that connect the bridge to the present.

Through the years people in your life fall off along the way, take different roads, and end up in changes that often leave the relationships of the past in a "dust cloud." And, if you manage to reconnect with such people, there is no bridge to connect them to the present. However, there are always those who manage to stay ahead of the "dust cloud."

One such friend is a woman who was part of a discipleship group we were overseeing in the state of Washington in 1995-96. Carol Stribling, a woman of beauty and grace, is one such person who ever connects the lessons and blessings of the past to the present. Our present age reminds us that over two decades have passed since our time together, but Carol has ways of bringing the past into the present as if there is no time or space. She never forgets a birthday and you always know she is there for you even if you rarely communicate.

She has taught me good friendships are like fine wines, they become more refined and valuable through the years. This priceless connection serves as an example of how Christ wants the same type of friendship with us.

So many of us linger in the shadows of His cross; rather than coming into the full light of it to first seek to serve Him in faithfulness in order to prove we can be His trusted friends. As trusted friends He will be able to share the intricate parts of His kingdom with us. It is at such times we can connect the past work of the cross with the present work of the Spirit that not only greatly benefits us but others as well.

Prayer: Lord it is a great honor to serve You, but my heart has found such delight when You have shared the heart of the Father with me. Lord, I want to be found to be one who is capable of being a good friend to You, a faithful comrade, and a trustworthy confident. Amen.

August 28

Precision tune-up mechanic. That's what my dad was when I was a little kid. He opened up his own business in Ballard, Washington, and was very good at what he did. His keen hearing could tell him if a car was finely tuned or not. If it wasn't, he knew how to discover the reason why it wasn't running right, and he knew just how to fix it.

Every time my dad, my mom and I made a trip on the old two-lane highway between Seattle and the Bitterroot Valley in Montana where we went to visit family, he was listening to the car engine every inch of every mile. I was not allowed to make any tapping, thudding, clicking, or snapping sounds, or any other noises in the backseat. Neither was our Cocker Spaniel, or Dad would instantly ask, "What's that noise?" to which my mother would try to quickly explain whatever was going on in the backseat.

Technology today has pretty much taken the place of gifted auto mechanics and a host of other specialized and skilled people. It's all a bit unnerving to watch robots and computers being used to replace human beings on a large scale, but none of these soul-less and unnatural inventions can ever replace God's creation of mankind along with the God-given abilities, skills, gifts and talents He has given us. In the spiritual realm, it is "practiced precision" that each of us needs to be able to discern spirits.

Hebrews 5:14 says, *"But strong meat belongeth to them that are of full age, even those who by reason of use have their senses exercised to discern both good and evil."* If we are to be "precision tuned" in this evil day, then we need to ask God for wisdom, and the gift of discerning of spirits. *"BELOVED, believe not every spirit, but try the spirits whether they are of God: because many false prophets are gone out into the world"* (1 John 4:1). – J. Haley

Prayer: Lord, we live in a world that requires us to be "spiritually" tuned up so we can walk properly in this world as Your witness. Thank You for giving us Your Spirit who does a perfect job in making and keep us fit for Your service. Amen.

289

August 29

"And Jonathan said to the young man that bare his armour, Come, and let us go over unto the garrison of these uncircumcised: it may be that the LORD WILL work for us: for there is no restraint to the LORD to save by many or by few" (1 Samuel 14:6). In a past post, I wrote about Saul sitting under a tree. However, we have a clear contrast between the spiritual complacent and those who walk by faith. The contrast of Saul was his son, Jonathan. I love the soul of Jonathan. He was a man of faith. How can God show Himself mighty on behalf of people when the king tarries under the tree, and soldiers are being overcome by such fear that they are either hiding or fleeing.

At such times, people do not need a new leader but someone who will become an example, an inspiration. Jonathan was not a man to wait around for something to happen. He went out to scope the enemy and the landscape. He came upon some enemy combatants and instead of zealously attacking or hiding, he put forth a test to see in what way the Lord wanted him to handle it. He clearly proved to be a man of faith.

Jonathan was willing to take his sword, his armor, and allow God to fight for him, knowing the victory would be the Lord's, and he would be the overcomer. Clearly, there is no overcoming until there is victory over the enemies.

The truth is many of us as Christians do not overcome because we do not allow God the means to be the Victor by bringing forth the victory. We fail to take up the sword and lift it in expectation of risking all to witness the miraculous intervention of the unseen world on our behalf.

It seems that many Christians are shaking, running scare, and hiding because they lack the heart and faith to stand on who the Lord is, and stand because of what He did for each of us on the cross. Keep in mind standing gives us the best view of our enemy, while making us the most vulnerable. However, standing on the Word of God makes us immovable.

Prayer: Lord, we know that you are on the move. We cannot see the fruition of all matters, but we know that it will be unveiled at the right time. Amen.

August 30

Likewise all the men of Israel which had hid themselves in Mount Ephraim, when they heard that the Philistines fled, even they also followed hard after them in the battle" (1 Samuel 14:22). I have said this many times through the years, "Heroes are forged." Cowards are simply those who won't step over their fears to see the bigger picture and accept the challenge to take the road of self-denial and choose the way of faith and sacrifice by giving God permission to determine the outcome.

In yesterday's post, I spoke of Jonathan who was a man of faith. His faith allowed him to trust the Lord with impossible odds and as a result, he is an example of one who was victorious. We can't obtain victory unless we are willing to risk it all. We must not care about our personal well-being, but our vision must be honorable and bigger than our small world of self-importance and self-preservation.

The key to heroes is that they see beyond any personal sacrifice to the prize that is worthy of any and all sacrifice. Jonathan went in the confidence of God to the enemies' location. He was a man of real faith. Faith always allows one to advance forward because the results rest in God's hands and not in man's hands.

Jonathan knew who held his life and the events, and as a result, he was able to allow God to show Himself mighty through him. Jonathan's example of bravery and victory shows us heroes ultimately will inspire the fearful and the cowards to take heart because it allows them to stand in the shadow of victory, trusting that it will be secured because God takes the ordinary and does the extraordinary through those who believe Him, and who take refuge in His shadow, while clinging to His promises.

Today the kingdom of God needs to see a few Jonathan's come forth to face present enemies in the strength and power of the Lord's might.

Prayer: Lord, You have enabled me to make so many strides in this world. The current of the world is always hitting against me, but You have delivered me through each one. Thank You for being faithful. Amen.

August 31

"So the LORD saved Israel that day: and the battle passed over unto Bethaven" (1 Samuel 14:23). The Lord is always waiting for His people to step forward in faith, whether they are lost in sin, they are facing insurmountable odds, or they are coming up against the formidable force of their enemy so He can show Himself mighty. In essence, He is waiting for people to believe Him and His Word so He can move on their behalf.

I have watched many Christians who are in terrible situations wondering why God is not doing something about their plight, but I must always consider whether they are stepping in faith towards God, stepping forward in faith because of God, and standing in faith knowing all battles belong to Him. I have to admit, what I see are those who are wrestling with God to do it their way to avoid the test or the mess, instead of letting Him be God and tear up the turf if He needs to.

There are also those who are sitting and bemoaning their plight, but they are not standing by faith and ready to trust God to take their hand and lead them victoriously through the dark night of their soul. There are also those who say to themselves that such miraculous events were for "that time," but now we live in a time where man has the knowledge and tools to solve his own plight.

The truth is, two things never change, man's need to be saved from not only his worthless devices and means, but from himself. And the second thing that never changes is God and how He does things. If we are not seeing the miraculous, the difference does not rest in the times we live in but in the lack of the faith of His people. They may be wrestling in prayer and lamenting in a pool of tears and self-pity, but how many are seeking God's face about the battle before them, and no matter how great, are ready to stand by faith to watch the Lord secure the victory?

Prayer: Lord, I remember the day when I had to get up from being on my face in complete distress and stand by faith on Your promise to save me in the battle and from my real enemies. From that moment on, every time I stand by faith, I have watched You cause obstacles and enemies fall like dominos before Your feet. Thank You for Your salvation. Amen.

SEPTEMBER

September 1

"For scarcely for a righteous man will one die; yet peradventure for a good man some would even dare to die" (Romans 5:7). What are people waiting for when it comes to facing their enemies? Most of the time they are waiting to see if they will be on the winning side of the battle. No one wants to risk life or limb if they think that they are on the wrong or losing side. After all, if they are on the winning side their odds of surviving are better.

They must also feel whatever sacrifice is required of them against any enemy or in any battle must be for a worthy, honorable cause. If they are unsure about the end results or the grand purpose winning out, that is when many will run back to their original lives or hide in caves of utter despair and hopelessness.

For Christians, they have three enemies, the world, the flesh and the devil. However, for the unbeliever they have one enemy: The God of the universe. There is only one great battle going on and that is between the kingdom of light and the kingdom of darkness. There is only one battleground where the battle is intense and that is for and in the souls of men. There is only one prize to gain and that is truth and there is only one winning side in the end. For believers, they are assured as to what side will win and they also know it will be the right side.

As a Christian, one of the most humbling aspects of my faith was to realize Jesus Christ, the perfect, sinless man, who was sent from above to become the Lamb of God died on the cross, not for good people, not for a winning cause, and not in an honorable way; rather, He died for His enemies. Jesus' enemies were not only doomed but many would oppose and fight against His righteousness, mock His truth, reject His sacrifice, and cast off His love as if it was worthless and trample on it with animosity.

To the world the kingdom of light is on the losing side. It notes that out of many who declare their loyalty to Christ, only a few are willing to stand and die for Him. After all, by their actions it appears that many are convinced one must make peace with their different enemies if they are going to survive this world. However, you can't gain this world without selling your soul and you must lose your life here and become crucified to the world to gain Jesus. (See *Galatians 6:14.*) God is clear, those who befriend the world are His enemies.

What side are you really on?

Prayer: Lord, it is easy to become confused because of the many battles going on. The battle is the same—it is for the souls of men but the attacks are many and coming from different directions. The enemy has different arsenals that are used, whether it is temptations of the flesh, catering to the pride, or causing many to become attracted to the power of darkness, Satan has been successful. However, it is who is standing in the end that will determine who wins and I know You Lord, Your Word will be standing in the end. I choose You regardless of what I lose in this life. Amen.

September 2

"Thou therefore endure hardness, as a good soldier of Jesus Christ" (2 Timothy 2:3). Have you ever wondered why the world can never be a friend of God? Let me ask, what kind of causalities are associated with the battle taking place in this present age

between the two unseen kingdoms of light and darkness? There are a couple of casualties: Souls lost to darkness and lives offered up as sacrifices.

The world looks at the empty cross of Jesus and is convinced that it has won, it looks at God's long-suffering and uses it to verify its conclusions, and it points to Christians who hide in fear when it comes to standing for and on truth, believing that their actions confirm that there is not anything of the kingdom of heaven that is true and worthy when it comes to the aspect of one losing any part of their life for it.

As the darkness becomes greater and wickedness reigning seems to remain unabated, it is as if the kingdom of light is being consumed by the kingdom of darkness. The demons rejoiced at the Son of Man's death on the cross, thinking it was the end to the conflict. They were blinded to the fact that at Jesus' resurrection, He would come forth holding the keys of hell and death, signifying that the real war had been won, not by great armies, but by His death, burial and resurrection.

Consider soldiers of the cross. How many have been tortured and martyred through the years in the name of the god of this age and all of the idols erected because of ignorance towards God, rebellion abounding in the hearts of the lawless and unbelieving, and the desire for man to be a god of his own little kingdom? However, these soldiers know their kingdom is not of this world.

It is natural for Christians to be excited about their citizenship in heaven, but not their call to duty as soldiers to stand and fight on behalf of their kingdom. Even though the war has been won by Jesus, the battles for souls continue to rage. As soldiers, we not only have been given the means to stand against the unseen forces, but we possess the authority, power and weapon to cause the enemy to flee.

Prayer: Lord, we rejoice over our heavenly citizenship, but can often cower before our enemies who are in all reality subject to You. Forgive us for failing to remember the victory of the cross so that we can stand in assurance of overcoming, knowing that our victory awaits us when we finally come home. Amen.

September 3

"But the word of the Lord endureth for ever. And this is the word which by the gospel is preached unto you" (1 Peter 1:25). Yesterday, I talked about casualties in the war between the kingdom of light and the kingdom of darkness. The first two causalities mentioned are souls and lives. However, there is another casualty and that is truth.

Consider the deception of this age and how great it is as many fall into line with its lies because they want their own reality that is void of righteousness, judgment, and consequences. After all, they just want to live their life and not be bothered with that which might shake their world, penetrate the darkness of their fantasy, and remind them that after this life is eternity, and if the Bible is true: JUDGMENT awaits.

When you look at the kingdom of light from the perspective of the world, it seems like it is always on the losing side in the skirmishes and battles taking place. The Leader of it crucified and His followers constantly being offered up on the different altars of this world.

This brings us to the believer's sword, the Word of God. In every age of lies, the truth established in God's Word becomes a luxury that costs much to possess. Even though in the end God's truth will be the only reality left standing, many in the camp of God, out of fear or indifference, have allowed it to become a casualty. After all, it seems as if the enemy constantly puts its foot on the necks of those who are "stupid" enough to believe the Bible and turn the other cheek when falsely accused, remain silent when mocked, slandered and beaten instead of being defensive and angry, forgiving instead of bitter over the unfairness of it all, and loving instead of vengeful.

As believers we already know the war has been won, but to gain the prize we must be willing to endure the hardship of soldiers in an unforgiving, formidable world where skirmishes and battles will occur, the causalities are great on both sides as is the case of all wars, and it will continue to be so until Jesus comes back for His Church; and as King of kings judges the world and puts His foot on all of His enemies' necks once and for all.

Prayer: Lord, You came as a Servant, the Lamb of God the first tIme. It seemed that as a servant, You had no rights and as a Lamb you had no say. That was all necessary to secure our redemption, but the next time You come it will be as victorious Lord, King, and Judge. Hallelujah! Amen.

September 4

"Wherefore come out from among them, and be ye separate, saith the Lord, and touch not the unclean thing; and I will receive you" *(2 Corinthians 6: 17).* As we all know, there is only one winning side, but in this world, its "winning side" is not always the "right side." In the end the right side will win because our God is powerful and just, but meanwhile the evilness of the world seems to be winning.

The truth is that in this world, it matters little who is right because it is surrounded, encased, and tied up in lies. To the world what matters comes down to ending on top of the pinnacle of arrogance no matter what is sacrificed along the way. The debate of the world is not about truth, but about who can outshout the other the loudest that counts. This world's systems are about money, power, and control and not about righteousness and justice.

We Christians need to keep these matters in the right perspective. We lament about the unfairness in the world, but what do we expect from Satan's system? We play footsie with the world to keep some semblance of peace with it so we can be comfortable in our worlds.

However, one of the greatest tricks of the world is something called "compromise." A little leaven leavens the whole lump, you can't serve two masters, and what agreement does the temple of God have with the temple of Baal? The more one compromises with the world the more they lose their edge, as their light of truth becomes dim and they lose their ability to discern. It is for this reason we are told to come out and be separate from it.

How can we come out and be separate from the world? After all, we are in the world, and the world provides our physical needs. The Bible tells us we must not love the world, but rather to set our affections on things above and choose to love, trust, and obey our God.

Clearly, we must not look to the world for our life and we must choose to always remember that our life is in God's hands. We must remind ourselves that Satan has used the world's systems to take captive what rightfully belongs to God, and regardless of how he uses it to oppress, enslave, and control people, God is still our Provider.

The world complicates things to bring confusion, but the simple truths of God will bring such blessed clarity as to what is right even in the midst of great spiritual darkness. As believers, we need to quit trying to adjust to or lay down for the world to keep peace with it, and stand up by faith and stand firmly on His Word, knowing that in the end, God's truth will be the only thing left standing.

Prayer: Lord, the world can easily catch us away or cause us to take detours from what is true. Lord, I give You permission to put necessary blocks in front of me when I fall or slip into the tumultuous waves of the world because I failed to step by faith in the current of the flow of Your Spirit. Amen.

September 5

When they leave us, they leave behind poignant and cherished memories. I'm thinking of beloved pets. Take our cute, smart, fluffy Chihuahua, Bell, for example. When we first moved into our current home, everything was in bad shape. The backyard had very little grass and was mostly weeds which had to be removed by a rented turf remover.

All of this upset little Bell because, to her, this was her yard, and she didn't appreciate losing even the scant grass that we had. Finally, all that was left was a small patch of grass which she decided to lay on in order to try and protect it for herself. She guarded her little "island" and looked at us as if we were all nuts. Finally, we had to carry her into the house while she sadly watched the removal of that last bit of grass. What she didn't know was we had nice, green turf all ready to lay down so she would have a whole yard of fresh green grass to enjoy.

Whenever I think of that day and Bell's tenacious "hold" on the remnant of something so important to her, it brings to mind how true that can be for us humans when it comes to the bits and pieces of our lives that we try to guard, cling to or save. The truth is we are not meant to live in this temporary world, in these temporary bodies while clutching our temporary pleasures and possessions forever because, if we belong to the Lord, He has far better things for us—far greater and more wonderful and glorious than words could ever tell.

Therefore, let us be willing to let go of that which we are afraid to lose in order to gain that which shall never be taken away. *"But what things were gain to me, those I counted loss for Christ. Yea doubtless, and I count all things but loss for the excellency of the knowledge of Christ Jesus my Lord: for whom I have suffered the loss of all things, and do count them but dung, that I may win Christ." (Philippians 3:7)*– J. Haley

Prayer: Lord, we can become so focused on what we might lose, we end up missing what we could gain. You have a storehouse of spiritual blessings and promises for us, but in some cases, there are those that only receive a small trickle because they won't let go of the world. Lord, prepare me to never settle for the trickles but to desire and stand under the waterfall of Your blessings. Amen.

September 6

"But avoid foolish questions, and genealogies, and contentions, and strivings about the law; for they are unprofitable and vain" (Titus 3:9). We Christians have a hard time not falling into the unprofitable debates about non-essential doctrines that have nothing to do with the salvation of one's soul. After all, as prideful individuals, in our minds there is no way we can't be right about this particular belief, which automatically makes the other guy wrong. However, that is not the issue.

The issue is are you in a right spirit lining up to the Word of God because you love the truth? Are you doing all you can to possess truth no matter how many times it offends you and puts a spotlight on what is not right in your attitude and thinking?

Let me state, the only place we will always win any argument, establish we are right about our conclusions, and be able to maintain the serenity about our reality is in the courtroom of our own minds, otherwise, we are going to be challenged in every other arena of life. We are going to find ourselves in conflict with others over opinions and theories. We are going to be agitated and offended by people who insist their reality or take on something is right, leaving us wrong. We are going to wrestle over minor details while at times missing the major issue of a matter. We are going to find ourselves wounded and bruised when we fail to stand on the rock of God's truth because we have moved away from it in order to defend our own personal pinnacles or small mounds of truth.

I often tell people to beware of what mountain they insist on dying on because their sacrifice may prove to be all in vain. We are told in *1 Peter 3:15* to be able to give a reason for the hope in us. The hope in us is not some church affiliation, pet doctrine or belief, or the latest teaching or revelation from the latest prophet who often turns out to be a heretic, but Jesus Christ who is in us and is our hope of glory.

Jesus is the truth, and when He is left standing in His glory in a matter, as well as exalted in light of His great work of redemption, you can be assured you are standing on the Rock itself and in the end that is what will silence any and all useless arguments.

Prayer: Lord, our religious pride often causes us to be like dogs fighting over a meatless bone when it comes to the endless debates we can get into over insignificant religious issues. Lord, I don't have time to waste such breath and energy over that which is non-essential. Keep my focus right, my heart quiet, and my mind disciplined to hear the voice of Your Spirit and recognize the vanity of man's endless religious debates and avoid their alluring attraction to my pride to prove that I also know something about spiritual matters. Amen.

September 7

"Whosoever is born of God doth not commit sin; for his seed remaineth in him: and he cannot sin, because he is born of God (1 John 3:9)." Christians make many different assumptions about their spiritual well-being. They think once they say the sinner's prayer, have some religious affiliation, and try to live a somewhat decent life, they are good to go. If they sin because it falsely promises some personal happiness that they think they well deserve, they figure grace will cover it, and that even though it is outright rebellion God's love will overlook it.

Such individuals believe once they have freely partaken of sin, that if they confess the sin, He will forget it. However, any such casualness towards sin causes one to put God to a foolish test. In such cases it is not the sin that these people foolishly walked in that causes them to be on dangerous ground; rather, it is their irreverent or complacent attitude about sin, which shows disrespect towards God, contempt towards His Word, and reveals that in the right situation they prefer the way of sin over Him. The Apostle John makes it clear if one is born of God, they will not be able to walk in sin without deep conviction that will cause them to flee it and run back to God in repentance.

It is easy to get caught up with debates over the matter of salvation. However, salvation is not the issue at this point; rather, it is the matter of the heart attitude. There is nowhere in the Bible where God is caught up with the narrow confines of man's theological understanding about such matters. He is testing the heart of man because the attitude of the heart towards Him, along with sin, and righteousness is what is really at the heart of all spiritual issues.

People who are casual towards sin and feel they can walk in it long enough to get what they want and then they will make it right,

303

lack the fear of God, do not love the truth, and are throwing decaying crumbs at God. It is obvious that they have never repented of what ails them in the first place: their attitude towards sin.

Clearly, they have not been broken over sin, sin that breaks God's heart, sin that cost Him His Son, sin that wounds others, sin that leaves despair and hopelessness behind, and sin that ultimately breaks any fellowship with God and destroys relationships with others. It is also obvious they have never come to a place of true repentance over their selfish preferences and wicked ways.

Jesus is clear, 'repent sinner or perish fool.' We are all born sinners, but we do not have to perish like a fool who may declare with their mouth there is a God, but with their life deny that He even exists, is holy and can have no part with sin, and will ultimately judge each of us for what we do in these bodies.

Prayer: Lord, we start out sinners with foolishness bound in our hearts and if we fail to repent of our sin, receive You as our Redeemer, and crucify daily the influence of the old disposition in us, we will fail to be overcomers and victorious. Forgive us for our foolish ways and selfish dictates. Amen.

September 8

But sanctify the Lord God in your hearts: and be ready always to give an answer to every man that asketh you a reason of the hope that is in you with meekness and fear" (1 Peter 3:15). I mentioned this Scripture in another post. Peter tells us to be ready to give a reason for the hope that is in us. "Reason" in this Scripture points to motive, computation, account, reckon, tiding, or treatise for the hope in us.

How many people are able to give a reason or testimony for their faith in Jesus? How many people who wear the label Christian, stand in sure confidence that God's Word is true and they have reckoned it as so? How many of them are motivated by the love of God when it comes to their life in Christ to stand by faith, to declare the Gospel to others with an urgency, to withstand with truth, and to continue to advance forward to their final destination?

The answer rests with whether Christians have sanctified the Lord God in their hearts. "Lord" here points to our owner, and "God" points to Him being our Creator. We must sanctify, set Him apart in our heart through consecration as we mentally venerate or exalt Him to a place of preeminence in our life.

We must realize He is our only hope, and that hope is identified because He is in us. Since Jesus is who He is, God Incarnate, He is the sum of heavenly glory to us and because He is in us, He is our only hope of experiencing that glory.

Exalting the Lord also points to us being in a place of humility where we can receive truth, proper instruction, correction, and direction in our life. If humility is present, meekness becomes the manifestation of it when it comes to others, and all of it will come out of a healthy attitude of the fear of the Lord, which is the beginning of wisdom.

Are you ready, willing, and prepared to give a reason for the hope in you. If not, perhaps you need to go back to square "A" to see if Jesus is truly your Savior and if you have made Him Lord of your life.

Prayer: Lord, we like to think great things about our knowledge of You and life, but if we fail to know You and sanctify You in our heart, we will find ourselves holding nothing in the end but empty air and wasted time that can't be recaptured. Amen.

September 9

"But seek ye first the kingdom of God, and his righteousness; and all these things shall be added unto you" (Matthew 6:33). What is your main emphasis when it comes to your spiritual understanding? I ask this question because it is not unusual to talk to Christians and hear more about other religious books, the latest trends when it comes to religious authors and shows than the Word of God. I have heard of Christians taking pride in reading the religious materials of cults and yet not know where to find the different books in the Bible.

If the secular influence is not bad enough with its various forms of unscriptural religious entertainment, then you have the religious influence that produces religious pride with its rigid rules, its unobtainable standards, and a false smugness that lacks the love of God where others are concerned. Keep in mind, Jesus never said that we would know people by their religious knowledge but by whether they have love for one another.

In religion we can hide behind pet doctrines, declare certain creeds, and stand on certain humanitarian causes while openly judging everyone with unmerciful cruelty who is not on the same bandwagon as we are. After all, no matter how small, limited, and foolish our religious corner of knowledge is, we still think we have a corner on particular truths or theology.

What many fail to realize is, it does not matter how much religious knowledge they may have, they still can miss what is important. The reason we must be careful as to what we expose ourselves to is because we are developing preferences and tastes as to what we will end up pursuing. The fleshly, worldly understanding will play on our conceits, but it will never develop a love or pursuit for unfeigned truth.

We are to hunger and thirst after righteousness. Faith is accounted for righteousness, and faith comes by hearing and hearing by the Word of God. The only thing that will produce a hunger and thirst for righteousness is a love for the Word of God. If God's Word is going to have the type of effect on us that will produce a hunger and thirst for righteousness, we must cast aside all influences whether secular or religious and give the Holy Spirit a clean slate to write on.

We must forget about what we think we know and ask the Holy Spirit to not only reveal what is truth in His Word, but to reveal THE TRUTH, Jesus Christ. The more we know Christ, who is the essence of righteousness to and in us, the more we will hunger and thirst after it for we will be pursuing to know Him.

Prayer: Lord, we are told what to seek for, but we have a tendency to think if it is religious enough, have a few scriptures attached to it or Jesus' name tacked onto it that it is good enough. The truth is, anything that falls short of leading us to You and establishing us in Your righteousness is not even close to hitting the mark as to what is acceptable to You. Forgive us for failing to seek You. Amen.

September 10

Be of the same mind one toward another, Mind not high things; but condescend to men of low estate. Be not wise in your own conceits" (Romans 12:16). Pride is a door that our enemy can easily enough come through. Conceit is a covert type of pride. It is not outwardly boastful, but when you encounter it, you'll find its very smug in what it thinks it knows. It will not brag about being superior, but it silently revels in its intellectual knowledge as it looks down on those who have no idea as to just how superior it is. Conceit thinks there are few who may know, or understand, that could possibly match its wisdom.

The problem with conceit is that it takes pride in what the Bible calls sensual wisdom and puffed-up knowledge that in the end will leave the conceited individual falling off their smug pinnacle right flat on their face. Such individuals failed to connect with the reality around them. After all, they are above such inferior ways, but they end up looking clueless and foolish in the end because much of life and reality passes them by.

The problem with people who take pride in what they think they know is that they fail to discern the influence of the flesh and world in their thinking. When it comes to spiritual matters, it seems to be obsolete or out of touch. As a result, If they do know truth, they will come into some type of compromise with the world's philosophy or substitute what seems simple with the profane. They do not understand that intellectual pride will set them up to become the jester who ends up playing the fool in the court of the world.

These individuals will eventually hit intellectual confusion, causing them to run back into the world, whether it is back to its philosophies, methods, or intellectual rationalization. This causes them to fall into the world's destructive traps. They do not understand how vulnerable their conceit makes them to the world's influence and how dangerous it is to expose themselves to the spirit of the world, Satan.

Since conceit thinks it stands above all, it must bow down to what it considers of the lower nature of things so that the person can gain real perspective in light of that which is all-knowing, and became wisdom personified in Jesus Christ.

Prayer: Lord, the Christian life is always on the decline in order for You to exalt it into high places. Whether it is kneeling before Your cross in repentance, falling before You in brokenness, or being overcome by Your majesty, we are ever descending in order to be brought higher in You. Amen.

September 11

"And it came to pass, when Jesus had ended these sayings, the people were astonished at his doctrine" (Matthew 7:28). If you are like me, you read both testaments. Perhaps you read the Old Testament in the morning, and the New Testament in the evening. In one of my Bible readings of both testaments, two things stood out. They were: 1) That God blessed Isaac because of Abraham's faith in *Genesis 26*. God's grace denotes that blessings are given to us for the sake of another. For Christians, we are blessed for the sake of Christ. It is indeed a matter of grace, and one that should produce a bit of sobriety and thankfulness in us.

The second thing that stood out to me was found in chapter *5* of *Matthew*: The precious truths of this chapter highlight the attitude, the practicability of righteousness, the character of godliness, and the manifestation of unhindered truth that establishes inward character. We must keep in mind that the Sermon on the Mount is about doctrine. The truth about doctrine is summarized in *John 7:17*, *"If any man will do his will, he shall know of the doctrine, whether it be of God, or whether I speak of myself."*

It is natural for religious people to major in doctrine without realizing that discerning whether doctrine is of God comes down to doing the will of God. Godly doctrine is about doing what is right. It requires you to first line up to God's will according to Scripture and then it entails carrying it out in child-like obedience in the right spirit and with the right attitude. Much of acceptable obedience is practical and can be easily missed when man complicates godly obedience with his religious, fanciful notions that highlight his noble best and not God's love and grace.

It is easy to overlook the practical while we search for the spiritual. However, the spiritual manifests itself in transformation of the inner man, while the practical is an outward manifestation of obedience to what is simple and right before God.

Prayer: Lord how many times are we told to keep things simple, but we want the glory so we have to add our two-cents of importance so people recognize how smart and wise we are. Forgive us for trying to compete or touch Your glory with our pathetic ways. Amen.

September 12

"...and Joseph brought unto his father their evil report" (Genesis *37:2c).* Today I read about Joseph's plight in *Genesis 37.* Joseph reported the evil ways of his brothers to Jacob. He received dreams from the Lord and in his immaturity cast them before those who would prove to be pigs in their attitudes and ways and would trample them under in jealousy and resentment.

For the most part, Joseph's brothers lived comfortably in the pigpen of their world. They resided in the decaying remains of envy and allowed roots of bitterness and mocking to take place. In the end, they tried to rid themselves of the stench of their wicked attitude and devious plans by selling Joseph into slavery.

However, the stench followed them in a couple of ways. First, they caused great sorrow to come upon their father. They had no regard for him, and how the loss of Joseph would affect him, but they were now entangled in their pigpen of deception. It was clear in their foolishness they did not consider the cost or the consequences that would follow.

The second thing they did not consider is that what Joseph saw was truly from God. They didn't care to discern it because it would not be a pleasant situation to bow before who they considered to be a cocky, immature boy. However, they would eventually bow before him, seeking grace and mercy. As I consider this situation, I realize that Joseph's brothers were a big part of fulfilling Joseph's dream.

Think about it. Is this not true when it comes to the many attitudes people have towards Jesus? Many refuse to bow before Him as their Lord, Savior, and God. They have mocked Him and become bitter towards Him. They have sold His truth, oppressed those who truly consecrate their lives to Him, and close their ears to the many warning cries about the end results.

We know God used the actions of Joseph's brothers to bring forth the dreams He gave the young man. We also know He used people to carry out the prophecies surrounding Jesus and His sacrifice on the cross, and continues to do so when it comes to the prophetic events that will usher in His second coming, BUT woe to those who have to live with the fallout of their own sinful actions of rejection, envy, anger, and betrayal!

Prayer: Lord, through this life we as believers will encounter many, like Joseph's brothers, who for one reason or the other become envious, unjustly angry at us and will have no trouble betraying us. However, I can see how You use such people to refine me and sometimes to get me where I need to be for You to fulfill Your plan in my life. Therefore, all I can say, "Amen, so be it."

September 13

"For where envying and strife is, there is confusion, and every evil work." One of the great enemies I have encountered in my life and ministry is jealousy. Jealousy can create such an unpleasant, tormenting environment from within, that to make some type of

peace with it, we have to transpose it elsewhere by placing the problem of this sin of iniquity at the feet of the one who our jealousies are focusing on.

To the mind of many their jealousies are present because there is something wrong with the other person; therefore, such envies become a twisted definition of discernment to these individuals and not a problem that is highlighting some character deviation in them. It is easy for envy to take anyone captive. Anytime we fall into this trap, it is natural to secretly think at such times that we are being treated unfairly or that we should be in that person's position, or have their recognition because we are more equipped and have earned it in some way.

We don't realize how envy works. It starts out from the pinnacle of pride. Pride is the door in which all jealousies enter. It calculates that we are not being treated properly as to our perception of importance in a situation, which often leaves us either feeling judgmental or smaller, insecure, and uncertain as to our place in the situation, causing confusion. Since we are not getting the proper attention, we take offense and this is where certain power plays or manipulation comes into operation, which often confuses, causes suspicion and mistrust.

If we fail to silence the cries of "foul" within us, we began to become angry, which is a door that Satan uses to bring in greater division. However, envy at any level will prove to be an evil working that wounds the innocent, bruises relationships, causes division, and thwarts the work of God.

We are all prone to envy, but we must discern it and immediately put it down as a liar and trap of darkness. And, to make sure it does not make any inroad, we must turn our attention towards the one that we are jealous of and see in what way we can encourage or help them in whatever their ministry, task, and responsibility is. You not only silence the envy in you because you step over self and leave it in the dust, but you overcome it by turning it into an opportunity to lift the arms of those who, out of envy, you were about to judge for trying to do the business of God.

Prayer: Lord, I can't stand the feeling of tormenting jealousy from within or the unbearable games and demands of those who are jealous. It is a green-eyed monster that has a very slanted perspective. Forgive me for giving it any space to cry "foul" or for giving in to it because in the end it will consume the one who harbors it. Amen.

September 14

"But covet earnestly the best gifts: and yet shew I unto you a more excellent way" (1 Corinthians 12:31). Jealousies are a major challenge for the "old man," because they are a natural response. Pride is in competition with others, ego desires to be exalted, vanity wants adoration, gifts require to be distinguished, and abilities want recognition. Because jealousies are prevalent in the old man, we must recognize them and step over them by adopting the attitude of Christ towards all things.

Jealousy and covetousness are the same except covetousness will cause one to pursue it where jealousy will simmer in toxic juices of resentment and anger. It is for this reason we are told to covet earnestly the best gift. This means we are not to settle for less, but desire what is best and pursue it with everything in us.

We are to covet the best gifts but yet God wants to show us a more excellent way. In other words, He does not want us to stop at what is best, but go on to what is excellent.

And what is the excellent way? —that of love. Godly love does not covet something; rather, it rejoices in what is honorable and godly. It is selfless; therefore, it is willing to give way to that which will prove to be beneficial for others.

313

I want to pursue and possess heaven's best gifts for His glory but I also want to walk the excellent way of love to make sure that I do not give way to the selfish base ways of the "old man" and bring a reproach on my testimony, leave a sour taste of hypocrisy and confusion in the mouths of the vulnerable, and leave Christianity with a black eye.

Prayer: Lord, You only allow covetousness when it comes to believers desiring that which is excellent. Give me that great desire that will cause me to pursue it regardless of where it takes me and what I have to leave behind of this world to possess it. Amen.

September 15

"But who may abide the day of his coming? And who shall stand when he appeareth? For he is like a refiner's fire, and like fuller' soap" (Malachi 3:2). I was learning about the Refiner's Fire in purifying silver. What caught my attention was that the silversmith sat in order to keep his eye on the process and make sure the silver was not destroyed.

Our Lord is sitting on the right hand of majesty, waiting for that time that He is sent once again by the Father to gather His people. The work of redemption was done at the cross, but the process is still taking place to bring forth a purified people. I know this is true because the work being done in my life is ongoing. It is clear it is all about timing and using the right circumstance to bring forth the desired results. The process is tedious, which is hard for many of us to accept.

As I have shared in the past, the other fact I learned is that the silversmith does not consider his work to be done with the silver until he can see a reflection of himself in it. Is this not true in the case of the Church? God is patiently trying to bring out the reflection of His Son in each of us so as part of His Body, we will reflect Him in this world.

King David talked about waking in His likeness in *Psalm 17:15.* I am aware that the work being done in my life is the Refiner's way of separating me from the dross in my life, refining me to be molded and shaped to His image.

This process is what it is and I embrace His glorious work for there is no greater legacy than to reflect Jesus, and no greater inheritance than to end up possessing His life and glory.

Prayer: Lord, I knew You fell down and prayed at Gethsemane, and You quietly stood before Your accusers so You could go by way of Calvary. You were lifted on up the cross to secure our redemption, but now the work has been finished, and You now sit on the right hand of Majesty watching over the process of Your saints to ensure that we each come forth by reflecting You in this dark world. Praise Your Holy Name. Amen.

September 16

"Also now, behold, my witness is in heaven, and my record is on high" (Job 16:19). I love this verse. This reminds me that what will be used to judge me in the end is not found in this biased world. Job is going through such trying times and it appears as if God is truly judging him, but he knows God is not behind it and he is struggling to figure out what is going on. He does not know why he is in such a personal struggle. After all, there was no conviction of sin and even though his situation was unbearable, he still found ease and peace with it at the point of his faith towards God.

Yet, his three friends who came to comfort him, proved to be miserable comforters as they tried to set the "record straight" according to their opinions. Clearly, they did not comfort him but ended up judging and falsely accusing him.

Job stood firm because he knew there was a witness in heaven that knows all and a record that had been properly kept. The only thing he was missing was a mediator or what he referred to as a days-man who would stand in the gap for him (*Job 9:33*). The truth is Job would in the end have to stand in the gap for his friends, even though they were falsely accusing him.

This brings us to the witness in heaven. John tells us who these witnesses are in *1 John 5:7*. Remember it takes two or three witnesses to confirm a matter. Who are the witnesses? The Father, The Word, Jesus and the Holy Spirit. We also have a Mediator, intercessor who stands in the gap for us, the Man Christ Jesus (*1 Timothy 2:5*). As believers we have it all and like Job, we can stand according to the witness of heaven and not falter before the false witnesses of this world.

Prayer: Lord, have mercy on us, Your pathetic people. Job had no sense of a days-man who could stand on his behalf, and I am so thankful that You are our intercessor who stands in the gap for Your people in the courts of heaven. Amen.

September 17

A few days ago, I made a comment that I can't stand stupid. That sentiment still holds, but it's also true of myself. That's the problem with living a long time—that just means you have more time to do "stupid" things and prove that your common sense likes to take trips to the dark side of the moon.

One such time occurred back in the early 80's (and I've only shared this with a couple of people, and definitely with my mother) when my husband and I took a drive up into the Cascade mountains in Washington (which we lived close to.) It was mid-January and for some miraculous reason it had quit being cold, overcast and wet. That, in itself, should have served as a huge caution sign, but oh no!

We decided to hike, with our two wonderful dogs, about 3 miles or so up to a small mountain lake. It was so exhilarating, so beautiful, and so peaceful. Too peaceful, in fact. There was not another soul around anywhere! About half way up, we became uncomfortably hot, so we took off our cold-weather outer jackets, and stashed them in some bushes by the trail to retrieve when we hiked back out. On we went, enjoying the rare beauty and weather, and not thinking (at all) about the time of the year and how early the sun sets.

Finally, we made it, I took a series of pictures of the lovely scene so I could later paint it in my studio, and then we noticed that the light was growing dim. Hastily, we began the long hike back down the mountain, but it was too late. It got pitch black! Did we have a flashlight, matches, water, or anything that people with an ounce of common sense would carry? NO!!!

That's when I began to pray and quote every scripture that I could remember about the Lord being a "light unto our path" and how He keeps our feet from "falling" (yes, I know that refers to sin, but I assure you, He answered my prayer because it was so dark you couldn't see roots, rocks, holes or anything!) Our two dogs led the way back down that mountain, my husband followed them, and I came last. Did we see our jackets? No! Was it cold? You bet!

Finally, we came to a fork in the trail and then we knew our jackets were back up the trail somewhere. So, my husband left me standing there for what seemed like an eternity while he somehow managed to go back up through the woods to look for our jackets. (He must've had good night vision).

I remember looking up at all the stars, and words can't describe the "all alone in the Universe" feelings you can experience in such a plight. It was dead silent. What if my husband got lost, or hurt, or attacked by something and never came back? What if I got attacked by a mountain lion or...? I couldn't hear anything. Nothing! Total silence.

Only God could help us, but would He? More exactly, does God help people who make stupid decisions? Oh! Definitely, especially when you're totally helpless, humble, repentant, and crying out to Him with everything in you. At last, I finally heard my husband when he was maybe ten feet away, and miraculously he had found our jackets! I was chilled through and through by then, and so thankful to have a jacket, the husband and our two dogs.

But we still didn't know which fork of the trail to take, and our dogs (who, I have to admit, were obviously quite disgusted with us by this time,) turned on to the right trail and led the way back to our pickup. *Psalm 107:8* says, *"Oh that men would praise the LORD for his goodness, and for his wonderful works to the children of men!" Just pray to be wise enough to pray for wisdom!"* – J. Haley

Prayer: Lord, we can prove to be foolish when we fail to seek You about matters or discern what is going on around us. However, I remember Your promise, "When we are faithless, You prove to be faithful." That holds true when we find our foolishness has led us astray. Thank You for being faithful. Amen.

September 18

"Let us hold fast the profession of our faith without wavering (for he is faithful that promised;) And let us consider one another to provoke unto love and to good works" (Hebrews 10:23-24). How many gems has God put into your path to enrich your life? Some of the most valuable gems are the saints that remind you of those stout-hearted individuals in the Bible who will not be moved from the Rock of ages no matter what besets them.

Donna Spencer is one such saint. She has a testimony of God's faithfulness and intervention that shines through the darkness. Her dedication to the Lord has served as an example to many including myself. Her prayer life has shaken heaven many times on behalf of others, her steadiness in her Christian faith has become a pillar to lean on, and through her examples of Bible reading, ministry to others, and maintaining the right focus, she reminds those around her that there are necessary disciplines in the Christian life that must be adhered to, to keep nourished, sharp, and ready to do the Master's bidding.

Although her tabernacle of almost nine decades is beginning to show wear and tear on it, she will not give up on victoriously finishing the race. Her eyes are growing dim but her goal is to read the Bible through one more time before she loses her ability to see it. Even though she is having problems walking, she keeps running to her prayer closet. She clearly misses being involved with her Christian family, but she knows her real fellowship is with the Lord.

The Lord always will give us examples of stout-hearted saints. They can be found in the Bible, but they can also be found among us. God always has His remnant, His witness, His saints that will never be moved from the Rock. In the end, there will never be any excuse for those who call themselves "Christian" for being ignorant or a spiritual slacker about what it means to be a committed believer that endures to the end.

Prayer: Lord, You are faithful to give us examples but for many of us the temptation is to look to the world for the examples of greatness and not with the spiritual eyes to see the heavenly examples that You have set before us. Forgive us for our arrogance, worldly standards, and fleshly and idolatrous attractions. Amen.

September 19

"Be not deceived; evil communications corrupt good manners" (1 Corinthians 15:33). We can't determine the people that cross our path, but we can determine how they impact our lives.

The influence of others will be determined by if we keep company with them or not. Communications point to "companionship." We are clearly told here that evil companionship will corrupt any good manners we have been taught or established in our conduct.

The first thing evil companionship perverts is authority. It will mock true authority and cause rebellion. It will encourage one to challenge authority which will end in lawlessness.

The second thing evil companionship will do Is cause a restlessness to rise up in the soul. It implies that the only excitement in life is to keep pushing the "rigid bars" of the establishment, whether it be home, the church or the law of society because we have RIGHTS. It becomes a sick game that will always escalate if there are no real consequences to be paid. Eventually it will become an appetite that will live on the edge of destruction, ending in ruin of relationships, reputations, and lives.

The third fruit of evil companionship is communication itself. Bad companionship always brings the worst out in us. Our attitude becomes belligerent, good conduct goes out the window and our language begins to sound like it has come out of some manure pile. We begin to act like the world, sound like it, and look like we belong to it.

Righteous living will have a clear distinction from the world. We, as Christians, need to quit conning ourselves that we can run in and out of the world without smelling like the pigpen in the end.

Prayer: Lord, we want the best from both worlds, but the world will choke out our life in You and Your Word demands that we come out and be separate. It is obvious we can't have it both ways; therefore, I choose You. Amen.

September 20

"And what concord hath Christ with Belial? Or what part hath he that believeth with an infidel?" (2 Corinthians 6:15). Who do you seek out or prefer to be with when it comes to companionship? It is natural to seek out those we think have something to offer, prefer those we like, share with those we trust, and fellowship with those we have agreement with.

Successful relationships are two-sided and find their strength in agreement. Through the years I have discovered there are people I would like to seek out, but they are not interested in me. I have loved certain people, but very few had the same commitment as I did. I have shared with those I thought I could trust to only be betrayed. As for those I had real agreement with, there were very few.

It is important to point out that because people do not share the same attractions, the same likes, or the same attitude about matters, it does not make them unreliable, untrustworthy, or unapproachable. It simply means they have different values, are on a different path and possesses a different focus.

What we need the most as people is true fellowship. So much of our conversations are surface at best. Man for the most part is lonely and longs to find someone with whom he can have a deeper and more satisfying time of fellowship.

I often wonder with today's indifferent technology how many people can even understand or have ever experienced real fellowship. Healthy verbal exchanges are few as communication is becoming a lost art. The more we hide behind screens, fellowship will become extinct, causing greater isolation.

This brings us to real fellowship. To have it, people must have the same spirit. For Christians, they learn fellowship at the feet of Jesus, but they must first seek Him out. They experience it in a place of humility, but they must be willing to be brought low; and, they begin to know its satisfying qualities when they truly learn to listen and hear what the other person is saying so that they can interact with them.

Prayer: Lord, so many people are lonely, isolated from human interaction and companionship. Sadly, although they may greatly fear being alone, many end up alone because they do not know how to reach out to others and interact with them, and that includes You. You are the only One who can fill every empty, vacant spot in our lives. Fill me with Your Spirit. Amen.

September 21

There he proudly stood with all four paws firmly planted on the rock that marked the highest point in the backyard that he could reach. As I watched our little Yorkie-Poo survey his kingdom from his personal rock, and announce his importance with a couple of barks, I couldn't help but burst into laughter. He may think he's "on top of the world" in his own small territory, but then, how many of us have thought the same thing about our lives?

I remember back to when youthful zeal along with a great deal of "vim and vinegar" would suddenly rush through my entire being like a great gust of wind on the open seas that would "hit my sails" and send me flying over the waves on the wings of my imagination—an imagination that wanted to literally pick up the whole world and shake it awake. To be sure, there is an old saying, "Youth is wasted on the young."

As a person grows older, physically weaker but hopefully wiser, that saying means much, especially as you watch the youth waste their strength on nothing but vanity; however, if we learn anything at all in this life it is this: we must learn of the only sure foundation—our Rock, Jesus Christ.

If ever there was a need and a time for people to come to the Rock for the saving of their souls, to the Rock for an indestructible foundation that shall never be moved, to the Rock upon which to build their lives so that when the storm comes—and come it will—they will remain steadfast, strong and unmoved, that time is NOW. *"He only is my rock and my salvation; he is my defence; I shall not be greatly moved." (Psalm 62:2.)*

Are you anchored to the Rock? – J. Haley

Prayer: Lord, we know that man's exalted place can be a mere platform, a small mound, a bandwagon, or a hill, but in the end, it will prove how small our world and understanding is. Give us Your perspective so we can soar in the heights of Your wisdom and glory. Amen.

September 22

"He answered and said unto them. When it is evening, ye say, It will be fair weather: for the sky is red. And in the morning, It will be foul weather to day: for the sky is red and lowering. O ye hypocrites, ye can discern the face of the sky; but can ye not discern the signs of the times" (Matthew 16: 2-3)? When summer's heat becomes unbearable, I begin to look forward towards fall. Fall is a time of the year that not only creates a special array of colors but it has a certain smell to it. There is a crispness to the air which lingers in your nostrils. There is also the smell of burning pine needles and leaves floating on the currents of the wind.

I love the feeling of fall. The changing of seasons reminds me change is in the air. Everything in creation adjusts and prepares for the next cycle of life. In fact, creation is never caught off-guard by the abiding laws of nature that are in operation.

It is easy to see that there are changes occurring in the political arenas on the national and international scenes. These changes were prophesied long ago. However, the Bible tells us many will not be prepared to confront the winds and storms that are looming on the horizon.

Even though the changes can be discerned according to the air and landscape, many will live in denial or ignorance of it. As a result, the waves of destruction will destroy the landscape of the lives of many people.

I, for one, choose to heed the signs of the times we now live in. They are exciting because they speak of the great countdown to the coming of our Lord and Savior. It will not be long before we see Him face-to-face.

Prayer: Lord, Your people should live for the time they see You face-to-face. According to the signs, it will not be long before You part the eastern sky and make Your entrance into this world to rule and reign. Quickly come! Amen.

September 23

"Teaching them to observe all things whatsoever I have commanded you: and, lo, I am with you always, even unto the end of the world. Amen" (Matthew 28:20). Ministry can prove to be a revolving door. When you are in it, people come in and out of your life. Some are for a season. They come in and go out with some wave or event to never return, while there are those who ride out storms with you and then go elsewhere because of their calling. Others are the ones who create the storms to be used to test and refine you.

There are a few that after going out of your life, God brings them back. You find there is not only greater refinement in your life, but they likewise have been refined like fine wine. Like John Mark was to Paul at the end of his life, such people prove to be a wonderful blessing and you pray that you also will prove a greater blessing to them.

Then there are those few relationships that remind you of a ship treading through dangerous waters and you hear "steady as you go." Such individuals bring stability to your life. They know what to do when your environment is in chaos.

I have learned through life that the currents of this adventure called "life" are unpredictable, but what causes life to be thrown up in chaos, creating all kinds of different winds, waves and storms in your life are people. They add the spice in your life and some of the spice can prove to be bitter, too hot, and unpleasant but all is necessary to bring the right mixture to your soul.

However, there is one closer than a family member, who desires to be the closest of friends. He is the One who never changes with the seasons, never leaves with the challenges, never forsakes you, or leaves after causing some type of turmoil in your soul, and that is Jesus.

Earthly relationships are important but our relationship with the Lord is priceless. Regardless of the storms that come and go, it is His voice that reminds you, "Steady as you go, because I am with You and I have this under control."

Prayer: Lord, we find ourselves in much tossing and turning about because of our relationships with others. We can trust that You have allowed the people in our life to be there, and we are often reminded that in all storms and challenges that the one anchor that holds true is You. Thank you for never leaving or forsaking me. Amen.

September 24

"Multitudes, multitudes in the valley of decision: for the day of the LORD is near in the valley of decision" (Joel 3:14) It sometimes shocks you how relationships turn out. I remember when my mother and stepfather were newly married his brother Max and his wife Doris came to live with us for a couple of months. They had two children Patrick and Linda who were both close to my brother and my age. In fact, I was exactly ten days older than Linda. After they left, we did not see them for a few years but a not-so-pleasant situation surrounding my stepfather caused us to end up at their door in need of some assistance.

That door is what opened the way for my cousin Pat to come and live with us for the last years of his high school. Pat was the type of person who wanted more out of life and knew he had to make certain choices to bring about his goals.

My relationship with Pat was like a brother. We had sparks, laughter, and some interesting memories. Pat went on to become a teacher and principal. He had five children and now loads of grandchildren.

My cousin Linda had a certain sweetness about her, and she also had an opportunity to come and live with us, but she made a different choice that led to the natural bent of other decisions which caused her to have a challenging and somewhat difficult life at times. Due to ill-health, she passed away at 49 years of age.

Pat and Linda remind me that it all comes down to the choices we make, and it is often that one important choice that changes or corresponds with the bent of the direction we end up going. We either choose to look for the opportunities that will allow us to come higher as we pursue our destiny, or we choose to settle for what we are used too and find ourselves the victim of an unseen current that can lead to regret, sorrow, and despair.

The one thing I am constantly reminded is that our Lord is always calling us higher. The currents are different. For the Christian it is the current of the Spirit that causes us to ever ascend upward but when it comes to the world, the current is that of a river that descends to the lowest points of despair, hopelessness and ruin.

Prayer: Lord, we stand at the crossroad of decisions about our life and the direction we are going. We choose the way we walk in and the bent in which we will naturally go. Lord, we need to make the true and only real choice to always follow You. Amen.

September 25

"Wherefore, my beloved, as ye have always obeyed, not as in my presence only, but now much more in my absence, work out your own salvation with fear and trembling" (Philippians 2:12). In a previous post I spoke of man's sweat. When it comes to salvation there are no personal attempts on man's part that could earn him his salvation. It is true our physical body needs to sweat out the impurities, and when strength is exerted in the right temperature we can sweat, but when it comes to our life in God, such sweat points to our personal attempts to work out something with God. The Bible is clear our best efforts are as filthy rags before Him (*Isaiah 64:6-7*).

When it comes to salvation, we must walk it out in fear and trembling. This means we must have a healthy fear of displeasing God and we must tremble before His Word to avoid taking on a casual attitude when it comes to obedience to Him. We must have enough respect for who our God is that we take nothing for granted and we must have enough sobriety about the things of God that we walk uprightly (*Ephesians 5:15*). I must point out that the burden of obedience is light because it is a matter of love for

God and the yoke is easy because Jesus is the One who already has carried the heavy end. It is clear that there is no sweat in the walk, just an abiding confidence and liberty to advance forward by faith towards God.

I think it is important to note where Jesus sweated: in the Garden in prayer. It is not unusual to sweat in the different gardens of the world when we are truly interceding for souls. It is the weeds of worldly influence that sucks out the joy and essence of life, the changes of seasons are trying to the soul, and the traps of the world are many; therefore, we must be prepared to stand in the gap for others, but even standing does not exert any strength that would produce personal sweat. This standing may turn into a wrestling match before God that brings one into true identification with our Lord over the burden which carries an urgency for souls, but it should never be with God.

We must remember the real wrestling match in prayer was summarized by Jesus, "Not my will, but Your will be done." The great sweat that occurs even in prayer is to get self out of the way so God's way in a matter is understood and His will be carried out.

I have learned that as a child of God I can come to the Father without fear of rejection, as an heir of salvation I can stand before Him in assurance, and as one hid in Christ I can be assured I will be heard as long as I line up to the Father's heart and will about a matter. Once again, I have learned there is no personal sweat in any of it.

Prayer: Lord, the only time I sweat in my walk with You is when I begin to struggle against Your will, wrestle with You when it comes to Your way of doing, and refuse to advance forward as I stubbornly try to hold my ground or personal take on a matter. Forgive me for any and all obstinance. Amen.

September 26

"And Samuel said, What meaneth then this bleating of the sheep in mine ears, and the lowing of the oxen which I hear" *(1 Samuel 15:15)*. Every time I come to this chapter in 1 Samuel, I shake my head at the foolishness of man. I understand such foolishness for I have been guilty of it. Foolishness makes men fools and women silly. It creates a surreal environment that feeds fickle emotions, but is void of any reality.

Saul reveals how foolish men become when they lack faith and true character. Saul set out to obey the Lord's command but fell short of obeying all of it. He consoled himself that God would accept partial obedience in light of sacrifice, but such obedience is disobedience to God.

Obedience is not a test, but a responsibility. Faith is a test and when one fails this test, the fruit of disobedience will naturally follow. Obedience is not up for debate, and for one to be casual towards God is to show a half-heartedness towards the responsibility, which is a type of contempt. To fall short of obedience is to show a disregard towards God and His Word.

At the core of all disobedience is unbelief, which states, "God does not mean what He says." It is sad to think man is actually betting his very soul that God is not who He says *He is; and, like man He really is indeed fickle in what He says.*

Prayer: Lord, forgive us for being foolish towards You and Your Word. Your written Word may be established with black ink on white pages, but the truth of Your Word has been forever established in the courts of heaven, and will be used to weigh us in the balance of Your Law and in accordance with Your Redemption. Amen.

September 27

"And Samuel said, Hath the LORD as great delight in burnt offerings and sacrifices, as in obeying the voice of the LORD? Behold to obey is better than sacrifice, and to hearken than the fat of rams" (1 Samuel 15:22) Saul's disobedience led to irreversible consequences. His actions may have not seemed so bad, but they were in direct disobedience to the Lord. We have a tendency to judge disobedient actions based on what type of affect they leave behind. However, the Lord does not judge disobedience in the same way.

Certain disobedience harbors an abominable attitude when it comes to God. God's instructions are not complicated, and even a child can understand what must be done. When we decide to change the game plan on God, we are telling God we know better or have more compassion or understanding about a matter. God does not care about our opinions and conclusions about things that fail to line up to His way, will and plan.

Saul had even bragged that he had obeyed the Lord. No one should have to point such obedience out because it is our reasonable service, not a matter of great sacrifice. However, when Saul was confronted with the awful truth of his disobedience, he had to confess he had sinned. He sinned because he did not believe God meant exactly what He commanded. In a way it appeared as if he thought he could placate God with some form of outward obedience without going all the way.

In his admission, Saul confessed he feared man more than God. He had to acknowledge he spared the wicked king, even though he declared he had wiped all the people out as God commanded, lying to himself, the prophet and God. Saul lost his kingship, and the legacy he left behind was that the prophet mourned him and the Lord repented that he ever made him king.

May my legacy never cause any saint to mourn over what would be considered a wasted life and actions, and God to repent of entrusting me with any of the work of His kingdom.

Prayer: Lord, You entrust us with a great, lasting legacy. Please keep us from the steps of the foolish by not squandering it on the insignificant things of the world. I do not want to miss heaven because I want to determine when and how I obey You instead of just humbling myself and do what is right and honorable before You. Amen.

September 28

Today as I stood in our kitchen, I asked the Lord for an inspiration for a post. And, this is what He gave me: It was such a beautiful fall day. I watched out the window as puffy white clouds lazily drifted across the blue sky. A gentle breeze playfully teased the wind chimes and ruffled the American flag into a rhythmic dance.

Then, without warning, it hit! An angry fist of wind from seemingly nowhere suddenly punched its way across the landscape, forcing the flagpole, trees, bushes and anything else in its way to bend and bow in submission. Even more surprising was that in a split second it "changed its mind," whirled around, and angrily vented its strength from the opposite direction. Again, everything bowed before it as its fury blew through the yard. All of this took place in less than a minute, leaving me a bit stunned and mildly wondering if it was an omen of things to come.

This unnatural blast of wind was not representative of "winds of doctrine" blowing through the churches, because those winds are subtle, seductive, sensational and subliminal. But there is a wind of the judgment of the Lord in many prophetic Scriptures, such as *Jeremiah 23:19,* and *20* which states, *"Behold, a whirlwind of the LORD is gone forth in fury, even a grievous whirlwind: it shall fall grievously upon the head of the wicked. The*

331

anger of the LORD shall not return, until he have executed, and till he have performed the thoughts of his heart: in the latter days ye shall consider it perfectly."

Praise the Lord! Our God reigns. Be prepared. – J. Haley

Prayer: Lord, sometimes Your inspiration reminds us that You are all-powerful and that we must pause and see how we are walking before You. May we walk lightly out of fear, be discerning out of respect towards You, and be sober in our attitude towards You because matters of heaven entails where man will end up in light of eternity and swift judgment. Amen.

September 29

"Not with eyeservice, as menpleasers; but as the servants of Christ, doing the will of Gd from the heart" (Ephesians 6:6). Will God accept partial obedience or half-hearted obedience? Any obedience that is not complete, true, and what one would end up considering their reasonable service to God would be like saying one is almost saved, is partially saved, and attempted to be saved when in fact such a notion is not salvation at all. Salvation is complete and likewise obedience to God must be complete.

What does true service look like to God? The prophet in 1 Kings 13 was given specific responsibility to go to the king of Israel and prophesy against him and his altar at Bethel. He was told to go straight there, come back another way and go straight back to Judah without stopping along the way. The prophet did everything right except he stopped short of going straight home and sat under a tree to possibly rest. It all seemed innocent enough except temptation caught up with him, and he never completed the course and made it back home.

God never changes His mind about our responsibilities to serve Him in the way the Bible lays out. His Word is Law and according to His immutable character. Everything we do must be with our whole heart, a heart that desires to please God above all else. It takes whole heartedness to stay the course, because after we carry out what we consider the main responsibility, our flesh will want to dilly dally around, our pride with its "so-called" rights will want to take a detour, and a place of rest may catch our eyes. However, everything that would stop us from carrying out our mission is off-limits to us until the job is done.

As believers, we must keep in mind that God's instructions include keeping us from falling into traps of temptation before the mission is completed. Paul stated that he had finished the course. Obedience is not just a matter of doing God's bidding, but completing the course that is set before us, knowing that each step of obedience is taken because we do believe it is God's Word, and that carrying it out at that time is our sole responsibility. When it comes to whole heartedness towards God in all we do, it is not only a matter of obedience that walks in faith, but faithfulness that walks a matter out by faith, and endurance that will not be sidetracked until it has been completed.

Prayer: Lord, only that which is of faith pleases You. This means we must be faithful towards You, faithful in obeying You, and not content until a matter has been completed according to Your Word. Lord, I desire above all else to be faithful to You to the end and I thank You for giving me what I have need of to finish the course. Amen.

September 30

"I protest by your rejoicing which I have in Christ Jesus our Lord, I die daily" (1 Corinthians 15:31). The principle of obedience is clear: we must not rest until we see a matter through to the end. The problem with many of us is we do not have the urgency to see

such matters accomplished. We always think there is another day to do what the Lord wants us to do.

We are, in essence, waiting for the right circumstances, the right mood, or the right environment. However, such waiting has to do with the procrastination of the flesh and not the urgency of pleasing God first. Such waiting simply allows our life in Christ to pass without any real change or advancement towards fulfilling our high calling.

Christianity is not a title but it is about walking out the life of Christ. The light that needs to shine from our life is the life of Christ that is becoming more and more a reality because we are adhering to the call of discipleship.

Discipleship requires us to deny the claims and rights of the flesh to have life on its terms and to mortify the self-life daily on the cross in order to follow Christ into the disciplined life of a saint. This life pertains to all that constitutes true life that produces godliness. Paul even admitted that he "beat the members of his body," the flesh into all subjection so he would not be a castaway or a reprobate in the end.

I think there are other aspects of the religious environment that allows for a sentimental Christianity that often lacks heart, urgency, and clarity. It has to do with the presentations of "cheap grace" that fail to reign through righteousness, "love" that proves to be nothing but fleshly sentiment that fails to produce honorable responses and conduct, and "fruits" that would not benefit and honor the King of kings and Lord of lords.

These presentations have rendered the idea of obedience to God down to a mere footnote at best. Obedience of any kind is often touted as working for salvation, rather than working it out in our lives because of love for our Lord and Savior. It is a subject that is sidestepped to allow people to sleep comfortably on the pillows of Universalism, where all will be saved in the end, and in religious chairs of duty that have some thinking that by going to church once a week they have done their duty; therefore, they can live as they please the rest of the week.

Christianity is not surface religion, full of lifeless activities, or wishful thinking that all will turn out well as long as Christ is somehow tacked on. Christianity is a disciplined life where the life of Christ is being formed in us so that the witness we display is not our religious best, but Jesus Christ and Him crucified.

Prayer: Lord it is easy to sidestep the issue of obedience but You have made it clear if we love You, we will obey Your commands. Lord, I choose Your love, knowing it will compel me to obey You. Amen.

OCTOBER

October 1

"For consider him that endured such contradiction of sinners against himself, lest ye be wearied and faint in your minds" (Hebrews 12:3). I have watched the various rivers around me taking on many different poses during the fall and winter season. Frost highlighted their fringes, ice challenged their liberty, and the cold constantly affronted their resolve, but they remained unstoppable and their relentlessness has not been hindered by obstacles. They have maintained a steadfast flow regardless of the many challenges that have confronted them.

The one aspect about rivers is their ability to push through different challenges. When they are confronted with obstacles, they will find a way around them. When it comes to the frost, the water will take on its beauty, and with the ice it will outlast it until the environment warms, causing the ice to thaw and the flow of the water to revert back to its open, free-flowing ways.

There are countless things of this present world that can cause the ice of indifference to cause the love of God to grow cold in the heart. However, there is the revelation of the Son of God that will once again thaw the coldness of a heart.

Obviously, it is vital that I do not let this world cause me to faint in my mind as the veneer of indifference grips my heart with a stiff but fragile resolve to somehow survive this present age. It is the warmth of the Son of God that reminds me that I have an ark I can hide in. I do not have to face the rampant darkness of this world with the cold indifference of a "stiff upper lip" and a cold heart. In Christ, I will be able to endure to the end of the winter of my spiritual life.

Prayer: Lord, the winter season of this age that is coming upon us is proving to be an ice age. The darkness is causing such coldness to come upon the hearts of many. Cause Your people to look upward to see the real Sun of righteousness. It is Your presence and warmth that will melt the ice upon the hearts of people. Amen.

October 2

"And as we have borne the image of the earthy, we shall also bear the image of the heavenly" (1 Corinthians 15:49). One day I was discussing the beauty of the fall season with a dear friend. I shared how the various colors of the trees dotted our landscape with splendor and majesty. She likewise was sharing how she was witnessing the artistic beauty of fall in her area as well. She then shared with me that this time of the year proves to be the hardest time for the trees.

We never think about what the trees must experience during this season to express themselves in a different way. We know the changing of their color points to preparation for winter. But, I never thought about the tree's display of color actually signaling its last burst of life and beauty just before it takes on the lifeless pose of dormancy.

I can't tell you of the many stories I've heard of people who were dying on their last day, and moments before their death, they seemed to burst forth with life and personality, causing those around them to think they would be okay. My desire as a Christian has always been to have a strong finish regardless of how weak I might be. Like the trees in the fall, I want to display the greatest beauty of the life of my Lord just before I exit the door of death to embrace the glory of eternity. Clearly, the grave is the lifeless pose that marks the saint's life, but resurrection in the spring will reveal the real life and quality that was developed during the most trying times of their life.

Prayer: Lord, beauty comes out of trials and testing. I know I have complained about such trials, but I know that You are trying to bring out the beauty of Your life in my life in preparation to shine brightly in dark times. Thank You for Your faithfulness. Amen.

October 3

"Thou art beautiful, O my love" (Song of Solomon 6:4a). Although it has been raining, we have already had frost cover the landscape. Frost creates its own beauty as it covers the grass and hangs from the trees. As we all know there must be moisture and cold air to produce frost. There is nothing as beautiful as the frost that simply gives an impression of a white glassy look to the edge of a river.

Even though you would think frost is frost, the truth is if you consider its uniqueness in creation, it comes across as a brush stroke of God on the landscape. It sets up a certain environment where the emotions experience a sense of wonder that mere words cannot describe.

Such brush strokes of God are meant to heighten our senses. As a result, they cannot be easily captured by words. They are designed to bring an awareness of something that is to make you pause and consider God's incredible artwork.

The reality of frost is that, like snow, it is made up of various ice particles that represent a world of their own. However, together, these ice particles create a mosaic of beautiful

338

expressions that speak of a Designer who is beyond comprehension. Yet each particle reveals how personal the Designer is. He is meticulous in every way to bring perfection to His design.

I realize my life should be like that ice particle. Its various prisms should reflect the light of Christ as it expresses His incredible heavenly beauty.

Prayer: Lord, I so appreciate Your creation. It speaks of You in various ways. How can man look at it and say there is no God. Your Word answers that question by calling such a person a "fool." Lord, help me to see You in every bit of Your creation. Amen.

October 4

"Now Hannah, she spake in her heart; only her lips moved, but her voice was not heard: therefore Eli thought she had been drunken" (1 Samuel 1:13). One of the women that inspires me when I read about her is Hannah, Samuel's mother. Hannah, whose name means "grace," reminds me that we can easily enough miss a blessing because we do not understand God and His grace.

Hannah was mocked and misunderstood, while quietly bearing her sorrow that she was living a life of disgrace because she was childless. Eli thought Hannah was drunk because her prayer was a silent heartfelt prayer to the Lord. He even accused her of being drunk. Eli's assumption almost cost him to miss an important blessing.

When Hannah explained that she was pouring out her sorrow before the Lord, Eli instructed her to go in peace for the Lord would grant her, her petition. And, what was her request—the answer came in the form of Samuel, who would minister to Eli and before the Lord as prophet and the last judge of Israel.

One must ask, how many of our assumptions have kept us from being part of the blessing, causing us to miss benefitting from God's intervention in a matter? For those who mock the things of God, they will miss the Son of God and heaven. For those who cast aside His servants, they will miss the blessings of God, and for those who make assumptions about the work and ways of God, they will miss being part of the miraculous.

I know in my life I have missed many opportunities and blessings in the past because I was trying to dictate to the Lord how He must bring a matter about according to my judgments and calculations.

How silly we often prove to be in our fallen, finite state!

Prayer: Lord, we have much to be thankful for. We spend a lot of time operating according to our foolishness instead of the wisdom of heaven. I am thankful that as God, You are infinite in Your qualities and willing to go an extra mile with us when You could easily enough become weary with our foolishness. Amen.

October 5

Besides the winds of judgment that I wrote about in one my last post, September 28, there are other "winds" to consider such as the one today that I was unaware of until I noticed that there were only two of three big planters full of thick, tall petunias sitting on the deck.

Closer examination revealed that the third one had been completely knocked off of its pedestal onto the ground. Those petunias had stood a bit taller than the other two pots because their heavy pottery planter was situated on an ornate iron "stool." Looking ridiculously helpless, and greatly humbled, it lay there on its side in the grass until I hoisted it back up onto the deck where it can stay instead of sitting on top of its former platform. Since it's "shorter" now than its companion flowers, there shouldn't be another toppling situation.

I have to admit, this little incident reminded me of a certain day, many decades ago, when a strong "wind of rebuke" from the Holy Spirit served to knock me off of the religious pedestal that I had worked so long and hard to erect. It was such a grand pedestal too—all white and fashionable. But when God, in His great mercy and wisdom, knocked me off of it, I "hit bottom" so hard that I have never forgotten His chastening rebukes concerning my foolish pride. *"A man's pride shall bring him low: but honour shall uphold the humble in spirit" (Proverbs 29:23).* - J. Haley

Prayer: Lord we often fail to realize when we think we are on top of the different matters of life that out of Your mercy You will knock us off such pedestals. I don't know how many pedestals You had to knock me off of before I learned humility is the safest place to be when the winds of testing come our way. Amen.

October 6

"And the men of Israel were distressed that day: for Saul had adjured the people saying, Cursed be the man that eateth any food until evening, that I may be avenged on mine enemies. So none of the people tasted any food" (1 Samuel 14:24). I have made mention of Saul and Jonathan in past posts. The Bible always brings a contrast so we can be rightly instructed in the ways of righteousness. The story of Saul and Jonathan reveals the difference between a righteous man and a fool, something we clearly need to take note of. Jonathan was a righteous man. He had right standing with God and walked according to faith in light of God's ability to bring forth a victory.

Saul was a fool, waiting under a tree instead of seeking the Lord, and when victory started happening because of Jonathan's faith, he zealously jumped in with both feet to claim it. It was all about avenging HIS enemies for making him look inept and not proving victorious over God's enemies because God had stepped on the scene. He suddenly tried to show a bit of piety by demanding the men to fast in battle instead of before the battle that would call for a type of prayer and intercession on their part.

The problem with fools is that they are out of step with the circumstances and as a result they always put others in jeopardy. Being in an intense battle never calls for fasting. You might have to eat on the run, but you are never too fast, for you must keep up your physical strength.

As a fool Saul proved to be out of step with what was realistic and needed. He made a foolish vow that not only set his men up to be vulnerable, but caused them to sin even more. He not only endangered his heroic son, but he set him up for condemnation because of his foolish vow.

Prayer: Lord, it is easy to fall into the traps of foolishness. The only weapons against it are prayer and truth. We can only stand in the battle when we have been prepared to do so by prayer and stand when girded up by truth. Saul was not ready to be a leader spiritually or politically; therefore, he would prove to be a fool. Lord, keep me from the traps of foolishness because of pride and indifference. Amen.

October 7

"And the people flew upon the spoil, and took sheep, and oxen, and calves, and slew them on the ground: and the people did eat them with the blood" (1 Samuel 14:32). I was talking about the foolishness of Saul. Fools sadly never "really get" how ridiculous their thinking and way of doing is. These individuals can become complacent in challenging situations because they lack wisdom

from above. They can become casual because they have no expectation or vision. They can become easily bored because they have no real substance or desire to choose the way of sacrifice and excellence. They also can be easily excited and rush in without counting the possible cost.

As we see with Saul, he became zealous when things started to go his way in a battle that was at a stalemate because of his inaction before God and the enemy. At such times when the miraculous is intervening, fools can acquire a sense of infallibility and as a result, they can't be reasoned with. Instead of showing wisdom, they reveal that their greatest strength is their ability to trouble people, hinder them from doing what needs to be done, and cause others to sin or come under condemnation.

Saul built an altar that was the same as his first altar, but what did he do at that first altar? Altars vary and are built according to whether they are to deal with sin, become a place of worship, serve as a memorial, or witness. Did he thank and worship his God for His great intervention before that altar? Did he prepare to wait for the priest to make a sacrifice for sin on behalf of his inaction of unbelief and his foolish vow? Did he establish a witness of God's greatness?

Fools may build altars but not in light of God's intervention. It may be out of show or out of duty, but a fool falls short of seeking the Lord first. He fails to wait before Him in prayer or to make sure he is in step with the Lord in events, and to ensure that nothing will hinder him from advancing forward to seek the complete victory that will in the end serve as a witness of God's greatness and intervention.

Prayer: Lord, we miss Your victorious way in our foolishness, pass by opportunities to honor You in our ridiculousness, and fail to see the importance of Your great works because we are caught up with how such victories will make us look before others. Lord, my heart is my altar and whenever You move, my next move, when it comes to my altar, must be that of humility, praise, consecration, and worship for what You have done on my behalf. Amen.

October 8

"And Saul said, Draw ye near hither, and the chief of the people: and know and see wherein this sin hath been this day" (1 Samuel 14:28). Words often fall to a wayside but when one makes a vow, they better mean it because the witnesses of that vow will remind that person that a vow has been made and they are to keep it or pay the consequences because it will be considered a sin not to. In the belly of the fish Jonah told the Lord that once set free from his predicament he would pay his vows. One can only summarize that Jonah's vow as a prophet had to do with obeying God and that would include Ninevah (*Jonah 2:9*).

Sadly, words mean nothing to a fool or the half-hearted. This is why words often judge and condemn us because they represent our heart condition. Every time these types of individuals give a vow, they perhaps start out with their best intentions but their character is like a sieve, where everything becomes filtered by what serves their purpose and what proves comfortable and convenient. Once all the zeal or feelings are gone, they will easily enough forget and renege on it. Like marriage vows that are made at some height of zeal and sentiment, few realize that such vows are not made for the good times, but to stand as a witness to endure the not so pleasant times.

Vows are to remind us that our words represent the true nature of our character and that to keep our end of the vow we must endure until it is fulfilled. In a sense we are putting our "money" where our mouth is. We must remind ourselves vows must not be surface but a heart determination.

344

In yesterday's devotion I noted how Saul built an altar like his first altar. It was clear that he never learned from his past rebellious actions. If you remember, at the first altar Saul built ended in him becoming impatient while waiting on the priest, Samuel, to come. The problem with foolishness is it is like a restless wave on the ocean, there is nothing to bring stability to it.

At the first altar Saul acted as the priest, which was a serious offense towards the Lord's instructions that only priests can do the work of a priest, and ended with Saul losing the kingdom for his descendants (*1 Samuel 13:13-14*). His failure to obey even after this situation with making a foolish vow ended with God rending the kingdom from him before his death (*1 Samuel 15:28*), but in this episode Saul's noble gesture of foolishness almost cost him his heir, Jonathan, a righteous man, his life.

As Jesus stated, let your words stand at "yes or no" and do not let them fall to the wayside because in the end each of us will be judged for every word lightly spoken, in jest, or foolishly.

Prayer: Lord, the world is wrapped up in so many lies, and the endless stream of words from many are rhetoric that are used to seduce, con, flatter, or threaten. It has become evident that there are very few words that would stand when tested to the end. However, Lord, I want my words to be established on You, the Rock, and what I say will be a valid witness for You and not a witness against my foolishness. Help me put a guard on my lips and cause my heart to be pure and my determination sure. Amen.

October 9

"But when he saw many of the Pharisees and Sadducees come to his baptism, he said unto them, O generation of vipers, who hath warned you to flee from the wrath to come (Matthew 3:7). It

is not my goal to shake people out of their comfortable lifestyles but how many sense the winds of judgment upon us?

Every generation has been faced with the reality of the times they lived in. Whether it was during the different world wars or the plagues, many felt they were in the last generation. Such warnings became like a type of lecture where every time the next generation heard the term "the last generation," they began to close their ears to it. The reality is that every generation is the last generation in the sense that that particular generation will never pass this way again. Man is like the chaff of the wheat of his generation. The wheat will eventually be gathered and used while the chaff will be driven by the winds to never pass this way again.

It is clear that like the days of Noah the whole world seems to be caught up in a whirlwind that is causing many societies and nations to spin out of control. Even in the smallest of worlds, foundations are being shaken. Whether we live in the last of all generations or not, I long go realized that the generation I have been part of is dying out and what will be left may be briefly mention in history, but like generations before mine, the winds of time are wiping out the footprints and memories of each one.

I was reading what John the Baptist said to the Pharisees in *Matthew 3:7-12*. It is easy to recognize that the Pharisees were the chaff that possessed no value or substance. They would be pulled downward from the narrow pinnacles of religion by winds of judgment, revealing that they were not identified to the immovable Rock of heaven.

John was clearly pointing out that the wind of judgment was coming and would not spare their generation, but would separate and cast their unbelieving souls and reprobate works into the air to be carried away by the winds of destruction.

Whether we are the wheat that will add some substance and life to those we encounter or the chaff tossed by winds of judgment it all will come down to whether we are anchored to the Rock of

Jesus. It is only the Rock of Ages that will enable us to withstand the winds blowing in the judgment of our particular age. The believing will cling to the Rock as the chaff is taken up by the winds. This makes it apparent that in each generation, the tribulations will come, ultimately testing everyone's faith, resolve, and foundation.

The question is, is this present generation ready, prepared, and able to endure the winds of judgment because many are wisely anchored to the Rock?

Prayer: Lord, Your abiding protection is always upon us. We are a blessed people who take for granted Your protection but find ourselves encountering challenges that make us aware that we are ever needful of You at all times. Amen.

October 10

The reason I posted the thought on discipleship ("there are many sons and daughters of God, but few disciples") was to hopefully give pause for Christians to ask themselves IF they are willing to pay the price of being a disciple of Jesus, or if they want to merely "sit in the boat" until the Judgment burns up their works as wood, hay or stubble.

Jesus didn't say "IF you want to get saved and get to heaven"...but "IF any man would follow Me." We are commanded to "go and make disciples" but you can't make a disciple (follower of Christ) until you've been discipled yourself. The great failure of the church system today is the failure to make sold-out disciples while bearing in mind that some will receive a "better resurrection" *Hebrews 11:35.*

Wake up, Church! We have battles to fight, and a race to run if we would be victorious overcomers in Christ. – J. Haley

Prayer: Lord, we have the "buts", the "whys" and the "how's" in our interactions with You, but You have the "ifs." The "ifs" tell us there are no "buts", "whys" and "how's" because there are no other options but to trust You, knowing that You enable us to do what we need to do to be Your attentive disciple, Your studious student, and Your committed follower. Amen.

October 11

"But every man is tempted, when he is drawn away of his own lust, and enticed" (James 1:14). In my studies I always come to the word, "temptation," in various Scriptures. God's Word clearly approaches this subject from different angles. In this Scripture, James is making it quite clear that temptation has to do with lusts.

In my teenage years, a certain saying was made popular by the comedian, Flip Wilson. In my brother, David's senior year, he was called to the principal's office to answer for a certain discrepancy that many other seniors had been involved in. However, my brother was caught having the evidence along with one of his friends.

My brother responsibly took the correction without implicating anyone else, but as he was leaving the principal's office, he took hold of the door handle and upon exiting through the door, he turned back to the principal and used Wilson's famous saying, "the devil made me do it!" and quickly closed the door behind him.

Everyone likes to get the last word in and in doing so we can even leave a smile behind. In considering this saying, is it scripturally right? According to James it is not. Satan cannot draw us into his web unless there is bait to do so.

Whether we like it or not, the bait that is often used to tempt us are heightened lusts that were produced because our imagination started swinging from heights of possible ecstasy. However, the ending is always the same. Such heights have set us up to fall into the deep cesspools of wickedness and judgment.

The other aspect of the "devil made me do it," is the fact it alleviates personal responsibility. It is natural to excuse sin away, and our preference is to make that which is an offence to God into something else less convicting. These tricks are because our prideful desire is to cause a divorce in our lives from recognizing sin for what it is and taking any responsibility for it; therefore, doing away with any obligation to do something about it.

The problem with this divorce is that there is no call for repentance, no need to humble ourselves, and no responsibility to come to the cross of Christ for deliverance. We must keep in mind salvation is about deliverance from sin and death in order to be delivered into the liberty of the Holy Spirit who brings forth the life of Christ in us.

Prayer: Lord, we often try to defuse the real issues of personal discrepancies with light heartedness, but when it comes to matters of life and death, there is no light heartedness but a fearful awareness that we could fall into the hands of an angry God. Forgive us for such flippancy because it points to unbelief. Amen.

October 12

"If it be possible, as much as lieth in your, live peaceably with all men" (Romans 12:18). It is not in the heart of most men to be at odds with their neighbors. They just want to live their lives in peace. For the most part they are not busybodies that go around trying to cause trouble for they just want to be left alone. The problem is man can be easily bent by the few who are trouble makers and since they are sheep, they can easily be driven by the instigators to become the sacrifice for the sake of wicked agendas.

It is amazing what damage the enemy does, but he is able to bring such destruction because there are instruments in this world who are open to do his bidding. Some are evil and ever ready to carry out his plans, others are trying to get ahead and are willing to sell their soul if necessary to obtain the illusion, and there are more than a few who, in the name of some heretical, hypocritical religion, zealously accuse, persecute, and taunt the true servants of God.

How do we Christians live in hatred while maintaining our lives and testimonies? It comes down to trust and obey. If people do it God's way, they avoid many pitfalls, but many Christians fail to obey what the Bible says and as a result fall into the deceptive and destructive traps of the world. Some of it could be ignorance, but most of it is stiff-necked rebellion that reeks with fierce independence that declares that no matter what, they are going to do it their way. They don't realize that this attitude brings them under the spirit of the world that works all disobedience into those who fail to humble themselves in repentance and draw near to the Lord.

Prayer: Lord, there is no place of agreement between me and this doomed world. Keep me from falling for its lies, into its traps, and away from You. Amen.

October 13

"Let us hear the conclusion of the whole matter: Fear God, and keep his commandments: for this is the whole duty of man. For God shall bring every work into judgment, with every secret thing, whether it be good, or whether it be evil" (Ecclesiastes 12:13-14). Being realistic about my conceits has proven to be a humbling process that continues to this day.

I don't know about you, but at a young age I asked questions because I knew nothing. In my adolescent years I had to learn to listen, and in my initial ascent into adulthood I thought I was clever because I had listened enough to figure out how to play some of the games of the world. As a whipper snapper starting out on the adventure of my life, I thought I had the world by the tail only to be slapped down by those who were not fazed by my so-called "cleverness."

The older I have become I realize that there is very little I know and what I do know is a drop in the ocean of wisdom that often fails to rise above man's best to meet the heights of eternal wisdom. I had to face that my worldly knowledge was very, very limited and often manipulated, proving that I lacked any real experience to confirm it one way or the other, and that any real expertise was a drip in some cauldron that became lost in nothingness.

When I consider the difference between God's wisdom and the world's wisdom, God's wisdom is about knowing Him and the more I know and experience Him, the greater my wisdom. His wisdom creates humility and awe in me, while the world's wisdom can prove to possess common sense, but it often becomes some pinnacle that arrogance can stand on to declare its superiority about something. Godly wisdom is able to look past the present to calculate the consequences, while the world's wisdom becomes an avenue where fools often rush through to their own destruction.

The main key behind the different types of wisdom is attitude. The attitude that operates through heavenly wisdom is the fear of the Lord. Solomon points out the necessity for this attitude in Ecclesiastes because one day God will bring every work and secret thing into judgment.

I have to admit that the fear of consequences sometimes kept me on the right path, and that is true for most of us. The only reason we wisely avoid dumb decisions, or stop from doing wrong or foolish things, is because of the negative results that might follow. However, when it comes to the fear of the Lord, love is also present and if we love the Lord, we will obey Him.

Prayer: Lord, without the discipline of godly fear towards displeasing You, we will ever play the fool which will often put You to a foolish test. Lord, I so want the Holy Spirit to shed abroad in my heart Your godly love so that obedience from me to You will be my natural response to Your Word and Ways. Amen.

October 14

"Knowing, brethren beloved, your election of God" (1 Thessalonians 1:4). My co-laborer Jeannette made a statement, "The Bible does not say we are the elite, but the elected." There is a difference, the main one being that of attitude. The elite come across as being the exception to the rule, but the elect realizes their position is a matter of grace.

The elite see themselves as being superior, the elect know that they are in their present status as saints because of the work of Christ on the cross, thereby, equal with the rest who have come to the cross, seeking forgiveness and salvation.

The elite do not think they are in need of healing but the elect realize they need healing to be part of the kingdom of God. The elite are blinded by their own religious pride, but the elect are aware that they are standing on the immovable Rock of Ages.

The elite are quick to judge while the elect are aware that their sins have already been judged and are now under the blood of Jesus. The elite are like the self-deluded Pharisees, white-washed tombs, but the elect know they were sinners from the beginning and only the grace of God could reach them in their miserable state of damnation, and save them unto eternal life.

It is because of God's work through Jesus Christ that the elect have been seated in the heavenlies, sealed with the Spirit, washed by the blood, identified to an everlasting covenant and an eternal inheritance. We are no longer sinners identified to the law of sin and death, but saints that possess the life of Christ who are standing on promises that will never fade, cease, or be done away with by the change of times, dimensions, or seasons.

Prayer: Lord, we are saints. We often think small, aim low, and look down because we do not know what we have in You. We often keep the same requests before You because we do not see beyond this world to discover the heights we can soar in. Clearly, we must keep the matters of Your kingdom before our eyes, knowing that we have the authority to stand before You and with faith pursue a matter until it is brought forth for Your glory. Amen.

October 15

"And the LORD said unto Samuel, How long wilt thou mourn for Saul, seeing I have rejected him from reigning over Israel? Fill thine horn with oil, and go, I will send thee to Jesse the Bethlehemite for I have provided me a king among his sons" (1 Samuel 16:1). Samuel had great hope for King Saul, but Saul was rebellious and stiff-necked. Samuel mourned greatly for Saul but there is only a short time allowed for such mourning over the fools of the world.

It was time for Samuel to once again get into the flow of life and do the work of God. How many of us have put great confidence in a person to only be greatly hurt and disappointed? Man's greatness depends on the work that he allows God to do in him and through him.

God told Samuel it was time to cease mourning and go forth to anoint another person to be king. God's work and kingdom will go on in spite of those who fail to fulfill their calling. God does not need any of us, but desires to use us. However, after taking hold of the plow of God, if we insist on running back to our familiar pigpens, the Lord will leave us there.

Many people are mourning because the world can't provide a reliable king. It often rejects honorable men while embracing the dishonorable because they have some talent or ability that is highlighted and promoted by the world. We need to keep in mind that the world conditions us to accept the Sauls of the world and not the King Davids who may not fit our criteria but will fit God's.

Eventually men will let people down regardless of character because like King David, man will always be humbled by tests that come his way. But then there are always those who cry after becoming disillusioned with some despot, greedy, power-hungry, tyrannical, cruel dictator who has proved to be an utter failure and a complete fool in the end. They are the ones who can't get off of the mat and keep going because they have no heavenly vision.

Saul was man's choice as far as being king, while David was God's choice, but man's choice always falls short of what is beneficial to everyone, while God's choice proves to be excellent and honorable even though such a person may not stand tall among others, and inevitably who proves to be a mere man after all, a man God has simply used in extraordinary ways.

Prayer: Lord, it is easy to fall asleep when things seem to be going well, but the truth is there is always disruption going on in the unseen world that is affecting everyone in one way of the other. Keep me awake and focused on You and what is really going on. Amen.

October 16

"Even him, whose coming is after the working of Satan with all power and signs and lying wonders" (2 Thessalonians 2:9). Yesterday I talked about how Saul was the people's preference for king while God's choice was David. It is important to note that people preferred Saul because he appealed to their senses. He fit their criteria as to how a king would look but they had no real concern if he had the goods to be king. They were not interested with his character, whether he could effectively lead men, and if he had the necessary grit that would cause him to stand when facing the enemy. All they could see is that he looked the part of the king and that was good enough for them.

The world is now looking for a leader. When I listen to who people prefer as their leader, it often comes down to how the person has affected their senses. To some it is how they present themselves, while to others it is what they hear these people say. It is important that we understand the world conditions us as to our preferences. I say this because what we prefer according to senses is not what we would ultimately choose if we could see behind the veneer of a person and know the motives and agendas of that individual. That is why the Bible is clear we are to test their spirit and their fruit and not how good they look or sound.

What kind of leader are you looking for and what is the criteria you are adhering to as to your considerations? We must remember in the end days there will be many seducing spirits and doctrines of demons that will be deceiving people. We know that the one who will step on the scene will use flatteries that will tickle people's ears. We also know he will attract people with signs and lying wonders.

It is clear that the world is conditioning people to embrace the anti-Christ and as Christians we must not have any of it. We must discern who God is using as honorable vessels to bring forth His judgements, and who He is using as dishonorable vessels to bring forth the prophetic times that will usher in the coming of the real Lord Jesus Christ.

Prayer: Lord in the past I thought I was clever and wise when it came to who I thought was right for the different leadership positions in churches, communities, and nationally, but I have learned man at his best will fail, and man at his worst will create devastation. It is clear I must trust that You are establishing the right vessel for the right time to do Your bidding, ever being mindful that the only true leader that is going to do it right and get it right is You. Amen.

October 17

Maybe it can be associated with the "call of the wild," but then again, maybe not. I'm way too much of a sissy to launch into some no-man's land of raw, untamed wilderness; however, there definitely has always been a "call of the woods" whispering to me.

This lure to follow a path into a forest, to walk among the trees, to discover new vistas, listen to nature's sounds, to breathe cool fresh air, and enjoy the subtle mystery of it all has captivated me since I was a small child, much to the chagrin of my mother. I got the lecture of "Stay out of the woods, and watch out for the boogie man" from both parents quite regularly.

Even though I grew up in north Seattle, back in that day there were plenty of vacant lots with towering "Scotch Broom" bushes and evergreen trees that were just perfect for little kids to play in. One day when I was maybe kindergarten age or so, the "call of the woods" overcame my fear of any "boogie man."

I knew my mother was busy inside, so since I was already outside in our front yard, I heard that alluring "call of the woods."

Naturally I gave in to it and dashed across the street to the forbidden evergreen trees and Scotch Broom that bordered a small ball field. But instead of finding the privacy I dreamed of, I ran smack dab into a group of older kids.

My intrusion into "their" space didn't set well with them, and in no time at all they ganged up on me and tied me to a tree with some rope. Now I was in double jeopardy—first from the mean kids, and secondly from angry parents. Needless to say, I survived both, but I never ever ventured into another Scotch Broom "forest." And, just for the record, it seems that adventuring into forests just isn't my calling anyway.

I've managed more than twice to step into a ground yellow jacket nest; once a wood tick attached to me; a spider bite gave me a swollen hand; and then there were the stings from deer flies not to mention all the blood I donated to hordes of mosquitoes. Stinging nettles and other nasty plants didn't make the call of the woods so attractive either.

Nevertheless, in spite of all this, there are times when I see a movie or a beautiful picture of forests, and that old compulsion rises up, tempting me to "head for the hills." All of this can be likened to the mesmerizing "call of the world."

Those world systems that dazzle the unsuspecting with promises of fascinating and luxurious lifestyles of wealth and power, and all manner of exotic, fleshly satisfactions. It can be especially tempting to the very young, those who haven't yet been corrupted by the serpent's sting, but who are overwhelmingly attracted to the self-serving offers he makes.

Irresistible temptations to sin and death, yet through the thick blackness of it all a faithful light still shines like a beacon reaching out to the lost. God's Word is that never-faltering light as through it the Voice of the Spirit woos, *"Love not the world, neither the things that are in the world. If any man love the world, the love of the Father is not in him. For all that is in the world, the lust of the flesh, and the lust of the eyes, and the pride of life, is not of the Father, but is of the world. And the world passeth away, and the lust thereof: but he that doeth the will of God abideth for ever" (1 John 2:15-17).* – J. Haley

Prayer: Lord, we have so many different temptations that attempt to lure us into forbidden areas. We need to resist by fleeing them, but sometimes the call is great, the flesh is convincing and the spirit waning in resisting it. Lord, you told us to pray that we would not be led into temptation; rather, that You would deliver us from evil. That is my simple prayer. DELIVER me from evil. Amen.

October 18

"And the LORD said unto him, What is that in thine hand? And he said, A rod" (Exodus 4:2). Moses' rod represents the Word of God and how many of us own a Bible but it collects dust, or remains unopen except maybe on Sunday and even then most leave their Bibles where they lay. We may own a Bible but fail to recognize its authority, and if we do bother to hold it, we still may never experience its power because we fail to walk it out in obedience.

The Lord told Moses to take the rod up in his hand to prove the authority that had been entrusted to him. This reminds me of how we must take up the Word of God in faith to use it to establish what God is declaring as being true. Once we take it up by faith, we must cast it down in obedience to see how it works.

The power of God's Word can be overwhelming, but we must face the reality of its authority and power in order to pick it up by faith so others will believe that the Word is from God and that God is the One who appeared to the saints of old and confirmed His identity, covenant, and promises when they believed Him, picked up the rod or mantle of His Word in order to victoriously advance forward in obedience.

Moses' first encounter with the rod made him flee, but once he took it up, he could stand before Pharaoh in the authority and power of God. We often try to stand in our own power, while minimizing or ignoring the need to pick up God's Word in order to learn what it means to stand before our enemies.

Moses quickly learned the significance and importance of the rod and did not leave for Egypt without it. We as believers could learn a lot from Moses' example when it comes to walking through this world.

Prayer: Lord, forgive us for being indifferent towards Your Word. You have entrusted it to us so we can walk before You in good faith, walk before our enemies in authority as overcomers and victoriously walk through this world with power. Amen.

October 19

"And Moses returned unto the LORD, and said, Lord, wherefore hast thou so evil entreated this people? Why is it that thou hast sent me? (Exodus 5:22). Moses addressed the LORD (Jehovah) as Lord (Adonai-owner) as an intercessor. The people were crying in their affliction and the Lord sent Moses to deliver them. However, before there is great deliverance the various taskmasters of this world will bring greater oppression because they have no intention of letting their slaves go.

The oppression will add to those enslaved with greater affliction, but the tendency of the oppressed is to give in to the demands and come under greater oppression while mourning in their affliction. They may become angry at those who have tried to stand on their behalf to secure their release, but they will prefer slavery when it puts greater demands on them because the great taskmaster of this world, Satan will not let his slaves leave without a fight. At such times it is the slave's tendency to succumb to it instead of standing when the oppression becomes greater, withstanding when it becomes unbearable, and continue to stand when it threatens to take away everything they have in this world.

However, oppression prepares the people for greater deliverance. Deliverance has no meaning unless oppression reigns. People may mourn under affliction but when they are delivered from great affliction, they have a greater appreciation toward the One who has delivered them.

Today many people do not see how oppressed they are and see no need to be delivered. If they cry out, it is often for relief from the unpleasantness of oppression and not for true deliverance from it. Sadly, they fail to realize they are being given a taste of the world that is yet to come, a world of not only unbearable oppression, but torment of the soul and suffering of the spirit in a place called "hell."

Prayer: Lord, we are more comfortable in our misery than we are in our deliverance. We are apt to settle for crumbs of this world than pursue You as the Bread of life. We will cry over the oppression of our bondage, but never rise up in faith to possess what we have in You. Lord, forgive us for being cowardly slaves that prefer the bitter bondage of this world instead of Your deliverance from its darkness into Your liberating light. Amen.

October 20

"And God spake unto Moses, and said unto him, I am the LORD" (Exodus 6:2). The children of Israel began to experience greater oppression after Moses made God's intention and demands known to Pharaoh. Pharaoh did not know the one and only true God of Israel. He didn't care if this God existed, because Egypt had a god for every important occasion, including him. Their gods

made them sufficient enough that they certainly had no need for any other god, especially a God to a bunch of slaves.

To try to humble the God of Israel before their eyes, Pharaoh would make the Jewish people pay for believing that they had such a God who was aware, personal and would be up front with a Pharaoh who considered himself to be deity in human form. After all, it made no sense to this arrogant man why God would care for slaves and call them to journey into the wilderness three days to worship Him.

It might have seemed to Moses and the children of Israel that God was playing some cruel game, but the Lord was setting up circumstances to prove that He was the I AM, God Almighty, Jehovah, covenant keeping God of Abraham, Isaac, and Jacob, as well as Adonai, the real owner of the children of Israel.

Sadly, this has always been true about man. He prefers the god of his own making that provides enough religion and sacrifice while allowing for idolatrous altars where lustful worship, pagan practices, and the worst abominations can take place in the name of deities. Needless to say, such wickedness is overseen by evil and God will judge it all in the end.

The Lord would prove who was and is the only true God by sending various plagues upon Egypt to humble their gods before them, and before it was over the Egyptians would know that the God of Israel, was the only true God of heaven and earth.

Egypt during this time is a good example to remember. The world is full of endless so-called "deities," of their different ages and there are many Pharaohs about who is oppressing those who dare to believe in the God of the universe. Their oppression is wicked and their overseer Satan is evil. However, like Moses before us we must stand and like the children of Israel endure to the end for God will deliver His people while humbling the false gods of this world.

Prayer: Lord, You alone are worthy of all worship and service. There is no god before You, after You, or beside You. All will come into submission to You and declare what we already know. There is no God but You. Amen.

October 21

And Moses said before the LORD, Behold I am of uncircumcised lips, and how shall Pharaoh hearken unto me? (Exodus 6:30). Moses was a mere instrument to God, but he struggled being a mouthpiece for Him. He felt unworthy to be such a mouthpiece to a Holy God. God does not ask us to be perfect in delivering His message; rather, He asks us to deliver such a message from a pure heart, to ensure its deliverance through prepared lips.

We know that Moses was almost killed because he failed to circumcise his sons after some successes. It was clear he felt unworthy to speak because he saw his lips as being uncircumcised. Moses' vision was still on the world. He was looking up, but not ready to ask the Lord what He wanted to entrust to him.

It is natural to consider our shortcomings when it comes to carrying out the Lord's instructions. We can look at our speech and believe it will not be eloquent enough to speak forth God's truths. We can consider what we see as an overwhelming task ahead of us and debate with God if He made a right choice, and perhaps someone else is more equipped. It is easy to create mountains in front of us that would justify why God's choice has to be wrong when it comes to using us in an uncomfortable fashion. We fail to realize God is the One who will move all mountains before us to ensure He receives the glory.

In *Isaiah 6*, the prophet Isaiah knew he had uncircumcised lips and confessed it as being so, but the Lord had the prophet's lips purged by a coal of fire from the altar. As a result, Isaiah was able to say, "Send me" to a people who would not even be able to hear his message. However, Isaiah was not concerned with people hearing the message; rather, he was concerned about obeying the Lord and speaking the message through pure lips.

Prayer: Lord, You are working everything out, but Satan has to put his two cents in it. Lord, help us keep our eyes on You, in order to prevent Satan from robbing our joy and standing in the way of doing Your bidding. Amen.

October 22

"And the Egyptians shall know that I am the LORD, when I stretch forth mine hand upon Egypt, and bring out the children of Israel from among them (Exodus 7:5). Why is it important for the Lord to show Himself mighty through His people, through you and me? How does the Lord show Himself Mighty? First of all, He is about to establish a witness of Himself among and through His people. This witness will magnify Him in not only the eyes of those who believe, but those who do not believe.

We are told that the Lord's eyes in *2 Chronicles 16:9* run to and fro through the whole earth, to show Himself strong in the behalf of them whose heart is perfect toward Him. However, the tragedy is He often can't find those who have the authority to stand in the gap for His people to serve as a viable witness. He must often go outside of the religious camps of the world to find an instrument who can stand in the gap, and then lead His people out of bondage. Once the Lord delivers them, He will be able to confirm the message of His servant, as well as the faith His people put in Him. (See *Ezekiel 22:30-31.*)

We often want God to simply insert Himself into our midst to deliver us from irritating matters. However, God must set up unpleasant circumstances that require a miraculous intervention.

363

Such intervention always proves to be glorious, but trying to one's faith.

Pharaoh would harden his heart towards the truths and warnings of God because he had no intention to believe or obey God. Each time God showed Himself to be mighty, He rendered all of Egypt's idols as being inept, lifeless, and powerless.

In the end God delivered His people, and Pharaoh tasted terrible judgment because of his rebellion and unbelief towards the one true God. Today there are many Pharaohs in this world who continue to resist the Holy Spirit and the truth. Eventually the Spirit will lift from such individuals, and the truth will cause them to become hardened towards it, setting them up for judgment.

Prayer: Lord, I have encountered the hard-hearted in the harvest field, the stiff-necked in the courts of the world, and the half-hearted riding the waves on the ocean of life. However, the hard-hearted will be broken, the stiff-necked brought low to the ground in humility, and the half-hearted will crash on the shorelines of reality. Lord, keep my heart pure, my mind open, and my neck flexible before You and Your Word. Amen.

October 23

"For they cast down every man his rod, and they became serpents: but Aaron's rod swallowed up their rods" (Exodus 7:12). Aaron had the rod of God, but the magician of Egypt had their magical rods that could no doubt be traced back to the black arts or witchcraft. The magician's rod was a counterfeit rod and was for the most part an illusion and limited as to how much it could control the natural laws of God. The truth is such rods are limited, but God's rod is an extension of His hand and power.

Egypt represents the world and it is hard for even Christians to understand that God does not have to prove Himself to an unbelieving world. We often want God to be an entertainer or a competitor in the arenas of the world to prove who is stronger and better. We believe that if He did, people would believe. However, those who have no intention of believing will remain in their state of unbelief just as Pharaoh did.

God does the miraculous to establish a witness among the unbelievers. This witness will come after all gods have been humbled before them, and then with a mighty hand God delivers His people as a final act to confirm what is so.

The Bible is clear, God does not have to prove who He is for He is the Great I Am. The witness He leaves is so that when all is said and done, those who refuse to believe have no excuse for their unbelief.

Our rod is the Bible. It is not only the revelation of God, but it is an extension of His power in the hands of His people who know how to lift it up by faith and are waiting to obey the next command. It is for this reason no counterfeit will match the power and victory of the Rod of God once it is lifted up by faith at His command.

The power of Satan's rod will eventually be swallowed up by the rod of God as all matters will eventually come into submission to His authority as Sovereign Creator.

Prayer: Lord, we get so caught up with the circumstances of this present world, we often forget to lift up Your Rod by faith, knowing that it will overpower and eventually swallow all the concerns of this age. Amen.

October 24

"And he said, To morrow. And he said, Be it according to thy word: that thou mayest know that there is none like unto the LORD our God" (Exodus 8:10). We have a tendency when God shows His might we think He is flexing His muscles to prove He is tougher

365

and better than the next guy. However, this is worldly thinking. When God moves it is to establish and confirm a witness to unbelievers. If we believe, it is because we have already believed the record God has given about Himself and His plan of redemption, which makes us part of the witness that God is establishing to those who refuse to believe. And what is that witness?

Let us come back to the whole purpose of God revealing His power as God in Egypt. As stated, it was not to out show or to outdo Pharaoh and his magicians. Such competition is for the arrogant of the age and not the Sovereign God of heaven and earth. We must always remember the Lord does not have to prove anything and when man asks Him to prove that He is God, the great I AM, it will prove to be a foolish test. At such times He is never provoked to prove His identity or intentions, but He is sometimes provoked to judge those who dare put Him to such a fool-hearted test.

It is clear that the reason God did what He did in Egypt was to be magnified in the eyes of His people, before those of Egypt, and ultimately be exalted over the gods of Egypt, including Pharaoh. "Magnification" means to exceed any expectation, to reach states of excellence, to pass all ideas, and to tower above all notions and concepts. In the end God will make everything look small, insignificant, foolish, and lifeless.

When God has His way, He alone will be standing. There is no other God but Jehovah, but for God to be exalted in this way, all idols have to be debased. We are not just talking about the fact there is no validity when it comes to worshipping and honoring idols but we are also talking about how man exalts idols in his mind and heart, and how God must bring them down before those blinded by their false glory so they can see the one true God of heaven.

Prayer: Lord, You have been faithful to debase all idols in my life, but at times I either fall over them because they have been placed in front of me or I am drawn aside by the temptation to erect another. However, You alone are God and the only One worthy of worship and service, and You alone will be left standing when all else falls before Your throne. Amen.

October 25

"And Pharaoh sent, and called for Moses and Aaron and said unto them, I have sinned this time: the LORD is righteous, and I and my people are wicked (Exodus 9:27). God humbled Pharaoh, but he was not broken. Pharaoh's type of humility occurs when all strength abandons you and you are left with the reality that you can do nothing but surrender to the present situation. The different judgments of God were whittling down Pharaoh's strength. He was forced to surrender out of necessity to spare him and his people from greater loss and discomfort.

It is clear that Pharaoh had been humbled, but not broken. Everyone has to be broken at their pride before they will concede defeat. Pharaoh surrendered to the situation but he was not about to concede defeat. His pride was still intact. Granted his strength had failed but the pride of his life was still in place to always raise its head in defiance once the relief came from the torment of another idol being brought down before the eyes of the Egyptians.

Pharaoh claimed repentance without conversion and transformation. Moses understood the character of Pharaoh. He knew he was confessing his sin to get God off his back and that he had no intention of letting the people go. We are quick to accept a verbal repentance when we need to wait for a heart conversion to reveal itself in attitudes and actions. Keep in mind, a heart is only converted when a person properly fears God, comes into agreement with God's attitude about something, and truly hates the evil that plagues their lives.

Through the years we have met many people who may have been humbled along the way by the overwhelming challenges of life, but they have never been broken at the point of their pride. As a result, pride will always exalt itself in another way or fashion to once again stand in defiance of God.

Prayer: Lord, life has knocked me down, adversity has put me in a headlock, and sorrow has made me depressed and complacent. I know what it means to be humbled, but I also know I must be broken over sin in order to be established in a state of humility. Search me, reveal iniquity, and break me so that You can put me back together as a vessel fit for Your use. Amen.

October 26

"I shall see him, but not now: I shall behold him, but not nigh" (Numbers 24:17a). The blind song-writer, Fanny Crosby, penned these words in her song, "Saved By Grace", And I shall see Him face-to-face, And tell the story—Saved by grace." Fanny knew she would never see the beauty of the world, but she was assured of seeing the beauty of her Lord's face because of grace.

I cannot imagine what it would be like not to be able to physically see. I so much enjoy the beauty around me and the ability to express what I experience on paper. It often serves as my inspiration behind my writings. However, Fanny's life teaches me there is an even greater inspiration that comes from within. The natural eyes can enjoy the beauty of the physical world, but the inner eyes of faith will at times see the beauty of heaven.

I realize when there is a handicap in one area, that other senses can be developed that are able to overcompensate. When it comes to the kingdom of God, we do not need physical eyes to see into the glory that is awaiting us. We have been given spiritual eyes; however, they can become glossed over by the things of the world. They can lose focus because of personal challenges and circumstances.

I have learned that I do need a bit of darkness to occasionally invade my soul to keep my spiritual eyes sharp and focused. I cannot afford to become blind to the spiritual darkness of this world. I must ensure that my eyes will always see enough of the unseen world that I will be prepared to look in the face of glory when the veil of my flesh is finally parted by death.

Prayer: Lord, I see through a glass darkly, but one day I will see the fullness of Your glory. I rejoice in the promise and hope of that day. Amen.

October 27

"A man's heart deviseth his way: but the LORD directeth his steps" *(Proverbs 16:9).* Life has a way of bringing different surprises into your life. A casual encounter here sometimes opens a door to new relationships, discoveries, and adventures that will greatly impact your life. The truth is we often just bump along with the waves of circumstances and events, while trying to make the best out of our encounters, and hopefully learning from our experiences, often without noting how so many times life does fall into place in an incredible way.

It is in the experiences of life that the unexpected can happen. I had the privilege of attending Girl's State in the summer before my senior year. Out of all the girls I noticed a quiet, shy person who I thought to myself, "I want to get to know her." I reached out to her as a friend and we became friends.

Her name is Norma and during our senior year we corresponded back and forth and she came to my graduation. My brother helped reciprocate her visit by taking me up to see her. To make a long story short Norma and my brother celebrated their 50th wedding anniversary in 2023 and my cousin Pat married her sister, Sharon, and they celebrated their 41st wedding anniversary the same year.

I do not believe life simply happens by chance. God is in control or He is not. He is directing the paths of His heirs or they are sitting ducks in the ocean of life. However, do we believe that He is in control? Do we stand on the assurance that God is using the flow of life and the experiences of life to touch, refine and bring us forth for His purpose?

As for me, I believe He is in control because there are too many incidents that fall into place in my life that assures me there is an unseen hand behind all of it.

Prayer: Lord, I know You are there, I know You are working, and I know You are in control. Thank You for all of those small and incredible touches and encounters in my life that makes the puzzle of my life fit together. Amen.

October 28

Guilt and a twinge of sadness began to creep into my heart as I took one last, long look at the beautiful petunias, geraniums, and verbena. Their "faces" seemed to be saying, "Look, and see! We've done our very best, blooming and showing off breathtaking colors, so rich and deep for the glory of our Maker! And now we have to go, never to return?"

I have to admit, it was not an easy thing to do, pulling them out of their special places and tossing them into big, black garbage bags, but the forecast for stormy weather and below freezing temperatures held steady. It was time.

The whole thing got me to thinking about the shock, sadness and sorrow we experience whenever we have to say "Goodbye" to a loved one, and especially to one who has yet to fade and wither away. We try to hang on, to steady ourselves, to deny the upsurge of emotions we can't control and wish that somehow, in some way, we had been spared of ever experiencing.

Then, in the midst of our soul's darkness a light begins to shine. It comes in the form of words. Not just any words, but living, eternal words; and hope, like droplets of pure honey and oil gently forming a calming balm of promise to ponder in our heart, and receive, believe and cling to in faith. Words such as, *"The righteous perisheth, and no man layeth it to heart: and merciful men are taken away, none considering that the righteous is taken away from the evil to come." "I am he that liveth, and was dead; and, behold, I am alive for evermore, Amen; and have the keys of hell and of death" (Revelation 1:18). "And God shall wipe away all tears from their eyes; and there shall be no more death, neither sorrow, nor crying, neither shall there be any more pain: for the former things are passed away" (Isaiah 57:1; Revelation 1:18; 21:4).* – J. Haley

Prayer: Lord, we do so much to hold on to this life, but our existence is fading with each year. Life has a cycle and it ends in death, but the key as to what existence will be present when I leave this world comes down to the type of life I possess. Thank You for sending Your Son so that everyone who believes upon Him will have everlasting life. Amen.

October 29

And that from a child thou hast known the holy scriptures, which are able to make thee wise unto salvation through faith which is in Christ Jesus. All scripture is given by inspiration of God, and is profitable for doctrine, for reproof, for correction, for instruction in righteousness: That the man of God may be perfect, thoroughly furnished unto all good works (2 Timothy 2:15-17).

One book that keeps pulling me back to its truths is Job. Job lays a foundation to God's sovereignty while exposing man's inept attempts to understand and explain it. The truth is that His sovereignty is the one aspect about His divine nature that remains mysterious and far from man's understanding. As God He has a right to choose what He will reveal to those He created.

However, God has revealed what we need to know and it is found in in His Word. To receive benefits from His Word we must approach it to believe it is His final Word on a matter and not judge it according to personal calculations, debate Him or others as to His judgments, or confirm personal concrete beliefs. As *2 Timothy 3:16* tells us, the Bible is here to instruct us as to righteousness and its instructions are not up for debate.

The problem with stepping outside of the Word of God is that it can make it into a lifeless book of theology or fables instead of truth. Man's theology is dead-letter because there is no place past our logic for the Holy Spirit to unveil its spiritual truths. If it becomes a book of fables, then it is rendered into a place of unbelief that ends in mockery.

God's Word is for our instruction and not for us to instruct God about His Word by twisting, adjusting, ignoring, or inserting it where it fits into our way of thinking. God's Word shows He is sovereign and to undermine that in any way by making Him understandable and His Word common is to show utter contempt towards both.

Prayer: Lord, we think we are so smart but in the end our contempt towards You and Your Words proves it is correct once again. Your Word remind us only a fool would act like a court jester towards You and Your Word. Amen.

October 30

"The way of a fool is right in his own eyes: but he that hearkeneth unto counsel is wise" (Proverbs 12:15). Yesterday I spoke of man's foolishness to show any disregard towards God and His Word because it is contempt to Him. This is quite dangerous because such disdain is directed at the One who will judge everyone in the end.

God's Word clearly states He is trustworthy, unchangeable as to His truth and righteous ways, and desires to have a relationship with us that comes only through the redemptive work of His Son. Sadly, it is because of God's sovereignty that many people choose to not believe Him.

Such individuals judge Him on what they would do in a situation even though they are limited in what they do know about the matter. They rage against God because He is not a tyrant that will overstep man's free will to choose who and what he is going to believe and do. They mock Him because they see themselves as wiser and more just in a matter, and would prove it if they could take all control from Him and call the shots.

This brings them to the most maddening reality of all, THEY ARE NOT GOD, and they can't influence God outside of who He is and His will. The harsh reality is their limitation and inability to change a matter is what creates an even greater anger that vehemently rejects everything about God, making them utter fools who say in their heart there is no God.

It is not enough to know there is a God, the demons know that much, and it is not enough to know about God, the realm of darkness also has such knowledge. The reality is we can know God and learn He is faithful to all He says, be confident in standing on His righteous ways, and trust His sovereignty regardless of whether it makes sense to us.

Prayer: Lord, You are God and it is because You are a loving, just God, I can trust You with all matters. You are Almighty and I can rest in You, and it is because You are sovereign, I can be still before You, knowing that You are in control, and You will bring about Your perfect will and righteous plan for my life according to Your timing. Amen.

October 31

"Then spake Solomon, The LORD said that he would dwell in the thick darkness" (1 Kings 8:12). The other day I talked about God's sovereignty. When we think we understand God, it is not unusual to suddenly hit a wall of confusion when something shakes our world because it doesn't make sense to us or seem fair. We think we are struggling with God's justice, when in reality we are coming up against His sovereignty. In our mind, since He is supposed to be in control of all matters, He surely wouldn't let the present crisis happen if He was truly in control, right? Think again. It is in darkness God is ready to go deeper as He enlarges and tests His people.

The darkness I am referring to might be a great loss, an overwhelming problem, a traumatic experience, or just the confusing mess of the world around us. In our utter despair, we even might say to ourselves, "Where is God in all of this?"

When I study Job, I realize Job is the only book that takes this question head on. The great debate that ensues shows how man wrestles with his understanding of God when everything he thinks he knows about Him is shaken, while contending with others' "so-called" expertise in understanding Him. The debate that man has never takes away the confusion; rather, it just adds greater darkness to it because it often turns into misunderstanding, judgmentalism, scoffing, and mocking.

The answer to the question, "Where is God in all of this," is He is still here. It's true that due to His sovereignty, He may be hidden by the darkness of our own understanding, enshrouded by the personal theology of others, and seem to be silent or deaf when the cruel darts of the judgment of others are unmercifully flung at us, but He is still there.

We need to remember that His darkness is to enlarge our faith and test the spiritual character of others, while the darts simply exposes man's iniquity so they can be called to repentance before God judges him. God is never AWOL regardless of what is going on.

Prayer: Lord, I must never forget that sometimes the darkness I see is Your light revealing the obscurity that is engulfing the situation in order to reveal that which is hidden from the naked eye. Sometimes Your light becomes darkness to enlarge our faith, test character, and reveal religious prejudices, but regardless of what is going on, You will never leave nor forsake us. Amen.

NOVEMBER

November 1

"Vanity of vanities, saith the Preacher, vanity of vanities: all is vanity" (Ecclesiastes 1:2). The holiday season is now upon us. Yesterday we finished with my least favorite day, Halloween, and now we are getting inundated with advertisement for Christmas as the commercial world begins to milks this tradition for all it's worth.

Keep in mind, Christmas is pagan at the core, but the religious world has tried to bring some semblance of meaning and purpose into it by directing the focus to the fact that Jesus took on flesh and came Into the world. Since He is God's great gift to humanity, we can seek to remember what the most important gift is, and it does not come from man, the world, or Santa Claus.

I realize inserting Christ's birth into this holiday has caused various debates. My goal is to talk about a whirlwind that takes us up into uselessness and flings us into nothingness.

As constantly brought out, Halloween celebrates the darkness of Satan's kingdom, the foolishness of paganism, and the vanity of man trying to grasp some purpose or meaning in useless traditions. It does not acknowledge God or the gift of life.

At the heart of man's traditions is vanity. Many times, man doesn't even know why he is celebrating something. For the most part, it is a way for man to have a day off, let off steam, or act stupid or foolish without being judged as such.

However, the one aspect of society that greatly benefits from such celebrations is the commercial end which comprises Satan's

376

system. In many ways man's traditions become an avenue for Satan to exploit, mock, and rob people of everything from innocence and money to their sanity.

As the tides of the vanity of the world come in with promotions, expectations, and ideas, we as believers must stay firmly on the Rock as we maintain that every day is a celebration of life in some way or the other. However, that celebration only finds itself in the reality of God and what He has done for us.

Christ's redemption is the only means that keeps us on solid ground when we are being bombarded by the thunderous waves of the world.

Prayer: Lord, thank You for being the anchor that never moves, the Rock that remains standing, and providing the mooring lines of Your grace that can't be broken by the crashing waves of this world. Amen.

November 2

"Knowing that shortly I must put off this my tabernacle, even as our Lord Jesus Christ hath shewed me" (2 Peter 1:14). Do you realize that the sunlight reveals that we only see in part? We are clearly limited in what we see because most of what we call life is operating in realms we cannot see with our physical eyes. Granted, we may see that which is around us but we can't see what is happening beneath the surface. Every living thing around us is covered by some veneer and underneath it is life. For instance, when it is cold long enough, the rivers develop ice that covers its many activities of life.

It is for this reason, ice on the river reminds me of the skin that covers our bodies. The real life that is present in me pulsates beneath the surface of my skin. There is no real life that is associated with the body. It is an outer shell that simply echoes the life that continues to run through the core of my inner being and through every tributary of my life.

My body simply houses the spirit and soul. It is from the spirit that the breath of life finds its source, and it is in the soul that the present life will pulsate through every fiber of who I am. It is because of the breath of the spirit and the influence of the soul that the body will ultimately manifest the character of the life that is present within me.

This brings me to the reality of the Christian life. The power of the Christian life depends on the depth in which the life of Christ has reached into my inner being. There is nothing surface to this incredible life for it is eternal. It not only identifies me to the depth of Christ's life in me, but to the eternal glories that will identify me to heaven itself in the near future.

Prayer: Lord, You are the essence of my life. It is Your life in me that brings significance to this outer tabernacle. Lord be glorified in my life. Amen.

November 3

"And when he putteth forth his own sheep, he goeth before them, and the sheep follow him; for they know his voice" (John 10:4). One of my heart's desires is to make an impact in the lives of my loved ones. However, you can only point them to Christ, lead them towards Him with His truths, and stir up hope in them with His promises, but you can't make them drink from the fountain of Living Waters. As a result, it can be hard to find true fellowship with some of your family.

I had the blessing of having a few family members that shared with me in my love for Jesus. One such family member was my cousin, LeNita Binam. I remember the time she wrote me the only real letter I ever received from her to tell me she received Jesus as her Lord and Savior.

It was true we did not see each other much through the years. We were both clearly on different paths in our lives. However, the Lord allowed me to take part in a special time of her life. In a sense, you might say I walked with her through the valley of the shadow of death.

LeNita had various physical problems which she openly admitted was due to her former lifestyle, but the last few years of her life I watched her bravely face the unknown in light of her child-like faith towards Jesus. She had to climb over doubts left lingering from her past, trust that Jesus held her time in His hands regardless of the bad reports of doctors, and come to rest that in spite of her rough edges Jesus had come to save one such as herself.

At the end she was in a coma, but before her last breath she opened her eyes as if someone had startled her by calling her by name, and then as the song declares, "flew away." After all, we all know that Jesus, the great Shepherd calls each of His sheep by their name when it is time to follow Him.

My dear cousin reminds me that we need to take the time to simply walk a while with those we share our faith with, share a bit of their journey regardless of the terrain, and know that no matter how bitter-sweet the journey may prove to be in the end, it will always leave those nuggets of memories behind that will continue to inspire a person in their journey to keep going until they hear that last call from their Shepherd to follow Him home.

Prayer: Lord, we need to learn to walk a while with some of Your sheep, but we most of all must remember to take time to walk a while with You to keep all avenues open for inspiration to mark our journey with precious nuggets of memories. Amen.

November 4

"And he said unto Abram, Know of a surety that thy seed shall be a stranger in a land that is not theirs, and shall serve them; and they shall afflict them four hundred years" (Genesis 15:13). I felt a need to sit down and write some type of explanation or challenge, or maybe some type of encouragement as each of us embark on the upcoming holiday season.

It is obvious that everything that man does in light of this holiday will end in vanity. The question I had to ask myself is, am I *trying* to make the best out of this time or am I *making* the best of this time, and remember that every day God gives me presents a gift of life.

Sometimes the gift of life comes with personal struggles as time seems to slip through our fingers. For me, the struggles and passing of time have produced some periods of silence in my life. The silence is when the spirit is quiet, sometimes a bit overwhelmed or vexed, and the soul is waiting to hear from only source of hope that comes from heaven.

For the people of Israel, they actually experienced silence for four hundred years between the Old and New Testaments before God brought forth a new revelation. I realize that silence has its importance.

Silence reminds me that I must separate from the vain activities of the world. It is easy to get caught up with such frivolous actions. In fact, the world can take me captive, causing much unrest in my soul as its many voices vie for my attention and my affections.

Regardless of what it taking place around me, I must maintain a strong stance against that which will invade my soul with false promises and the bitterness and hopelessness of vanity. I must maintain the integrity of what is true and right while seeking the place of rest and silence from a world that is clamoring to take every aspect of my soul captive.

Prayer: Lord, sometimes Your silence is to give me time to consider if I have been taken captive by the subtle ways of the world. Bring me to the place of quietness so that You can reveal where I am in my walk with You. Amen.

November 5

"It can't be in two places at the same time" I said to myself as I held the pretty retro alarm clock in my hands. After all, the turquoise border perfectly matched a couple of items on top of the dresser along with my lighthouse painting positioned on the wall above it; but then, on the other hand, I had purchased the little clock to fit perfectly in my bathroom.

Decisions, decisions, but not drastically important ones such as which country should we declare war on. However, this whole infinitely small dilemma brought to mind the times when I wished I could be in two places at the same time.

We've all probably had those times when we found ourselves forced to choose which invitation, activity or situation we would, should or could physically attend! What a comfort it is to know that our God is omnipresent; that is, everywhere present. He never has to choose between two locations as to where to "be" at the same time. *"Can any hide himself in secret places that I shall not see him? Saith the LORD. Do not I fill heaven and earth? saith the LORD." (Jeremiah 23:24.)*

When we feel small and alone, lost in the midst of it all, and when loneliness suddenly washes over us like an icy wave of the sea, threatening to sweep us out into some unknown cavern of deep darkness, quickly grab the "life ring" of *Psalm 139* and let the Spirit of God breathe love, joy and peace into your spirit and soul.

For has Jesus not promised, *"I will never leave you, nor forsake you" (Hebrews 13:5b)?* - J. Haley

Prayer: Lord, my weaknesses and ineptness reminds me that I am limited in all things, lacking in all knowledge, and have little strength when confronting the issues of life. Lord, I need to remember my great need for You every day to avoid being set up to find out how small I am when I fail, how inept I am when I can't change things, and how foolish I am when I realize I know very little about You and life. Amen.

November 6

Being confident of this very thing, that he which hath begun a good work in you will perform it until the day of Jesus Christ" (Philippians 1:6). As many know, living in North Idaho inspires me in so many ways to consider my Creator and His wondrous ways. This is no surprise since Jesus used creation to teach about God's provision and ability to meet us in every need.

Reading back on some of my diary entries during my time at Priest River, I found this entry, "I awoke to a light dusting of snow on the ground. The day was overcast, but in the afternoon, the sun broke through to reveal the beauty of the river. The gold and greens of the landscape greeted us with a melody of beauty. It was as the sunlight began to break through the overcast day that it highlighted the countryside while shading in certain areas to bring depth to the terrain.

"The highlight of the sunrays not only changed the countryside but the river as well. The river continues to reflect the change that creation is bringing forth with its different types of lighting. It is as though God was bringing incredible contrast with a stroke of light here and a bit of shading there.

"It is for this reason that the creation around me constantly reminds me of the Creator's handiwork, especially in relationship to my life. So much of my life has been covered by a drab blanket of mediocrity and drudgery. However, once in a while, the Lord's light breaks through my spirit to once again stir me up to consider the work of God upon my soul. I realize that under the drabness of everyday life, the Creator continues to work upon the landscape of my inner being. I have become more aware of how God will finish the good work He has begun in me."

Prayer: Lord, You have always been faithful to do the necessary work in my life. I can trust You in Your love, power, and grace to do an excellent work that will bring You glory. Amen.

November 7

"And that thou mayest tell in the ears of thy son, and of thy son's son, what things I have wrought in Egypt, and my signs which I have done among them; that ye may know how that I am the LORD (Exodus10:2). How will God leave a testimony of Himself in this dark world unless it is through the adversity of His people? We are so used to making our life about ourselves, we forget if we are believers, our life is about the God we serve. We are to leave a witness behind us about His greatness and not about how wonderful we think we are.

We often question why we go through challenging times, but we need to remember that God is not limited by the plans, ploys, and workings of men; rather, He sees such times as opportunities by showing Himself mighty on our behalf. God's greatness shines the most in our times of adversity.

Sadly, we do not want to go through such times. We are afraid of losing our rights and our reputations, but when it comes to these types of events, it requires a miraculous intervention on God's part and faith towards God on our part.

We need to change the way we look at adversity, remembering it is God's opportunity to establish a witness among us and in the midst of us in a world that will not even consider His existence. It is hard for some of us to remember we are here to bring a light into the midst of great darkness with our witness; therefore, we are not called to the common ways of the world but to the excellent ways of God that will cause the ordinary to become extraordinary in what is often considered the normality of this present world.

Prayer: Lord, it is easy to become rebellious and stiff-necked as we insist on our ways. However, I want to be a David, possessing a heart after You, and not a heart that leans towards the world. Lord if we don't get it right because You are the only way, we will prove to be absolute fools to an unbelieving world and fail to leave a viable witness behind for others to consider. Amen.

November 8

"And though the Lord give you the bread of adversity, and the water of affliction, yet shall not thy teachers be removed into a corner any more, but thine eyes shall see thy teachers" (Isaiah 30:20). Why do we avoid adversity, secretly fear it and sometimes openly resent it with bitter tears? I am sure everyone who is honest with themselves knows the answer. Adversity may show God's greatness on our behalf, but it will expose our weaknesses as it becomes a grave test to our faith.

Unless our faith is refined in fiery ovens, our flesh remains subject to its lusts, our resolve fickle, our pride self-serving, and our character soft like butter under heat instead of proving to be like steal that can withstand the heat and come out better for it. It is often because we want to leave impressions of our best and convince others just how good we are in our religion and before God. However, adversity reveals just how pathetic we are.

Today we are living in a time that we are tasting the bread of adversity and the water of affliction. If you don't believe me, just look outside of your small world and you will see a world full of troubles.

The reason for such affliction is because many in the Church prefer teachers who will tickle their ears with foolishness about how good they are or how good they are going to have it. They often choose the court jester of fantasy over truth because they do not have to give up the limelight that allows them the luxury to live in denial about the environment that has been created by a terrible mixture of the world with the matters of a holy God, corrupting what is pure, rendering many inept to stand under the pressure of adversity. They flock to hear the motivational speakers and cheerleaders so they will feel good about a life that is falling apart at the seams.

It is time for us as believers to decide if we want to eat the bread of adversity and drink the water of affliction with the rest of the world or whether we turn to God in repentance, fling ourselves on His mercy, and be still before Him as He cleanses us so that He can deliver us through our adversity and be glorified in it.

Prayer: Lord my spirit is vexed over the condition of this world, causing me to taste the bitterness of my anguished soul through my tears. Lord, I do not want to simply survive the present adversity, I want the things of this world to be consumed in my life by it so that You can raise out of its ashes a powerful witness of You to a lost, dying, doomed world that needs to see Your reflection and light in my life. Amen.

November 9

"And Moses said unto the people, Fear ye not, stand still, and see the salvation of the LORD, which he will shew to you to day: for the Egyptians whom ye have seen to day, ye shall see them again no more for ever" (Exodus 14:13). I have been studying Nehemiah when *Exodus 14:13* came to mind. It is clear that Nehemiah had to WAIT *ON* the Lord, WAIT *BEFORE* the Lord and WAIT *WITH* the Lord. That meant he had to *stand still* as he waited *on* the Lord, *sit still before* the Lord, and *be still with* the Lord until He moved. It was when the timing was right, Nehemiah stepped into the flow either to make sure he did not end up behind his LORD, but with Him as to His plan as well as beside Him in advancing His will.

We must stand still and wait on the Lord to see His salvation. It is hard to stand still, but when I was in the military, we had to come to attention in order to direct everything towards what we were about to hear and commanded to do in order to carry a matter out in correct form. Standing still is about recognizing that God has timing and that He must prepare the way before entrusting us with marching orders. However, we cannot properly move unless we are standing and ready to put one foot in front of the other without being tripped up.

Many people are tripped up because they are not standing when the orders come down. You can try jumping up but you will find out that you are not necessarily prepared to march forward in order to come into step with the orders and plan. It is easy to be unprepared when we are not expecting anything to happen. Without expectation, we will find ourselves asleep and far from being ready to stir.

I had to ask myself when was the last time I stood still in my soul, allowing for my spirit to move forward in the flow of God's Spirit?

Prayer: Lord we can be caught up with business and not be prepared to hear Your marching orders. Lord, cause me to be still in my spirit and attentive in my soul to what Your Spirit is saying. Amen.

November 10

"Be still, and know that I am God: I will be exalted among the heathen, I will be exalted in the earth" (Psalm 46:10) To be still allows one to know God, to sense God, to be overwhelmed by His holiness, be humbled by His great grace, to fall on one's knees to seek mercy, and to experience a love that is all-consuming, **to ultimately know God in the end.**

Being still means waiting with the Lord until He moves. The truth is the Lord must prepare the way in order for me to advance forward in my life and the conflict. To stand has to do with salvation, to sit has to do with God preparing us to receive the promises, but to be still involves encountering God.

We want to direct our life in God, but it is God who prepares us to come into a place where He can reveal Himself to us in a powerful way. We want instant everything, but the sweet, priceless things of God entail waiting. Whether it is God preparing the way or preparing us, we are not always prepared to receive things in the right spirit or in a way that will prove to be beneficial for us.

Being still in our spirit and quiet in our souls can be very challenging, but it is necessary if we are going to be in the right state to encounter God in such a way that our faith and understanding of Him enlarges to the point that we allow God to be God.

Prayer: Lord, keep me from settling for surface Christianity, just getting by in my life before You, while skipping across the water of immaturity instead of learning how to walk on it during the stormy times and good times of life. I know in the storms I must ask You to take my hand so I won't sink and in the good times, I need to discipline my focus by keeping my eyes on You so I don't take some detour and sink into foolishness. The Bible tells me You are the one who guides my steps and I desperately need your guidance every minute of each day. Amen.

November 11

"Then said she, Sit still, my daughter, until thou know how the matter will fall: for the man will not be in rest, until he have finished the thing this day" (Ruth 3:18). It is hard to be still because if you are like me, there are so many things, according to my thinking, I must do to redeem the time, but the one thing I must never forget is that being still before the Lord is never a waste of time. In fact, when you enter into that place with the Lord, time stops as you stand in the presence of that which is eternal.

What does it mean to sit still before the Lord? I long ago learned that I must sit still until God reveals what He wants me to do. I must not be concerned about sitting still in my spirit until I hear from the Lord because until He does give the instruction, it is and will always be in His ball court to make the next move.

Clearly Ruth had to sit still because it was not her move when it came to Boaz. This is another important lesson about sitting still. We do all we can and then we must sit still until God makes His move. The problem is we want to hurry up the process, but once again timing is involved. Before we move, others must be prepared. It is like a chess game.

A player must sit and wait until the opponent makes his move before making any other move. However, while the player is sitting and waiting for the next move, they are occupying as they prepare to properly respond.

To sit still before the Lord is to ensure that a matter is verified. We can try to guess what He will do, but I have never been right yet. I often complicate the matter while He always simplifies it in ways I could never imagine.

To sit before the Lord means waiting before Him in a quiet state until you hear His invitation or command to move. In the case of Ruth, she had to sit and wait before she could realize the full extent of her life in the Lord.

She would discover the invitation to get up has to do with receiving the Lord's promises. What a glorious expectation that awaits those who truly learn to sit before the Lord, and like the five wise virgins in *Matthew 25* are ever ready and prepared to rise up when the invitation finally comes.

Prayer: Lord, we have our timing which is according to our comfort zones, but Your timing is all about people being prepared to move into the right place at the right time to ensure that all matters are carried out in the right way. We are so busy trying to get our imperfect way, we skip those steps that bring us into perfection. Forgive us for wanting to rest in assumptions while secretly presuming our way is right and superior to Your way. Amen.

November 12

Some of us remember what we fondly recall as "the good old days" when we were kids. Those days were "good" because we got to be kids; in other words, most of us got to keep our innocence, through the childhood stage at least; we got to play with "normal" toys that didn't mess up our minds with perverted, occult, or "subliminal" brainwashing agendas; we got to be outside in the fresh air and sunshine without wasting time on cell phones, video games, or watching too much television even though most of it was simple, and the "good guys" always won, and we even experienced the joy of reading decent, character-building books.

We got to use our imaginations to "invent" games and figure out how to entertain ourselves such as playing "dress up" for girls, and for both boys and girls pretending to live in the Old West where we rode our imaginary horses. Some were even "lucky" enough to have cowboy hats, western boots, fake guns or other cowboy paraphernalia. It seemed that looking the part served to give you a certain "advantage" over the other kids. (I never looked "the part" because my mother didn't want me to grow up to be a cowgirl.)

Fast-forward to today and the nominal churches in conjunction with the spiritual realm wherein the wolves, heretics, hireling shepherds and false workers play. Just as everybody knows that the wolf in Little Red Riding Hood looked like Granny because he wore her clothes, so too, we're told the wolves among us wear sheep's clothing, so there's no problem in picking them out, right? WRONG!

Satan is shrewd and he knows that we think we know what a "wolf's clothing" looks like; but because the virtuous sheep's clothing made up of the fruit of the Spirit and truth has morphed into a "new style" while still sporting the same label, he "dresses his wolves up" in "clothing" that Christians can accept, approve of, enjoy, and even admire. Let's try some of these on for size.

First, there's the alphabet soup suit. It's tailormade to appeal to those who only trust people with enough accreditations to fill fifty boxcars and then some. No need to discern the spirit or test the fruit on this person. Everything they think, say, or write just has to be believed, hands down.

If that doesn't impress or fool some folks, the enemy has come up with a second style that fits well on the other end of the spectrum, and that is a non-accreditation, one-of-a-kind, super sensational, colorful "new revelation-mystery-hidden-'hath-God-said,'" one-size-fits-all, barely there, feel-good "thing." This new "thing" is very effective garb for a wolf because it's always in motion to attract attention and keep sheep too busy and entertained to check the fruit or discern anything.

Finally, the third new style of wolf-wear for Satan's workers is the ever-popular, soft, cozy, warm and pliable sleepwear. It comes with ear-tickling feathers, a complete set of jokes, humor, repetitious self-songs, and a guide to church social events, and even a warm blanket in matching pastel colors that any wolf would be proud to wear while lulling the passive Christian into a deeper sleep into La-La Land where nothing is ever discerned.

Of course, all three wolf, heretic, false workers' clothing styles are guaranteed to succeed wherever the Bible and discipleship are not a priority; where self-interest and pride are the norm; and where man and his programs, ideas, achievements, and selfisms are exalted instead of the LORD Jesus Christ! *"But there were false prophets also among the people, even as there shall be false teachers among you, who privily shall bring in damnable heresies, even denying the Lord that bought them, and bring upon themselves swift destruction." (2 Peter 2:1)* - J. Haley

Prayer: Lord, Satan is subtle and he uses our arrogance to blind us to our vulnerability, our unbridled curiosity to go where his traps await us to take our minds captive, our ignorance to remain in darkness, and lack of knowledge to ensure we will perish in our foolishness. Lord, give me an unadulterated love for Your truth. Amen.

November 13

"For the Egyptians shall help in vain, and to no purpose; therefore have I cried concerning this, Their strength is to sit still" (Isaiah 30:7). Whenever I look back on my diaries, I can't help but notice

there are many empty spots in them. I often wonder if they represent days that are lost to time. Time has always been an interesting subject to me. It simply marches on and emerges into seasons of changes and hopefully growth. Time is marked by small seconds, gauged by fast clicking minutes, highlighted by days that become years.

Diaries are not about years but days. In many ways, seconds are lost, minutes considered insignificant, and days a waste because there is so much normalcy and worldly demands that swallow each day up into a vacuum what appears to be more than nothingness lost in the midst of vain activities.

I try to make my days count, but they merge together. Dairies often mark events and personal discoveries. It is for this reason I try to mark time with projects and important events, ever being aware that I am preparing for eternity. In Isaiah, the children of Israel were always looking to other countries to help them instead of God. Such attempts ended in vain, and that is when the Lord reminded them of where their strength came from.

It is Scriptures such as these that have made me realize that empty spots or spaces can represent those times one has become still in their soul. Perhaps they were waiting for matters to fall into place or maybe they were waiting because they were too overwhelmed to speak or move because of what was happening around them. Or, they could be waiting for God to move in some way.

I have realized that empty spots for me do not always represent lost time, but sometimes they represent a stillness that took place because God was doing something while I was waiting in preparation to properly respond. At such times, there are no words to describe what is happening and no means to even begin to explain what is going on.

Waiting on the Lord is never "Wait and see;" rather, it is about waiting in expectation of what God is doing to prepare me, to prepare the way in which I am to walk, and to prepare the circumstances that will often discipline the way I am to walk in to ensure the right results for my benefit and His glory.

Prayer: Lord, we get excited over various things that end in vanity because they have nothing to do with learning about You, doing Your will, and ensuring Your ways are being upheld. Forgive me for getting caught up with those empty spaces of my life, knowing You so often have always filled them with a greater revelation of Yourself. Amen.

November 14

"For I say unto you, Till heaven and earth pass, one jot or one tittle shall in no wise pass from the law, till all be fulfilled" (Matthew 5:18). In the last post I spoke of God filling the empty spaces. In this Scripture Jesus is making reference to such a concept when it comes to His Word, His Law, and His promises.

One jot points to the smallest letter in the Greek alphabet and can be compared to the Hebrew letter "yod" or "y" which is formed like a (') comma, and is used to express the minutest thing. Tittle points to a "horn like" mark or an apex or point. It can refer to a diacritical dot placed over abbreviated words and some letters. It can also reference the apex or point of certain Hebrew letters called a tag (taga).

As you can see, regardless of how small or big a detail is, the right accent marks must be present in the right place to keep things in the right context. We have a tendency to become sloppy when it comes to ensuring that everything is being presented in the right place, but without the right emphasis even mere words will be rendered lifeless; but with it, it will speak volumes without having to write out a great discourse.

It is important to realize that God is in the smallest details and in the moving and shaking of our times. There is nothing too great for Him to use and nothing so small He overlooks it. Sadly, we put our own slant on what we think is necessary, important, and worthy of our attention when it comes to the matters of God's Word and kingdom. In the end, we leave out some of the jots of His truths and ignore many of the tittles that mark His ways.

We often summarize that we know enough about God without realizing we do not know Him. We fail to see His faithfulness in the jots, and His goodness in the tittles. We forget that Paul stated that Jesus fills our all in all with not only the miraculous but the jots and tittles of His ways and promises.

Prayer: Lord, we minimize who You are and the uniqueness of all You do. We want and look for that which will entertain us, but we miss what will inspire and encourage us in the midst of challenging realities. Thank You for always being that truth that will fill in the empty places and put the right emphasis where needed to maintain the spirit and intent of Your Word and Ways. Amen.

November 15

"But I am poor and needy: make haste unto me, O God: thou are my help and deliverer; O LORD, make no tarrying" (Psalm 70:5). What does it mean when God is our help? According to Strong's Concordance, the same word that was to describe Eve as Adam's help-meet is the same Hebrew word used in this text when it comes to God being our helper. Does that mean He is subservient to us and must do our bidding, or does it mean He is there to ever aid us in our journey, encourage us in our life, point us upward to what is excellent for our well-being, and try to guide our steps in the right path to ensure the best results?

It is clear in this text that "help" has to do with those who are poor and needy, and not in light of being the tail that can be wagged at the whims of others. However, to be on the receiving end of God's help, we must see our state for what it is in order to seek the help that will aid, support, and benefit us. We must see our need before we seek our helper and be able to receive His assistance in the proper way.

In the kingdom of God, every believer is a servant not only to God but to others. Greatness in God's kingdom is not a place of elitism or one that allows us to lord over others. Greatness in the kingdom of God has to do with being the type of helper to others that God is to us. We are not here to run the show but to make sure that we are part of what God wants to do and is doing when it comes to the affairs of His kingdom.

We often speak of the Church being the Body of Christ, but we forget Jesus is the head, and we as the body can't function outside of the head. Yet, how many of us do not understand the mind of Jesus, know His will and instructions, and are prepared to aid Him in the affairs of His household and kingdom. I am thankful for God's faithfulness to help me, but am I that type of helper when it comes to being a servant in His household?

Prayer: Lord, I thank You for Your abiding help. Without it I would not be here today, and my prayer is that I can be that type of support to the saints of the household that You are to me in my time of need. Amen.

November 16

Whosoever therefore confesses me before men, him will I confess also before my Father which is in heaven" (Matthew 10:32). How important is confession? We are told if we don't confess Jesus before others, He will not confess us before His Father.

Clearly, this is in relationship to a public confession of one's faith, but it must be backed up by obedience to His Word to bring any credibility to it. In a sense "water baptism" is a public confession, but it also has to do with identification with Jesus in His death, burial and resurrection into a new life. It also points to the work of justification because of His death, speaks of the present work of sanctification because He lives, and reminds us of the future promise of glorification with Him in new bodies.

In *1 John 1:9* we are told if we confess our sins, He is faithful and just to forgive us our sins, and cleanses us from all unrighteousness. According to the Greek language "to confess" our sin in this manner means to "acknowledge," "profess", "come into agreement," "to speak the same," "surrender," "make an assent," and "an admission." But, the most interesting meaning of it comes in the form of a noun where it points to "contract."

Clearly, confession is agreeing with God about how He looks at a matter, especially in the case of sin, which many avoid or prove quite weak in due to pride that refuses to be humbled. However, it goes on a step further in making a contract to never do it again.

It is clear that the word, "confess" has been watered down in today's weak, compromising, worldly Christianity. People hide behind a worldly idea of God's love to cover up their rebellion and hatred towards His immovable, moral Word and Law. They have cheapened His grace to embrace sin, stand on heretical doctrine to justify their bad fruit, and stand behind a religious garb to hide their unbelief.

Jesus made it clear in *John 15:22* that He came to take away the cloak that hides sin in order to expose and address it. After all, we stand doomed in our sin and will not see the Lord without coming into a state holiness before Him by partaking of it in repentance, conversion, and obedience (*Hebrew 12:10-14*).

Prayer: Lord, I so appreciate Your precious Word and examples. There are so many examples of how sin is handled and what we can do to obtain Your forgiveness and overcome our spiritual enemies. Thank You for Your Word of truth and promise. Amen.

November 17

HEADS UP, Christians, it's absolutely chilling, and I'm not talking about the shock produced when someone sticks ice cubes down your back on a hot summer day. What is "chilling" is mankind's incredible and (for most of us) the hard-to-fathom increase in knowledge that has the power to exterminate every living thing on this planet if God doesn't "shorten the days" and Jesus returns to set up His kingdom on earth.

What is of utmost importance for God's people is to have a "love for the truth" (2 *Thessalonians* 2:8-12). We live in a time when we must "stay awake" and realize that we cannot believe everything we hear or see. Discernment is not a "luxury" for some believers, but an absolute necessity for all.

One of the many evil inventions that can be used against all mankind to spread deception is AI (artificial intelligence) such as, for only one example, that created by Deepdub, which has developed AI-driven audiovisual dubbing and language localization technology. To quote an article in the June issue of "News From Israel" magazine, "With advanced generative AI algorithms, it is now possible to emulate a person's voice with remarkable accuracy, creating a synthesized speech that sounds almost identical to the original."

Therefore, when we view a video of someone whom we follow, trust, respect or even admire and suddenly hear his or her voice speaking terrible words that are totally out of character, moral persuasion, or deep-seated beliefs, are we to automatically shut down our discernment, believe it's really that person, and wrongly judge them? Or, on the other hand, if we hear a voice that we recognize as being an enemy of God, but they are suddenly speaking uprightly, are we to throw out our discernment and trust them? ("Ye shall know them by their fruits.")

The magazine's commentary, in part, concludes "This development shows the increased difficulty in determining whether one hears or sees an original or an AI-generated one. This process is part of man's attempt to marry the human with manmade structures. Most of us know only little about this type of technology." *Matthew 24:24* warns, *"For there shall arise false Christs, and false prophets, and shall shew great signs and wonders; insomuch that, if it were possible, they shall deceive the very elect." Revelation 13:5a "And there was given unto him a mouth speaking great things and blasphemies...."* – J. Haley

Prayer: Lord we are living in frightening days but You told us not to fear and to be of good cheer for You have already overcome the world and You will be coming back to straighten out this doomed world. Thank You for reminding me You are the Victor and that the war has already been won by You. Amen.

November 18

"Not that I speak in respect of want: for I have learned, in whatsoever state I am, therewith to be content" (Philippians 4:11). One of the themes for a series of articles I have written for the newsletter was "Spiritual Survival." Even though we are embarking on the holidays, there are many lessons we can learn during such times when it comes to spiritual survival. This brings us to the first lesson we have to learn in order to survive. It involves developing an attitude of thankfulness.

Every Thanksgiving we are to remember where we have come from, where we presently are, and where our faith walk will ultimately lead us. As believers, we should possess the greatest type of personal contentment. The reason for such contentment has to do with possessing an attitude of thankfulness.

The problem is that we are too busy regarding what we think we do not have, that we completely overlook what God has blessed us with. When we overlook what we have and focus in on what we do not possess, we become morbid people. The morbid pose we take on can only bring gloom to our environment and restlessness to the poor souls who have to put up with it. And, to think such a morbid state is due to ingratitude.

If we would only repent of such an attitude, we could begin to learn to be content in our state, knowing that God knows where we are and how to preserve us.

Prayer: Lord, thanksgiving is part of the sacrifice of praise we are to offer You. Forgive me when my state is morbid and my mood foul because I am being a spoiled child crying for the many pacifiers of the world to temporarily satisfy my lusts rather than a saint of the Most High who recognizes what I have in You. Amen.

November 19

"Be careful for nothing; but in every thing by prayer and supplication with thanksgiving let your requests be made known unto God" (Philippians 4:6). As believers in America, there is much to be thankful for. There is our spiritual heritage of redemption as children of God, our physical heritage of freedom as Americans, and our eternal promise of life as saints of the Most High God. In reality we have it all.

When you consider what we have in Christ, every base has been covered in regard to our lives. Yet, there are many Christians who are not content. They live in the mire of regrets, wallow in the pigpen of self-pity, and lament in the cesspools of "Woe is me." They cry over the spilt milk of the past, while ignoring the precious moments of the present, allowing the hope of the future to slip through their fingers.

The truth is most people are missing God's blessings while they look for the illusive "carrot" of life according to their fanciful take on it. They want life on their terms without realizing that they will not find life in any of it. It is a fantasy at best and a tormenting nightmare at worst.

There comes a point where even God's people must choose to add faith to what they know about Him to find His true peace in a matter. At that time the situation may not be void of conflict, but it will be standing sure on the promises of God in light of an eternal peace.

Prayer: Lord, I so thank You for Your sure promises. The world offers no hope, but Your promises remind me that You are true to Your Word and You will bring forth a matter for Your purpose and glory. Amen.

November 20

"In every thing give thanks: for this is the will of God in Christ Jesus concerning you" (1 Thessalonians 5:18). I do not have to tell anyone we are living in trying times. I have been told that such times will either bring the best out in us or reveal the worse about us.

I learned long ago that how I react to trying times depends on the attitude I maintain towards God and life. If I think that I deserve the best from God and happiness from life, the pose I will take on towards both will be a type of contempt. My attitude will reek with ingratitude as I consider God useless to my cause or non-existent to my way of thinking. I will mock life and those who try to bring any reality check to my selfish ways. In the end I will learn how to play people, while I tempt God and try to manipulate life.

If we are going to survive the times that are looming in front of us, we must learn to walk in thankfulness towards what we have in Christ. In order to develop an attitude of thankfulness, we must repent of living in the mire of our thinking, wallowing in the pigpens of our godless lifestyles, and lamenting in the cesspools of our ways. We need to awake from our spiritual dullness, rise up out of our foolishness, and flee from the insipid vanity of it all. We must choose to be thankful in all matters, knowing that it is God's will and that our Lord has a purpose for everything that comes our way.

Prayer: Lord, I want the trying times to bring me forth as a precious gem, ready to be placed in Your crown. I want to be able to reflect the passion of Your heart, the fire of Your holiness, the zeal of Your righteousness, and the perfection of Your ways. Amen.

November 21

"Unless the LORD had been my help, my soul had almost dwelt in silence" (Psalm 94:17). There is something about silence that has the ability to heighten people's senses. Sometimes it actually puts people into a mode of expectation where they become aware that something is about to happen.

Although there is much clamoring going on in the world, my soul has experienced a time of silence. Even though silence can be unnerving in many ways, for believers it should cause a state of alertness and expectancy.

As I embark on this season of celebration, I perceive that the silence of my soul is marking important events. Depending on how I perceive these events will determine the type of attitude I will adopt in regard to my present status and my future hope. My hope is that as believers each of us has already come, or we are coming, to the place of expectancy in our soul towards the matters of heaven as we each embark upon this time of Thanksgiving.

It is vital that we find our Lord in the midst of the activities. He must become our help for He is the only One who our souls can come to rest upon as we celebrate the many gifts of life with thanksgiving in our hearts for His many blessings.

Prayer: Lord, You are my help, but I first must come to a place of silence so that I can locate You in the midst of a busy, unproductive world of useless activities. Amen.

November 22

"That I may publish with the voice of thanksgiving, and tell of all thy wonderous works" (Psalm 26.7). Celebrations always carry with them certain expectations. The question we must ask is what are we celebrating? The type of celebration we are having should dictate to us our attitude towards it. Perhaps it is a joyous occasion because two special people are going to be united in marriage. Maybe we are celebrating the birth of a child or some important transition in our lives. We can't have a proper attitude until we have an understanding of what we are marking as a point of importance.

There is a difference between a celebration and a holiday. People are constantly taking holidays to relax, have fun, and get away from the usual, but a celebration marks something of significance that we are not to simply pass by. The Old Testament bears this out.

God marked certain days for the Israelites to come apart and celebrate His intervention and provision for them. These celebrations were to serve as "living" memorials and were centered around certain events such as Passover. At such times, these celebrations were to cause the people to take time to soberly remember what God did on their behalf so they could truly celebrate the life and blessings they had been given.

These memorials were to not only cause them to remember, but it was to create an attitude of gratitude towards God and the life He had entrusted to them. It is important to point out that a thanksgiving offering was often given along with other offerings. After all, why offer something that has no understanding, meaning, or gratitude behind it? Gratitude is the only thing that acknowledges and reminds us that all we have comes from God; all we receive is a matter of grace, and the hope that we can rest on is a matter of His mercy.

Is Thanksgiving a holiday or a celebration? Is it a day we take off or is it a memorial that causes us to pause and truly remember that as a nation we have been greatly blessed by our Creator, as a people we have been shown incredible mercy, and as individuals, we have indeed tasted His glorious grace.

Prayer: Lord, we take much for granted, and as a result we have forgotten or push aside memorials that remind us that without You we have nothing, without Your intervention we end up with nothing, and without You there is no hope to be found anywhere. Thank You for Your many blessings that continually grace my life with the awareness of how great You are. Amen.

November 23

"For when for the time ye ought to be teachers, ye have need that one teach you again which be the first principles of the oracles of God; and are become such as have need of milk and not of strong meat" (Hebrews 5:12). Through the years I have taught many Bible studies and I noted three groups of people.

There are those who act fragile and just want to skim the surface of the Word by staying in the "kiddie pool" of doctrine in order to leave feeling good about themselves and not with a greater sense of the Lord Himself. If challenged they will skip right out of the study with an attitude of being insulted that later becomes judgmental because you dare challenge the flimsy reality of their Christianity.

The second group are willing to go a little deeper, but they are holding onto some anchor of personal beliefs or an agenda that they will not let go of instead of grabbing a hold of the Rock of Ages that allows them to go deeper. Eventually these individuals will be taken away by some storm that will challenge the strength of their anchor, exposing its great weakness.

Finally, there are those who come hungry to know His Word, not on a surface level but on a deep level. In some cases, they have been skipping across the surface of the water because of how the Bible has been taught to them, but they want to go deeper into the ocean of God's Word. They want to study the riches left by the great cloud of witnesses, find the nuggets left by God's abundant provision, and discover eternal treasures left in the wake of those who have explored the possibilities of God's truths by exercising their faith towards Him.

I am excited to see when a Christian receives that "wow" revelation that lifts them onto another plane when it comes to God's Word. The Holy Spirit connects some dots as He brings revelation to the person's spirit about some aspect of God's character, work and/or way. Suddenly, the person's eyes open wide, followed by their mouth saying "Wow!"

God truths are simple, yet profound. They are pure, but deep, they are true but mysterious, they bring awe to the heart, challenge the "mental boxes" of the mind, and cause the emotions to overflow in indescribable wonderment as one realizes that there is even more to discover.

I love His Word and I love Him for being everything the Word describes and more, which always proves to be a glorious revelation of the eternal, the incredible, and the indescribable.

Prayer: Lord many are in love with their idea of You, but I am in love with You because of what Your Word reveals about You. Thank You for being the Living Word and for being the reason and inspiration behind Your written Word. Amen.

November 24

"Wherefore, come out from among them, and be ye separate, saith the Lord, and touch not the unclean thing; and I will receive you. And will be a Father unto you, and ye shall be my sons and daughters, saith the Lord Almighty" (2 Corinthians 6:17-18). How much do you think the world has influenced the Church? There are so many warnings in Scripture about how the members of Jesus' church need to come out and be separate from the influence of the world, but what has become obvious is that the visible Church has adopted the attitudes, methods, and philosophies of the world.

It is clear that those of this fleshly, worldly church evaluate matters according to the world and not the Spirit of God and His Word. The matters of God can only be discerned because it comes down to the spirit that is in operation.

These misguided individuals use worldly methods to grow the church numbers when it is the Lord that add souls to His kingdom. They integrate some of the world's philosophies such as psycho-babble, New Age Yoga, "contemplative" prayer, visualization, political correctness, and now the "latest woke" into their practices and ideology to attract people, instead of becoming the method that is submissive to the leading and work of the Holy Spirit.

I could go on and on about how the world has come into the church to corrupt, defile, and render it powerless. This invasion is nothing new and it has been an ongoing battle since the church's inception. This encroachment started out subtle, cleverly ebbing away the Church's authority, power, and testimony with compromises here and there, while adding a bit of pagan practices while touting a Christian veneer.

There was higher criticism during Spurgeon's time that demoted the wisdom of the Bible, and now we have psychology that cast the counsel of the Word aside, relativism that gave the absolutes of truth a black-eye, along with "pet doctrines" that managed to override its intent and principles with their own interpretations. What we have ended up with is smorgasbord of weak Bible versions that have created spiritual malnutrition resulting in a spiritual famine in the land, while making the different forms of literature and entertainment lame substitutes for reading and studying the Word.

The battle has always been over the truth of God. It comes down to unbelief versus faith, darkness verses light, wickedness verses righteousness, and deception verses truth. In the end truth will win because it is righteous, as well as a matter of transparent light, and is received as being so by genuine faith.

Prayer: Lord give me a love for the truth, child-like faith to embrace it, a boldness to display its light, and like Job the integrity to hold true to it, regardless of the darkness that surrounds me. Amen.

November 25

"For consider him that endured such contradiction of sinners against himself, lest ye be wearied and faint in your minds" *(Hebrews 12:3).* Life is a current that takes us through the terrain

of this world. It is a journey of discovery but not of this world, but of the character of one's soul. If you could put a spotlight on your soul, what would it tell you about you? Would you see your soul as being parched, wearied, lifeless, or patiently trusting and waiting. I say this because the great challenge is to possess our souls in patience to endure to the end (*Luke 21:19*).

It is easy to become weary with life. Life has challenges and drudgeries. It can feel like a barren wilderness one moment as our souls become parched from the endless realities of the world we live in and in the next become consumed by floods of problems that seem to contaminate and rob us of any purity and purpose.

As we look at the different tides of life, we have to remember in the parched times, the Lord knows how to uncap the Living Water in our soul, in the uncertain times we have enduring promises, in the floods we have the Rock of safety, in the swells of difficulties we know that He is in the boat with us, and in the battles, He has already won the war.

In simple terms, the only way we can avoid weariness in this life is to consider what Jesus endured in His life on earth so that our hope can rise out of the ashes of despair and take flight, bringing us into a new realm where the Lord's presence will sustain us, His light will shine forever, and His glory will enfold us.

Prayer: Lord, we take much for granted about Your many blessings, but it is in the challenging times of life that we are reminded we have great need of You and it is the drought that brings us to the realization we can't live without You and the Living Water that You uncap in our souls. Amen.

November 26

"In whom are hid all the treasures of wisdom and knowledge" (*Colossians 2:3*). It is obvious that once the snow comes to the

rivers, the mist must also make its entrance. It may dance on the water or it may lay as a light blanket on the surface.

The mist reminds me of the moisture that must be present to not only highlight the incredible phase of winter, but it is also part of the cycle of life. The mist, the steam, and the fog must come to bring needed water to the earth. It sometimes hides the workings of the rivers in order to define the landscape.

As the mist dances on the surface of the water, it reminds me that life comes from above not from below or around me. It must cover the terrain to separate the warmth from the cold to ensure a balance of life.

The mist also reminds me of the mystery of life. Life fascinates me with its endless flow of surprises. Some are pleasant and some not so pleasant, but life reminds me that it is moving forward regardless of the past consuming the present with its ever-changing reality, and advancing forward with expectation of experiencing its various treasures.

I know the life I possess from above is the life of Christ and it is leading me to a heavenly destination, an eternal home, and a wondrous end.

Prayer: Lord, I know all of the treasures of heaven and life can be found in You. Become my all in all so I will possess as much of the riches of heaven as I can before I leave this sin-sick world. Amen.

November 27

Old shoes and old hats. How many times have you felt like playing Taps over your preferred old, worn-out shoes when you had to part with them, or maybe even an old hat you favored? Let's face it, sometimes the "old" is more consistently compatible, convenient and comfortable than the latest "fashion" the world has to offer.

Then there's the up and down realm of relationships with others where many times you are taken for granted and treated like "old shoes" while your warnings and exhortations are waved off as "old hat." While some friends stay close and dear, others drift off on the currents of the world in order to find satisfaction in all that they think the world has to offer; however, when an ominous storm threatens to cause a leak, or even sink their "pleasure boat," all of a sudden, they reach out for their "old shoes" friends for prayer.

Then, after the crisis is past, they quickly float back out on the ebbing tide to avoid any words of wisdom, exhortations, or godly advice that their dependable "old shoes" friends may have for them because, in their minds, it's just "old hat."

The question is, how many times do we treat our great God and Savior as "old hat" because we know that He is "always there" if we really need Him; and, how many times do we close our ears, minds or hearts to the truth of His Word because it has become "old hat" to us?

Think about it. The Great Day of the coming of the LORD, and the Day of Judgment grows closer with every "tick" of the clock. On that day it will be too late to undo what we did, and too late to do what we didn't because of our "old shoes" and "old hat" attitude. *"Therefore we ought to give the more earnest heed to the things which we have heard, lest at any time we should let them slip. For if the word spoken by angels was stedfast, and every transgression and disobedience received a just recompence of reward; How shall we escape, if we neglect so great salvation; which at the first began to be spoken by the Lord, and was confirmed unto us by them that heard him; God also bearing them witness, both with signs and wonders, and with divers miracles,* and gifts of the Holy Ghost, according to his own will?" (Hebrews 2:1-3). – J. Haley

Prayer: Lord, we treat you like an "old hat" because You are trustworthy and You seem to always be there when we call out. However, there are times when You will withdraw Your presence to let us know what it feels like when You are not there to be taken for granted like an "old hat." Lord, forgive us for our selfish, ungrateful attitudes and ways. Amen.

November 28

"A man that hath friends must shew himself friendly: and there is a friend that sticketh closer than a brother" (Proverbs 18:24). The type of impact a person makes on you will be determined by the type of history and relationship you share with them. I have a history with various people, but there are those who actually are the instruments that the Lord uses to write more than a paragraph on my mind, but an actual story on my heart.

One such person is an individual I occasionally call "Sis." She is actually a foster sister who lived with me and my family in my senior year. Her name is Deborah Zitterkopf, Debbie or Deb for short. She was in my class and she was without a stable residence during a period of transition and wanted to finish her senior year at my school so my mother invited her to stay with us so she could accomplish that goal.

She brought a certain spice to our home that included a bit of joy, a willingness to be part of the team effort, and a sense of humor that always left a smile on our hearts. Like all young people ready to embark on new adventures, we went in different directions after graduation, but years later we did come back to the same place together, Jesus Christ.

She became a believer. Instead of miles apart as before, we now live less than an hour away from each other. We get together when we are in her vicinity to do shopping and recently, she joined our Bible Study via phone.

Debbie has taught me that it is not where you have been that counts but where you end up in the end. We all must start out somewhere with a person. In other words, there needs to be a history with an individual before there can be a present with them, and hopefully the history is not some footnote, sentence or paragraph but a sweet story that not only becomes an important part of who you are, but becomes a mirror as to how far you have come as a person, a friend, and most of all a Christian.

Prayer: Lord, You have brought so many different blessings to my life. These blessings are not just needs or things, but people. Although there are always few incidents I would love to have avoided with some people, I am thankful for each one for You have made them part of the mosaic of my life to fine-tune the work You are doing in me. Amen.

November 29

"Come now, and let us reason together, saith the LORD: though your sins be as scarlet, they shall be as white as snow; though they be red like crimson, they shall be as wool" (Isaiah 1:18). It has been snowing! In fact, the heavens have been letting down the white stuff for a couple of days. Every time the snow covers the ground, I am reminded of *Isaiah 1:18.* The snow makes everything clean and pure. It covers up the dirt, filth, and residues left behind by the other seasons of life. It not only makes everything look clean, but it makes it look new.

Isaiah tells us that before God can cover our sins with the purity of righteousness, He must first reason with us about sin. We need

411

to come into agreement with His evaluation about a matter. It is clear we must take on the same attitude about sin that God has towards it. If we fail to do so, we will start to dance around it, then we will parlay with it to the point we will justify its presence in our life.

I must admit this Scripture in Isaiah was always used in relationship to what God can do in regard to sin, but the fact that He first wants to reason with us about sin is rarely highlighted. Without reasoning about it to bring it to the light there will be no sense of conviction, and without conviction there will be no need to repent.

People must not only understand the sin that besets them, but the spiritual ruin it will bring to their lives. Without the changed attitude that leads to true repentance they will not turn away from it in disgrace and flee its lies and influence on their lives.

Prayer: Lord, You are the only One who can deal with our sin. There are many marks left by sin, but I know that I have been cleansed by Your blood and stand chaste in Your righteousness. Amen.

November 30

My beloved is white and ruddy, the chiefest among ten thousand" *(Song of Solomon 5:10).* The first phase that marks the winter season is the presence of snow. A couple of weeks ago we had a combination of rain and snow. Rain creates a gray that looks like a shade, but such a tinted shadow is needed for growth. So much of our spiritual growth takes place in the overcast day that produces a type of shade or shadow over our lives like it does the countryside. We are reminded of *Psalm 23* that it is in the valley of the shadow of death that we know He is with us.

Snow gives, especially the rivers around here, a certain beauty. Even though the light will cast shadows on the landscape, the snow will define the shapes that emphasize the rivers in a stunning way. At times the fog hangs low on them and as it begins to lift like a curtain, you begin to see such beauty that brings wonderment to your soul.

The light breaking through the fog highlights certain aspects of the river's beauty while causing some of the other parts of the landscape to be obscured by a bit of darkness. In some cases, shadows are more defined as each aspect of the river is clearly outlined by the white of the snow.

This is how the righteousness of Christ has marked my life. It is in the dark valleys that I sense His presence but when it comes to snow it highlights places of darkness. My flesh clearly causes areas of the fog of confusion and uncertainty in my life. I must seek the Lord, who is the light of the world, for any real clarity. There are certain aspects of His righteousness that have brought a cleansing to my life. But such aspects have also outlined the darkness of my discrepancies. It is for this reason that I embrace the perfect ways of God's righteousness.

I want Christ to be reflected in my life as well as those troubled areas highlighted by His patience, mercy, and grace so they can be addressed in a proper way.

Prayer: Lord, my prayer is simple, I want to be marked by Your righteousness. I know there is no good thing in any aspect of my flesh. I submit to the precious work of Your Spirit. Amen.

DECEMBER

December 1

"And now men see not the bright light which is in the clouds: but the wind passeth, and cleanseth them" (Job 37:21). In the area in which I now live I have had the opportunity to watch the stages rivers go through during the winter season. As I meditate on these stages, I've often noted the affect that ice has on them in my diaries and posts. We know that standing water turns into ice when the environment is right, but it takes a greater amount of extreme weather to create a veneer of ice on running water.

It's fascinating to watch the ice edge its way from the shorelines of the different rivers to take as much of the water captive as it can, creating a transparency that speaks of a beauty which refuses to be hidden. As the ice edges its way out, it seems to be stopped by the rushing water that refuses to be cornered and corralled by the encroaching ice. Thus, the river maintains its openness as the water hurries towards its destination.

Life carries the cold wind of indifference. Such indifference can cause us to become cold to everything around us. Even though ice can be transparent and beautiful when it comes to water, it is destructive when it enters into the heart of man.

As a believer, I must never let the cold winds of indifference create an icy veneer over my heart. Such a veneer will stop the warmth of God's love from flowing through my life. The beauty about God's love is that it will always lead me back to the warmth of His mercy, grace, and promises.

Prayer: Lord, keep the warmth of Your love flowing through my heart and life. I never want to be rendered indifferent by the cold ways of this present age. Amen.

December 2

"Awake, O north wind; and come, thou south: blow upon my garden, that the spices thereof may flow out. Let my beloved come into his garden, and eat his pleasant fruits" (Song of Solomon 4:16). I have often found myself in awe with God's creation by watching the different changes that take place with the rivers that flow through the landscape.

During extremely cold times it appears as if the ice will win the battle of the smaller rivers. The combination of snow and coldness will create conditions that will cause some rivers to completely disappear under what appeared to be chunks of ice. But upon examining such rivers, you realize that the water remains flowing underneath the ice.

I marvel at how the elements of nature can change the face of creation. In each change there is evidence of a new cycle of life emerging to maintain the function of the whole.

This is true for my spiritual life. It seems that at times my life has been consumed by that which is overwhelming, but the reality is God is doing a greater work. Unbeknown to the physical eye, life is pulsating in greater ways underneath the various surfaces that obscure the deeper and finer work of God.

I have come to realize that this is part of the cycle of regeneration. Therefore, I welcome the cold wind from above because what will follow are the fruits of a new life.

Prayer: Lord, You give us so many examples of how the matters of life work. We can learn so much by the terrain around us. Give us the wisdom and means to learn the valuable lessons of life. Amen.

December 3

"And he shall be like a tree planted by the rivers of water, that bringeth forth his fruit in his season; his leaf also shall not wither; and whatsoever he doeth shall prosper" (Psalm 1:3). When I think of a garden, I can imagine smelling the spices which point to Jesus who is the fragrance of heaven. When I think of flowers, I think of the Shulamite girl who, like a bud, was opening up and revealing the beauty created in her by the love for her king and shepherd to the world, and when I think of trees, I think of godly men that stand tall in the world and upright before God.

I have some good supportive Christian brothers that are like trees in my life. There is Mike Kropp who has such a big heart that he brings so much "shade" from the intensity of the trials of this world and comfort to the weary soul that needs encouragement and direction. There is John Wulff whose greatest desire is to be a Berean of the Word and teach and challenge others to be one too.

Two of my latest brothers are Bill Castle and Jeff Vullmahn. Bill has a fierceness towards what is right, a gentleness towards what is heavenly, and such integrity he is a lot like a strong, established castle that will not be moved from what he knows is true. There is Jeff who has such zeal about Jesus saving him that he wants the whole world to know, but he is wisely learning to allow the Holy Spirit to temper him in the ways of righteousness.

Each brother reminds me of the different aspects of Jesus. Whether serving as a pruned, but fruitful tree for others to run to, turning over the money-changers' table to expose the sham of man's religion and ways, or ever ready for the Spirit to move Him, Jesus is the ultimate tree and example. I know that it is the trees that shade the gardens of the world and we each need to recognize such trees and discern when we need to run to them for shade, direction, and encouragement.

Prayer: Lord, thank You for positioning Your trees in our midst. They are necessary to ensure the well-being of the gardens of this world. Amen.

December 4

"Again, a new commandment I write unto you, which thing is true in him and in you: because the darkness is past, and the true light now shineth" (1 John 2:8). After Thanksgiving, I used to put up my Christmas village as part of the decoration for the season. I especially loved to look at it at night when the small buildings were highlighted by lights that revealed the detailed work that had gone into each one of them. You could see different activities taking place in many of the pretty miniature buildings that marked the holiday season.

I have since given the village away, but I used to study it because it brought a bit of sentimental nostalgia to my memories of a more innocent time when I was young and my eyes were full of excitement and anticipation. It was much like watching the classic movie, "The Christmas Story." Even though the movie was made in the 1980's, it represented the time I grew up in, the late 1950's. It seemed as if it was a more innocent time for our nation. It was between the Korean conflict and the height of the Viet Nam conflict.

I realize that the village created a certain sentiment towards Christmas that was a bit childish. However, there is nothing sentimental about where Christmas should lead us. If we are going to establish a memorial of Jesus' Incarnation during this time, we must cast aside the vanity of the demands and activities of this season and pause in order to meditate on what it meant for God to become man. Granted, innocence came by way of a baby born in Bethlehem, the light parted the darkness, and heaven rejoiced, but all of this occurred in light of an ominous shadow that would later be cast upon the countryside by an old rugged cross.

It is not wrong to be sentimental about this time of the year, but such sentiment becomes silly, a veneer to cover up worldly attitudes and activities, and wrong when Jesus is left in the manger, while commercialism takes center stage, and Santa is exalted. Clearly, Jesus is never allowed to fulfill His destiny in our minds and hearts as the Lamb of God who was born (mostly likely in September), to take away the sin of the world. After all, Jesus' great sacrifice became a gift of life that provided the means for His blood to cleanse the repentant sinner from all unrighteousness as a means to reconcile each of us back to God.

Prayer: Lord, everything You have done on our behalf stirs up emotions, but I must never let sentiment towards the world keep me from going forward to embrace the unexpected, the incredible, and the eternal. Amen.

December 5

Food! It's definitely one thing all people have in common. And if you've ever observed how people consume a meal, then you know that while some gulp it down at the speed of light, others have learned the art of savoring each bite.

Somehow, they've discovered that washing down chunks of meat, or a large mouthful of "everything-at-once" with a beverage just isn't all that satisfying to the palate (plus it causes indigestion and weight gain). Such hearty eaters have missed the joy of savoring the tantalizing nuances of subtle flavors and textures that seductively dance on the tongue.

Cultivating the art of "savoring the moment" is a much more satisfying and pleasurable experience, but food and drink aren't the only life experience we can savor with our senses. What about the beautiful, harmonious tonal range of an inspired masterful instrumentation?

Great music is a gift from God with the power to intimately touch and profoundly move upon the soul of man by lifting the spirit to soar in lofty heights, calming the troubled heart, and producing both mental, emotional and sometimes physical healing. In addition, there are exotic, mesmerizing and beautiful-beyond-description visual wonders, both great and small, all around us to appreciate, enjoy and "savor" as well.

That leaves two of the five senses—touch and smell. Both can offer "savor moments." For example, I used to "savor" the incredible softness of our little, long-haired Chihuahua, Bell. As for smell, what is lovelier than the amazing fragrance of roses, hyacinths, or lavender? Of course, there is the aroma of food cooking on the BBQ, and that brings us back to where we started--food!

To savor these things results in a greater satisfaction; however, the most important and valuable possession we have to "savor" is the Holy Bible, God's personal letter to us. We need to truly take the time and effort to "savor" it by meditating on it, and believe it, receive it as truth, hide it in our hearts, keep it in our thoughts, apply it to our life, and walk it out in obedience. Savoring God's Word will result in spiritual satisfaction. Jesus said, *"I am the bread of life: he that cometh to me shall never hunger; and he that believeth on me shall never thirst" (John 6:35).* – J. Haley

Prayer: Lord, we start out savoring much of the world, but until we learn to savor You and Your Word, the world will be the main source of attraction to us. Lord, change my taste from this world to that which is heavenly and eternal. Amen.

419

December 6

"Seek ye me, and ye shall live: But seek not Bethel, nor enter into Gilgal, and pass not to Beersheba: for Gilgal shall surely go into captivity, and Bethel shall come to nought" (Amos 5:4b-5). As we wade through the busyness of holidays, I realize that the end of the year seems to come quicker than the year before. Regardless, of the fact that the stores gear up for the commercial push of everything "Christmas" after Halloween, this time of the year comes like a locomotive train, heading down the track at high speed. People basically run as fast as they can to keep ahead of the impact it can leave in its wake.

For me, this time causes me to want to wrap up my pending projects for another year. In a way it is like trying to be able to prepare for a new year where I run the race with less commitments clinging to my back. But I have learned in the past that I must always push past tendencies to accomplish all, set the demands of the world aside, and begin to seek God's perspective. It is at this time I remind myself that upon embracing the gift of God in the form of Christ's redemption that I rid myself of past baggage.

You realize much of the activity during this time is not a flow but a tidal wave that grabs you and takes you out into a mass of wasteless activities, causing you to wisely realize that you must take time to seek Him in order to enjoy the life and the many blessings He has given you regardless of the activities, projects, and responsibilities.

This reality should become a standing lesson to me each year, but I am forced to remind myself of the lesson when I begin to lose my sense of humor. It is then I must remind myself to take time in my relationship with the Lord and enjoy who He is, not only during this time, but every time the world begins to make more demands on my life.

Obviously, the Lord must be put to the forefront as a means to secure a right perspective and to avoid the wastefulness which comes with the fleshly activities of the world. He must become my prize that I desire, seek, and pursue with my whole heart.

Prayer: Lord, sometimes my attempt to do good things causes me to miss that which is best and excellent. Help me to get my priorities right. Amen.

December 7

"And have put on the new man, which is renewed in knowledge after the image of him that created him" (Colossians 3:10). When you read diary entries, memories are stirred up as well. I remember the time when I was excited about getting out of my warm bed to check out the scenery of the river. The reason for such excitement was to see how the Artist's great brush had changed the landscape of the river. The change would occur because of the snow that had blanketed the countryside the night before.

To witness how, "with the stroke of a brush" the great Creator dusted the landscape with a bit of snow is humbling. The white on the fir trees and its beauty on the bushes added a different dimension to the majestic scene. Even the gray color of the sky and water seemed to showcase the beauty of the snow on the picturesque scene that lay before my eyes.

This all reminds me of how God changes my inner man. Sometimes under the covering of darkness, He adds a bit of white, that of truth, purity, and righteousness. Even with the grays of uncertainty, His artistic ways bring beauty to His abiding work in my life.

Admittedly, I am amazed about the changes that He has brought to my life. My desire remains the same that His glory is manifested through me.

Prayer: Lord, You are the artist and I am the canvas. In spite of the marks left by sin, You can use it to bring glory to You. Have Your way, oh Lord, because this is the only way my life will become a masterpiece that brings You glory. Amen.

December 8

"But we have this treasure in earthen vessels, that the excellency of the power may be of God, and not of us" (2 Corinthians 4:7). Do you feel the race today is intensifying? The one thing that I constantly wrestle with is being human. I want to simply do my best and know it is perfect so I can go on to the next mountain peak that must be scaled so I can see the next one that I need to be prepared to climb.

The reality of life is that the terrain varies with mountain peaks of fading accomplishments, rushing rivers of challenges, deep valleys of testing, still waters of drudgery, and storms that threaten to wipe out everything that is not rooted in the eternal.

For years I have been busy trying to tie up loose ends. I think that is my last name, "Loose Ends." However, I have felt that the loose ends I have been dealing with for years will never be tied up to my way of thinking. One of the reasons that I have never felt that any project was complete was because I wanted to present everything I do in a perfect state to my Lord.

We live in an imperfect world, are born into a fallen state, possess a carnal, fleshly mind, and are limited in our flesh. Death works in the members of our body ever ready to stop any progress. I have always known the best of my offerings will not be perfect when it comes to the Lord but that does not keep me from trying to press forward to that "imagined perfection." As Paul stated, he was pressing towards the prize of his high calling.

My ineptness reminds me that I am a simple vessel that has no value apart from Jesus. It is Jesus in me who adds purpose and value to my life. It is the work of sanctification through the Holy Spirit in each believer that reveals His blessed perfection and not our best. After all, the vessel has no purpose outside of what it possesses within.

Meanwhile, I must accept my humanness that reminds me that I am nothing more than clay that possesses imperfections that needs to go through the process to even be made useable to the Lord. My imperfection also clearly shows me my need for a Savior who saves, a High Priest who intercedes, and a Holy God who is mighty to do the impossible, even through imperfect vessels. He is a forgiving Lord who is always ready to once again restore a wayward servant, who occasionally loses their focus and way to His household.

Prayer: Lord, we want to get it right, have everything perfect, and skim through life, but if we could, we would not need, consider, or regard You. Your cross shows us everything is foreboding when it comes to this life and that the only hope we have is the light of redemption that has illuminated the way with Your love, while sending forth the invitation to come to partake of the rivers of Living Water, and live. Amen.

December 9

"I do not frustrate the grace of God; for if righteousness come by the law, then Christ is dead in vain" (Galatians 2:21). What does it mean to frustrate the grace of God? It means a person is declaring that Jesus' death on the cross was all in vain because man has

the means to please God without Jesus' sacrifice. Man can usher in the work and promises of God without the cross.

We live in a day of mass confusion about truths that have been firmly established from the beginning. There are two diverse kingdoms of God, one is tied into the covenant God made with Abraham in *Genesis 12:1-3* and the other one is part of the covenant established by Christ's redemption. One is attached to a national identity and the other one is attached to an unseen kingdom.

Those of each kingdom have the same high calling to be separate from the world and the same distinction that is to shine through the darkness of idolatry and paganism to bring contrast. (See *Exodus 19:6; Deuteronomy 14:2* and *1 Peter 2:9.*) For one kingdom there is a biological DNA from Abraham that identifies them to national Israel, but for the other they are spiritual children identified to the same type of faith Abraham had when God reckoned it to him for righteousness. Those who are faithful make up an unseen kingdom that is not of this world (*John 18:36*).

One kingdom was an avenue in which the Messiah would come forth (Israel), and the other one is the avenue in which He would work through (the Church). It is important to point out covenants are perpetual until all is fulfilled.

Although the blessings and promises allotted to the Church came out of the initial covenant God made with Abraham, the two covenants (law and grace) are distinct in their ministrations and are not interchangeable. The ministration of the law goes back to Moses but proved oppressive, while the ministration of grace goes back to Jesus Christ and ends in spiritual liberty (*2 Corinthians 3:6-18; Hebrews 3:1-6*)

Jesus told the woman at the well that salvation came by way of the Jew because God chose national Israel through which He would bring forth the Messiah, and as the Church we are commissioned to share the good news that Jesus died for our sins (transgressions) as a sacrifice to make atonement, took our sin (iniquity) to the grave to bring forth reconciliation between God and man. He ultimately took the sting out of sin, by paying the necessary wages with His life, and rose again to prove victorious over death.

We are told in *Colossians 2:14-17* that the Jews had shadows of the work of redemption in their observances, which Paul referred to as beggarly elements in *Galatians 4:9*, but we as believers have the actual manifestation of those shadows in Christ. The question is, why would those who claim to be believers run back to mere shadows instead of by child-like faith embrace the manifestation, the promise, the glory, and the hope of redemption found only in Christ, unless as Paul stated in *Galatians 3:1*, they have been foolishly bewitched by another gospel that stands accursed before God and will ultimately frustrate His grace.

Prayer: Lord, we are prone to run back to the pigpen of the vain, dead works of religion, the vomit of pride that tells us that grace is too simple and archaic, accept the regurgitation of heretics that add their poison to truth, and be caught up with the glitter of the old while failing to simply walk in the light of Your grace. Forgive us for our ignorance towards You, our pride that wants to share in Your glory and our unbelief that refuses to humble itself in light of Your great work of redemption. Amen.

December 10

"I say then, Have they stumbled that they should fall? God forbid: but rather through their fall salvation is come unto the Gentiles, for to provoke them to jealousy" (Romans 11:11). Is God done with Israel? Some declare that the church has replaced Israel. If they dare study *Romans 11* in the right spirit, they would see this is not true. Israel became the means in which salvation would come to

Gentiles such as myself, but now the Church needs to be a visible witness to provoke Israel to consider the truth that Jesus is their Messiah. We know according to *Zechariah 13:8-9*, national Israel will go through a great purging but in the end, those remaining will receive Jesus as their Messiah.

The explanation to clear up this confusion about who is who can be found in "The Parable of the Trees" in *Judges 9*. This parable reveals how Israel is a special tree, a vineyard planted by the Lord in a land He promised to Abraham and His descendants. In this vineyard, God had a plan to bring forth a certain Vine (Jesus) and from this Vine, many branches (Church) would spring forth to produce precious fruits for His glory. This Church would be one Body made up of both Jews and Gentiles and instead of having a physical inheritance of the Promised Land, it would have a spiritual inheritance attached to heaven itself.

The parable of the trees poses a very important aspect, "Why would a chosen people, a prized nation of ordained priests want to be something other than what it was called to be? Why would its calling, sweetness, and joy be traded in for harsh yokes and thorns of paganism to become useless and later purged by fire in order to bring judgment, clarity and distinction?

We may think Israel foolish but what about the Church? Many who call themselves Christians want to come back under the Law to claim the promises God made to Israel instead of standing on the promises that God has given to the Church. Why would those who have been promised great liberty in the Spirit want to come back under a heavy yoke that the fathers of Israel could not bear, thereby frustrating the grace of God (*Acts 15:10*)? Like national Israel, why would we, as His Church give up our high calling and commission to fit in a world that is full of thorns, and will one day be burned up by the wrath of God? Anyone with common sense and vision would not want to trade such promises for vanity, foolishness, and judgment, and yet man often proves to be a fool because he wants to have salvation on his terms, his way. He wants to claim positions and promises that he has no right to in the first place.

My question is since we are in Christ and we possess everything we have need of to stand in this world, withstand its temptations, and continue to stand in light of eternal blessings attached to salvation, why would we not believe that Jesus is not sufficient enough to not only meet all of our needs but fill all of our empty spaces with the presence of His Spirit and His promises?

Prayer: Lord, the emerging picture of the past into the present reveals that man has the same spiritual challenges, and that his solution has not changed. Thank You for being our solution to sin and my solution to a broken life where yokes of religion were great, the spiritual prisons strong, and the hopelessness of all immeasurable. Amen.

December 11

"...but there be some that trouble you, and would pervert the gospel of Christ. But though we, or an angel from heaven, preach any other gospel unto you than that which we have preached unto you, let him be accursed" (Galatians 1:7b-8). In the last post, I asked if Jesus is enough to rest in when it comes to all we have need of to be saved and survive this age.

I have had a couple of people tell me Jesus was not enough for them so they looked to greater enlightenment or works to add on to Him and His work of redemption; or, that He was not worth losing any aspect of the world over because the world promised satisfaction, even though it will prove to be temporary. I have heard all the reasons why man chooses not to believe what God has done on his behalf, not to trust Him with the matters of life, and not to rest in Him when it comes to the storms and challenges of life.

The tragedy of Jesus not being enough, or being worth losing any association or identification with the world, is that such individuals will end up perverting the true Gospel. "Perversion" is simply an addition to Christ's redemption, whether it be some New Age enlightenment, religious affiliation, or works, or a subtraction of who Christ is as God in the flesh, the Promised Messiah, the Son of God, and the Savior of the world.

The truth is man prefers religious shadows of old because he can create his own ideas of goodness and salvation within them, or the false lights of enlightenment that entangles his pride, making him superior in some ways to the ignorant masses. Oftentimes such beliefs allow him to work his way to some "state of perfection" or "deity," or the intellectual means to affect his own salvation and others as well. Why does man insist on perverting what is pure and simple?

The reality is man simply does not want to believe God's Word, repent of his arrogance, and humble himself before God in complete brokenness and desperation seeking forgiveness and salvation first from himself, next from the influences of the world, and finally from the claims of Satan on his life. He would rather quibble, debate, and become insulted by the simplicity that salvation is the complete work of God and man has no part in it other than believing it is so with child-like faith, trusting it must be so in sincere assurance, and in the end knowing it will prove to be just as God and His Word declared it to be: We are saved by grace through faith and not of any works that we can take credit for before our Holy, Almighty God.

Prayer: Lord, our lack of faith towards You is a choice of unbelief. We choose NOT to believe Your Word, Your examples, and Your promises. We may claim we believe but our inaction and our wrong actions prove we do not because true faith is active, faithful, and obedient. Forgive me for any unbelief and help me to choose the child-like way of faith. Amen.

December 12

"But he is a Jew, which is one inwardly; and circumcision is that of the heart, in the spirit, and not in the letter, whose praise is not of men, but of God" (Romans 2:29). The question is what is more important being identified to that which is of the flesh and the world or that which is of God?

The Jews were set apart by such things as circumcision, keeping the Sabbath, and observing certain rituals. This may have identified them to Moses and the Law, but not to Abraham or faith. Granted, they had the DNA that would trace them back to Abraham, but the faith that justified this patriarch before God was long before the Law that could only point out man's transgression.

There are Gentiles who desire and claim to be Jews, and Jews that prefer to not be burdened with such an identification due to the persecution. We know there are those who are biological descendants of Abraham, who was called by God, and they can be traced to Isaac the chosen son who was promised by God, and through Jacob (Israel) whose seed was selected in which the Messiah would come forth from Israel's son Judah. But this physical identification will not justify or save them.

As a believer I am part of a Church, a Body that has been called, chosen, and selected to be part of the plan and move of God. As a believer I am identified not by outward tokens of circumcision, particular days of rest, or rituals, but by the unseen seal of the Holy Spirit. I have been spiritually circumcised by the Spirit. My Sabbath is not a day of rest but a place of rest in my Jesus. I stand justified not because I have tried to keep the Law, but because I have become identified to Abraham by way of faith towards God and by placing my faith in His plan of redemption.

We always want to have something to say or brag about when it comes to our spiritual heritage. I think this desire has something to do with earning the right to stand before God and insisting He must save us because we have something that we can point to such as an act, a family tie, or some religious identification, and that regardless of how much we live like the devil, pursue the world, and hold on to our idols and pagan ways, God must save us.

When we stand before God, it must be according to His work of grace, for outside of it, our claims will prove empty, our attempts foolish, and our high opinion of our greatness a pinnacle that will be easily toppled by God's consuming fire of holiness and judgment.

Prayer: Lord, man is a confusing mess. He will not accept who he is and refuses to see that You have no favorites. You have offered all of us salvation and You have made it clear and simple enough a child can understand what it means to be saved. Lord, the more man tries to make himself acceptable to You, the more he perverts the truth, shuns real hope, and misses the real opportunity to get it right through brokenness and repentance. Forgive us for insisting on being fools who, for the most part, act and live as if You do not exist. Amen.

December 13

"Now these things were our examples, to the intent we should not lust after evil things, as they also lusted" (1 Corinthians 10:6). Consider this statement: Not everything in the Bible is written TO us as New Testament believers, but everything in it has been written FOR our edification. One of the problems is that God has

given certain promises to the nation of Israel, Abraham's biological descendants, that He will bring forth in due time, but there are many in Christendom that are claiming those promises and causing confusion and discord in the Body which are not part of the fruit of the Spirit.

It is important to discern what applies to Israel while noting that there are principles, teachings, lessons and examples that we can greatly benefit from when it comes to Israel. We get glimpses of this in the examples that are brought out in the New Testament. Jesus brought out examples such as Abraham, Solomon, Jonah, and David. Paul spoke of Abraham's faith in Romans, the son of a bondwoman, Ishmael and the son of promise, Isaac of a freewoman in *Galatians 4:23*. He mentioned the baptism of the Red Sea and the Rock in the wilderness being Jesus in *1 Corinthians 10:1-6*. Hebrews speaks of many of those in the Old Testament in *Hebrews 11* and points out that Esau had no place of repentance in *Hebrews 12:16-17*. James talks about Rahab's active faith and the patience of Job.

It is for this reason Paul tells us we must rightly divide the Word of truth. We must discern what promises belong to Israel, which mainly has to do with restoration of them as a nation to the full inheritance of the Promised Land so we can appreciate the spiritual blessings attached to the promises concerning the Church.

My question is why would we desire the earthly promises of Israel surrounding their nation and land when we have a spiritual inheritance that is a matter of His grace that we will be unveiled to us for ages to come in the heavenlies?

We are living in days that requires us to be sober and watchful about what we choose to believe and what we expose ourselves too. May it always be based on the sincere, true Word of God and the grace He has so abundantly bestowed upon us.

Prayer: Lord every time we try to mix our understanding and interpretation to Your truths, we pervert them. When will we just let Your Word speak without trying to interpret it according to our understanding, and when will we let You be God and trust that Your ways are right for us and perfect in all You do? Amen.

December 14

"How shall we escape, if we neglect so great salvation; which at the first began to be spoken by the Lord, and was confirmed unto us by them that heard him" (Hebrew 2:3). What does it mean to neglect salvation? I have asked myself this question because you can't neglect something you don't have, you can't lose something that you hold in your possession, and you can't misplace something that you are focused on. Let us be clear, this Scripture is clearly not directed towards those who have not experienced salvation.

We Christians take much for granted about our salvation. We assume much about Jesus and make foolish presumptions about His work of redemption, while hiding behind unrealistic, often worldly teachings on God's love and "cheap grace." It seems like there are those who are operating in "wishful thinking." After all they said the "sinner's prayer" and have some religious affiliation, but the question still lingers, "What are they doing with their salvation?"

It is important to point out salvation is not some mental understanding or some religious affiliation. Salvation means you have the life of Christ in you. You are saved because you exchanged your old life with His life, you are being saved because His life is being worked in you by the Holy Spirit, and you will be glorified with Him because the glory of His life is being unveiled in you.

If you don't have His life, you are not born again which means you are not saved and you are still doomed in your sins. After all, we have been born in an ungodly state, we have sinned in some way or manner which makes us sinners and enemies of God and it is only the life of Christ in us that makes us new creations and changes our status.

It is clear that if we are neglecting our salvation, it is because we are not nurturing the life of Christ in us by soberly growing in our knowledge of Jesus, being perfected in it by the Spirit, and walking in its light through obedience to His Word. We must cease to move with assumption about God, but instead with the leading of the Spirit. We are not to operate according to presumption about truth, but according to the complete counsel of God's Word, and we are not to hide behind some worldly and fragile concepts of love and grace when we must learn to hide in Christ where our life in Him will be firmly established.

Prayer: Lord, we often want to skip, slide by, or sit on our religious laurels as we wait for You to pour out some blessing on us, rescue us from our faith being severely tested, or to avoid the refinement of our inner character, but active faith calls us deeper in You, inspires us to ascend higher in Your excellent ways, and will cause us to arise out of complacency to begin to walk out the life in us so we can experience Your goodness, faithfulness, and sweetness. Amen.

December 15

"They are all gone out of the way, they are together become unprofitable; there is none that doeth good, no, not one" (Romans 3:12). What does it mean to nurture the life of Christ in You? Is it about having some religious affiliation, being exposed to Bible teaching, or being around the right people? To nurture something

433

means you have to make some type of personal investment. In essence, YOU must cultivate Jesus' life in you so that it will be brought to maturity.

We are told to work out our salvation with fear and trembling. We need to have a healthy respect and understanding that our salvation is about handling the life of Jesus. We are clearly born with a wrong bent towards the matters of life. We are selfish and prefer our dark ways, our perverted reality, and self-serving agendas. We are inclined toward sin and have a propensity to justify it in our own minds.

We must change that bent, but how? We know we must read and study the Bible, but to make sure you make a right investment you must be aware of WHY you are doing it, WHAT spirit is present, and WHERE it must lead you. Why are you studying the Word? To impress some people, hide some moral bent behind the knowledge of Scriptures, justify spiritual complacency, or to know Jesus?

What spirit are you approaching it in? Are you approaching the Bible to have knowledge about it or gain revelation about Jesus? I know a person who could quote the Bible, but there were blatant discrepancies in her life. It became clear that she wanted to be a person of the Word but not a person of God. Is there a difference? Yes. The Bible is all about knowing the author of it and not just being able to quote it.

Are you approaching it so you can debate about doctrinal matters, or so that it can instruct you in the ways of righteousness that are a matter of faith? After all, only faith can please God, and obedience to His Word that comes out of faith will glorify Him.

Where should it lead me? It should change my perverted bent from the flesh and this world to Jesus. The bent comes down to my heart attitude. And the more my heart attitude is lined up to who God is and His Word the more my conduct and countenance will reflect the life of Jesus in me and through me. It is clear the

434

"why" in my cultivation has to do with faith, the "what" has to do with the right spirit and the "where" has to do with having a right attitude towards the Lord by always coming into agreement with His attitude about the matters of truth and life that have been clearly established in His Word.

Prayer: Lord, You are always challenging our perception in order to reveal our attitude about a matter, but we skip over our attitude, slide past the real issue of a matter, and convince ourselves that our religious theology, reforms, and activities are good enough. It is true such measures may be good enough to me and others, but it will never be good enough to You. Thank You for Your longsuffering towards Your poor creatures, but we must never forget Your Spirit will not always strive with us. Amen.

December 16

Hast thou heard the secret of God? and dost thou restrain wisdom to thyself? What knowest thou, that we know not? what understandest thou, which is not in us? (Job 15:8-9). One of my big challenges as a Christian is to avoid making assumptions out of pride, religious zeal, and personal judgments about the plight of others.

Eliphaz made many assumptions about Job in the arrogance of his mind. He tried to reason with Job that what he had to secretly know in his heart, but was hiding or living in denial about, that his three companions would perceive it as well. This may sound logical, but these companions of Job were looking through the untrustworthy dark glasses of their own biased thoughts and conclusions.

The reality is that many people know similar things due to culture, language, known facts, and certain insights. However,

435

when it comes to spiritual matters, it is not about how much you know, but how well you know God.

We may know many facts about God because of similar religious experiences and teachings but few know God past their theology. Granted, theology may be correct, but that does not mean one understands what is going on, especially when it comes to another person's relationship and interaction with God. Since theology is limited, it can do nothing more than judge according to what a person understands based on its influence on them.

Eliphaz was taking on a religious pose in order to judge Job, but his judgments were wrong; therefore, his accusation became slanderous. If we could strip away the religious pose of Eliphaz, I wonder how much jealousy we would find. There is nothing crueler and more slanderous than jealousy that finds a self-righteous platform from which to judge, while hiding arrogance behind religious garbs.

Prayer: Lord, it is easy to become an Eliphaz. Arrogance can convince us we know a spiritual matter when in fact, we know nothing. Lord bring me down from any high pinnacle of nonsensical arrogance into the dark valleys to show me that my conclusions are not trustworthy and in the end will not stand when the light finally reveals the real crux of the matter. Amen.

December 17

All people, and even most pets, love to receive a delightful gift from time to time, and I also believe some people possess an "art of giving." They seem to have an uncanny way of knowing just what type of gift will delight another, but the heart that receives the greatest blessing belongs to the giver for "it is more blessed to give than to receive" *(Acts 20:35),* and "God loves a cheerful giver" *(2 Corinthians 9:7).*

However, at this point there is a big "Caution sign." Through the years I have learned that at the very moment you hand someone a gift, no matter how much you may have invested in it, or hunted for it, sacrificed for it, or even created it yourself, it is THEIRS and whatever they do, or don't do, with it after that is totally up to them. By doing so, you not only offer freedom of choice to the recipient of your gift, but you also free yourself of any emotional entanglements, personal expectations, or attachments that could develop into a type of unsavory bondage, and hurt feelings, for both your friend and yourself.

Simply put, let it go without expecting anything, in any way, in return. Consider our example in *James 1:17 "Every good gift and every perfect gift is from above, and cometh down from the Father of lights, with whom is no variableness, neither shadow of turning."*

The greatest gift ever given is the Son of God. *"For the wages of sin is death; but the gift of God is eternal life through Jesus Christ our Lord."* What are we doing, today, with this great Gift, and *"How shall we escape, if we neglect so great salvation....?"* (See *Romans 6:23* and *Hebrews 2:3.)*

Are you ready for a "gift exchange" with God? – J. Haley

Prayer: Lord, to give a gift means we give it freely, but whether others prize that gift will come down to their attitude. We can use, abuse, or discard the gift. This is what many have done with Your Son and in the end, they will not only miss the benefits of such a wondrous gift, but it will become a point of judgment to them as well. Amen.

December 18

"Neither give heed to fables and endless genealogies, which minister questions, rather than godly edifying which is in faith: so do" (1 Timothy 1:4). As I enter my seventh decade of life, I have

437

seen a lot of history. Looking back it is like a movie that has been speeded up to keep up with the pace of change.

In the 1970s when I became a Christian, eschatology was a big thing. In the 1990s you could see the expectation that some people had about Jesus coming waning down from a roar to a mere mention. Today there is skepticism, scoffing, silence, and debates about it, but there is little or no place where one can reason or simply discuss it.

In the first decades of the 21st century it seems many have developed itching ears. They do not want to hear the truth and it seems the waves that are sweeping into Christendom are creating an environment that is becoming more averse to truth and righteousness. It appears that many prefer to believe in fables, false promises, false prophecies that lead them to nowhere, and doctrines of demons that are shrouded in seduction.

In fact, I often wonder how many people who call themselves Christians know the basic tenets of their faith? How many know how to properly use their sword, the Word of God? I guess a better question is how many have read the Bible through, studied it to show they know how to properly handle it and are actually capable of discerning the times because they know what the Bible says about the days we are living in?

We all have opinions, assumptions, and presumptions about religious issues which in many cases will prove mere theories in the end and not the truth of the Bible. Don't get me wrong, I have my opinions, and I have assumed I understood something because when I heard it the first time, it sounded good to my way of thinking, as well as maintained presumptions about matters, but all proved to be shifting sand when tested with the actual reality of the times. Instead of being taken out by some wave, I would let the wave take out my notions as I clung to the Word of God.

The Bible, which was written for our instruction warns us of being deceived. Our foundation is not based on opinions about spiritual matters but on the Truth, the Person of Jesus Christ. Beliefs must not be mere assumptions but sound doctrine, confirmed by the complete counsel of God's Word. And our stands must not be according to presumptions but on what has been verified as being eternal.

Prayer: Lord, when Your Word challenges us in our faith, we often transpose it on the next guy. After all, all those warnings about being deceived do not apply to me. However, I have learned they do apply to me. They are warnings to me and I need to own each one if I am going to examine my faith to see if I am hid in You, standing on You, and ever coming to an abiding confidence in You about what is so. Amen.

December 19

"...for if righteousness come by the law then Christ is dead in vain" *(Galatians 2:21b).* At one of our Bible Studies a lady shared how she thought she was a Christian, but three years prior she learned she was not truly born again because she had not repented of her sins. Sadly, many people assume they are saved because of a sinner's prayer once said, an affiliation with a particular denomination, good deeds they are doing, or the people they associate with.

The cry even from Jesus' lips was to repent or perish! Many people have a façade of piety, but there is no real godliness to be found in any of it. In other words, the activities and works they do can't be traced back to a love for God, the upright standing of faith towards God, and the right standing of obedience because it is a matter of righteousness established by the Word of God.

Most of religion is about how man feels about himself and not about how God sees a matter. Man offers carnal worship, lifts up concepts of God, which are idolatrous, and adheres to a social

439

gospel of works that exalts man's deeds, ever frustrating the grace of God that alone saves underserving man.

Christians are saved by grace, but to understand how grace works a person must repent, turn, and seek real mercy from a holy God because of sin, rebellion, and unbelief. This lady got it right and now sets out to contend for the souls of others, including those who are planted in church pews, where roots have grown into lifeless doctrine, indifference that has petrified them in their state, religious affiliation that gives a false sense of salvation, and works which will be considered profane by a Holy God who did not ordain them.

Sadly, those who seek a false sense of salvation are settling for some flimsy "fire insurance," instead of seeking the only One who can save them from the fires and damnation of hell.

Prayer: Lord, we want to feel some personal sweat when it comes to our salvation so that we know we have a part in saving ourselves. Your grace sets the record straight, we are saved by what You have done and it is that measure of faith You give us that we can be assured of receiving it as the great gift You have offered each of us. Forgive us for thinking the filthy rags of our best could ever be accepted by You in Your holiness. Amen.

December 20

"And thee appeared an angel unto him from heaven, strengthening him. And being in an agony he prayed more earnestly: and his sweat was as if was great drops of blood falling down to the ground" (Luke 22:43-45). Years ago, a man who was praying for me stated that I would move into my gift without any sweat, and without realizing it I did come into my gifting without any effort.

Yesterday I mentioned that many want to somehow put their sweat into salvation so they can take some credit for it. In fact, the concept that we are saved by grace has caused some to walk away from the salvation that God has so abundantly and freely made available to us.

When I think of sweat, I remember what happened to Jesus when He was in Gethsemane, He sweat great drops. In a way, Jesus was pouring out what represents the best of man's efforts on the ground so that the great work before Him would be about that which was without sin, fleshly strength, and would take divine intervention to serve as an example to us. In the great battle in Gethsemane, it appeared Jesus wrestled over the reality of whether He could endure Calvary in His humanity. The truth is only that which is without fleshly strength can understand the sustaining enduring beauty and work of grace.

You might say Jesus sweated for all of humanity so that we did not have to sweat when it came to salvation and service. Even the priests of old wore linen that would keep them from working up a sweat in their service to show man that when we are serving God, there is no sweat, just a sweet abiding confidence that all stands well for those who are truly serving their Creator out of love and devotion.

The truth is man works up a sweat over the notions that he can somehow earn his salvation, please God with his own doings as he tries to get his way with his Creator. However, the contrast of Gethsemane and Golgotha shows us salvation comes by way of Jesus blood, not man's sweat; and serving the Lord is no sweat because of loving Him. After all, such service is the least I can do in my body, and He alone is worthy of such adoration and worship.

Prayer: Lord, we work up a lather when it comes to our ideas of You and our "so-called" worth before You. We feel we must always do something, but Your example is to pour all of our

441

notions about our best at earning brownie points with You to the wayside, and just give way in submission to Your way, trusting You with the details, while walking in obedience to Your Word. It is Your work on Calvary that shows us You have gone before us, while preparing a way for us so we can embrace Your work of grace by childlike faith. Amen!

December 21

Alone. Alone is a word that we usually associate with sadness, despair, sickness and suffering, accompanied by feelings of hopelessness and discouragement because "alone" can chill us through and through with the desperate feeling that "nobody cares." Granted, there are those times when we look forward to a temporary "alone" time so we can enjoy the silence that allows our hurried thoughts to settle, our emotions to become calm, and our spirit to rest in peace. When we're undone and frazzled by circumstances both near and far that are beyond our control, it's not unusual to withdraw for a time of aloneness.

However, there's a vast difference between suddenly being thrust into a state of aloneness due to events, circumstances or tragedy and deliberately carving out some "alone time" for oneself. In addition, most of us have experienced that all-consuming, dreadful "alone" sensation even when we're surrounded by others.

In order to get past ourselves and right a wrong perspective, our wonderful God has given to us a place of refuge, understanding, knowledge and comfort, and it's called the Holy Bible. From Genesis to Revelation we can read, study and meditate on the plight of man from the first man, Adam, alone except for the animals, to the Apostle John who was alone on the Island of Patmos. Consider the life of Joseph, sold by his brothers to slave traders who took him to Egypt; and Moses who fled to the back side of the desert for 40 years; the prophet Elijah who spent

442

40 days and 40 nights isolated on Mt. Horeb, and who also lamented that only he alone was left who worshipped Jehovah God and not Baal.

Remember David, who tended his father's sheep alone in the hills and who wrote, *"I watch, and am as a sparrow alone upon the house top" (Psalm 102:7)*. Jeremiah spent much time alone, even in prison and deep in a well. The other prophets spent much time alone, including John the Baptist. The Apostle Paul spent years alone in the desert of Arabia receiving divine revelations in preparation for his ministry (see *Galatians 1:11-24*).

We all know, or should know, that the Lord Jesus spent much time alone in addition to the 40 days and 40 nights in the wilderness. He went alone into the hills to pray to His Father, and He prayed alone in Gethsemane while His disciples slept. Jesus said, in *John 6:32, "Behold, the hour cometh, yea, is now come, that ye shall be scattered, every man to his own, and shall leave me alone: and yet I am not alone, because the Father is with me."* Finally, we come to the cross of Christ and the greatest, ultimate, all-consuming loneliness that a soul can ever suffer and which Jesus suffered, "My God, my God, why hast thou forsaken me?" *(Matthew 27:47)*.

So, my friend, consider this: When you are overcome with fear and the dreadful, consuming feeling of being all alone in the Universe, and that "nobody cares," instead of withdrawing into yourself in search of some kind of solace, instead cry out to the Lord. *"Seek ye the LORD while he may be found, call ye upon him while he is near; Let the wicked forsake his way, and the unrighteous man his thoughts; and let him return unto the LORD, and he will have mercy upon him; and to our God, for he will abundantly pardon."*

God allows extreme "alone" times in our lives so that we will seek to draw near to Him, to know Him, to be able to hear His voice, and to come higher in Him. There is a chorus I love that

443

goes like this: "Shut in with God in the secret place, There in the Spirit beholding His face; Gaining new power to run in the race; How I long to be shut in with God!"

If we belong to Jesus, we are never alone! – J. Haley

Prayer: Lord in the world we stand alone, feel alone, and know the hollowness of it, but in You we are never alone. Keep us from looking about and teach us to rest in You and Your promise to never forsake us. Amen.

December 22

"Glory to God in the highest, and on earth peace, good will toward men" (Luke 2:14). There are two ailments that people can suffer from during this time: commercialism and wishful thinking. Both of these conditions can prove to create misery and great disappointment. They can push one into absolute despair, while setting others up to fall into an empty vacuum of nothingness that leaves a bitter taste in their mouth.

Now before you accuse me of being a "humbug," my question is where can you find peace and good will when these two ailments exist? I was, in a sense, asked this question the other day. There are parts of our society that will heap all kinds of things upon themselves and no one will be better for it, especially mankind. On the other hand, there will be those that will taste bitterness because their lack is apparent or their loneliness greater, creating a dark pit of hopelessness. Where is the peace on earth for them?

Granted, there are organizations and dedicated individuals who try to bring some relief to close the great gap between the "haves and the have nots" during this time. However, even in our attempt to close the gap, we never will because it is not a social problem, but a spiritual one. It is not a status problem, but it has

444

to do with the general state of mankind due to spiritual poverty brought on by sin.

The night that the angels made this declaration was in relationship to bringing glory to God. It had to do with the Prince of Peace coming into this world.

Mankind tries to bring relief to the less fortunate the best way he can. It is usually nothing more than putting band-aids on a bleeding artery, but it becomes quite obvious that they can't save individuals from what really ails them whether it is selfishness or being lost, nor can they fill a lost soul with life and hope. The truth is Jesus alone is the only one who can address the spiritual problems of mankind.

Clearly, it is obvious that the core of the angels' declaration is not about man's best of trying to create good will, but rather God addressing man's worst, his lost state, and his hopeless plight in order to establish good will, or that which will truly benefit mankind. Jesus' death is God's good will towards men and Jesus' ministry of reconciliation is what will bring lasting peace to man's empty, tormented, lost souls.

Prayer: Lord, man may have the best intentions towards others, but he lacks the power to change the inward state of man where the greatest battles and problems take place. That is why You came into the world. Amen.

December 23

"And when they were come into the house, they saw the young child with Mary, his mother; and fell down, and worshipped him: and when they had opened their treasures, they presented unto him gifts, gold, and frankincense, and myrrh" (Matthew 2:11). The present presentation of Christ's entrance into the world does not really hit the mark.

It may be sentimental and sweet, but we know that the wise men did not show up at His birth. They found Him in a house and not a manger. Jesus could have been at least two years old. The only reason we suspect this is because Herod asked the wise men how long they had been following the star and afterwards he ordered all the boys up to the age of two to be killed in Bethlehem to rid him of any competition. This implies their search for Jesus had been for at least two years.

There is one part of the presentation surrounding the wise men that I can agree with and that is "Wise men still seek Him." The question is, what will guide the "wise men" of each generation to the Lord?

The Star of Bethlehem was the guiding light for the three wise men. Keep in mind stars are to serve as signs and only shine in the darkness. Without the lights of heaven, we are all in darkness and only a guiding light from above can guide us through the darkness.

It is amazing how at this time in considering the incarnation of Christ that the star often takes center stage. Clearly, it is a vital part of the events that took place so long ago.

It is important to note all other stars have a name, but the one that led the wise men to Jesus is referred to as the Star of Bethlehem. I know that as Creator, Jesus created every star, named them and walks among them, but the Star of Bethlehem had no known name. Its identification is what matters. It is identified to Bethlehem, to the place of Jesus' birth, to the Son of God.

It would make sense that it would have no identity apart from Jesus. It was His star, and it was simply there to point the wise men to the One whom they would worship and who would later become the Morning Star that would be dawning in the hearts and souls of those who were/are heirs of salvation.

446

I am one such heir, and the light of Jesus has guided me to the place of salvation. Now that precious Star—the real Star of Bethlehem resides in my heart, shining forth His glory in my soul.

Prayer: Lord, like the wise men of old, I need to keep looking up and focus on You as the light of the world. Amen.

December 24

"And suddenly there was with the angel a multitude of the heavenly host praising God" (Luke 2:13a). After being overcast for a few days, the shining sun brought such a contrast to the landscape. Since we are in that time when snow can cover the landscape, I am reminded how the light can cause the different aspects of the snowy countryside to sparkle as if it was one big diamond glittering in the light. It is amazing how the light from above illuminates God's gems.

This is the time we talk about gifts. As I watch the way many get caught up with gifts, I realize how most gifts have little lasting meaning to them; and, that the most priceless gifts are overlooked and rarely enjoyed.

The key to real gifts is that they can highlight any day. Perhaps the gift is a moment where one was touched in some small way, a kind gesture that broke through the terrain of drudgery, a caring smile that brings a bit of sunshine to a weary heart, or a listening ear that took the sting of indifference out of the day.

The sparkling landscape reminds me of God's present to all of us. He provided a gem for each of us to possess. The gem came from above. Fashioned in heaven, it was only proper for the heavens to highlight this treasure as the angels proclaimed this gem's value that would be brought into the dark, barren wasteland of sin, sorrow, despair, and death. We know this gem to be the Lord Jesus Christ.

As I observe the beauty about me, I remember the beauty of God. Heaven not only parted many centuries ago to declare the glory of God, but it also illuminated that small bundle lying in a manger.

In that manger the gem of heaven would eventually light up the world with the light of hope. His light would sparkle like diamonds through the darkness, highlighting the message of heaven and the promise of life and peace.

Prayer: Lord, You came into this world as a small bundle, but You died as a sacrifice on a cross to save my soul, but left as a living, ascended Lord. You are my source of peace in this world and hope in the next. Amen.

December 25

"And behold, there was a man in Jerusalem, whose name was Simeon; and the same man was just and devout, waiting for the consolation of Israel: and the Holy Ghost was upon him. And it was revealed unto him by the Holy Ghost, that he should not see death, before he had seen the Lord's Christ" (Luke 2:25-26). The question for this day is did you get what you were looking for? Did it meet your expectation? Or, are you happy and glad it is over with, and are ready to really celebrate with a tired sigh of relief? Are you emotionally left up or down or feeling inside out because you are overwhelmed by the reality that now the excitement is over with and what is left is nothing more than vanity. Perhaps you feel sideways, stuck between a rock and hard place because you are now in some type of bind.

We Christians try to put God's stamp of approval on our sometimes worldly or fleshly attitudes and activities. We try to take the lemons this life presents us and make it into lemonade, but we must be honest that in spite of breaking a matter down with our logic and adding what we call justification to it, that in most cases out type of lemonade will be considered sour to God, and He will spit it out.

When I consider the events surrounding Jesus coming into this world, I note the angels' declaration, and the humility of the manger and shepherds, but to me the purpose of His entrance is found when He was dedicated at the temple. Simeon was told he would not see death until he saw the Lord's Anointed One. When he saw Jesus he stated, "For mine eyes have seen thy salvation." My question is, have you seen the resurrected Jesus, the One who saves? If not, are you still lost?

There was Anna, an 84-year-old prophetess who had served God with fastings and prayers night and day at the temple, and upon seeing the baby Jesus, gave thanks to the Lord and went forth to proclaim Jesus to those who were looking for redemption in Jerusalem. Are you in the right place of service to see the reality of Jesus that causes great thanksgiving to rise up in you, compelling you to declare Him to others?

What about Mary, the mother of Jesus. She kept all the prophecies surrounding Jesus and pondered them in her heart. She was told the great price her Son would pay, revealing the hearts of men. In the end, just like her Son's heart on the cross, her heart would be pierced and broken as well, becoming identified in His death, burial and resurrection. If you have Jesus in your heart, do you ponder His sayings, workings, and teachings? Has your heart been broken over sin, your spirit vexed over darkness, and your soul burdened over man's spiritual plight?

Jesus' coming into this world as man was not about His birth, but about His great work of redemption. Like Simeon, as believers we have seen in our spirit our consolation hanging on a cross, and like Anna we are seeing the promise of redemption being fulfilled but have we shared it with others? Have we been a Mary, pondering His Word and ways in our hearts and identifying with His work in order to land on His everlasting promises? This time should remind us that our life of Christ begins at the birth of His life actually taking place in our hearts.

Prayer: Lord, we focus on outward activities and not on the events that shape history, lives, and man's destiny. The great line has been drawn by Your cross that cast such a huge shadow, there is no history before or after it, there is only opportunity to choose life or death, heaven or hell. I choose You, Lord Jesus. Amen.

December 26

"For which you, intended to build a tower, sitteth not down first, and counteth the cost, whether he have sufficient to finish it" (Luke 14:28) Sometimes this time of the year reminds me how it is easy to be taken by the wave of vanity out into the ridiculous promises of the world. If you have this, you will be happy. All you need is this, or that, and you will have more time on your hands. I do not want to miss the real message or blessing that each day should bring and not just this time of year.

For years I have enjoyed the treasure of heaven, but at times I have taken it for granted. I let it get tarnished by being casual with it. I have neglected it by not regarding it in the proper way. I often become despairing over the fact that I can become forgetful or casual about the things of God. The things I often value are temporary, the things I find myself focusing on are illusive, and the things I pursue end up proving to be a waste of time.

Through the years I have had to pull myself back and take stock. As the new year inches closer, I realize that God was taking stock of this world when He sent His only begotten Son. Even though He already knew the verdict, His Son would become the measuring stick to show mankind just how far away from the mark they are. In the end, Jesus would pay the necessary price to close the gap between God and man.

When I consider what Jesus had to do to pay the price for my soul, I begin to realize so much of what I do is small and insignificant. Admittedly, it brings humility to my spirit, but I also realize how vain much of my activities really are.

Prayer: Lord, save us from the endless stream of pettiness that often takes us captive with the cords of vanity. Keep me focused on what is eternal. Amen.

December 27

"Folly is set in great dignity, and the rich sit in low place. I have seen servants upon horses, and princes walking as servants upon the earth. He that diggeth a pit shall fall into it; and whoso breaketh an hedge, a serpent shall bite him" (Ecclesiastes 10:6-8). Sometimes the people who inspire you the most prove the most untrustworthy.

For me there was one such individual who was rich materially, but poor spiritually. This person loved places of dignity but was a slave to great darkness. This individual rode upon the high horses of society while mocking those who were of heavenly royalty. They built "barns" at the expense of others, lied and cheated to hold on to their preferred lifestyle of greed and decadence.

In this person's mind, they had every right to their lifestyle and those who did not play their wretched game and did not fit in were foolish. Even though they were selfish and unloving, they perceived that they had enough religion and experiences with God that they were okay.

This person's pursuit of the physical set her up to miss what was valuable. That which was priceless involved two relationships. One was with her Christian daughter and the other one was with her God.

The daughter had prayed for her parent's salvation and God had shown Himself to this individual more than once, but neither commitment seem to give this person a reality check about the seriousness of her eternal destination. At death she had to leave the riches of this world behind while facing the harsh reality she was wrong and her daughter was right. This no doubt happened as she faced the emptiness of her life and realized she was spiritually clothed in common, foul-smelling rags.

Prayer: Lord, You give us living examples of what is true when it comes to riches, and I choose heavenly riches over the temporary riches of this world. I choose You over the idols of greed that will set people up to fall into an endless pit of vanity and judgment. Amen.

December 28

There were tears in his eyes, and there were tears in mine as well. This is what happened: I had stopped to pick up the hard copies of our newsletter at the print/copy shop, and the owner, a kind young man, stepped up to the counter to wait on me. I could feel that something was very wrong, and asked where his big "shop dog," Nyla, was.

Nyla was my friend, and she always greeted me, then jumped up on her chair, bowed her head, and lifted a big paw so I could coddle her and tell her how wonderful she was and all the words dogs love to hear. That's when the tears began to form as he told me she was gone—that she had died of a big stomach tumor.

I was stunned, and even though it was a busy day for me, I lingered to enter in with him as he told me all the details. What I want to emphasize in this writing is men and tears.

452

Culture tells us that "big boys and men don't cry." That is a horrible, damaging, LIE out of the pit of hell. Why do I say that? Because, for one thing, our LORD wept in *John 11:35* and you get a sense He was weeping over His beloved city, Jerusalem in *Luke 13:34-35*, but how many Christians are aware of all the men mentioned in the Bible who wept, cried and shed tears?

The references to weeping and crying in Scripture are numerous, so here is just a brief list of some of the men of God who wept and cried: Jacob, Joseph, King David, King Joash, King Hezekiah, the priests, Levites and old men in Ezra (plus women and children); Nehemiah, Mordecai, Job, valiant men and ambassadors in *Isaiah 33:7*; Jeremiah ("the weeping prophet"), Micah, Zechariah, and the children of Israel. Of course, we know that Peter wept, the Apostle Paul wept, and the Apostle John wept, *Revelation 5:4, 5*. And, there were many, many more.

When was the last time you saw weeping in a Christian assembly over "sin in the camp?" Maybe I should ask, when was the last time you stood and wept and cried out, "God, forgive me a sinner!"? When was the last time the Spirit of God moved so powerfully during praise and worship that you wept? When was the last time the Word of God moved you to tears? When was the last time you wept over the sins of the people around you, your city, state, nation or the world? And, when was the last time you entered in with a hurting, weeping, broken soul and wept with him or her?

Let's face it brothers and sisters, we have become so "civilized," and so "proper" with our "stiff upper lips" and tough "I've got it all together" facades that the Church in America, with few exceptions, in spite of all the "happy clappy" hype, motivational speakers and cheerleaders for Jesus, and upbeat "me, myself and I" "worship," is like a pile of dead, dry bones rattling on about some make believe "revival."

Until the Church REPENTS of losing its first love, (and the love that esteems others better than self with no respect of persons), REPENTS of its disobedience, REPENTS of its lukewarmness, pride and idolatry, REPENTS of failing to feed God's sheep the WHOLE COUNSEL OF THE WORD OF GOD and make disciples, it will continue to be a dead, dry social club, and never regain, or fulfill, its commission to be the salt and the light in this dark world, but instead will continue on playing church until the Lord comes and says, "I never knew you." God says, *"For my people have committed two evils; they have forsaken me the fountain of living waters, and hewed them out cisterns, broken cisterns, that can hold no water" (Jeremiah 2:13).* – J. Haley

Prayer: Lord, weeping reminds us of loss, sorrow of what has become lost to us, and mourning as to what will never be. However, weeping reminds us of the morning, sorrow that twilight is temporary, and mourning will be turned into joy because of the light of Your presence to comfort, Your abiding faithfulness to hold us, and Your glory that will cause all to become dim and flee away in the end. Amen.

December 29

"If a man therefore purge himself from these, he shall be a vessel unto honour, sanctified, and meet for the master's use, and prepared unto every good work" (2 Timothy 2:21) Often times, when I am beginning to wake up, the Lord speaks to me whether it is with impressions or pictures or even with a small still voice as to what He wants me to share. At such times it is sweet, but I also know I must get up and record it or prepare to deliver it so I will not forget what He has shown me.

This morning, He spoke to my heart and reminded me that all greatness comes out of sacrifice. It is not just any sacrifice but a consecrated sacrifice.

A consecrated sacrifice is one that has been prepared to be set apart for God's good pleasure. It is not a showy sacrifice that others can admire. It is not a ritualistic sacrifice that is required. It is a sacrifice just for the Lord, prepared for Him with a pure heart, a sacrifice that does not come out of the best we have to offer, but like the widow with her mites it is all that we have to offer.

It is a sacrifice that will prove to be acceptable and will be consumed on His altar by Him, an offering that when the fire is done a sweet fragrance will come out of it and ascend to God. For the Christian the fragrance is the life of Jesus (*2 Corinthians 2:15-16*).

All we have as Christians to present to God as a sacrifice that would prove to be acceptable, when pressed against the altar and as fire is being put to it, is our bodies and our lives. When Paul speaks of presenting our bodies in *Romans 12:1* as a living sacrifice, he is instructing us as a vessel to offer all of our life as a sacrifice for God's pleasure and glory.

We must not preserve our life for ourselves, or maintain our life to hold onto this world, but offer all of it up so that in the end, we gain the real and complete life we have in Christ.

Prayer: Lord, we need to offer our bodies up daily to You so You can do as You will in and through our lives for Your good pleasure. A body was prepared for You to become a Lamb, and now as part of Your Body, I offer up all that I have been given by You for Your use and glory. Amen.

December 30

"Preach the word; be instant in season, and out of season; reprove, rebuke, exhort with all longsuffering and doctrine" (2 Timothy 4:2). I have been in ministry for four decades. To some, that may seem like a long time, but for others it may not look that long after all because some have been in service to the Lord longer.

It seems like my years of serving the Lord have passed me by like a flowing river. There are times that the flow has been leveled off, leaving me with a time of peace and rest to meditate a while, while at other times it has been rough due to storms that would take me down, except the Lord was in the boat. And, there are the times that we have found ourselves in the rapids descending down into some unknown destination to always come out with a greater awareness of God's abiding faithfulness upon our lives.

The Bible speaks of remembering, remembering who God is, His Word, and His works. For the most part I don't remember the 40 years of service, except for those times where God touched a matter with eternity allowing me to witness the extraordinary, experience the miraculous, and partake of the glorious. Such times are simply moments when the touch of eternity stopped time, leaving an indelible mark on my heart.

The reality is that world can consume us with its drudgery of trying to survive its challenges as well as its incessant demands that choke out the Word of God. More often than not it is the world that leaves one weary with it all. I must admit I have never been bored in my service to the Lord, but I have become weary with the world's ridiculous ways and demands.

When I find myself too much encumbered by the world, I will stop to consider why I am here. It is so easy to get off track and caught up with the fool trickery of the world that is forever offering

456

mere imitations of even spiritual realities. When I stop to get my bearings, I remember a picture of the first evangelistic meeting held in Romania in 1990 after 70 years of darkness under Communism on a cold November day. It takes three legal sized papers to capture the 60,000 souls that showed up to find hope in the great light of Christ and His Gospel, that alone could penetrate the darkness of their hopelessness and despair.

Why are we here? Because there are people wandering in the darkness of hopelessness and despair. Why are we here? We carry the light that can penetrate that darkness and have been commissioned to share it with those who are seeking. We must remember why we are here lest we forget that we do not belong to ourselves and we have been commissioned to carry out a life-and-death mission. We are here to contend for the faith that was first delivered by the saints of old. We are here to pull some out of the grips of hell with the Gospel, guide some away from the abyss with the hand of compassion, and take the hand of the lost and lead them to the Shepherd.

We may become weary with the world, but not with our calling in the Lord. I wrote this to remember why I am here and I want to share it with you today. It is called *Lest We Forget*.

Lest we forget why we are here,
   Oft sitting in comfortable pews of indifference.
Lest we forget we have been saved,
   Not to sit idly by, but to march forward.
Lest we forget we have been given a vision,
   Never to be content with the ordinary,
   Always pressing forward to the extraordinary.
Lest we forget we have been marked for excellence,
   Ever striving towards the miraculous.
Lest we forget we have been called to greatness,
   Not to a mediocre life on worldly plateaus.

Lest we forget we have been set apart,
　　To be lights in the dark world.
Lest we forget we are in the race of a lifetime,
　　Carrying a torch of Life.
Lest we forget that people are dying without hope,
　　Lost souls crying in the night.
Lest we forget why we are here,
　　To be laborers in the harvest field.
Lest we forget we have been commissioned,
　　Never to be content until the mission is finished.
Lest we forget, Jesus died so man could live,
　　Jesus rose so man could hope.
Lest we forget, we have been entrusted,
　　With a message that changes the destiny of man.
Lest we forget who we are living for,
　　Failing to bring Him honor and glory.
Lest we forget who we are, what we are called to,
　　Lest we forget why we are here.

Prayer: Lord, never let us forget why we are here: for Your purpose, to do Your will and for Your glory. Amen.

December 31

"My days are swifter than a weave's shuttle, and are spent without hope. O remember that my life is wind; mine eye shall no more see good" (Job 7:6-7). How would you end this statement? "It is the last day of the year. Since we are creatures of time, we have a beginning, and a beginning points to the reality of an ending.

As an author, I understand the importance of a good start that leads to a great ending. In between the start and the ending is a crescendo that is trying to reach heights of accomplishment, success, purpose, and calling to discover or unveil the potential, or greatness that will make any end memorable and lasting.

Today we can finish the statement with, "it is the last day of the year." However, what if it read, "it is the last day of my life here on earth?" Would you play the fool and taste as much of this world you could before the night overtakes you, or do you have enough fear of God that you would be wise enough to seek His face and make sure you are right with Him to be assured of awakening to look into the face of the light of the world?

Each year reminds me my "starts" are becoming less but the biggest ending, when it comes to the end of my life here, is closer. I am aware that until I see Jesus coming in the clouds or enter the door of eternity, my life as I know it is closer to coming to an end. Life has taught me that if there is any real fanfare it is at the beginning, but for the majority that last day is just another day, where without any fanfare, the night of death will quickly overtake them to mark an end.

There is only one consolation when it comes to my life here, for it is always marked by the night overtaking each start, each day, and that is marked by the cross of Christ. That is when life really started for me. The crescendo I have experienced is not based on the ups and downs of life, but revelations of Jesus that take me higher and higher. And regardless of the challenges of this present life, I have the assurance that God remains sure as the Immovable Rock. He sits on the throne and will always have the last say as to the events of my life and my time here.

We live in precarious days, but as believers we are waiting for the greatest fanfare to happen and it will mark an end to this present age. For saints of the Most High, we know we will encounter the greatest ascension ever for we are assured that we will see the face of our glorious Lord, whether in eternity or in the sky, that the spiritual night will not overtake us, and that our Lord will right what has been made wrong since the fall of Adam.

Prayer: Lord, we are approaching a New Year, but each year teaches us it is not the years that we must make count, but the days. Years mean nothing unless we have lived out our past days in light of eternity. Amen.

Other books by Rayola Kelley:

Hidden Manna (Original)
Battle for the Soul (Book & Workbook)
Stories of the Heart
Transforming Love & Beyond
The Great Debate
Post to Post: (1) Establishing the Way
Post to Post: (2) Walking in the Way
Post to Post: (3) Meditations Along the Way

Volume One: Establishing Our Life in Christ
My Words are Spirit and Life
The Anatomy of Sin
The Principles of the Abundant Life
The Place of Covenant
Unmasking the Cult Mentality

Volume Two: Putting on the Life of Christ
He Actually Thought It Not Robbery
Revelation of the Cross
*In Search of Real Faith
Think on These Things
Follow the Pattern

Volume Three: Developing a Godly Environment
Godly Discipline
Prayer and Worship
Don't Touch That Dial
Face of Thankfulness
ABC's of Christianity

Volume Four: Issues of the Heart
*Hidden Manna (Revised)
Bring Down the Sacred Cows
The Manual for the Single Christian Life
Parents Are People Too

Volume Five: Challenging the Christian Life
The Issues of Life
Presentation of the Gospel
For the Purpose of Edification
Whatever Happened to the Church?
Women's Place in the Kingdom of God

Volume Six: Developing Our Christian Life
The Many Faces of Christianity

*Possessing Our Souls
Experiencing the Christian Life
The Power of Our Testimonies
The Victorious Journey

Volume Seven: Discovering True Ministry
From Prisons and Dots to Christianity
So You Want To Be In Ministry?
(These two books found in **The Journey of a Lifetime**)

Devotions
Devotions of the Heart: Books One and Two
Daily Food for the Soul: Books One and Two

Gentle Shepherd Ministries Devotion Series:
Being a Child of God
Disciplining the Strength of our Youth
Coming to Full Age

Nugget Books:
Nuggets From Heaven
More Nuggets From Heaven
Heavenly Gems
More Heavenly Gems
Heavenly Treasures
More Heavenly Treasures

Gentle Shepherd Ministries Series:

The Christian Life Series
What Matter Is This?
The Challenge of It
The Reality of It

The Leadership Series
Overcoming
A Matter of Authority and Power
The Dynamics of True Leadership

Books By Jeannette Haley

Books co-authored with Rayola Kelley:
Hidden Manna (original)
The Many Faces of Christianity (Volume 6)
Post to Post 3: Meditations Along the Way
Post to Post 4: Inspirations Along the Way

Other Books:
*Rose of Light, Thorn of Darkness (Volume 7)
The Pig and I
Reflections of Wonder (Devotional)

Angelus Assignments Includes:
(Both books in Volume 7)
Interview in Hell
Interview on Earth

Children's Books:
Little Stories for Little People
Traveler's Tales
The Adventures of Zack and Mira
The Adventures of Paul and Dana
(A House on the Beach)
The Monster of Mystery Valley

*Books that have been separated from the volume and now are under their own title.